# Lines of the Nation

Cultures of History

Cultures of History

Nicholas Dirks, Series Editor

The death of history, reported at the end of the twentieth century, was clearly premature. It has become a hotly contested battleground in struggles over identity, citizenship, and claims of recognition and rights. Each new national history proclaims itself as ancient and universal, while the contingent character of its focus raises questions about the universality and objectivity of any historical tradition. Globalization and the American hegemony have created cultural, social, local, and national backlashes. Cultures of History is a new series of books that investigates the forms, understandings, genres, and histories of history, taking history as the primary text of modern life and the foundational basis for state, society, and nation.

Shail Mayaram, *Against History, Against State: Counterperspectives from the Margins*

Tapati Guha-Thakurta, *Monuments, Objects, Histories: Institutions of Art in Colonial and Postcolonial India*

Charles Hirschkind, *The Ethical Soundscape: Cassette Sermons and Islamic Counterpublics*

Laura Bear

# Lines of the Nation

*Indian Railway Workers, Bureaucracy,*
*and the Intimate Historical Self*

Columbia University Press   New York

Columbia University Press

*Publishers Since 1893*

New York    Chichester, West Sussex

Copyright © 2007 Columbia University Press

All rights reserved

Library of Congress Cataloging-in-Publication Data

Bear, Laura.

Lines of the nation: Indian Railway workers, bureaucracy,
and the intimate historical self /Laura Bear.

p. cm. — (Cultures of history)

Includes bibliographical references and index.

ISBN 978–0–231–14002–7 (cloth : alk. paper) —

ISBN 978–0–231–51151–3    (e-book)

1. Indian Railways—Management—Historiography.

2. Indian Railways—Officials and employees—Social conditions.

3. Indian Railways—Officials and employees—Economic conditions.

4. Railroads and state—India—Historiography.

5. Eastern Railway (India)—Archives.  I. Title.  II. Series.


HE3298.B38      2007

331.7'613850954—dc22        2006036065

Columbia University Press books are printed on
permanent and durable acid-free paper.

This book is printed on paper with recycled content.

Printed in the United States of America

c 10 9 8 7 6 5 4 3 2 1

*To Subhrasheel and Thalia*

# Contents

# Acknowledgments

This book has been a long time in the making and has been enriched by the contributions of many people. It started in the vibrant atmosphere of the doctoral program in anthropology and history at the University of Michigan. There, Val Daniel, Tom Trautmann, and Ann Stoler inspired me to set out on this path of research, and their ideas guided me through it. Nick Dirks, as my adviser, has since provided both constant intellectual challenges and invaluable support. Without his belief in my project, this book would not have been able to grow into the form it takes here. My fellow students and friends from Michigan, in particular Clea Finkle, Anjan Ghosh, Riyad Koya, Rama Mantena, Gita Rajan, Anupama Rao, Lee Schlesinger, Parna Sengupta, and Tom Williamson, may recognize echoes of our stimulating discussions held long ago in the pages that follow.

My research in India and London was funded between 1993 and 1996 by the American Institute of Indian Studies, the Social Science Research Council, and the Wenner-Gren Foundation. I received further funding for more time in India in 1996 and 1997 from the Rackham Dissertation Grant and Sawyer Research Fellowship at the University of Michigan. In India, my work and life were changed completely by the companionship and ideas of Anglo-Indian and Bengali railway families in Kharagpur, Adra, and Kolkata. Indrani Chatterjee, Rohit Chopra, Bhaskar Mukhopadhyay, Aditi Sen, and Sufia Uddin were generous with their friendship.

I started to rework this book while lecturing at Goldsmiths, where Nick Thomas, Olivia Harris, Steve Nugent, Simon Cohn, and Eva Berglund all contributed much to my work with their support. Versions of chapters were presented at seminars in the departments of anthropology at Sussex, Goldsmiths, the London School of Economics, Edinburgh, and in the South Asia group at Oxford and were greatly enhanced by the suggestions given. Janet Carsten and Jonathan Spencer have been particularly kind with comments and encouragement. Mukulika Banerjee has been a constant friend throughout the writing process.

I can't thank my colleagues at L.S.E. enough for providing a nurturing environment for the final stages of this book. Chris Fuller and Johnny Parry have had an important impact on the arguments presented here thanks to their thought-provoking questions and support. Fenella Cannell has pushed me to think anew about Anglo-Indian religiosity. I am particularly indebted to her ideas on the Christianity of genealogy and secular institutions. Stephan and Miranda Feuchtwang have helped me to understand the emotional power and significance of Anglo-Indian experiences. Veronique Benei has been a wonderful friend, sparring partner over ideas, and reader for some of the chapters in other forms. Also thanks to my colleagues—Catherine Allerton, Rita Astuti, Maurice Bloch, Matthew Engelke, Deborah James, Michael Lambek, Martha Mundy, Norbert Peabody, Michael Scott, and Charles Stafford—in the writing group and weekly departmental seminars that provide such a stimulating atmosphere in the department.

I would also like to particularly thank the two readers for Columbia, Thomas Blom Hansen and an anonymous reviewer. They have had a great impact on the book. They have enabled me to hone my ideas and gave me the confidence to make its central argument. At Columbia University Press, I would like to thank Peter Dimock for his suggestions for final revisions, which were very liberating comments for a writer. Also thanks to Kabir Dandona for working hard to get the manuscript through the process of review.

Most books are written in a "free" space and time that is carefully sustained by the love of friends and family. It was the love of Jeremy, Griselda, Subhrasheel, and Thalia that meant these pages could come into the world.

# Lines of the Nation

# Introduction

The two headed stationmaster
belongs to a sect that rejects every timetable
not published in the year the track was laid as apocryphal
but interprets the first timetable
with a freedom that allows him to read
every subsequent timetable between the lines of its text
Finally he nods like a stroke between yes and a no
And says
All timetables ever published
Along with all timetables yet to be published
Are simultaneously valid
At any given time on any given track
Insofar as all the timetables were inherent
In the one printed
When the track was laid

—Arun Kolatkar, "The Stationmaster," from "Jejuri"

We have never been rational, scientific, disenchanted. This is a story we tell ourselves in order to produce and purify the hybrids modernity has produced.

—Bruno Latour, *We Have Never Been Modern*

The railway in India, from the first accounts of its history, has been described as a vector of capitalist modernity. British entrepreneurs and bureaucrats argued that it drew Indian society—composed of agriculturists suffering under the tyranny of moneylenders, landowners, and caste—into the world of enterprise and work discipline.[1] Colonial histories prefaced their descriptions of the progress of lines and the technical feats of engineers with accounts of how travel and work on the railways dissolved traditional social ties.[2] From the 1870s, economic nationalists challenged these accounts of the progress created by the railways. In images of fatal blood loss and poisoning they argued that the railways destroyed the Indian national economy. Commentators such as Naoroji, Ranade, Joshi, and Dutt provided a powerful critique of colonial claims of benevolence by their detailed enumeration of the drain of wealth from India to Britain and the role of the railways therein.[3] But this new, nationalist version of colonial economic history, which combined with *swadeshi* (self-rule; literally, "own country") and socialist dreams to provide the basis for the Indian National Congress's economic policy, did not challenge the fundamental premise of railway history. The assumption remained that the railways and their bureaucracy produced an economic modernity in India that dissolved ties of caste and community.

Commenting on the introduction of railways to India in 1853, Marx provided the foundation for later debates within the Indian Marxist tradition by suggesting that they would be the "forerunner of modern industry," adding that "modern industry, resulting from the railway system, will dissolve the hereditary divisions of labor upon which rest the Indian castes, those decisive impediments to Indian progress and Indian power."[4] Drawing on this statement, Indian Marxists were forced to explain why issues of caste and community recurred in labor disputes. Tied within this transition narrative, they recurrently attempted to address the reasons for India's inadequate passage from precapitalism to capitalism.[5] Strikes on the railways from 1890 to 1929 that openly challenged racial and economic inequalities did not lead to a reinterpretation of the social effects of the railways either. Instead, much of the early intellectual discussion of these strikes was guided by the orthodoxy provided by the *Report of the Royal Commission on Labour* in 1930. This inquiry was the response of the colonial state to widespread agitation against its exclusionary economic strategies. The report enshrined a version of the Indian laborer as bound in networks of community and tradition that had to be accommodated in state policies. The traditionalism of workers also justified a continuation of the administrative presence of British supervision and governance. In the Royal Commission on Labour the railway bureaucracy once more defined its role as that of educating a precapitalist laborer in modern working practices, now defined as Taylorist worker welfare. This view of the precapitalist nature of the working classes was made popular in nationalist and Marxist circles by Radhakamal Mukherjee's influential book, *The Indian Working Class*.[6] Affected by this framework, historians of Indian labor have long challenged the racial exclusions and mercantile capitalism of colonial workplaces. Yet they have not overturned the notion of railways as a project that transferred laissez-faire individualism and capitalism into India. The insights provided by more recent anthropologies and histories of labor in India that have revealed the complex emergence of community and class in different workplace settings have not been extended to this arena.[7]

Historians of the railways for a long time have only added details to these founding debates about the impact of the railways on Indian society. They have turned the speculative and moral arguments of colonial administrators, Indian

nationalists, and colonial commissions of inquiry into detailed analyses of investment, price differentials, tariff rates, market forces, managerial strategies, precapitalism, and class conflict.[8] These accounts have repeatedly focused on the
issues of the transfer of capitalism, modernity, and technology into an alien social
landscape.[9] In recent years work has started to depart from this model by examining the coloniality of the railways as an arm of imperial government control that
radically altered perceptions of national time, space, and economy.[10] Yet we still
have not charted the historically variable impact of the specific practices of the
railway bureaucracy, nor fully questioned the association of the railways with the
introduction of a technological and economic modernity to India.

This book rethinks the modernity of the railways by focusing on the local archives of the Eastern Railway and by reinterpreting these archives through the experience of workers and their families, who have worked for several generations on
the railways. My rewriting of this history and reinterpretation of the contemporary
railway bureaucracy are based on ethnographic research in the railway colony at
Kharagpur in West Bengal, with networks of railway families spread across several
locations, and in the Eastern Railway Headquarters in Kolkata.[11] Seen from the
perspective of the quotidian practices of the bureaucracy and from the accounts of
workers, the promised form of modernity that the railways were supposed to have
brought with them to India is shown to have never existed. Instead, the bureaucracy and workplaces generated distinctions of community, nation, caste, respectability, and race, turning Indian society into a new kind of target for state policies.
The practices of the bureaucracy, as we will see, drew upon a complex ethical vision of race, nation, and community derived in part from Protestant and medical
models. The bureaucracy also traded in distinctions central to English kinship of
pedigree, transforming these into markers of class and nation. It articulated these
concepts to a naturalization of both colonial and national projects of rule and to
attempts to administer sentiments.[12] In turn these practices affected in unintended
ways the political visions and intimate reckonings of ethical and genealogical selfhood among railway workers and their families. These bureaucratic practices also
became suffused with meanings running at a tangent to their intended effects and
associations. In particular in the context of this institution, ideas of *jati*, a term
commonly translated by anthropologists as "caste," became a complex indexical
and iconic sign of new forms of social distinction and political solidarities.[13] *Jati*
has now come to incorporate multiple and historically produced meanings of species, nation, race, kinship group, community, pedigree, and caste.

The Indian railways ultimately have a significance for our broader understanding of the transformative power and mesmerizing symbolism of railways in general.
It has been widely argued that railways radically altered perceptions of time and
space; were understood as proof of nineteenth-century cultural ideas of progress;

generated new kinds of modern subjectivity; and provoked new forms of representation in art and film.[14] Some of the discontents of this process have been explored as well, for example, how fears about railway accidents and concepts of railway nerves were expressions of anxieties about capitalism itself. The Indian railways raise interesting and different questions for our understanding of modernity and the railways in general. How did both the railways and institutions of modernity build on older practices of rule and social distinction? How were the new personal and collective experiences produced by the railways suffused with troubling sentiments and anxieties from sources that were supposed to have been banished by the power of modernity itself? How was the promise of railways that they would lift people out of localized places of origin and introduce them to a new, democratic era as individuals free from constraint always undercut by practices that embedded them in social distinctions that were improvised from older forms?[15] Why is it that utopian visions of radical and liberating breaks in the social order forged by technological change are never fully realized? Railways were mesmerizing because they appeared to materialize individual liberty and social progress, but ultimately this promise wasn't realized in India or elsewhere.

## KHARAGPUR AND ITS DISCONTENTS

My ethnography was carried out with Anglo-Indian and Bengali families in the railway colony at Kharagpur and along the networks that linked them to relatives in Kolkata and other railway towns in Bihar and West Bengal. Kharagpur was constructed between 1898 and 1900. Located eight miles from the district headquarters in Midnapur, it was designed to be an important intersection between Kolkata and the lines that traveled south to Orissa and west to Chattisgarh on the new Bengal-Nagpur Railway. This line was part of a phase of construction after the Famine Commission of the 1880s, which sought to prevent the problems of distribution that caused widespread suffering and provoked the attacks of economic nationalists. It was intended to open the territory of the Central Provinces to external trade and to lead to an outflow of wheat and seeds from Chattisgarh to the two ports of Kolkata and Mumbai. It was also planned to link Bilaspur to the Umaria coal mines and to provide a line that would join the East Indian, Great Indian Peninsula, and Indian Midland railway systems. In 1908 a connection to the new steel-producing town of Tatanagar was built. Until Independence, when the railways were nationalized, this railway was run by a private company carefully overseen by the state bureaucracy because its income was in part guaranteed by tax revenues.

The layout of Kharagpur followed the pattern of colonies built in the 1860s to house European and Eurasian workers, such as Jamalpur. Today the colony remains largely unchanged from this original plan. Within it hierarchies of rank and public spaces are still marked by colonial buildings. It remains distinct from the surrounding bazaars and unplanned settlements. On the south side of the railway station is the railway colony proper, consisting of a series of roads in a grid of six main avenues crosscut with smaller roads. On the southernmost limits is the long street of widely spaced bungalows with large gardens for senior officers. So uncrowded and deserted is the area that it is known among lower-ranking employees as a nighttime lovers' lane. Next to these bungalows is the old railway-volunteers ground, where employees used to be drilled in how to defend the colony, which is now owned by the Railway Protection Force. Moving northward back toward the station from this outer avenue there is a sports track and arena, the Railway Institute, the Masonic Lodge, and Protestant and Catholic churches. Closer to the station are rows of old single-story cottages and two-story flats with balconies for drivers and guards. These have been added to by modern, concrete, two-story blocks. In keeping with old theories of ventilation and ethnoclimatology there are large, open, grassed areas between each street of buildings. In this area too is the old railway primary school. Most children of railway employees above the rank of lower-level workshop workers now attend the large English-medium school run by St Agnes' Convent and built in the 1930s on the southwest outskirts of the colony. Right next to the station and opposite the Railway Guest House is the single official liquor shop, Billmorias. Near the station as well are the offices of the railway and the small Raj-era hospital. Across the railway tracks on the north side are a few rows of barracks for low-level employees and a Catholic cemetery. There also are the large workshops, which opened in 1904 for the overhaul of steam locomotives, passenger cars, and freight cars. Now these repair the full range of diesel and electric engines and carriages. Kharagpur also has a small separate workshop where a dozen female employees manufacture specialized components for locomotives. Across a short stretch of open ground is the sprawl of the bazaar and of the unplanned satellite settlements that grew up alongside the colony. Outside the limits of the colony there are temples, mosques, and a hotchpotch of old and new construction that houses various workshop and nonrailway employees. These are areas where land was allotted for workshop employees from 1911 on a community basis. Beyond the southern boundary of the colony and across paddy fields to the southeast is the more rural settlement of Hijli. There, interspersed with an *adivasi* (commonly, "tribal") settlement of mud-brick houses and unpaved roads, are houses that Anglo-Indians, who acted as guards, drivers, and supervisory staff in the workshops under the British, have built or retired to. There is also a village compound of mud-brick houses owned by Anglo-Indians. Part of the railway line going south to Puri curves around this area, providing its outer limits.

The colony is self-contained in the sense that it has its own water supply, municipality with sweepers, bottling plant, and bakery. Fifty percent of the staff of the railway is housed in the railway colony. Priority is given to people who are needed at short notice, such as senior officers, drivers, and guards. Houses are categorized in a rank from one to six. The allocation of houses is based on rank and salary levels. The lowest level consists of barracks that usually have one room, a veranda, and a bathroom. Level-two houses usually go to skilled workshop employees such as hammer men (metalworkers). Junior supervisors in clerical or technical positions and junior locomotive drivers usually receive type-three houses. Type-four houses go to senior supervisors, drivers, staff nurses, probationary officers, office superintendents, and stationmasters. Type-five houses go to administrative-grade officers with ten years of service. Type-six houses go to those who have been in service more than twenty years.

Despite the addition of functional, yellow-concrete two-story flats and houses in a blank modernist style, Raj-era architecture still predominates in the colony. Bungalows for senior officers have large verandas and steep, sweeping roofs familiar from colonial British architecture across the tropics. The houses and flats for middle- and lower-ranking employees are usually just two or three rooms with high ceilings and a balcony or veranda framed by arched windows and Victorian ironwork. A few houses emulate small, stockbroker Tudor cottages with brick-lined paths. Since Independence no temples or mosques have been built within the colony as part of a policy of "secularism" practiced by the railway administration. Instead, the public spaces at the heart of the colony remain the Masonic Lodge, sports ground, Protestant and Catholic churches, and Railway Institute. Most of the ground floor of the old Railway Institute has been converted into a cinema for showing Hindi movies, but upstairs dances and *housie* (bingo) games are still regularly held. The film shows and *housie* games are largely attended by male employees of the railway. Only Anglo-Indians and Indian Christians attend the dances. Some railway officers are members of the Masonic Lodge, and there are frequent meetings there. Athletics and soccer events at the sports ground draw modest crowds.

On one of my first days in Kharagpur I was given a guided tour by Abdel Ahmed, a recently retired workshop foreman, who later became my friend and introduced me to all the families I came to know in the colony. The additional divisional manager, the second-highest-ranking officer in the town, had just introduced me to Abdel. He had instructed Abdel to show me around all the important places, and he had put his official ambassador car at our service. I expected a trip to the workshop, the Railway Institute, maybe the hospital or the railway school, but Abdel chose to give me a quite different kind of tour from this itinerary of public buildings. What I learned that morning continued to puzzle me throughout my research, especially because the anxieties and dilemmas it highlighted recurred in a wide range of archival and ethnographic contexts. Each chapter of this book, in fact, contributes to a layered understanding of this event, the broader discontents among railway workers it revealed, and, more generally, the emergence of railway colonies and work environments such as Kharagpur.

First, we crossed the bridge over the railway tracks to the old, Indian, north side of the colony. Abdel chose to take me to the freshly painted Ram Mandir. Its head priest sat with us inside the temple and told us his version of its history. He said that the temple was built in 1902 by a local contractor, Mr. Rao, in penance for constructing a butcher's shop for the railway colony. The priest said that this act had made his family issueless. His service to the railway had polluted his lineage. The priest added as an afterthought that the land for the temple had been granted by the railways. Ironically, the railway authorities had helped Mr. Rao to regain his purity. He eventually had a son, but this son remained without children; as the priest said, the curse continued. This was in spite of the fact that the son extended the temple. The priest added with some force that after Independence the son had become a grand master of the Masonic Lodge, implying that this was connected to his infertility. As we were leaving the temple Abdel pointed out a series of European faces carved onto the arch above the door of the temple. The priest looked irritated that Abdel had drawn attention to them. The priest quickly said that these had been painted over in the recent renovations, and that they had needed "Indianizing" like the railways had after Independence. Next, Abdel took me to the Kali Mandir, where there was an image of the powerful and fearsome Shamshan Kali, the incarnation of the goddess associated with burning ghats. The priest there told us that Kharagpur was one of the few railway colonies where temples were officially encouraged by the railway. The land for this temple had been given in the 1920s by the agent, who had visited it on its opening. The funds for the building were provided by Mr. Nath, an Indian railway officer, who had given up his whole provident fund on retirement to construct it. He had turned his wages into spiritual currency. He also served his duty to the civil society of the railway colony by building an institute for Indian officers in the 1930s on the north side of the tracks. The priest told us that in spite of all his good deeds and respectability, still Mr. Nath's son had turned out to be a waster. In this oblique manner he hinted at a similar problem for the lineage of railway employees as that mentioned by the priest in the Ram Mandir.

Next, Abdel took me to the Catholic graveyard, between the railway station and the old Indian barrack lines. There, we met Clarence Vanjo, a retired Anglo-Indian guard, who was crying by his wife's grave. He told us that every day he goes to the cemetery. He washes the grave, decorates it with flowers, and then burns candles and incense on it. He repeats daily the practice associated with All Souls' Day when Anglo-Indians and Indian Catholics commemorate their ancestors. He told us that he has to go each day because his wife's ghost calls him there. Mr. Vanjo complained about the state of the graveyard, saying that it was hatred that had made the Indians smash the faces off the angels and take the iron crosses away to make supports for *paan* (leaf parcels of betel nut) stalls. His public space of grief and memory, and his intimate past, was disappearing into fragments in the streets of the bazaar.

Finally, Abdel took me back toward the south, into the old European side of the railway colony, to show me the Masonic Lodge. Mr. D'Souza, the caretaker of the lodge, said that he and his family were old railway people. He agreed to let me look into the secret room upstairs where he told me railway officers go for their ceremonies. He added that they go there to conjure up spirits of the dead. Abdel said that the Masonic Lodge was known as the *jadu bari* (magic house) or *bhut bari* (ghost house) by railway workers. There, the railway officers are said to call up the spirits of the past to control the present and future. He added that all the local railway people say that when you walk past it at night you lose the sense of where you are going and what your destination is. You are controlled by the spirit of the house and wake up hours later not knowing where you have been. At the top of the stairs was an antechamber with an ancient Egyptian–style arch guarding the secret room. Inside the room were two wooden thrones and plinths with mason's hammers. On tables were whips, a skull with measuring calipers next to it, and a copy each of the Koran, the Bhagavad Gita, and the Bible. Against the wall was a picture showing a railway line with cross-shaped signal arms next to it leading up to heaven. The guided tour was over.

Abdel's tour was perhaps idiosyncratic, and he had his own particular reasons for it, which I address later in the book. Yet he did provide a vivid introduction to the anxieties and uncanniness that, as my longer-term research confirmed, suffuse the railway bureaucracy and its workplaces. These places are seen as filled with moral perils and transcendent forces that act outside of human agency. The malign influences arise from the colonial past and threaten the intimate integrity of genealogical lines, polluting and corrupting them. These presences demand rigorous practices that act as a bulwark against their influence. The places of the railways are also sites of disintegration and personal loss, in particular for the Anglo-Indian, Mr. Vanjo. His railway colony is full of ruins populated by domestic ghosts who seek to remake ties across the break of death and in spite of the public disappearance of their memorials. The riddle of these ethical sensibilities and of the emergence of the material and social landscape of the railway colony is what shapes the inquiries into the history of the railway bureaucracy that follows in this book.

## ANGLO-INDIANS AS A "RAILWAY CASTE"

At the core of my account of the moral universe of the railways is the intertwined history of the Anglo-Indian community and the railways.[16] My focus is on the formation of the Anglo-Indian community as a railway caste and the ethnography of its present predicament.[17] From the first operation of the railways in India, domiciled Europeans and Eurasians were preferentially recruited to upper subordinate posts, and Indians were excluded from all but the lowest levels of the hierarchy. Despite periodic efforts to reduce the expenditure on expensive European and Eurasian labor and an official policy of Indianization implemented in 1870, the railways remained the only arena of the colonial state that continued to give preference to domiciled Europeans and Eurasians in recruitment to upper subordinate posts. Even as late as 1923 nearly half of the Anglo-Indian community was employed by or associated with the railways as dependents of employees, and in 1932 almost 100 percent of the upper subordinate positions on the state-managed railways were filled by Anglo-Indians and Europeans.[18] As this book shows, the preferential recruitment of Anglo-Indians for upper subordinate positions on the railways, regulation of their social spaces in railway colonies, and cultural loyalties in educational institutions attempted to produce distinctions between the physical and moral qualities of British civil society and Indian forms of sociality. The history of these measures reveals the ways in which the administrative project of the railways made community, racial, and family affiliations into commodities at the heart of colonial capitalism, part of the public sphere, and a problem for governance. The railway bureaucracy also drew workers into new calculations of community identities and led them to forge forms of nationalism and self-fashioning that fused ideas of *jati* with political sentiments and class sensibilities. Therefore, a focus on the Anglo-Indian community reveals the hidden history of the effects of colonial bureaucracies and popular responses to them on both intimate and public forms of life.

Histories of the Anglo-Indian community written by Anglo-Indians themselves and the public rhetoric of their political organizations reveal the close relationship between their "marginal" status and the formation of apparently more "authentic" Indian community and national identities. They also indicate the personal dilemmas this formation has produced. From the 1890s, when Anglo-Indians began to write accounts of their history and to form political organizations to plead their case to colonial authorities and nationalist politicians, they were faced with two problems that reveal much about the nature of the colonial and nationalist public sphere. To enter politics they first had to argue that their private ancestral origins were respectable, traceable, and legitimate. Anglo-Indian leaders such as Stark, Maher, Dover, and Anthony, in their historical accounts of the community, attempted to remove all suspicions of their bastard, illegitimate, and low-caste status.[19] This reveals the significance of private community lineage to the politics and public life of late-colonial India. The second problem that Anglo-Indians faced was that nationalist politicians refused to build alliances with the Anglo-Indian community on the grounds that their blood, loyalty, and habits of life marked them as outside the project of a nationalism that demanded a peculiar kind of genealogical "Indianness" on the part of its members. In the pages of the *Modern Review* and other nationalist journals, in Gandhi's speeches, and in debates in the Legislative Assembly, Anglo-Indians were disqualified by their dress, "mixed" culture, and "blood-line" from taking part in the formation of a modern independent India. They surface as a curiosity whose Britishness is revealed by nasal indexes and stature in the ethnography of Thurston and statistical inquiries of Mahalanobis.[20] After Independence the Anthropological Survey of India described them as possessing a "spurious" culture that posed a problem for national integration.[21] For a long time historical inquiries written in India have continued to write Anglo-Indian history as a separate story from the history of the rest of India.[22]

Left outside the definition of nationalism, Anglo-Indian political leaders allied themselves with other excluded constituencies such as Muslims and low-caste and *dalit* groups. This alliance was forged and the principle of economic reservation for minority communities was first suggested by these groups in the Simon Commission in 1928. In their petition to the commission, the Anglo-Indian Association argued for the protection and reservation of upper subordinate positions for Anglo-Indians in the railways, customs, post, and telegraph services and constitutional safeguards for fifty years that would give the community temporary economic protection while it attained the level of education achieved by other Indian communities. At Independence the Anglo-Indian community shared the fate of scheduled tribes and scheduled castes. The Constitution of India granted to Anglo-Indians reservation in public services, including the railways, post and telegraphs, and customs, and the right to separate educational facilities for a period of ten years from 1950. Until 1960 they were placed under the administrative authority of the commissioner for scheduled castes and scheduled tribes, who continued to inquire, as the colonial state had after 1930, into the antecedents and legitimacy of members of the community.

In the decades following Independence, nationalist and more localized regional and class-inflected images of inauthenticity continued to affect the social conditions of the Anglo-Indian population. Once the guarantees of preferential employment expired in 1960, the economic fortunes of the Anglo-Indian population declined sharply while negative representations of male Anglo-Indians prevented easy access for them to other avenues of employment. Indian films and literature depict the Anglo-Indian woman as disreputable, and the resistance of Hindu families to intermarriage demonstrates the salience of this public failure to be Indian to private family alliances. For Bengali middle-class society in Kolkata and Bengali railway workers in Kharagpur, Anglo-Indians are immediately identifiable by their dress, Christianity, accented English, Bengali, and Hindi, and most of all by their unrespectability. They are often described in fiction as anomalous "survivors" who are marked by their improper sexuality and degeneration. In films such as *Chowringee Lane* they are the lonely and lost remnants of a colonial order. They also represent inappropriate and immoral forms of modernity. In Satyajit Ray's *Mohan Nagar*, an Anglo-Indian woman guides a middle-class Bengali housewife forced into the public space of work by her family's poverty by giving her the insignia of *adhunik* (modern) female sexuality—lipstick and sunglasses. Her husband is shamed when he sees his wife wearing these in a cafe, talking to a male customer, and he feels he has forced her into new kinds of degradation. On the streets of Kolkata and Kharagpur, Anglo-Indian women are more widely seen as public property to be "eve-teased." When I was walking through the streets of the city and the railway colony with Anglo-Indian women, the prurient gaze of male members of the public was palpable to me. In conversations with Bengali middle-class women I was told stories of the degeneration of *bongsho* (family lines) by the intermarriage of members of their family with Anglo-Indians. Bengali middle-class men told me of their extramarital affairs with Anglo-Indian women, which symbolized for them the fact that they had strayed too far from their Bengali roots. One explained that his relationship with an Anglo-Indian girl had been based solely on his quoting of Shakespeare to her as she sat "entranced." Bengali railway workers complained that the problem with Anglo-Indians was that they had no *desh* (village home) and therefore no country of origin. Bengali railway workers and middle-class Bengalis were all united in their assertions that Anglo-Indians were *tash*, a term applied equally to Indian Christians and Anglo-Indians that suggests that they are low-class, too Anglicized, rootless, sexually disreputable, and cheap imitations. Given this context of declining economic fortunes and unclear status, it is not surprising that half the Anglo-Indian population (estimated at 200,000 at Independence) has emigrated from India looking for a new life in Australia, New Zealand, or Britain.

One of the few spaces that Anglo-Indians can claim as a home territory, equivalent to the originary *desh* of Bengalis, is the railway colony itself. Among members of the Anglo-Indian community in Kolkata, railway families are immediately distinct in their identity. "Railway girls" were described as homely, respectable, simple in their habits, and a little too rustic for the evils of Kolkata. "Railway boys" brought up in the colonies or former railway employees were often seen as daringly cosmopolitan, with experience of a variety of locations due to their education in a network of boarding schools and job transfers. Members of these dispersed railway families return to the colony for seasonal dances at the Railway Institute or just to spend time in them as a change from the city. The fact that one's family had worked on the railways is also taken as proof of British lineage. It gives one access to a kind of authorized origin that nonrailway Anglo-Indians do not automatically possess. Anglo-Indians argued that in the railway colonies it was less easy to fake your identity because everyone knew you and your lineage and the railway authorities checked your antecedents before employment. Railway Anglo-Indians proudly offered to show me the certificates issued to them or their male relatives by the railway bureaucracy for good service in order to indicate their authenticity. One eighty-year-old Anglo-Indian woman, Phylis Daniels, described her movement outside the railway colony as a difficult loss of status. She moved with her husband from the railway colony at Jamalpur to a slum near the railway tracks on the outskirts of Kolkata. She said she managed to survive and to keep up her daughter's respectability in this environment. But she added that almost every month other Anglo-Indians, those who could not bear this change, committed suicide by throwing themselves on the railway tracks nearby. Anglo-Indian families who had left the space of the railway colony far behind remembered it as a place that had provided them with a kind of industrial *desh*.

Anglo-Indians in Kharagpur tell more complex stories about the history of railway colonies and their contemporary predicament. For them there is a radical and perplexing disjuncture between their sense of self and their present existence. They do not have the luxury of Kolkata Anglo-Indians of resting secure in a self-hood ascribed to them by the past of the railway colony, and their situation is usually economically precarious. They remember the past of the colony in a less nostalgic vein, recalling the ambivalent status of their family members under British rule. They struggle to make material their British origins and family history and to negotiate their place as Indian citizens with their fellow workers. It is on their attempts to try to produce proof and substance for their family histories, kinship connections, genealogies, memories, and political affiliations that I focus in large parts of my ethnography.[23]

In this way, my work joins a group of recent studies inspired by Stoler's work on sexuality, respectability, and empire that have used the history and contemporary situation of Anglo-Indians to reveal the relationships between imperial rule and the intimate politics of domestic spaces. Some of this work has focused on attempts by the colonial state to gather moral authority to itself and to carefully control access to rights to economic and national status through legal rulings on Eurasian families.[24] This has contributed to a broader project that is exploring the radical restructuring of notions and practices of family, attachment, and property under colonialism in India.[25] Other work has looked at the situation of Anglo-Indians in the present, analyzing them as, in Caplan's words, "children of colonialism" in "a post-colonial world."[26] These studies move between the large-scale spatial politics of decolonization and the microcosm of domestic practices within families. All of this work has profoundly questioned assertions that imperialism and nationalism worked via a separation of gendered spheres of either public or private, or in Bengali terms *baire ghare*. Instead, this separation is shown to be a profoundly polemical claim that produces a series of reshapings of domestic life by state institutions, reforming organizations, and family members.[27]

My approach to Anglo-Indians as a railway caste shares this emphasis on the politics and distribution of privilege in the domain of domesticity but attempts to take the arguments further. I use the marginalization of Anglo-Indians also to explore the idioms and ethics of colonialism and nationalism and their grounding in transformed concepts of kinship. In contexts other than India, the situation of "mixed-race" communities has been used to trace various historically and morally structured links between nationalism and exclusionary practices of racism.[28] So in the United States, for example, the rule of hypodescent, or the one-drop rule, in which any child with one drop of black blood is automatically classed as "black," provides the racial underpinnings for the myth of the immigrant melting pot. It is also no doubt grounded in the naturalization of blood as the source of the substance of kinship that is then crosscut by the order of law as described for American kinship by Schneider. In Trinidad, in contrast to this, the image of racial hybridity as a national moral form then marks East Indians as distinct because of their "retrograde" attempts to remain "pure." It is particularly striking that these issues have not been explored in relation to the attitudes of both British colonial officials and Indians toward Anglo-Indians. The marginalization of Anglo-Indians reveals much about the cosmologies of the nation and the ways they have been rooted in transformed notions of kinship, natural inheritances, and descent.[29] In my account here I trace the specific history of the ways in which nation and race have been made part of intimate genealogies and family practices in transactions with one colonial bureaucracy. My analysis does not stop here; it also addresses how people attempt to give substance to their genealogies in their everyday lives and maneuver within or around this history of intimate interventions. In these attempts to make ancestry and inheritances, structural dilemmas of social status (linked to class, nationalism, and race) meet other more existential issues of death, love, care for family members, and commemoration of ancestors and interact with religious and other idioms. It is in the realm of genealogy that social positionings including those of being or not being part of a nation, community, or class are linked into intimate experiences. For Anglo-Indians and other Indian railway families, their attempts to bring forth origins, commemorate them, and give them physical and nonphysical substance are marked by the history that I uncovered in the railway archive in the Eastern Railway Headquarters.[30] They traffic not simply in idioms of relatedness or even of nationalism imagined as kinship, but in historically and institutionally produced techniques for suturing and severing connections to other human beings and to the past.

## THE RAILWAY ARCHIVE AND ETHNOGRAPHY

The Eastern Railway Headquarters, from which the network of the Eastern Railway that stretches through Bengal and Bihar is managed, stands at one corner of Dalhousie Square—the old administrative heart of Kolkata. The building was constructed in the 1870s, and its architecture presents a curious mix of references to Mughal rule and the long march of technology toward a bright future. The red-brick facade of the building is topped by a white Islamic dome that stands above a frieze that trumpets the progress of technology from the discoveries of the ancient Greeks to the Industrial Revolution. The building is separated from the street by huge, sharp, cast-iron railings, and its entrances are guarded by the Railway Protection Force, the dedicated police force for the railways well known among employees for strike breaking and petty pilfering. Outside one can find hawkers selling old railway-service exam papers to clerks who are eager to improve their rank. The hawkers are frequently joined by union-led sit-ins protesting the failures of the railways to live up to their promises to recruit and promote scheduled castes and tribes or to honor wage agreements. Inside and away from the main grand entrance and central corridors the building is a warren of windowless corridors and stairways, built by the British to conceal the movement of clerks and peons. In these clerks cluster, smoking and gossiping, around *paan* stalls. Files stained black from dust and red from betel-nut juice are dumped haphazardly on the stairs. In the main corridors the atmosphere is that of a formal waiting room. The sunlight pours from the open verandas onto people sitting on benches below signs leading to the air-conditioned rooms of the railway officers. On my first day in the headquarters I sought permission from the deputy general manager to look for colonial records in the building. From that moment I became a member of those crowds of clerks, workers, and businessmen. I was drawn into networks of favor and friendship in a manner that made it clear that I was working in a living archive. This wasn't because the documents I read were still consulted. On the contrary, the record books and files I looked at were forgotten in the dark, subterranean Agent's Record Room and in the loft of the Mechanical Engineering Library. They were clogged with dust and chewed by rats. The Agent's Record Room was supervised by aging or injured athletes who had been originally taken on as part of the sports quota for the railways to fill their various athletics and soccer teams. During my time working in the record room they were called upon only once, to deposit some files on the shelves. Usually they sat around chatting or left their posts to attend sports events. No one other than myself ever looked at the files stored there. This was a living archive for other reasons.

First of all, the Eastern Railway Headquarters was a place where documents did not just create authority or record events, but were the medium through which social relationships were contested and formed. This became clear to me in part because of the long process of extracting a letter of permission from the deputy general manager to allow me into the Agent's Record Room. This letter was negotiated with numerous visits to his office in which I usually just sat forgotten in a corner until my novel presence had conveyed his authority over foreign scholars to the assembled clerks and clients. Once the letter was disbursed he very kindly signaled the new grounds of our relationship by inviting me to his huge Victorian railway flat in Colvin Court near Howrah station so I could interview him about his years of service. The rooms were the largest I had ever seen in a private residence, and the balcony was so big you could have played cricket on it. It overlooked the Florentine towers of Howrah station, which house the running-staff rooms crammed with bunk beds and the bungalows of junior officers. He told me that the rooms were so empty because he and his family couldn't afford enough furniture to fill them. There, I met his wife and two young children. He introduced his daughter and son by saying, "this one is from Battinkarna" and "this one is from Ondal," naming the railway colonies in which they were born. The intimacy of my visit, news of which spread fast among the clerks in the headquarters, as well as my possession of a one-line letter from the divisional general manager, gave me tremendous status. And this called forth further favors and attempts to use my influence. Clerks often interrupted my work in the record room with offers of help, adding that they had heard that I had used my influence to get other clerks better positions elsewhere. This was all a very direct lesson in how the documents I was reading had been caught up in similar processes of negotiation. I began to read them not just as sources, but also as material artifacts that embodied power and forged selves. In this context and in many others, they did not just create a transcendent idea of the bureaucratic authority of the nation-state, but became extensions and materializations of persons circulating and transmitting elements of their essences and qualities.[31] This insight was reinforced by the fact that the librarians who oversaw two of the collections I consulted (the Mechanical Engineering and Personnel Libraries) acted as advisers to railway workers on writing petitioning letters to officers when they had been demoted, dismissed, or treated unfairly. Documents were part of elaborate strategies to redirect the social indifference and depersonalization of responsibility of the bureaucracy through networks of personal connection.[32]

The headquarters was a living archive in another important sense. The railway morality that framed the gossip about fellow workers and myself was a precipitate of the historical processes I was researching. Clerks warned me not to associate with the deputy general manager or with other staff members because they had bad morals and were alcoholics. They suggested that I was safe with them instead because of their unimpeachable behavior. I was lectured on the immorality of Western women and Anglo-Indians and then congratulated on my unusual demure manner, married status, and wearing of a *salwar kameez* (long dress and trousers; often worn by young professional women) and *shakha pola* (bracelets that are a Bengali sign of marriage). Stories were confided to me about low-ranking clerks and how their vices of gambling or other faults of alleged corruption had led to their demotion. When Anglo-Indian workers accompanied me to the offices, staff members—who were friendly with me—cut them dead or ignored them. In conversation Anglo-Indians often came up as an ethical and professional reference point. For example, a Bengali junior officer in his thirties gave me an account of his career progression as follows. He was brought up in the railway colony at Bilaspur, where his father was an accounts clerk. As a child he envied the Anglo-Indian community for their liberty, sportsmanship, and musical abilities. But as he grew up, left the railway school, and progressed through various positions until he became the head of a training school for junior officers, all his Anglo-Indian friends "disappeared." People like himself had replaced them, or they had been left behind. He described how he had even replaced his own Anglo-Indian teacher, who had been head of the training school before him. He added that he thought that their disappearance and decline was due to a degeneration of their family life and morals. This, of course, implied that his own domestic and personal probity had led to his rapid rise. In this environment there was an immediate resonance between the documents I was consulting and the everyday practices of distinction and tales of morality at work around me. This traffic in ethical stories has, as I discovered, a particular historical frame. These stories speculate on a long-standing tension in the railway bureaucracy using idioms of bureaucratic honor, race, and *jati*. This is the contradiction between its claims to social indifference and fairness and its practices of personalized power and moral judgment.

The Eastern Railway Headquarters was also a living archive in a quite different respect. People who worked there attempted to explain their present situation with stories about the recurrence of the past. Publicly, officers tended to emphasize a dramatic break with the past at Independence and the new national project of running the railways. However, clerks puzzled over the not quite complete realization of a modern Indian national time and place in the railway headquarters. They were troubled by the colonial roots of the institution they worked in and felt as if time in it was out of joint. They suggested that anything that was wrong with it was due to a fatal and irresistible inheritance from British colonial rule. For example, if officers had high-handed manners this was described as an automatic outgrowth from their British forebears. Clerks felt too that the headquarters building itself acted as an agent that collapsed times together, rejoining in particular the despotic and excessive past of Muslim rule to the present. The General Manager's Office was at the very top of the building under the "Islamic"-style dome that crowns it. The approach to it is framed by pink keyhole arches and columns most reminiscent of Moorish Spanish architecture. I passed it quite often because the Mechanical Engineering Library, where some of the old records were kept, was tucked away down a corridor next to it. Whenever clerks accompanied me they whispered that this section of the building was constructed from part of the Mughal palace, on which the Eastern Railway Headquarters had been built. Later, I was also told that at night the Railway Protection Force officers who guarded the building heard the ghostly sound of *ghazals* (Urdu songs of lost love) and the laughter of men and women coming from that place. These tales were interesting for clerks because they could use them to explore the sense they had of working in a peculiar time and place. The bureaucracy in this setting did not simply manifest a routinization of work in which every action took its place in a national chronotope.[33] Instead, it seemed to preserve other places and times. Clerks attempted to explain how their surroundings had come to feel like a living archive. In turn, in this book, I explore why railway workers have this sense of the inappropriate irruption of the past in the present.

The unusual quality of the Eastern Railway Headquarters as a living archive made me think carefully about the stories we tell about the immanence of colonial history in the present. On the one hand there appeared to be a direct similarity between some of the material I was uncovering in the record rooms and the present. In particular the files I found of petitions demanding redress from the bureaucracy, and from workers requesting the bureaucracy to verify their national and racial identities, seemed to be connected to contemporary railway moralities and to the dilemmas facing Anglo-Indians. On the other hand, to explain this resonance as simply a continuation from the colonial past seemed inadequate. This would not really be an explanation, but a variant of the sense railway clerks have of the supernatural emergence of the past in the present. Researching in this context pushed me toward a careful tracing of exactly which elements of the colonial past of the railway bureaucracy are revived at a quotidian level by the practices within the institution in the present. It also led me to focus on the accounts by workers of the relations between the past and present as the product of dispositions toward the past that have been shaped by the history of the railway bureaucracy. These accounts often work at a tangent to historical events, sometimes obscuring them in ways that help to reproduce the influence of colonial practices.

Inspired by the resonances I experienced between archive and ethnography, the chapters that follow trace the historical emergence of ethical sensibilities, orientations toward the past, and institutional forms that structure the daily lives of railway workers today. The first part of the book retells the history of the railways.

This history provides a unique window onto the process of the spatial and institutional formation of the colonial and postcolonial state in India—of the creation of its verticality and encompassment of Indian subjects through its reach along the tracks of the railway.[34] The railway bureaucracy in all its minute practices attempted to assert the transcendent legitimacy and moral authority of British rule. Railway workers were drawn into these new kinds of moral reckonings in their workplaces. Travelers on the railways also experienced new kinds of public places. Long before the mass travel of tourists or electronic global flows of capital the Indian railways restructured experiences of landscape, space, and time, as well as the flow of income and goods to and from the subcontinent. This restructuring in a colonial context was marked by attempts to discipline, contain, and put people back into their places and strata of origin. The experience of modernity in India and elsewhere was not and still is not experienced as a simple escape into laissez-faire individualism or into neutral national or global citizenship.[35] As we will see, the railways diffused the authority of the colonial state throughout India. Yet they also provoked ethical outrage about this authority, helping to form nationalist communities of sentiment and creating new contexts for the emergence of political solidarities and social distinctions based on adaptations of ideas of bureaucratic honor, domesticity, and *jati*.

The second half of the book is an ethnography of contemporary railway morality and of the dispositions toward the past among Anglo-Indian and Bengali railway families. Although my work was based on broader research, in this section the experiences and narratives of particular families and individuals figure largely. These people are at the core of my argument because it is only through a map of their specific longings, hopes, family romances, and discontents that it is possible to destabilize some of the past and present reifying practices of the railway bureaucracy. As Michael Hertzfeld has argued, bureaucracies are often key sites for routinized procedures that attempt to produce social indifference, taxonomies of belonging, and the transcendence of the nation-state. The experiences I recount both show the impact of these practices and unravel their reifications by personalizing the effects of the railway bureaucracy and tracing its relation to intimate life.[36] It also becomes clear from the predicament of Anglo-Indian railway families that kinship, genealogies, and memories in India, and elsewhere, have become entangled with archival technologies and the moralizing taxonomies of bureaucracies.[37] As I explore further in the conclusion, now when we tell our family histories and family romances of sentimental and natural kinship connections we inevitably engage in a negotiation of the terms of this engagement with the institutions of the nation-state. Often we also attempt to forge our own political and ethical projects in order to create a trajectory apart from the kinlike moralities of, administration of sentiment by, and attempts to control social reproduction by bureaucracies.[38]

# Part I

## Chapter One

# The Indian Railways and the Management of the Material and Moral Progress of Nations, 1849–1860

*Reader*: Be that as it may, all the disadvantages of railways are more than counter-balanced by the fact that it is due to them that we see in India the new spirit of nationalism.

*Editor*: Only you and I and others who consider ourselves civilized and superior persons imagine that we are many nations. It was after the advent of railways that we began to believe in distinctions, and you are at liberty now to say that it is through the railways that we are beginning to abolish these distinctions.

—M. Gandhi, *Hind Swaraj*

The origins of the railways in India are usually traced through the negotiations among entrepreneurial dreams, manufacturing interests, and the administrative ambitions of the East India Company.[1] Their story is then continued with an account of the technical and managerial feats of track construction.[2] More critical work then outlines the effects of the railways in the terms set by economic nationalism. Nationalist politics in the period from 1880 to 1905 was catalyzed by attacks on the economic policies of the colonial state as unrepresentative and undemocratic.[3] In these challenges to the legitimacy of the government, nationalists such as Naoroji, Joshi, Ranade, and Dutt first began to imagine a national economy and to calculate its losses in statistical forms.[4] In the case of the railways, their calculations showed that they were profoundly detrimental to India. These nationalists argued that they could not bring prosperity to India as they had to other countries because their profits were siphoned off into British hands. Even worse than this were the terms of the guarantee arrangement between railway companies and the government. On their formation, railway companies would deposit a certain amount of capital with the government of India, on which they would be paid 5 percent annual interest from the pockets of Indian taxpayers. If the railways proved unprofitable and had to be closed, then they would be given back to the government and the capital sum would be returned in full to the companies. Nationalist calculations also showed that large sums of money were extracted from circulation within India in the forms of payments for imported materials, expenditure on offices in England, and salaries to expensive European staff. The effects on internal trade were shown to be a disaster too. Railways facilitated the export of food grains, which meant that there was insufficient supply during times of famine. Their rates policy favored imports from ports and therefore helped to destroy local manufactures and underwrite the expansion of consumption of British commodities. Their employment of only British and Anglo-Indian workers in positions of responsibility meant that there was no transfer of industrial skills to Indians. Railways only served to impoverish Indians and hold them back from any form of industrial progress. Some commentators even suggested that railway management in India was designed to turn the country into nothing more than an agricultural colony of Britain.[5] These long-standing critiques of the railways have recently been supplemented by work that suggests they were a colonial institution of command and governmental control.[6]

Yet the standard origin point for the railways and the critiques of them do not address two other essential aspects of the project of the Indian railways. From the 1840s, they created a new sphere of government action materialized in a highly centralized bureaucracy. The railway administration forged a form of rule in which governance was not about the creation of forms of political life—rights and duties or the representation of interests—but about the sustenance of the prosperity of India through the action of bureaucratic experts.[7] Even more importantly, from 1857 they were part of an economic vision that centered on the complex problem of managing the physical and moral well-being of populations as well as on balance sheets and imperial military control. The railways in India were entangled in projects of imperial governance that, as Gandhi argued in *Hind Swaraj*, led to the emergence of new kinds of social distinctions.

## A NEW TECHNOLOGY FOR GOVERNANCE

The infamous guarantee agreement signed in February 1849 between the East India Company and the East Indian Railway Company and the Great Indian Peninsular Railway Company can be seen as an important beginning for the railways. Yet its significance is different from that usually depicted. The contracts with the companies tied every transaction and decision the railways made to the scrutiny of East India Company officials. The East India Company (and after

1858 the government of India) had the right to choose or alter the route of each line and approve rolling stock, schedules, rates, and fares. The boards of the railways in Britain had to include a government representative who could veto all of a railway's decisions. In India a consulting engineer to the government of India would oversee all company transactions and plans. A new field of action and intervention opened *in potentio* for the East India Company, which could—if successful—silence its free trade critics at home and secure the legitimacy of its project of rule among Indian subjects.

It was the governor-general Dalhousie who turned this financial agreement into a grand project of reconstructing the technology of rule in India. Lord Dalhousie's minute written in 1853 provided the charter for the first period of major railway construction. Dalhousie insisted on the commercial and social advantages that India would derive from railways, which he said were "beyond all present calculation." He divided India into a series of markets, ports, and great tracts of land "teeming with produce they cannot dispose of." Railways would inevitably lead "to the same encouragement of enterprise, the same multiplication of produce, the same discovery of latent resource, to the same increase of national wealth, and to some similar progress in social improvement that have marked the introduction of improved and extended communication in various kingdoms of the Western world." This process would be speeded up by the cooperation with private companies because they would act as agents of "English capital and English energy" that would rectify the fact that "the spirit of enterprise still shows so feebly in India." But this transformation according to the universal laws of political economy aided by the special genius of "English capital" would not be the only consequence. The map of India did not only show resources and markets in Dalhousie's panoramic vision; it also showed hostility and threats to the security of territory. Dalhousie wrote:

> A single glance cast upon the map, recalling to mind the vast extent of the Empire we hold,—the various classes and interests it includes,—the wide distances which separate several points at which hostile attack may at any time be expected,—the perpetual risk of such hostility appearing in quarters where it's the least expected—the expenditure of time, of treasure and of life that are involved in even the ordinary routine of military movements over such a tract,—and the comparative handful of men scattered over its surface, who have been the conquerors of the country and now hold it in subjection—a single glance upon these things will suffice to show how immeasurable are the political advantages to be derived from a system of internal communication, which would admit of full intelligence of every event being transmitted to the Government . . . at a speed . . . five-fold

its present rate; would enable the Government to bring the main bulk of military strength to bear upon any given point in as many days as it would now require months.[8]

Dalhousie dreamed of the scale and reach of the railway as a new technology that would make the government present everywhere, all-seeing, efficient in its concentrations of force, and parsimonious in its expenditure of treasure and the lives of its soldiers. Now the state in India had acquired a new technological form that would allow it to be profitable in a much wider sense. Its influence would circulate like the capital and commodities carried on the railways into the transactions of everyday exchange.

To realize this new technocratic vision, Dalhousie fully utilized the potential for government control that existed within the guarantee contracts. Earlier in his career, in Britain, he had been head of the Railway Department of the Board of Trade. This had been a frustrating experience for him because every attempt to reign in the practices of railway companies was overturned in Parliament. Railway interests were just too wealthy and well represented by MPs to be controlled. But in India there was no parliament to restrain government action, and Dalhousie himself described his role as that of a benign despot.[9] All of Dalhousie's actions in fact centralized the railway bureaucracy under the decision-making power of the new Public Works Department and ultimately the governor-general. Initially, in India the railway companies were supervised by a consulting engineer for guaranteed railways appointed by the central government. He was the head of a small railway department that was part of the Central Public Works Department. All matters of importance were ultimately referred to the governor-general and later the secretary of state for India. From the outset, the Railway Department scrutinized every transaction the railway companies undertook, from the composition of the workforce, provision of housing, and station buildings and stores to regulations used to govern traffic and railway workers.

Under successive viceroys the character of the autocratic bureaucracy Dalhousie had established continued with greater elaboration. In 1866 a railway branch separate from the Public Works Department was created, and it was headed by a special deputy secretary. In the late 1860s as the railway network expanded provincial consulting engineers were appointed for each region. They had to inspect every line before it was opened and regularly examine it afterward. They also had to inquire into all accidents and injuries, matters of safety on the line, the convenience of the public, and well-being of the staff. All matters that were not routine were referred for decision to the government. These officials worked on behalf of Indian subjects to reduce risks to their lives and infringement on their commercial transactions and to ensure the smooth running of the lines for the movement of troops and government information. In comparison with the power of officials in Britain, their power was almost despotic. For example, Dalhousie applied the Land Acquisition Act of 1821 to the purchase of land for railways. As a result, unlike in Britain, in India there was no recourse for landholders to question the provincial governments' definition of the taking of their lands for "public purpose." The successive Railway Acts of 1854, 1871, and 1890 did not include any provision for Indians to protest against the choice of routes for lines by the government or the rates for goods offered by railway companies. Such provision to protest the practices of private railway companies and their choice of lines existed from the 1840s in Britain.[10] However, in India government officials and companies acted on behalf of an absent public.

The bureaucratic chain of command remained the same until the viceroy, Lawrence, in 1867 advocated direct state construction of new railways. Lawrence's successor, Mayo, introduced this practice in 1869 for the newly planned lines from Lahore to Rawalpindi and Carwar to Hubli. As the guarantee arrangements with other companies expired some of these, such as the East Indian Railway, became state-run lines. This experiment necessitated a greater centralization of the bureaucracy. In 1870 state railways were taken away from the Public Works Department and placed under a state consulting engineer for railways. In 1874 a state railway directorate was formed. Some state railways such as those in Burma, the Central Provinces, and the North West Provinces were left in charge of local governments. By 1881 a director-general of railways oversaw the running of the Imperial State Railway of Scindia, the Punjab-Northern Railway, the Indus-Valley Railway, and the Kandahar Railway. The railway branch of the Public Works Department oversaw the East Indian Railway, the Eastern Bengal Railway, the Oudh-Rohilkhund Railway, and the Sindh Punjab and Delhi Railway. Smaller railways were overseen by the respective provincial governments in Madras, Bombay, Bengal, North West Provinces, Central Provinces, and Burma. None of these developments undermined the pattern laid down by Dalhousie of making government control central to the running of railways in India. When new lines urgently had to be built in the 1880s, the government turned again to a guarantee system, but their control of companies remained as tight as ever.

After 1857 this powerful bureaucracy was guided by a new vision of the Indian economy and the significance of railways. In the postrebellion period debates about the importance and management of railways focused on the reproduction and security of British populations in the hostile climate of India. The differences between the Indian economy and its populations and those of Britain began to be specified in detail in a manner that they had never been before. The absent public on behalf of whom bureaucrats and entrepreneurs saw themselves as acting was coming into view. But this public was not the same as that in Britain; it was made of multiple populations with diverse qualities of life and moral conduct. This vision made morality, nationalism, and race explicitly part of the railway's business. The railways would now be part of an economic project that involved social engineering on grand and intimate scales.

## AN ECONOMY OF MORALS

The postrebellion vision of the railways and template for their management is to be found in the discussions of the colonization and settlement of India. Dreams of European settlement in India were nothing new and had long been strongly resisted by East India Company officials.[11] But these dreams were given a new saliency in 1857 and 1858 as a result of two events. The end of East India Company rule gave laissez-faire projects for India a new lease of life. These had always included an expanded notion of the potential role of European settlers in India. Also, the rebellion of 1857 seemed to many to demonstrate the danger of a small British presence in India and the necessity of making the "interests" and "affections" of the populations that inhabited the subcontinent more akin to those of British rulers. But most importantly, these discussions were a response to the crisis of legitimacy of the Raj and shaken confidence of both bureaucrats and the wider public in Britain in the forms of rule in India. As we will see, they explored and affirmed the physical and moral grounds on which the British, and in particular the British middle classes, should rule in India at a moment of intense doubt. As the debates about colonization took off they became about much more than just the immediate issue of whether to allow settlement of India. They defined the nature of the British presence in India, the threats to British rule, the nature of Indian and British populations, and, most importantly, explored the relevance of these various factors to the management of the Indian economy. The settlement of working classes in India was ultimately rejected after extensive inquiries in the Parliamentary Commission on Colonisation and Settlement of India in 1858. However, the mapping of a peculiarly Indian economy that demanded specific kinds of management and self-management carried out in this debate had a much longer life in administrative practice on the railways.

The first clear statement of the potential importance of railways to the security of populations in India came in a pamphlet published by Hyde Clarke during the rebellion in 1857. Clarke, an influential railway economist, editor of the *Railway Times*, and agitator for railways in India, wrote a pamphlet dedicated to the East India Company titled *Colonisation, Defence and Railways in Our Indian Empire*.[12] This urged the government to construct railways to Darjeeling and Simla that would allow India to be governed from the hill stations and open up these regions for the entrance of English capital, laborers, and middle classes. Clarke argued that the heads of civil, military, medical, and ecclesiastical administration and the mint, post office, Public Works Department, merchant houses, and railway workshops should all be transferred to the hills. Pensioned soldiers, immigrants at a rate of 50,000 a year promoted by an Indian immigration department in London, and retired lower officials would all be given land grants in Darjeeling and Simla on the Wakefield system used in Australia. The Eurasian and European clerks and mechanics who worked on the plains could settle their families in the hills and visit them frequently with the aid of cheap second- and third-class return tickets. "By creating a home for the working classes of England in the hills, India would readily obtain the needful assistance of skilled labor in every department of industry, nor would the workmen be so much exposed to habits of intemperance and irregularity," without the "hazard of misconduct or death" (p. 136). In Clarke's scheme the proposed railways would secure the reproduction of British populations and capital, removing them from the debilitating influence of the Indian climate. He argued that in the hill stations everything from joint-stock companies, appropriate domestic influences, and Christianity to a militia to defend India from internal and external attack would flourish. Islands of British civil society, as Clarke called them "English Towns," and the colonial state would be planted in the hills, and "moral resources would be more largely developed in India and consequently the field for European labor extended" (pp. 3, 136). The new hill railways linked to the trunk lines would transcend the "pestilence" and demoralizing influences of India (p. 129). European travelers insulated from India would spread the theory of science, enterprise, and capital, developing "the machinery of civilization" (p. 137).

In his pamphlet Clarke adapted ideas of medical topography and ethnoclimatology that had first been applied to India in terms of the management of the health of soliders to the arena of political economy and the potential of the railways. In this political economy Indian and European populations were seen as profoundly distinct, and this difference was naturalized as the varying ability of their bodies to survive in different climates and locations. Clarke imagined a topography that would further materialize their separation. Europeans would be part of a kind of hilltop fortress state. This state would defend its security on the domestic, personal, political, and economic fronts while disseminating enterprise and enlightenment to Indians. All this would be achieved with railway technology, which according to Hyde had the double benefit of reducing the risks of loss of life and of commodities. Although extreme, his plan has echoes in more official documents, including those of the Parliamentary Commission on Colonisation and Settlement of India. Even when people argued against such schemes they used the same metonymical overlaying of the reproduction of race, nation, and capital as Clarke and proved these links with the laws of political economy. Race, nation, and the growth of capital were all seen as acting together as natural, or rather naturalized, forces. This was a new application of medical theories of ethnoclimatology and topography, which had first been applied to the management of the army in India, that made them relevant to economic calculations.[13]

Apart from a pioneering article by David Arnold, the Parliamentary Commission on Colonisation, which met from 1858 to 1859, has been sidelined in the story of the postrebellion state, but at the time it was as important as the discussions of the reform of the army, police, and land-tenure systems.[14] Backed by liberal members of Parliament who saw such a debate as an opportunity to fully discredit the old East India Company government and to set a new stamp on India policy, the liberal MP William Ewart called for an investigation into colonization and settlement in March 1858. Once the committee was in session its deliberations were eagerly watched by the British in India and widely reported in newspapers and journals. Committee members were mainly important East India Company bureaucrats and influential liberal MPs. They included R. D. Mangles, who had been chairman of the court of directors of the East India Company during the rebellion. There were also people who combined administrative clout with experience of the railways: for example, J. P. Willoughby, who had been on the original committee of the Bombay Great Eastern Railway and after many years of service on the Governor's Council in Bombay had been made a member of the new India Council. Similarly, there was Sir Erskine Perry, who had also been involved with the origins of the Bombay railway, was chief justice in India, and later joined the India Council, in 1859. The liberal MPs on the committee generally shared interests in free trade, philanthropic measures for the laboring classes, and imperial endeavors. For example, the MP Arthur Kinnaird combined a concern with helping working class women by setting up refuges and reformatories for them with a detailed knowledge of India. He was the author of a book on Bengal's landed tenure and police system and his wife was one of the founders of the British Ladies Female Emigration Society and the Zenana Bible and Medical Mission. Experience of other colonial settings was provided by people like Robert Lowe, who had been on the legislative council for New South Wales in the 1840s with special responsibility for financial and educational questions. In the 1850s he was given roles in Britain on the Board of Control, Board of Trade, and Council on Education.

This mixture of influential liberal opinion and old East India Company experience combined to produce a new orthodoxy on the dangers and potential of the Indian environment for European enterprise. For witnesses the committee members called upon a range of people, from planters to clergymen to medical professionals who had experience of India. Guided by these witnesses they established that domestic habits and modes of life were relevant to the security of state and economy in India. The railways emerged as a means of escaping the limits of this environment and of preserving the integrity of Europeans. They would also have to be managed in a manner that would take into account the particular dangers of India and the qualities of life among Indians. In addition this committee gave the British middle classes a unique destiny in India. Because of their pedigree and moral practices they were uniquely suited to produce a flourishing economy. Medical ideas of ethnoclimatology were enfolded in this committee into a model of Indian economic life. They were also combined with a contradictory understanding of processes of social improvement, which, although universal, had to be guided by a particular class and race group with innate moral and physical attributes.

The brief of the Parliamentary Commission on Colonisation and Settlement of India was to inquire into the practicality of introducing European settlers and commerce especially in the hill districts and "healthier climates" of India. Witnesses argued that "European skill and capital are independent of locality and . . . [it] . . . follows them whether in the eastern as well as western parts of the world,"[15] and they also advanced the proof of the greater value of indigo and cotton produced under European superintendence in "neutral" world markets. The construction of the railway trunk lines and more extensive branch lines would enable such "spirit of enterprise" to penetrate India "in all directions."[16] This would remedy the present situation in which

such capital as there is in India is hoarded up by native bankers for usurious traffic, or amassed by the native princes and zemindars, only to be lavished in the pursuit of sensual pleasure or in the celebration of the disgusting ceremonies and mummeries of paganism. No one dreams of spending any money on his land, and a native who would allot a large sum to bedizen his wife, or a hideous idol with costly jewels and ornaments, would grudge a few shillings to repair a road through his own farm.[17]

In these discussions entrepreneurial capitalism is seen as a natural characteristic of certain people because of their European pedigree. However, the project "to engraft European skill and energy and industry upon the practices of the natives and upon the country in which they are placed" appeared a more problematic task than it had at the time of Dalhousie's minute on the railways.[18] India now seemed to be filled with barriers to enterprise and could not become exactly the same as Europe or settler colonies such as Australia.

The wide range of witnesses who testified to the committee included indigo planters, barristers, army physicians, engineers, military officers, and missionaries.

Whatever position they had on colonization, they all argued that India provided an inhospitable environment for civil society and enterprise. They complained of the scandals of an unjust system of laws, inexperienced British magistrates and collectors, no representation in government, no commercial system of land sale, systems of land tenure and forced labor that resulted in social inequalities, and police administration that relied on torture. But their solution for these problems was not the reform of institutions and extension of equal legal rights, but to increase European superintendence of Indian labor at all levels of society. Democracy, liberty, and enterprise would ultimately be secured by the example of the superior moral leadership of Europeans.

Yet there was one further barrier to the spread of this European moral leadership through India—the climate of the country. As was typical in medical thought from the 1820s, the ethnoclimatological theories put forward by witnesses in the committee were combined with an emphasis on deep innate differences between populations.[19] As was the topographic medicine of the previous decades, the Committee on Colonisation was shot through with anxious questions about the dangers of the Indian environment for British populations, who were "fitted" for the temperate climes of their homeland. The testimony of experts circled around multiple speculations on these themes. They wondered whether Europeans could reproduce to a third generation in India. They explored which locations and elevations were the most favorable for European health because they most approximated their natural habitat at "home." They speculated on why the health of European men and women differed from each other and whether this reflected the varying abilities of genders to adhere to moral precepts. They wondered which mixtures of "races" produced the healthiest offspring. They addressed which kinds of Indian mothers produced efficient populations of Eurasians—Protestant, Catholic, Muslim, or Hindu. They speculated on why European railway laborers were so degenerate and Portuguese-Indian offspring so dark. They argued about which castes of Malabaris, Bengalis, or Indian Christians produced the best laborers. The witnesses tried to catalogue and statistically map on a large scale the implications of this topography and ethnoclimatology for the management of enterprise and labor. They discovered a series of peoples that each represented unique combinations of physical life, morality, and laboring efficiency. Provoked by the discussions of the committee, the English press in India began to publish articles on the moral life, habits, and economic potential of the Eurasian, Armenian, and Chinese "communities." In these discussions ethnoclimatology naturalized race as part of the inheritance and fate of the body—certain bodies were more suited to the Indian environment than others. It also created a "natural" link to the land of your birth that was expressed in the physical response of your body to other climates. The British could only naturally flourish and be productive of further generations within the specific territory of the nation. Elsewhere they were under dire peril. In this committee and the further discussions it provoked in the press in India and Britain, race and nation were perceived as inherited substances within bodies. The agricultural metaphors of English kinship based in notions of pedigree were in these ethnoclimatological discussions combined with medical theories to produce a form of English nationalism. The issues of breeding, fertility, and hybridity (understood literally as a combination of physical inheritances) that were so important as part of Victorian understandings of both kinship and nature were linked to the wealth of nations.[20] Ethnoclimatology and medical topography had a particular place in these discussions; they introduced the issue of the territory of nations to the calculations of political economy. Ideas of both pedigree and ethnoclimatology were reworked in a way that naturalized the links between the British and their territorial nation state. The fears of degeneration in ethnoclimatology and the certainty about the links between Europeans and entrepreneurial capitalism were part of a middle-class nationalism that attempted to naturalize the historical destiny of Britain to be a beacon of economic enterprise as a feature of specific bodies, lineages, and territories.

There was an important class politics to these nationalized and racialized forms of political economy as well.[21] All witnesses to the committee agreed that the only prophylactic against degeneration were middle-class temperate "habits of life," abstinence from alcohol, a European domestic environment, and residence part of the year in hill stations. The ascetic form and content of the habits necessary for the preservation of European life in India were derived from a combination of medical and religious opinion. Doctors testified on the importance of sobriety of all kinds to the physical health of Europeans whose bodies were only fitted for European or specifically British climates. Clergymen of all denominations suggested that moral control enabled Europeans in India to reproduce healthy children and to guard themselves against degeneration. However, there was some competition among them, with Protestant missionaries suggesting that Catholic and Portuguese mixed-race offspring had high rates of degeneration. In these combinations of religio-medical expertise, the nation and race were preserved by the practice of forms of moral asceticism. These forms of asceticism were unequivocally associated with the productive family sexuality and respectability of the middle classes. In this new political economy, British and Indians were imagined as possessing different moral practices, physical substances, and natural national habitats. In addition it was the peculiar features of the pedigree and moral practices of the middle classes that suited them for command both at home and abroad. Although social improvement was possible in India, it could only come under the guidance of the British middle classes.

Eventually these arguments led the committee to conclude that the empire in India should be as solidly middle class as possible since the working classes could not be trusted to govern themselves:

> The term "Colonisation" must, in this instance, clearly be limited to a class of superior settlers; who may, by their enterprise, capital, and science, set in motion the labour and develop the resources of India. The inducements to a settlement of the working classes of the British Isles are not generally to be found in India. Those inducements are high wages, the facility of obtaining land at an easy rate, the enjoyment of a constitution framed after that of the mother country, a temperate climate, and the prospect of forming a part of a community speaking our language and conforming to our manners and customs. . . . [India's] lands have mostly been appropriated; the wages of labour are low; its Government is absolute; its climate is generally unfavourable to the permanent residence and increase of the British race, and to labour in the open air; and its usages, languages, and religions are strange and repulsive to the English labourer.[22]

A new system of imperial labor control and governance was legitimized in this report and its speculations about the relevance of topography, morality, and physical capacities to enterprise. This was one in which the moral and physical qualities of the British middle classes made them naturally appropriate as supervisors and managers of empire. Similarly, the government would justify its existence by its ability to manage the diverse populations of India for the prosperity of all. Issues of political legitimacy were swept aside in a class-inflected calculus of physical and moral appropriateness for rule based on the biomoral qualities of people understood through adapted kinship idioms of pedigree and ethnoclimatological theories. The middle classes had a special destiny in Britain and India not because they could act with interests that existed apart from the domestic or private sphere.[23] On the contrary, it was their domestic practices and personal pedigree that made them peculiarly suited to be owners of capital, entrepreneurs, bureaucrats, and leaders. In the Committee on Colonisation a specific British idiom of class, nationalism, and racism was displayed. This suggested that the fertility of political economy and civil society could only be fully upheld by those whose pedigree and morals made it natural for them to do so. The generative power of individual lineages, the productivity of capital, and the prosperity of nation and empire were all collapsed together. The railways provided a technological form that would sustain the power of these lineages. They would allow the British middle classes in India to preserve their distinct qualities by making it possible for them to travel through the territory and climate of India without being affected by it. They would also make it easy for them to travel to hill stations to recuperate their productive powers. In addition the railways would be run on the template of this moral and racial calculus of productivity.

## CIRCULATING RACE AND NATION

Ideas discussed in the Committee on Colonisation and given wide publicity by the reporting on its evidence found practical expression in the management of the railways in the years that followed. Witnesses to the committee suggested that "the establishment of railways" would "give the traveler the advantage of passing rapidly through these districts where now he may be obliged to linger and so to avoid the danger of disease" and that they would provide easy access to hill stations that would secure the longevity of the European population and prevent them from passing through the "deadly terrain" that led up to these safe zones.[24] During the following decades branch lines were planned and built from the trunk lines, making the hill stations of Darjeeling, Niligiris, Ooty, and Simla accessible by rail, thus securing the healthy circulation of European bodies. The Committee on Colonisation argued against the large-scale entrance of working classes into India and recommended that a spirit of European enterprise should infuse industrial undertakings. Therefore, it suggested that the subordinate-level functionaries of railways should be Eurasian and domiciled European military orphans who had been educated in hill schools. Their wives would come from this source as well. Railway companies and other industries would pay a premium to the orphanages for those they would require. The railways from the 1860s began to train Europeans and Eurasians for upper subordinate positions gained from this source. As Arnold has argued, following the same logic as Clarke's schemes for English Towns and the committee's fears of European degeneration the railway companies constructed railway colonies that sought to morally discipline European and Eurasian workers. The railways also developed an intricate classification of laborers, attempting to enfold the opaque processes of Indian, European, and Eurasian populations into its political economy. From 1857 onward in India, nation, race, and morality were the business of the railway. The reproduction of capital and of life were seen as related natural forces that were linked to the well-being and sanctity of the nation. Their preservation required individual ascetic governance and the wise rule of morally fit British administrators, as well as the distribution of tasks to populations according to their physical and moral qualities. The sheer weight of evidence in the Parliamentary Commission and the widespread reporting on it helped to bring this new kind of Indian economy into being.

The formidable railway bureaucracy initiated by Dalhousie turned its attention toward the management of the forms of life that made up this Indian economy. Bureaucrats helped to forge new experiences of moral, national, and racial identifications. Travel and work on the railway involved Indians in an encounter with an institution that was part of the creation of the everyday colonial state and that marked them with new kinds of selfhoods. In the four chapters that follow I trace the history of these encounters. The encounters are an important part of the story not only of colonial India, but also of its postcolonial present.

## Chapter Two

# An Indian Traveling Public, 1850–1900

The engine is the source of fire.
How much strength the carriage has!
This carriage has six sahebs, two who shovel filth.
Two carriages push up against each other.
How many men fall under the influence of cum-juices!
A woman disembarks from the carriage at the station,
Running running rushing rushing.
The train stops its rhythm.
Panting, she says, "Help me, please give me water."
How much strength the carriage has!

—Pobon Das Baul, 1994

By the 1850s in Britain railways were widely perceived to be a source of social as well as economic transformation. Their public spaces were heralded by political economists and journalists as both the emblem of and a catalyst for the growth of a new, more democratic industrial era. Travel by train seemed to bring all passengers whatever their status under the sway of the progressive dictates of industrial processes. For example, an article from *The Edinburgh Review* in 1858 on the economic impact of the railways in Britain marveled that "the same loco-motive whirls along the same rail the duchess and the bag-man, the fugitive and his pursuer, the man of business who lives by saving time and the man of fashion who lives by killing it."[1] The piece continued to suggest that as these passengers traveled their "freedom of intercourse has already removed a thousand prejudices and contributed to the maintenance of those friendly relations which are the best security of mutual advantage, of common knowledge and general peace." The train was a leveling public space that would catalyze the growth of the principles of association, which formed the basis for joint-stock companies and civic life.[2] Yet rail travel also created new anxieties of forces out of control and social reversals. Railway accidents became a symptom of the potential crises of capitalism.

New illnesses were discovered, such as railway spine, which afflicted the commuter. Shock was invented as a measurable and insurable hazard that faced the railway passenger. The material culture of the station and train often attempted to ameliorate such anxieties. The middle classes bewildered by the experience of being hurtled along as part of a machine ensemble were cushioned by elaborate carriage furnishings. The division of carriages into first-, second-, and third-class naturalized social hierarchies. Station architecture and waiting rooms eased the transition into the industrial space of the train.[3]

When railways were introduced to India they were accompanied by similar dreams about their potential social effects. Entrepreneurs, government officials, and nineteenth-century histories of the railway were united in their expectation that the railways would spread new principles of association and help to forge a liberating public space. For example, Horace Davidson, in one of the first histories of the railways, wrote in 1869, "A more powerful agency than that of laws, roads, bridges, canals or even education was destined to arouse the Hindoo from his torpidity. The steam-engine was now advancing eastward and with its advance was overturning prejudices, uprooting habits and changing custom. . . . A sacred Brahmin now sits in a third-class carriage in contact with a Dome and preferring a saving in money to his caste exclusiveness, drops his prejudices."[4] But alongside this hope there were also fears among bureaucrats about the particular dangers of railway travel in India. These specific colonial anxieties gave a very different tenor to the public spaces and material culture of the Indian railways from those in Britain. Strange versions of technological, commercial spaces emerged, such as traditional, domestic railway carriages and railway stations that doubled as lock-ups and military outposts. This chapter explores the kind of public sphere and experiences of being a member of "the public" that the Indian railway carriage and station materialized.[5]

## THE RAILWAY STATION: SECURITY AND COMMERCE

In Europe the railway station in the 1830s began as a modest structure with simple wooden roofing and a single platform for arrivals and departures. But by the 1850s, with the increase in traffic and new engineering technologies, it had become a grand structure, especially in the great city termini. It now combined familiar tropes of architecture with a new space of glass and steel. The facades of stations used common if grandiose architectural references and therefore eased the transition from a nonindustrial cityscape into the technological space of the station and train. Waiting rooms sheltered passengers from too sharp a movement from one arena to another as well. By the 1860s such elaborate arrangements had become unnecessary as the city had itself become more industrialized and the public was used to the hubbub of the general mixing of social classes in the station. Yet the form, an ornate facade and then a vast industrial hall of glass and steel, remained the common practice.[6] In Britain smaller stations along the line echoed domestic architectural buildings of the period combined with gardens reminiscent of municipal parks. These stations announced the passengers' arrival at a fixed destination with familiar architecture. For those waiting on platforms they referenced easeful spaces of leisure and public mingling. The first railway stations built in India in the early years of the 1850s were similar to those of the 1830s in Europe. Their simple wooden beams and terracotta roofs rendered the station part of the landscape rather than apart from it. The use of local materials made them reminiscent of village and small-town structures. Engravings of the period show crowds assembled in attitudes of ease mingling freely.[7] These may have been somewhat idealistic representations, but they captured the aspirations of the planners of railway stations that they would unite all varieties of Indians and Europeans in a new public space of commerce. But after the 1857 rebellion the trajectory of development of railway stations in India diverged from that in Britain.

One of the many tales of horror circulated after the 1857 rebellion was that of the attack of railway engineers working on the new stations and railway lines at Etawah and Arrah. This attack seemed to crystallize the vision of the irrationality of Indian rebels because they had sought to destroy the agents and means of social progress. In fact some commentators thought Dalhousie's pace of reform, including an aggressive construction of railway lines, had in part provoked rebellion from a retrograde social order. These events, the general atmosphere of fear, and the significance of railway lines for military maneuvers led Lord Canning, the governor-general, in 1859 to call for an inquiry into the means of making railway stations defensible from attack. In the discussions that followed and later decisions on the construction of establishments the railway station subtly changed in nature from simply a place of commerce. It became an arena for the expression and protection of state authority and hierarchical relationships of command. Its architecture, location, and the law that governed it reflected a tension between a desire to materialize a neutral public sphere of commerce and a fear that Indian populations were hostile. The station therefore came to condense the paradoxical dual face of the colonial state as a liberal "reforming" agency and a military occupation.

When the architects and engineers consulted on the issue reported back to Canning on their findings they argued that it was practical to defend stations from attack. In fact they went further and suggested that stations should be planned to be the refuge for British people at times of civil war. The military engineers advised that stations near cantonments should be the "place de rendezvous" for the local British population "in preference to erecting forts."[8] Defensive ditches would be placed in front of the enclosing six-foot walls topped by iron railings. Flat-roofed buildings would be constructed with keeps "formed with projections so as to afford cross and flanking fire."[9] The location of railway stations would be chosen so as to enable them to fulfill their emergency, military functions. Already existing railway stations could be defended by constructing "sheltered communications" between the buildings, and towers could be added to existing structures.[10] One military engineer argued that a "loopholed palisading across the railway with openings sufficiently large to allow of the trains running in and out and capable of being instantly closed by a proper loopholed gate" should be added to the proposed towers and iron *chevaux de frise*.[11] But in the conclusion of the report, the officiating general engineer argued for the provision of "the required defence *without too much parade of means*. At the same time that there shall be that in the position and appearance of the buildings which shall convey an idea of solidity and an impression of safety."[12] This recommendation was approved by the lieutenant governor of Bengal, J. P. Grant, and passed on to Canning. The colonial production of capitalist circulation demanded an impossible condensation in the railway station of military command and a neutral public sphere. After this inquiry Canning prescribed the contradictory principles that should guide the construction and situation of railway stations as follows:

> 1. All railway stations must be designed primarily for the convenience of traffic and no distribution of buildings or ground that would tend to impair this should be permitted.
> 2. Traffic having the foremost place defensive arrangement should rank next. So far as is consistent with the convenience of traffic the buildings should be so disposed as to be mutually protective and they should be provided with . . . simple and inexpensive facilities for defense.[13]

All station plans were submitted to see if they met these prescriptions to the government of India before construction was allowed to begin.[14] Defensive military concerns continually resurfaced in the architecture and locations of railway stations. The first railway stations built, such as the one in Lahore, testified explicitly and fantastically to a defensive obsession. They stood as Norman castles in the landscape of India. Later constructions such as bridges, water towers in colonies (such as Liluah), and the details of station buildings (such as Ranchi) all referred back to this defensive obsession, telling the story of colonial occupation in the center of public space in a more subdued fashion.

The debates over the location of Jubalpur and Allahabad stations demonstrate these recurrent contradictions between a desire for the production of a neutral public sphere and military presence. They also mark a shift in the solution to this contradiction. This was to make the colonial state invisible in the physical features of the station while also dispersing the authoritarian powers of the state and military to railway employees. In 1865 the governor-general, John Lawrence, argued that since Jubalpur station would contain extensive workshops and was the junction of the East Indian and Great Indian Peninsula Railways, it should be built so as to be susceptible to defense. It should have an entrenched position between the city and the cantonment so as to be a line of defense for and within easy reach of the troops. Therefore, he ordered that construction of the station within Jubalpur city should be stopped. He later retreated from his decision on advice from the lieutenant governor of Bengal, William Grey, and the consulting engineer of the Public Works Department. Their argument was that

> the convenience of large cities need not be made the sole consideration in the selection of a railway site, but if the subject is closely examined it will, I think, be found to be very nearly of paramount importance. Financially natives are the mainstay of the railways. The system of trunk lines when completed will so greatly strengthen the power and hold of the government that it can I think safely afford to place each station with a view merely to commercial interests. The more the inhabitants of large and influential cites are identified with the railway thereafter will the stations and the country generally be. The people will see in the railway a developer of industry and the works that grow by peace and not merely an engine of war isolated as much as possible and kept to hold them in subjugation.[15]

The building of the railways was now a project that sought to empty railway stations of all visible signs of the colonial state as an occupying force. Instead, it aimed to create spaces that would produce and be protected by the self-interest of the Indian public. However, at the same time as these discussions were occurring Grey suggested an alternative to defensive arrangements at railway stations. This was for the English and Eurasian upper subordinates to be formed into a Railway Volunteer Infantry Corps. He argued that this measure "affording amusement to the men, would, at the same time not only give confidence to them and to the residents in their vicinity but would also effectually check any idea . . . of an attack on the station."[16] In this way, "more would be done for the security of the Railway Station than anything which is practicable in the way of fortifying existing buildings."[17] Lawrence "heartily approved" of this measure, and it was extended beyond its original implementation in Jamalpur to the whole railway network by 1866.[18] In an attempt to achieve the loyalty of Indian subjects defensive architecture would disappear. But it would be replaced by upper subordinate railway servants who would be granted the powers of the military in controlling and defending everyday traffic through the station.

This new project that aimed to attract the consent of Indian populations to British rule created a space for the growth of an aesthetics of the commercial, colonial public sphere. The removal of defensive features from stations was accompanied by an increase in associated recreational spaces and development of new architectural styles. A typical example of this is the discussion around the extension of the East Indian Railway station at Allahabad in 1868. The railway was advised by the lieutenant governor of the North West Provinces, E. Drummond, that it should create spaces for recreation. He argued that "it has long appeared [sic] to me that the space in front of the station and between the khoosroo bagh and the dispensary is singularly wanting in neatness, cleanliness and taste" and that Khusrau Bagh's position "close to the native town" recommended its transformation into a place of "public resort."[19] He added, "We have gardens and walks and drives in the new city and we must be careful to avoid the reproach that we are doing nothing for the embellishment of the native city and for the recreation of its inhabitants. . . . The native population should see and feel that we care for the aesthetical requirement of their side of the railway as well as for those of the European side."[20] Therefore, he recommended that the railway should take over the land between its station and the garden, which with the removal of the intervening "hovels" should provide an "elegant frontage" to the station.[21]

Architectural styles for stations multiplied from the middle of the 1860s in tandem with this growth of an aesthetics of public spaces. Station buildings and facades, especially at small- and medium-sized stations, usually contained references to Indian architectural styles such as mosques, palaces, and temples. The station announced itself as a specific local destination and a public space that belonged in India. For example, all along the East Indian Railway from Lucknow to Delhi buildings used adapted Indo-Islamic domes. At the larger termini in places such as Bombay, Calcutta, and Madras the station faced the city as an emblem of civilization. In some places the architecture was a mélange in the Indo-Islamic and Venetian Gothic style of Victoria terminus built in the 1880s in Bombay. At other places such as the 1868 building at Madras and 1890s building at Howrah this was unabashedly European with references to respectively Victorian Gothic and Italianate forms. What was important was not that these facades cushioned a transition into the industrial space of the platform, but that they announced the fusion of European technology and a generic force of civilization. This civilization was a world civilization that condensed and unified Indian and European styles. It often, as in Victoria terminus in Bombay, literally represented a cooperation between European architects and Indian businessmen. Most importantly, these facades no longer referenced the railway as part of an alien occupying force in the city and landscape of India.

Yet this concern for the production of a beautified and neutral public sphere for recreation and commerce was coupled with further measures that dispersed

STD STANDARD DAY SINGLE     Valid from 19 OCTOBER 2007

From LONDON TERMINALS     Valid until 19 OCTOBER 2007

To HAVANT     Adult ONE    Child NIL

Route ANY PERMITTED     ONLY VALID WITH YOUNG PERSONS RCD

Journey details (via codes see over)     Coach/seat accommodation reqmt

190CT 15.00 LONDON WATERLOO HAVANT     16.26 NO SEAT

Sold at 1749 36 *****6036 58974 150CT07 22.34 Y-P R

Issued at 1749 36 *****6036 58974 160CT07 06.16

387313723

C/CRD GBP ****14.35 For conditions see over

NOK 889

GB

state and military powers to railway staff. As architecture became less confrontational and defensive something else was happening in parallel. There was a silent, invisible return of the occupying force of the colonial state in the form of the bodies of railway subordinates who were trained to control the behavior of Indian passengers. It was not only as members of the Railway Volunteer Force that railway staff gained this authority. The Railway Act in 1854 had mainly been concerned with the behavior of employees of the railways, but its amended versions in 1871 and 1890 gave extended powers to railway guards, drivers, and station staff. As in Britain, the railways in India were encoded in the successive 1854, 1871, and 1890 Indian Railway Acts as common carriers, which meant that "a common carrier is a public carrier. In the carriage of passengers he cannot exercise any unreasonable discrimination neither can he do so in the carriage of freight."[22] But the railway in India produced a very distinct series of public offices and public rights from that in Britain. In this legal production of the public sphere the traveling Indian public would be criminalized. Control of it would remain in the hands of European and Eurasian upper subordinate officials commanding Indian station staff, and the public commerce of passengers would transform into scenes of authority and violence.

As soon as the traveling Indian public entered the space of the platform, it came under the authority of the railway acts and the station staff. Under British law, platforms were not part of the property of the railway, and there was no such offense as trespassing on a station platform. In India, the railway owned all land within the fences or boundary marks and could exclude from their premises persons "not having any business on such premises" and could "impose any terms they consider proper as conditions for admittance" (p. 32). The Indian Railway Acts encoded the authority of railway servants over this space. If a passenger committed any one of the offenses listed in the act, from being in a state of intoxication to endangering the safety of persons, any railway servant could take him or her before a magistrate, without a warrant. There was no such analogous law in Britain that granted this right to railway upper subordinates. Even for minor offenses such as not paying an excess fare, the authority of the train staff was absolute. If there was reason to believe that the passenger might abscond or the passenger refused to give a name and address, or there was reason to believe the name and address given was incorrect, any railway servant could arrest the passenger. In British law such an arrest, if proved unwarranted, could lead to a suit for false imprisonment or action for assault. However, under the Indian law even if the arrest was shown to be unwarranted the railway subordinate making the arrest was not liable in any way. If a railway staff member assaulted a passenger it was classified as being in excess of the staff member's authority and the company was not liable. The usual practice if an assault did occur was to transfer the employee or give him discharge on terms that meant he could be reemployed on a railway elsewhere. The traveling public's right to be protected from the excessive use of power by railway staff in the treatment of passengers or "trespassers" was severely limited. Section 120 of the Railway Act would seem to have offered some redress. This section made it illegal for any person in a railway carriage or any part of a railway to be in a state of intoxication, to commit a nuisance, to perform an act of indecency, or to use obscene or abusive language. But this section was only made applicable to railway servants in a legal case in 1934, and this ruling remained controversial. It was overturned in 1937 because such a provision would be "opposed to the maintenance of good discipline" (p. 644). The list of twenty-three offenses in the Indian Railways Acts that a passenger could commit was distinct from similar legislation in Britain. Most of the offenses had much higher penalties than those in Britain or were not considered offenses at all in British law. This wide definition of offenses and punitive nature of the law coupled with the discretion given to railway staff in defining trespassers and their wide powers of arrest made the railway platform a place of coercion.

In addition to its general nature as a place of disciplinary powers, the railway platform became a site for attempts by the government to control the movement of populations through India. The circulation of poor Europeans in the Mofussil, away from urban centers, was a recurring anxiety from the late 1860s to the 1870s. In 1869 lockups were constructed at railway stations to confine Eurasian and European passengers who were found to be vagrants or to be under the influence of drink.[23] The 1869 European Vagrancy Act gave a greater reach and scale to these measures.[24] It gave magistrates the power to transport people of European extraction without visible means of support or who had taken to the trade of begging from the interior to workhouses in the cities. From there, they could be sent to Australia or Britain if they did not reform or find employment after training. This act sought to prevent the growth of an itinerant white working class in India. As the various experts consulted when the act was being drawn up put it, the vagrant European sank into "forgetfulness brought on by drink," became "dependent often on the charity of Natives for his daily food," and lost all traces of his origin.[25] The vagrants could not be trusted to govern themselves in a manner that would prevent their degeneration. Their behavior would potentially blur the boundaries between British and Indians in a manner that threatened the whole theory of the Indian economy and British enterprise that shaped postrebellion governance.

The result of the Vagrancy Act was that any European who was spotted on the railway platform by station staff or the police was immediately under suspicion simply for traveling. In 1871, a bemused commissioner of police in Calcutta wrote to the Judicial Department complaining that he had been sent a Joseph Schkrabola and a John Brock who were "not of disreputable appearance and yet both were arrested and convicted of being vagrants."[26] Schkrabola's statement shows the overzealous prosecution of travelers:

> I came from Calcutta yesterday and am going to Dinapore where I have friends viz. Mr. Weber loco driver. He is a countryman of mine. I can pay my train line to Dinapore. I did not ask for money from the minister at Jamalpore; but the German minister gave me 1 rupee at Bhaugulpore 3 months ago. On my way to Calcutta I got a ticket from the minister at Jumulpore. I had three days work in Calcutta; no regular employment. I have got Rs. 2.[27]

Brock adds in his statement: "I am on my way from Calcutta to Nagpore to join my family. I came to Nagpore to see after my wife who absconded from there three months ago. I went from thence to Calcutta looking for the parties, but failing to find them I am going to Nagpore to arrange about my children."[28] The commissioner of police was severely reprimanded in a ruling by the junior secretary to the government of Bengal for discharging these "vagrants" from the workhouse in Calcutta.[29]

The railway platform also became a site of control during the measures taken to prevent the spread of plague in the 1890s. It was a short step from the existing powers of railway staff to the tight imposition of control over passengers during this period. Section 71 of the Railway Act had already placed in law the ability of a railway administration to refuse to carry persons suffering from any infectious or contagious disease, and under section 117 they could be removed from the railway carriage. No analogous law existed in Britain. In the appearance of the plague the dream of circulating commerce and passengers became the nightmare of the indiscriminate passage of disease in the bodies and parcels of the Indian public. Herbert Risley addressed the corporation of Calcutta in October 1896, when there were no cases of proven plague in Calcutta and recent reports from Bombay had suggested that the disease was contained in one section of the city, in the following terms, "with the communications which existed between the two cities a microbe which was so infinitesimal and so long-lived might come from Bombay at any moment and propagate infinitely."[30] He reassured the corporation that the "utmost precautions had been taken by the several railway administrations, even before the plague was stated to have been found in Calcutta."[31] The governor-general, in February 1897, when there were still no cases of plague in Calcutta, sought to cut off the entrance of passengers from infected districts. He urged that "the medical inspection of passengers in trains coming from the infected districts should be complete and . . . this can only be effected by the removal of the passengers to the platform and individual inspection there by the medical officers."[32] The government in Bengal also decided that "all station masters [should] be furnished with a list of infected places, and that ticket collectors should be required to stop all passengers presenting tickets from infected stations. Further, that such passengers should be required to give their names and addresses, and such an account of themselves as will enable their future movements to be watched."[33]

The Calcutta municipal corporation and some civil servants argued that third-class railway traffic should be stopped altogether. The government of India rejected this suggestion because it would "make invidious distinctions between classes and would cause great inconvenience and hardship."[34] Instead, they reintroduced this discrimination in another less obvious way. During the inspection on station platforms those passengers "who are at all suspicious, either by reason of his appearance, symptoms, or the dirty condition of his clothes or his effects, should not be permitted to proceed without being placed under observation."[35] In these measures we have the completion of the disciplinary function of the railway's public sphere. On the railway platform

all passengers are required to alight and be examined. . . . A European Station Master, a European Police Sergeant, two Head Constables and nine constables attend each train. Of these, three constables are stationed on the up-platform to see that no person gets out on the wrong side of the train. In addition there are a number of railway khalasis [driver's helpers, engine stokers] present to open locked compartments. . . . If any one is contumacious and declines to submit to the examination, time is not wasted in arguing with him, but he is locked in and the carriage is cut off, and put into a siding. . . . On arrival of the train, ropes with hooks attached are fixed on to both ends of the carriage and are held taught by the police. Male passengers are ranged in one or two rows nearest the ropes and facing the train. Female passengers are ranged on the platform near the train and facing it. . . . The police or stationmaster having reported that the compartments are empty, inspection of each passenger and his ticket begins.[36]

By the late nineteenth century the station was not a space of utopian laissez-faire individualism, of a frightening industrialism, or of democracy of commerce. Instead, it was a space suffused with the paradoxes of colonial rule, a place of leisure and beauty that referenced its location in India but which was controlled by railway workers who had the dispersed power of the state and military at their command. They had been given the right to exercise legitimate force yet this was not to deal with enemies of the state, but with traveling civilians. Their uniforms indexed this authority. European stationmasters and drivers wore with their suit and tie a military style cap marked with the insignia of the railway. European guards wore the pith helmet, military collar, and redundant sword sash of a soldier on dress parade. Indian staff members from cyclists to waiting room attendants were provided with the adapted versions of local dress characteristic of the Indian army. The Indian firemen, who shoveled the coal on the train, were dressed in shorts and military jacket and belt with a cap or *pagri* (turban), depending on religious affiliation. Their winter jacket had the round neck characteristic of *bandhgalas* (Nehru suits). Indian waiting room bearers and saloon attendants wore a long round-necked kurta and either dhoti or *salwar* (long shirt) with a military sash on their *pagri*. *Chupprassi* (platform attendants) wore a long kurta over bare legs with a military sash around their body and stripes on one arm. Licensed vendors and porters simply had a dhoti, *pagri*, and round-necked shirt without any military signs.[37] On the station military analogies and proximity to authority were clearly demarcated in a continuum from British stationmaster and guard to Indian porter. It is not surprising therefore that the railway station from the end of the nineteenth century became the site of challenges to the legitimacy of British rule.

## THE RAILWAY COMPARTMENT: DISTINCTION AND THE ZENANA CARRIAGE

During the early discussions around the introduction of the railway to India there had been limited speculation about the kinds of carriages that could be run on the lines because it was largely assumed that the only passengers would be Europeans. Those who did discuss such arrangements presumed that carriages would have to be divided along religious and caste lines. Upper-class Indian supporters of the railways argued that three separate classes of carriages would need to be provided for Muslims, high-caste Hindus, and low-caste Hindus, respectively.[38] William Andrew, who was also campaigning for railways in India, suggested in 1848 to the East India Company that five separate sets of carriages would be needed. These would consist of a single class for Europeans, a first and second class for Muslims, a first and second class for Hindus, and separate compartments for women from both these latter groups. When trains began to be run along the railways in the 1860s this particular version of social distinctions was not echoed in the arrangements for passengers. Railway officials had found that even without these arrangements Indians had flocked in large numbers to use the railways. They were also reluctant to provide accommodation that would reinforce prejudices against other groups in the space of a train, which was a motor for social enlightenment. Instead, the rolling stock that ran in the 1860s was separated along lines of class, gender, and race. There were first- and second-class carriages divided into compartments for Europeans, Indians, and European women. In addition there were open third-class carriages for Indians with a separate single compartment for Indian women. On some lines there was also a completely separate third-class carriage for Indian women. The design of carriages with compartments within them that had originated in Europe for first- and second-class passengers on the model of the cabins of coaches was perfectly suited for the segregations of colonial society.

The interiors of these various carriages also adapted the British pattern to the social extremes of an imperial setting. First-class carriages were lavishly upholstered like Victorian drawing rooms with beds that pulled down, their own bathing facilities, and a small room for servants. Such elaborate arrangements were not present in Britain. So grandiose were the furnishings that second-class carriages with their wicker and cane seating panels were in fact more comfortable to travel in. Third-class carriages took the British origin of working class carriages as freight carriers for coal to a further degree. They were long open cars with three tiers of wooden planked seating that were reminiscent of shelves used to stack goods. In 1862 some third-class carriages were divided into two stories so as to pack in even more passengers. In these there was not enough headroom to stand up. There were no bathing or toilet facilities, and doors were locked for the whole journey. In 1866 the doors began to be unlocked at stations. The barred and shuttered windows in second- and third-class carriages meant that passengers were enclosed in an interior space. First-class carriages by contrast offered panoramic vistas through larger windows at the expense of protection from heat. At one end of the spectrum was the British senior official who could gaze across the landscape from a carriage that echoed the ease of domestic interiors. At the other was the third-class Indian traveler shut in with a crowd and stacked up on benches. In the 1860s differences of caste and religion may not have been materialized in the space of the train, but the hierarchies of colonial society were.

Up until 1870 the designs of carriages were largely just extensions of British patterns. However, in that year an entirely innovative sort of carriage was introduced. This was the "zenana," or "family," carriage. It was designed to be particularly suited to the social mores of Indian society. As we will see, far from just reflecting these, the family carriage helped to extend the principles of middle-class respectability so that they were imposed on a wider segment of the traveling public. It also introduced social distinctions using metaphorical extensions of notions of *jati* fused with ideas of race and respectability into the spaces of the railway. The origins of the zenana carriage lay with a concern by the government of India under Mayo to encourage Indian women of all classes to travel by train. The railway authorities frequently received letters of complaint about the lack of proper facilities for middle-class women. Railway officers and bureaucrats felt that if Indian women of this class could be encouraged to travel it would have the dual effect of bringing a new kind of liberty to them and of expanding the revenue earnings of the notoriously unprofitable railways. In April 1869 instructions were sent out by the provincial governors to local commissioners that they should hold discussions with "native gentlemen" in order to find out how this could be achieved. Apparently it was not enough just to provide compartments reserved for women. In the discussions that followed, railway officials and government bureaucrats appeared to act as neutral arbitrators of the practicalities of tradition in the context of the modernity of the train journey. Yet in the measures that they subsequently implemented colonial officials helped to materialize Indian middle-class and high-caste social distinctions based on *jati* and class in the heart of the public spaces of the railway. Their measures helped to mark Indian women with signs of respectability or immorality depending on which ticket they could afford to buy for their passage.

The zemindars (landed gentry) and lower-level government officials approached for their opinions were united in their assertion that respectable women could only travel if they remained protected by their male family members and enclosed in a private sphere. They suggested that provision should be made for "family compartments" so that male escorts of women would have close and easy access to their compartments. Since ladies of the higher class "become quite helpless in the absence of their male relatives and protectors," these carriages would be constructed so that they had two end compartments filled with male kin and a middle carriage filled with the women of the family.[39] Otherwise, they argued, male kin should be allowed to reserve carriages for short distances in which they could carry their families together as an isolated group.[40] The internal arrangements of these carriages would not be the same as "Western" carriages with benches. Since these were "a form of seat they [Indian women] are never accustomed to and make use of them with the greatest reluctance," carriages should be emptied of seats and be "plain and unadorned so that the inmates may freely use it in their own way."[41] Such suggestions were greeted by government officials as "very practical" because women "within domestic circles feel greatest ease and comfort when sitting cross-legged on the smooth marble pavement or on carpets on the floor."[42] In these measures the public space of the railway carriage would be transformed into a domestic interior where only people who were related by blood and kinship would mingle.

The greatest anxiety expressed about train travel in the responses from the middle-class Indians consulted was that it exposed women to the public gaze of strangers unrelated by blood and kinship. They produced elaborate schemes of portable folding doors to shield the movement of women from *palkis* (screened carriages carried by servants) to compartments to prevent women's exposure to "many strange and new eyes."[43] They argued that *palkis* should be permitted on station platforms because "females in general (not to speak of those of rank and respectability) are quite averse to exposing themselves to the eye of the public and that it is death to them to walk up to the train."[44] They were concerned that windows should "be covered on all sides with shutters and venetians and such screens."[45] Some suggested that *palkis* should be placed on undercarriages on the train and act as compartments for shorter journeys. The public attention feared was not just that of lower classes, but of the upper subordinate railway staff. The railway staff, they suggested, "give themselves airs at every step and generally look down upon the passengers as if they were creatures of an inferior order or goods soon to be packed off."[46] Some even hoped that European and Eurasian railway staff could be completely excluded from interaction with middle-class women. They suggested that female, Indian railway guards and waiting room attendants should be employed. These arguments rested on a sense that the public spaces of the train were hazardous for women because they were occupied and controlled by unrelated people of different blood. One argued, for example, that "the social position of the native females, the etiquette they have to observe, their feelings their modesty etc. if we take all of these into our consideration it would seem quite clear to us that such a sex can never be accommodated by male officers of different families and blood."[47] In these discussions notions of *jati* became translated into the amalgam of respectability, class, and race that was characteristic of late-nineteenth-century and twentieth-century concepts.[48] Carriages and traveling arrangements would now apparently have to be designed in a manner that would help to further materialize this new version of social distinctions. Some of the gentlemen consulted also suggested that rooms for cooking should be built along the line with "regard being had as a matter of necessity for caste distinction."[49] The Etawah Native Reading and Debating Club argued that there should be two female carriages, one for Hindus and one for Muslims, in each passenger train.

These discussions also extended the relevance of upper- and middle-class respectability to all female travelers. The zemindars consulted assumed that no respectable woman would travel alone in a general carriage. In fact they claimed that if not enough third-class female carriages were run as part of the regular rolling stock then no women of "rank and position" would "make themselves willingly passengers of the Railway."[50] Honorable women, they suggested, would rather not travel at all than travel alone in general carriages. This was described as a kind of "degradation" because it would bring them into contact with "common male passengers of a different creed and colour."[51] The selective vision of female honor suggested that the principles of the upper-caste and middle-class family that confined women to the *ander mahal* (inner courtyard of an extended family house) extended to the whole population of India. The Bengali personal assistant to the commissioner in the presidency division wrote that the provisions to enable "native ladies" to travel "in privacy even by a public railway" affected "not the upper 10000 only who form the cream of native society . . . but a very considerable portion of the female population of the country; the whole in fact coming under the designation of 'Purdanusheen.' "[52]

Yet this description of a general population of women who required special arrangements also suggested that women who did not conform to these mores were less than respectable. In fact the native gentlemen consulted by the government worried about how honorable women could be protected from their less salubrious sisters. One proposed that female carriages should be divided into two classes, the first class for "passengers of gentry" and a lower one for "those of the commons." Another zemindar argued that it was vital that "the mere name of female . . . ought not to entitle one to the privilege of going with the ladies. I mean to say, females of ill repute ought to be excluded; it is true it would be hard to trace out which is which but still a hard ruling on the subject may prevent much."[53] The different ranks of carriage became associated in these proposals with different degrees of respectability. Honorable women would travel surrounded by their male family members in private reserved carriages as hidden as possible from interaction with other passengers. At the other end of the spectrum were the (by implication) dishonorable women who traveled alone and independently in general carriages or in all-female third-class carriages.

In response to these demands government bureaucrats and railway officials set about the task of adapting station and carriage accommodation to these newly formulated middle-class traditions. They regretted that so far travel arrangements had been "made with exclusive reference to European customs" and suggested that now they needed to be more in accordance with "Oriental society."[54] The lieutenant governor of the North West Provinces, William Muir, whose minute provided the template for the revised arrangements, argued that "the habit of female seclusion is not only practiced among the rich, but also among the vast majority of the respectable classes, whatever their means."[55] He urged that female carriages should be available to the masses because "we are bound to do so by every means in our power, not only as a duty to the native public, but also in view of the encouragement of traveling among the females of India. It is not perhaps too much to say that nothing would contribute more than this to the general enlightenment of the people and to the eventual introduction of a more civilized and rational treatment of the female sex in India."[56] This would be effected by the introduction of reserved first-class compartments for the upper classes; a first-class female compartment to which women could have access in *palkis*; third- or intermediate-class carriages with compartments at each end in which respectable men could travel together with their women as a family secluded by venetian blinds; a third-class female carriage for the commoner class; and retiring rooms for women in the *serais* (waiting rooms) next to the stations. The third-class female carriage was necessary because "even where there is no absolute seclusion or 'purdah' respectable females are unwilling to be placed in indiscriminate association with men or . . . prostitutes who should not be admitted into their reserved compartments. There would of course be no practical problem in this country in the recognition and exclusion of the latter class."[57] The vision of the "native gentry" and the expansion of their notions of respectability to cover all female travelers could not have been more fully realized.

The East Indian Railway implemented all the measures suggested by Muir.[58] For example, existing rolling stock was converted into a second-class family compartment. This carriage had a longitudinal passage in the center. On one side there was closed accommodation, with a bathroom, for ladies. On the other side was an open apartment for their male relatives. The railway also provided third-class family accommodation by separating two compartments from the rest of a carriage. One of these had its platform doors closed and was intended to be a purdah compartment. The adjacent compartment communicated with it and was for the male relatives of the family. New third-class all-female open carriages fitted with a bathing room were also added to local trains. In addition, *serais* were built at most major stations that gave separate accommodation for Hindus and Muslims. The only request that the railway did not accede to was to provide Indian female guards and ticket collectors because they felt that "if we set aside European Agency a door will surely be opened for fraudulent practices."[59] In their practical steps the East Indian Railway materialized problematic distinctions between respectable and unrespectable women. Those who traveled in the third-class female carriage or in general carriages would be suspect in some manner. New versions of *jati* built around distinctions of blood, respectability, and honor marking different kinds of class bodies were enfolded within the public spaces of the railway. The environment of the railway carriage that had originally been imagined as a public place where prejudices could be dissolved had become its opposite—a conveyance for families united by caste rank and a private domestic space in which women of wealth could be secluded.

Given this proliferation of carriages in order to incorporate the burgeoning hierarchies of colonial society, it is not surprising that by 1871 railway companies were instructed by the governor-general, Northbrooke, that they needed to simplify their class structures and rolling stock. In that year carriages ran across India marked as first-class European, first-class Indian, second-class European and Eurasian, intermediate-class Indian, third-class Indian, Indian female, European female, family, and fourth-class coolie. At the first conference of the railway agents in 1871 Northbrooke, worried about the unprofitability of the railways, instructed them to standardize carriage accommodation and to introduce a common class of nomenclature. In preparation for the conference, a memorandum was circulated by the joint secretary to the government of Bengal, Public Works Department, suggesting that a U.S. system of all class/one class carriages should be adopted in order to simplify the increasingly complex and uneconomical rolling stock. From the 1840s, the system of carriages in the United States had been distinct from those in Europe. Carriages were composed of long undivided rooms with a central passageway allowing freedom of movement with no locked, enclosed compartments. Wolfgang Schivelbusch shows that this style of carriage was considered unacceptable for Europe, despite its greater comfort for long distances and safety, because it did not suit social mores: "The classless open car was . . . the appropriate travel container for a democratic pioneer society."[60] In the 1860s, Pullman Palace coaches were introduced, which inaugurated a distinction between first and second class, but they retained the open interior structure of the older, U.S. carriages. In India, as soon as the suggestion for the introduction of this kind of simplified class structure and carriage was made by the secretary for the Public Works Department, objections multiplied.

The locomotive and carriage superintendents of the various railways completely rejected the proposals. They argued that the system was appropriate for the United States or Mexico, but that "in India where there are Europeans and Natives of various ranks and castes it would not be found to answer."[61] The new, lower-first-class carriages with dividers would not serve because they would impede the passage of the guards. They stated that the Pullman Palace cars should be used only for first-class European travelers, who required comfortable surroundings, or for the movement of troops, who were all of the same rank. For third-class and fourth-class Indian passengers the main issue was "getting more into one carriage."[62] They added that the coolie carriages (fourth class) did not require seats and that the most important concern was how to get forty to fifty passengers in them at once. Relatively more comfort could be provided to third-class passengers by adapting existing rolling stock so that it contained bulkheads to separate them and prevent overcrowding. One carriage superintendent reminded the conference of the necessity of separate carriages for females. Therefore, he suggested, if the U.S. method was adopted for third-class carriages, there should be separate carriages for men and women. The conference concluded by not making any alteration in the existing divisions in the traveling public. The only alteration was to provide first- and second-class European travelers with the comforts of the Pullman Palace car. Railway carriages continued to divide the traveling public and to materialize social distinctions. In 1888, the railway conference again complained that there were "four classes of carriages in India and some of these are further divided off for separate accommodation for Natives, Europeans and for Women. . . . The subdivision of carriage accommodation has been carried to a point that it is a detriment to the economy in working the lines."[63] The concern at the railway conference was that of all this diverse rolling stock only third-class passenger traffic produced profits for the companies. But the measures of reform introduced were again limited. They just consolidated first- and second-class European carriages. In India the profitability of the railways was less important than the maintenance of hierarchies within the traveling public. By the late nineteenth century the public spaces of the railway were a key site for the forging of social distinctions both within Indian society and between imperial rulers and their subjects.

## RAILWAY OUTRAGES: *JATI* AND PATRIOTISM

The wide-ranging authority of railway staff and emerging notions of respectability associated with the traveling public proved to be a problematic combination. The railway carriage and railway platform increasingly became places of injustice. By the 1890s the Indian-vernacular and English-language press were full of reports of incidents of what were called "railway outrages." These varied in severity, but they all showed evidence of the new moralities of travel and of railway staff abusing their wide-ranging powers. In some cases it was a simple matter of incivility and of staff overstepping their warrants. For example, reserved compartments, the province of families related by blood and caste, were thrown open to unwelcome strangers. In one such case in 1891 a carriage reserved from Howrah was unreserved by a European ticket inspector "with great insolence and rudeness" on reaching Asansol. *The Bengalee* reported that this was a matter that "deeply affects the members of the native community who when they travel with their families for any long distance always travel in 'reserved' compartments."[64] Other minor cases showed racial hierarchies at work. This was often particularly insupportable for middle-class Indian travelers because these incidents involved mixed-race upper subordinates who were from a group that was widely despised as degenerate. For example, in 1895 some Eurasian ticket collectors at Lahore station emptied an intermediate-class carriage of its Indian occupants in order to allow a few Eurasian women to travel alone in it. As a result of this three Indian women were left behind on the platform due to lack of room on the train. They were then taunted by the ticket collectors. *The Bengalee* reported that at the same place and time "a man who had gone to see a friend off and had purchased a platform ticket was driven out from the platform and afterward assaulted by a Eurasian ticket collector. . . . The veil of a purdanashin woman was lifted by a ticket-collector."[65] These incidents involving middle-class travelers were minor in comparison with the experiences of lower-status women.

When lower-caste and lower-class women traveled on the railways they were marked by the particular fare they purchased and carriages they traveled in as having a certain degree of respectability. Here the convergence of middle-class notions of propriety and the authority of traffic staff had more serious consequences. Some women were merely insulted. For example, in 1895 a booking clerk, Akshay Kumar Roy, verbally insulted the wife of a Mr. Ghosh, a clerk in the post office, when they were buying a ticket. Mr. Roy's reason was that he had suspicions that the woman was not in fact Mr. Ghosh's wife and he was trying to prevent them from continuing their journey.[66] Other women had more frightening experiences. Some were detained illegally when they failed to pay excess fares or had overridden their stations.[67] This had the potential to become a more dangerous situation. For example, in 1893 at Poonpoon a man, his wife, and their two children were unable to pay their excess fares and therefore were taken off the train and detained on the platform for the night. The assistant stationmaster, Dwarka Pershad, made advances to the woman and then attempted to assault her while she was sleeping on the platform.[68] At the Rajbundh railway station in 1891 Gokul Kahar, an *adivasi* man, complained that while he and his wife had been waiting for a train his wife had been raped by a traffic gate man.[69] At Hathras junction in 1891 the assistant stationmaster, Mohamed Mohsin, molested the wife of Damodar Das, a low-caste man. The assistant stationmaster ordered the man and wife to leave the waiting room. While the husband was carrying his baggage away the assistant stationmaster assaulted the woman in the waiting room.[70] A similar case occurred in the same place in 1894, this time involving a ticket collector named Jogendranath Ghosh. Yet it was lone female passengers traveling third class who were a particular target for railway staff. At Jamalpur station in 1894 a female passenger who had overridden on her fare was raped in the third-class waiting room by a railway mail service agent, Ashutosh Banerjee. At Howrah in 1892 the head ticket collector, Pereira, and luggage inspector, Bourhillon, were accused of molesting a young woman, who had been traveling by intermediate class on a third-class ticket, in the ladies waiting room with the collusion of the female waiting room attendant.[71] The third-class carriage and all-female carriages were also problematic spaces that marked some women as less than respectable and as a target for illegitimate acts. A ticket clerk, Panday Proshad, in 1894 entered a female third-class compartment between Damar and Kurja and insulted a female passenger. In 1895 a European guard on the Indian Midland Railway attempted to molest a Muslim woman whom he had taken out of the female compartment to the break van.[72] To travel in the public spaces of the railways uninsulated by the zenana carriage and unprotected by male companions was a hazardous prospect for women of limited means. The moralities of travel materialized in the carriage arrangements introduced after the debates of 1869 had yielded problematic results.

The cause of women travelers was widely taken up in the vernacular and English-medium press in the 1890s. It proved to be an important rallying point among the middle classes for the nationalist cause. This was a successful issue for agitation quite simply because travel by train was the arena in which people experienced the authority and paradoxes of the colonial state in their everyday lives. The most influential campaign was that of Surendranath Banerjee. In the pages of his newspaper, *The Bengalee,* and in the meetings of the Indian Association he combined an upper-caste moral disdain for affronts to female honor with a political argument against British control of Indian institutions. Banerjee was from a Kulin Brahmin family, but his father was a doctor and a man of liberal ideas. He educated his son at the Parental Academic Institution attended mainly by Eurasian boys. After studies at Calcutta University Banerjee went to Britain to study for the Indian civil service exams. He worked for some time in Sylhet as an assistant magistrate, but he lost his post by dismissal in unfair circumstances. He read the work of Burke and of the Italian nationalist Mazzini and formulated his own quite radical position on Indian self-rule and the tyrannies of the current government, which he taught at Ripon College in the late 1870s. He also founded the Indian Association in 1878, which became the center of an all-Indian political movement that bore fruition in the first session of the National Conference in Calcutta in 1883. This organization amalgamated with the National Congress in 1886. The intervention of Banerjee into the cause of female travelers was part of his larger attempts to build a groundswell of nationalist sentiment among the middle classes. Yet the moral panic that he provoked around railway outrages did nothing to dissolve the notions of respectability associated with or to alter the situation of women travelers. In fact his political arguments blurred the issues and problematically drew upon sentiments associated with new social distinctions of class status built around metaphors of *jati* and linked these with the public spaces of the railway.

In these debates as well the Indian nation was depicted as a collection of people united in the defense of women against the intimate pollution and degradation of their status by others who did not possess either purity of lineage or demeanor. It is through such public campaigns that *jati* came to acquire its contemporary and highly problematic meaning of "the nation." This is, of course, a meaning that can signal inequalities of both class and caste within the fold of the nation. These inequalities are certainly visible in the campaign by Banerjee, as we shall see.

Banerjee began his campaign in 1891 in the pages of *The Bengalee,* reporting on the case of Pereira and Bourillon. At least once a month new examples of various degrees of severity were reported in the newspaper. The articles describing these outrages were narratives of the dangers and violence lurking in the railways because they were unjust colonial spaces controlled by an immoral alien power.[73] They gave detailed accounts of the accidental circumstances that the railways provided for the isolation and defilement of women. The stories were framed by descriptions of how the loss of a ticket, an accidental overrunning of a destination, the lack of money to pay an excess fare, and the separation of a husband and wife into male and female compartments produced devastating violations. The perpetrators were always Europeans or Eurasians, and they were marked by the signs of colonial authority—wearing the cap of their office or dressed in the uniform of the Railway Volunteer Force. The Indian women, however, appeared as respectable widows, young brides, and innocent village girls. They would often be rescued, if they were truly respectable, just in time. They would begin "to cry aloud at the top of . . . [their] feminine voice for help—a woman's chastity is a thing which God guards zealously if the woman really be chaste and not seemingly so."[74] These stories aimed to appeal to sentiments among the readership that would lead them to unite in order to protect not just middle-class women, but all Indian women. Yet these women would only deserve this protection if they remained "feminine" and outwardly virtuous.

These narratives of rescue were not predominantly about the violence of rape. They expressed outrage about the potential contamination of respectable travelers, and they operated on metaphors of the pollution of *jati*. Stories about the offering of meat and drink by railway guards to female passengers were placed in the same category as more violent acts and were intended to provoke as much outrage. In an editorial written by Banerjee on the Asansol outrage case in which a low-caste woman was raped by five railway officials, the following case was included as equally monstrous:

> An incident that recently occurred at the Jamalpore station has been causing some stir there. On the 4th instant by the 9 a.m. train, a number of young Bengali ladies, accompanied by a few matrons, arrived there after the late full-moon bathing at Monghyr. Finding a Eurasian ticket collector there, they approached him and waited to drop their tickets into his palm from a little distance, so that their hands may not come in contact with his. But he refused to receive the tickets unless the ladies would hand them over to him in the usual manner. The women were in a fix when the Assistant Station Master came to the scene, and intervened on their behalf, but in vain. At last, an Honorary magistrate of the Monghyr Bench arrived by the same train, came up and told the ticket collector of the perils he was going to bring upon himself by his conduct. . . . The matter has been officially reported to the District Traffic Superintendent, Shahibgunj.[75]

The solution that Banerjee urged in his petitions and editorials to these railway outrages was that Indian ticket collectors and guards should be employed instead of European and Eurasian guards. This would mean that

> upon the same or lesser pay, the services of a better educated and a more respectable class of Hindoos and Mohamedans might be secured; and the public would hear less of these cases. They would, for the most part, be married men possessed of greater self-restraint and less exposed to the temptations to which so many half-educated European and Eurasian striplings have fallen victims.[76]

In his eagerness to inspire patriotism and protect the caste integrity of middle-class Indians Banerjee ignored the fact that a larger proportion of these rapes and molestations were committed by Indian subordinates than by Europeans or Eurasians.[77] All that was required, according to him, was a substitution of "blood" or biomoral substances, the appointment of respectable, married Hindu and Muslim men, to prevent these outrages. This argument had an admirable political goal—to overturn the racial hierarchies of the railway and by implication to delegitimize the colonial state. But the nationalist aims of Banerjee left unaltered the disciplinary space of the railway station and railway platform and the problematic definitions of class/*jati* respectability materialized in railway travel. In fact the way stories were reported intensified these values and made them more relevant to the patriotism of his middle-class readership. These accounts also projected idioms of *jati* into middle-class nationalism, expanding metaphorically the purity or impurity of lineages to the level of the purity of the nation.

Banerjee and other members of the Indian Association sent a public protest about the general pattern of abuse to the chief secretary to the government of Bengal in June and September 1895. They suggested that the East Indian Railway had an especially bad record of assaults and insults on female passengers and that measures should be taken to protect their honor. These would include the employment of Indians as station and running staff and of some female ticket collectors as well. Their letter was provoked by the outcry over a recent case, which was known as the Asansol Outrage. The various discussions of this case and the situation of the woman, Rajabala Dasi, at the center of it crystallize many of the contradictions surrounding women who traveled alone on the railways and reveal the limits of middle-class nationalism built around idioms of *jati*.

For the nationalist press Dasi was represented as a vulnerable, innocent child who had been horribly violated. For example, in the *Amrita Bazar Patrika* her case was described as follows:

On the 8th instant a Hindu girl of about 12 or 13 years of age Rajabala Dasi by name and a Boishnava by caste was traveling in the female carriage of an up-passenger which is timed to arrive at Asansol at 7:39 p.m. She was asked to show her ticket by some European employee. She said she had kept it tied along with some pice in a piece of cloth and that as she was going to untie it at the station the ticket was blown away by a gust of wind. She, however, entreated the official to let her go to Jamtara, which was close to her house. . . . The European official, however, forced her down and placed her in charge of a chaukidar with instructions to take her underneath the over bridge. After the train had passed away four European railway employees came to the spot, sent away the chaukidar and then having forcibly taken her into a neighboring house ravished her in a most fearful manner. It is said that the four brutes committed the outrage upon her person by turns, one of them gagging her mouth, and two of them catching hold of her two legs. At 10 o'clock she was driven out to the streets in a helpless condition when some kind-hearted man was moved by her piteous talk and took her to the stationmaster. Her case was immediately taken up by a head-constable, who happened to be there. Next morning she was sent to Raniganj for medical examination and the doctor was of opinion that she was hurt. In the afternoon she was brought back to Asansol and asked to find her ravishers from amongst a number of Europeans and Eurasians, who were collected together. You can easily imagine that it was no easy task for a village girl like her to recognize the culprits from a group of white men, who were dressed in the same fashion, still she was able to point out four men, who she said had committed the atrocious act upon her the previous evening.[78]

In the pages of the nationalist press Dasi appears as a tragic, violated victim, who could become a rallying point for outrage about the Europeans and Eurasians who command the space of the platform and carriage. There is only one sign here of the violence of notions of respectability that made her vulnerable in the first place. This is her description as of Boisnob caste, a term that had come to signify by the 1890s in middle-class urban and rural society a loss of caste. Yet this stain on her character is glossed over in nationalist accounts that drew on the sense of responsibility that the middle classes felt for the protection of the lower-class and lower-caste masses.

The report on Dasi by the assistant inspector-general of the Railway Police shows a greater complexity to her position than that suggested by the accounts of her in the nationalist press. It suggests also that simply by being cut off from ties of kinship, locality, and family she remains suspect in the eyes of all concerned.

This report concentrates on establishing her kinship and previous history, but it fails to do so simply because Dasi's life does not fit the expected patterns of either middle-class Indian society or those assumed by colonial officers. It begins with a citation from her statement under oath to the magistrate:

> I have since arrived in Asansol, being living under a tree (this is at the police lines). Government gives me to eat. I beg for food at Bengali's houses. The Babus who give me to eat are servants of the station. I don't know their names. Since I have been at Asansol I have not asked the police to take me to my father or husband's house. I have not quarreled with any of his family, nor of my father's household.[79]

Dasi appears as an anomaly for both nationalist and colonial observers. She is a woman who is alone and refuses for whatever reason to return to her male kinship group.

Given this strange position and the police's duty to try to find a group of people who can be held responsible for her, they continued to question her about her antecedents:

> With regard to her relatives not taking her back—Mr. Todd Inspector tells me that he asked her relatives names, but she said she had none. Even in her complaint she gives her address as Jamtara village Jamtar police station, Sonthal Parganas district. I learnt from her that her mother died when she was an infant, and her father remarried, turned her out after which she was brought up by her grandmother Rotunmani and uncle Sham Dass of Sirsa village, Deoghir subdistrict, who however, will not take her back till she purchase back her caste. Her husband died whilst she was away. They were so she says very fond of each other, and always went about together to the house of her uncle Sham Dass and Saroda Dassee her aunt and always lived together. Futher, that whilst at the house of Sham Dass she was enticed away by some cooly contractor. Saroda Dasee denies that she is any blood relation of Rajabala's and further that she never saw the girls' father or husband and that she has simply given the girl shelter till the case is over; and finally that she has not been outcasted by so doing.[80]

The police questions reveal that Dasi is not a young village girl in the romantic manner imagined in nationalist accounts of her plight. Her life has been a mobile one, passing from different households and into the pay of a coolie contractor. It is this kind of life unimaginable to Banerjee's middle-class readership that has led to her traveling alone on the railway. Unfortunately, the values of respectability perpetuated by the nationalist campaign for her cause and the third-class carriages she traveled in made such a mobile life hazardous. The refusal of Saroda Dasee to acknowledge her as a blood relative is more difficult to interpret, but indicates that Dasi's itinerant life and her subsequent rape were threatening to rural notions of respectability as well. The report in nationalist newspapers that Dasi was a Boisnob by caste gives a clue that she may have converted to this religious group after expulsion from her local *samaj* (community) as a result of a violation of caste codes or having become a widow.[81] But this term in Dasi's "case" remains radically uncertain in its reference. It is not clear whether it refers to a "crime" of widowhood or immorality committed before her wanderings. Is it perhaps a status assumed by Indian newspapers because she was a lone female traveler? Was it a "choice" on her part to take up this status in order to leave the kinship group? Or was a status given to her later as a result of her rape by European railway guards? What is clear is that her itinerant life placed her at the intersection of a series of judgments on her respectability—those of middle-class Indians, European and Eurasian railway employees, and village society.

As Dasi's story remained unclear after these inquiries, the police could not leave the case there, but included gossip about Dasi. This was added at the end of the report as a final conclusion on her status:

> Mr. Stark, subdivisional officer Jamtara, who was present when I was questioning the woman informed me that he had heard that the girls' husband had divorced her a year ago, and that she was living secretly in prostitution and the probability is that her husband turned her out for some immoral conduct. . . . As for her not going to her relatives none would have her and that she knew full well and intentionally concealed their names and would not go to them or return to Jamtara.

This conclusion that Dasi had, in fact, been a prostitute all along was taken up by the East Indian Railway officials in their report to the government on the general pattern of railway outrages on their line.

Provoked by the representations of the Indian Association to the government, the head of the railway bureaucracy, Major White, ordered the agent of the East Indian Railway to inquire into the circumstances around this case and the frequency of other outrages. In these accounts the conclusion of the police report is used to question the innocence of Dasi. The general traffic manager wrote in his report to the agent on Dasi's case, "the circumstances of her previous wanderings laid her at least open to suspicion and the reports received led to the impression that she was a consenting party."[82] He also discussed another recent case from Asansol in which it had been proved that a claim of rape by a woman was false and the complaint had arisen because of a dispute over payments for services. He suggested that Dasi was also a consenting party upset by nonpayment. He felt that her willing statement of the circumstances of her rape suggested this. He added that no measures needed to be taken to prevent the reoccurrence of such rapes apart from the issuing of memorandums to the staff that instructed them to observe courtesy to female passengers because "owing to the social customs of the country the cases where respectable females travel unaccompanied by protectors of the opposite sex must be rare."[83] The agent of the East Indian Railway agreed with his conclusion. None of the measures requested by the Indian Association would be brought into effect. Their claims about European and Eurasian staff were also shown to be false by the statistics that indicated Indian staff's greater involvement in acts of outrage. The agent did promise that the railway would try a few experiments with female ticket collectors, but that he did not hold out much hope, as women of the right "physique and intelligence" would be hard to find.[84] Therefore, the only outcome of the agitation by the nationalist and vernacular press was an intensifying of the notions of respectability associated with female travelers by rail that had made Dasi vulnerable in the first place. In particular the publicity around her case and those of other railway outrages served to bind patriotic sentiments tighter to a desire to protect honorable women alone from violation by specifically European and Eurasian officials. This ignored the intersection of multiple forms of power relationships that made the mobile lives of women like Dasi difficult to live. It also projected the unequal idioms of *jati* into the community of the nation.

The legal system did not allow Dasi any vindication either. The commissioner of the Burdwan division wrote to inform the government of Bengal of the outcome of her case. His opinion was that she had been "without doubt" "dishonored by four men against her will" and that the evidence of identification against two of the participants was accurate.[85] But he regretted that the case was dismissed against two of the men by a majority of the jury. Two of the others had absconded when released on bail, which was allowed because the committing magistrate had not believed the evidence provided of their identity and there was no jail accommodation at Ranigunj or Burdwan for Europeans and Eurasians. The case against one of the men was referred to the high court, but the man died in jail while awaiting trial.

## THE "SIX *SAHEBS*"

It was not until after independence that the individualistic democracy of travel in which passengers are divided from each other only by class that was imagined in the utopian visions of the 1840s came into being. Yet there continues to be one exception to this rule—that is, the all-female third-class carriage. This was unchallenged by the nationalist campaigns of the 1890s. In fact the campaign of Banerjee in the 1890s intensified the ideas of respectability that made this carriage necessary and the lone women who traveled in it open to suspicion. It is not surprising therefore that the railway journey remains fraught with issues of respectability and that lone female travelers have a problematic status.

Heading this chapter is a song written by Pobon Das Baul that expresses this contemporary situation. Pobon is a Baul who spent twenty years of his life making his living singing his songs in West Bengal, often in the setting of a third-class railway carriage. When I met him in Calcutta and told him that I was doing research on the railways he sang this song to me:

> The engine is the source of fire.
> How much strength the carriage has!
> This carriage has six sahebs, two who shovel filth.
> Two carriages push up against each other.
> How many men fall under the influence of cum-juices!
> A woman disembarks from the carriage at the station,
> Running running rushing rushing.
> The train stops its rhythm.
> Panting, she says, "Help me, please give me water."
> How much strength the carriage has!

With an eclectic mixture of Sufi and Vaishnavite theology, Bauls' songs explore, often through explicit sexual imagery, passionate devotion to God and the treacherousness of the body. A recurrent theme is the cage of the body and the six vices that control its actions. In this song this standard image is transformed into that of the body as a carriage mastered by six *sahebs*, or the six vices. Bauls mix their metaphors in a way that offends and confuses middle-class Bengalis. Although their performances are consumed at festivals near Shantineketan and elsewhere and are sanctified by the enthusiasm of Tagore for their "syncretic" imagery, their songs, like this one, offend. They contain a moral message about the body as a domain of distracting passions that can be appropriated to middle-class morality, but they deploy explicit imagery that questions the closing down of sexual passion as a route to religious ecstasy. When I showed the text of this poem to my middle-class Bengali teacher, who prided herself in instructing me in demure "Bengali" manners, she exclaimed in shocked exasperation, "These people, they are so crude, they don't know how to write proper Bengali; it's very difficult to translate." She proceeded to render *roshatol*, "cum-juices," as "destroyed utterly,

ruined." Thus she turned the fifth line into "How many men were destroyed utterly." Explaining the fourth line, she said it referred to a train accident in which
two carriages crashed into one another. However, there is another image suggested by this line; the phrase *dakka gele* suggests an explicitly sexual act of two
carriages/bodies "pushing each other."

In Pobon's song we find condensed the contemporary sense that the railway
journey is fraught with double-edged erotic dangers for both men and women.
There are temptations for men to follow the impulses of the body that will lead to
the violation of women. So far this could fit middle-class notions of respectability and travel. But where Pobon diverges in his interpretation is that he suggests
that these libidinal temptations are not produced by the deportment or status
of women. Instead, they are the result of traveling in the space of the train itself
and they are under the control of those who drive it. Those people are the *sahebs*,
by implication the educated middle classes and natural heirs of European rulers.
Pobon provides a current diagnostic that inspired much of my inquiry into the
history of the public spaces of the railway. The colonial railway station and the
railway carriage have helped to materialize a very particular kind of public space
and traveling public in India. This is a space suffused with notions of honor and
of class understood through idioms of *jati*. The traveling public is divided into
ranks of women who display the class degree and community sentiments of their
families. As we have seen, the foundations for the tense arenas of the railway
were laid by the unexpected consequences of emergent notions of *jati* among
middle-class Indians meeting the authority and concerns of the colonial railway
bureaucracy. The tremendous power of railway employees, the railway station as a
sign of an occupying alien force, and the intricate racial subdivisions of the public
have all disappeared. Yet the railway still materializes the hierarchies of Indian
society that emerged from nationalist responses to the coloniality of its spaces and
their idioms of the nation as *jati*.

## Chapter Three

# Governing the Railway Family, 1860–1900

It is laid out with military precision; to each house its just share of garden, its red-brick path, its growth of trees and its neat little wicket gate. Its general aspect is that of an English village . . . put under a glass case . . . with a holy calm. . . . No one can flatter himself that in the multitude he is overlooked or believe that between 4pm and 9am he is at liberty to misdemean himself.

—R. Kipling on Jamalpur Railway Colony, "Among the Railway Folk," 1891

Historians of the railways in India have argued consistently that labor on them introduced workers to new habits of industrial discipline.[1] In this they largely agree with the congratulatory speeches made at the opening of new sections of line in the 1860s. For example, in 1863, Bickersteth, the chairman of the Great Indian Peninsula Railway, announced the opening of the Bhore Ghat Incline in the following terms:

We all know what vast sums, chiefly of English capital, have of late years been spent in this country. Let us consider for one moment what has been the effect of all this money being spent, in giving a fair day's wages for a fair day's labour. . . . For the first time in history the Indian Cooly finds that he has in his power of labour a valuable possession. . . . the labourer works far harder, and acquires new and more civilized wants in proportion to the high wages he receives. . . . Follow him to his own home, in some remote Deccan or Concan village, and you will find the railway labourer has carried to his own village . . . new modes of working, new wants and a new feeling of self-respect and independence.[2]

Research in the records preserved in the India Office Library would largely confirm the perspective offered by such speeches and the standard historiography—that the Indian laborer in railway service had begun to be tutored in habits of capitalism.

Employment in the railways without doubt admitted the railway worker into a domain in which written instructions, rules, and lines of command would be the medium of work discipline. The 1854 Railway Act encoded this universal sphere of discipline and public duty, making sure that the minutest details necessary for train operation were made explicit to the workforce.[3] "Native servants" of the railways were issued with translations of the rules relating to their particular duties and had to carry them about with them and produce them when called upon to do so. Foremen and *mistries* (leaders of work gangs) were also expected to read them out to the men under their charge. The government quickly stamped out any practice that contradicted these regularized forms of work discipline. For example, in 1859, when a railway inspector of the East Indian Railway was discovered making up manacles and fetters to use on native workers under his charge, he and the agent of the railway were severely reprimanded by the head of the Public Works Department. The lieutenant governor followed up by asserting that "what the case discloses is the perverted ideas of this inspector and it may not be too much to assume of others also of his class as to the rights of his fellow native subjects and the social condition of this country under British government. If Mr. Duncan had been working in his own country . . . he would never have thought of making up fetters to be used under any circumstances."[4] He urged the agent and officers of the railway to instruct their less-enlightened staff that all classes in India had "equal rights of freemen, which they themselves have at home." If we wrote the history of the railways from these sources, then free labor under universal rules and procedures for a fair day's wage would seem to have been what was in operation in the railways. Yet if we turn to the history of recruitment practices on the railways and explore the history of the emergence of railway colonies, we gain a quite distinct insight into the effects of railway labor on social identifications and self-fashioning among workers.

## THE INDIAN RAILWAY ACCIDENT AND RACIAL HIERARCHIES

From the first plans for railways in India there had been speculation about the arrangements for their manning and control. For example, Rowland MacDonald Stephenson, the founder of the East Indian Railway Company, in 1844 had suggested that British personnel would be necessary to direct all aspects of train running in order to safeguard the investments made by British capitalists. The Parliamentary Commission on the Colonisation of India in 1858 added to such early proposals with its detailed imagining of the variable economic capacities of different groups and of the sorts of Europeans who would escape degeneration in India. Its recommendations argued that habits of industry could only be spread by British superintendence, but that this should be of a quality that could exercise the powers of self-control necessary in the hostile climate of India. When railway officials began to build up their personnel on the East Indian Railway in the 1860s, they followed this pattern of insisting on the importance of British supervision. All office-based work would follow the pattern in the Indian civil service of British managers and Indian subordinates. More surprisingly, any work that dealt with the running or repair of trains also had to be in the hands of British agency. To the earlier reasons offered for this management structure they added another—the impending danger of railway accidents. The threat of technological accident that hung over all railway enterprises took on a particular tenor in India. This was not just a fear of a crisis that was horrifying in itself and terrifyingly reminiscent of the uncontrollable nature of commodities and markets.[5] It was a specific colonial fear that Indians could not be trusted with the supervision of industrial machinery. The imagined otherness of their bodies made it uncertain that they had the traits necessary for such a task. Railway bureaucrats were unsure that the quality of their physical life and the moral practices that governed their maintenance of it were sufficient to prevent disaster. This sensibility placed railway bureaucrats in direct opposition to their superiors in the government administration who with their eye on the public purse constantly insisted that the companies should economize on their expenditure on expensive European and, later, Eurasian labor.

Conflicts over this issue began as soon as trains started to run regularly on the lines. Although the hierarchy in offices went unquestioned, the governor-general, Canning, and the lieutenant governor of Bengal, J. P. Grant, insisted in the late 1850s and early 1860s that mechanical labor should be increasingly Indianized.[6] They periodically called for reports from the various railways as to the progress on the training of engine drivers, guards, and stationmasters. Similarly, they took every opportunity to press home their point about ending the expensive importation of European workers or reducing the numbers of such highly paid employees on the books. The agent of the East Indian Railway and his traffic superintendent were more skeptical, but they began to attempt to train different groups that they thought might most closely approximate British workers in their physical and moral capacities. They experimented with Sikhs, Chinese, Bengalis, Parsis, and Eurasians as upper subordinates. Eurasians recruited from military orphanages and apprenticed to the railways and domiciled Europeans (often pensioned soldiers) were found to be most capable as railway guards, drivers, and stationmasters at large junctions. Indians, usually Sikhs or Parsis who were felt to most closely approximate the qualities of British workmen, were only used to drive stationary and pumping engines or trains in the enclosure of goods yards. Similarly, if they became stationmasters they were placed in charge of small stations with infrequent traffic. The reason for this restricted role was that traffic managers claimed that they could not exercise the necessary "judgment and presence of mind" to deal with emergencies and that they "seldom have character enough to enforce strict obedience."[7] For a man to become an engine man or guard, the locomotive superintendent suggested that he needed to be "a sharp, ready hardworking man with sound judgment, great nerve, when suddenly brought into danger. He must have in himself a natural turn for mechanics which makes him fond of his profession. He must be sober and of good constitution."[8] Similar capacities were required from stationmasters. Indians appeared to lack these essential British somatic and moral characteristics, although they were seen as capable of working in subordinate levels on the repair of lines or of equipment in the loco sheds if a close eye was kept on them by their British superiors.

This view that Indians were incapable of protecting public safety was reinforced by the occurrence of accidents. For example, in June 1861, a mail train and a goods train collided between Connagar and Bally stations after the mail train had lost steam and stalled. The European driver and guard of the goods train had been drunk and had fallen asleep, leaving the train to be driven by the fireman. The discussions of this case between Captain Hyde, the officiating consulting engineer to the government of Bengal, and Edward Palmer, the agent of the East Indian Railway, focused on the absence from their posts of Bengali stationmasters to whom the fireman could report the drunkenness of his superiors. This accident did not lead the railway bureaucrats to reconsider their view of the natural competence of Europeans; instead, it led them to further question the capacities of Indians. As a result of it the East Indian Railway did not appoint Bengalis to stationmaster posts until the mid-1870s.

Despite the introduction in 1870 of an official policy of Indianization as an economic measure due to the continuing failure of the railways to make profits, resistance to it continued. Indians were repeatedly found to lack sufficient "talent, energy, general knowledge and reliability" and to be unable to stand the hard work due to the "privation which caste rules subject them to" in order to drive trains and coordinate large volumes of traffic.[9] Other arguments were advanced that suggested that at least three Indians would be required to do as much work as one European, which on their rates of pay would double the costs of the establishment.[10] When a few Indians were trained as engine drivers in the mid-1870s they were only permitted to drive on level, noncurving branch lines and to take control of low-speed goods trains, because they could not be trusted with the responsibility of conveying the public.[11] Indian guards were only permitted on these goods and coal trains when their responsibilities were shared with a brakeman.[12] The further training of Indian engine drivers and guards was discontinued on the East Indian Railway in 1876, after a few years of experiments, because "men of the Baboo class have not the physique for the work or the spirit of loyalty which goes so far with the bulk of the European staff of Guards in ensuring hearty and willing cooperation in times of real pressure."[13] After this decision, when the existing staff of Indian drivers were employed on new branch lines or as pilots between the shunting yards and the main tracks, the lines were judged by the traffic manager and agent according to their degree of difficulty, and European guards were always placed in charge of the trains.[14] Unlike in Britain, there was no possibility of Indian firemen rising through the ranks to the level of mail train or passenger drivers, nor of Indian stationmasters being promoted to larger stations or of becoming traffic inspectors.

Each category of biomoral life on the railways had its own scale of pay and privileges. By 1900, in the regulations for pay, promotion, and suitability for jobs employees were subdivided into "European, Eurasian, West Indian of Negro descent pure or mixed, non-Indian Asiatic or Indian."[15] On employment the local medical officer would certify the race and caste identity of a candidate and write it on his history sheet, determining his future pay, leave allowances, and location in the railway hierarchy. The central role of the medical profession in this categorization shows the importance of the idea of visual physiological signs of the quality of physical life possessed by different race, caste, and religious groups. The body literally was a witness to the origins and moral practices of a person. As in the Committee on Colonisation in 1858, the health and efficiency of bodies was dependent on the quality of life they contained and on the nature of the self-governance practiced within the community of which they were a sign. Within the different railway companies officers developed local classifications of the suitability of Sikhs, Parsis, Madrasis, Brahmins, Punjabi Muslims, and Bengalis for particular positions.[16] In railway workplaces different races and communities were ranked on a "natural" scale of physiological and moral efficiency determined by their cultural and physical inheritances. The colonial political economy that emerged in post-1857 discussions about the impact of European colonization and capital on India was realized at a quotidian level on the railway. British ideas of pedigree—the natural capacity for enterprise, labor, and moral governance that inhered in certain genealogies—were central to the workplaces of the railways.

Fears of accidents lay behind another aspect of the work environment of the railways as well—its rigid discipline and moralized workplace regulations. Railway officers felt that the Indian context made disasters more likely to occur and therefore required that a particularly strong system of punishment for disobedience or carelessness was necessary. On the one hand this was in order to counteract the essential inadequacies of Indian workers. On the other it was also important in order to prevent European and Eurasian employees from degenerating into indiscipline due to their residence in India, which was seen as full of temptations for men of their class. As we have seen from the discussions around the Committee on Colonisation, there was deep distrust of the ability of the working classes to prevent the degeneration of their physical and moral selves. The rules of the workplace had a juridical and moral intent, which was designed to overcome the inherited moral and physical inadequacies of Indian, Eurasian, and European workers. In 1854 the first Indian Railway Act was passed in order to provide rigid procedures and punishments to overcome these peculiar dangers of running a railway in India. When it was passed the agent of the East Indian Railway wrote with relief to the board of the railway in London. He felt that the new regulations would remedy the current situation in which European workers had "been careless . . . and given much trouble," adding that he had asked for transportation for life to be added to the penal clauses of the act.[17] Each railway added its specific regulations, which were issued to every worker in a rule book in English and appropriate vernaculars. This rule book had to be carried by each employee while on duty, and if it wasn't the employee in question was punished with a fine. The duties of stationmasters, guards, engine drivers, pointsmen, and permanent way inspectors were all laid down in detail. Each of them had responsibility for the segments of the machinery they controlled and were required to have a military command of employees under them and to conduct daily inspections. They were responsible for their subordinates and were required to inform on their misconduct or inefficiency.

The daily routine of stationmasters was punctuated by the arrival, dispatch, and departure of trains. But they were also required to protect the station buildings and property, to detain passengers who had disobeyed rules, and to maintain the paper regime of orders that were entered into logbooks. They commanded all those who worked under them, from ticket collectors to *chaukidars* (watchmen). Guards governed the trains. All passengers and property were under their charge, and they were responsible for the safety and regularity of the whole. They were the keepers of the timepiece that measured the progress and punctuality of the journey. They also had the duty of regularly signaling to the driver that all was clear. If it wasn't they had to sound the bell on the tender to inform the driver that he had to apply the breaks. The engine driver inspected the engine and had the duty of obeying the guard. Pointsmen were guarded by a policeman who gave the all-clear signal to the trains. Permanent way repair gangs were governed in a chain of command from inspector and foreman down to the *mistries* and laborers. Each link was morally responsible for those below it. The relationships between persons were controlled by the terms of the Railway Act. Employees would be immediately sacked for the disobedience of orders, negligence, misconduct, or incompetence. For lesser faults they would be fined. If they were found to be drunk on duty they would be dismissed and liable for a fine or imprisonment by the magistrate of the district. The judgments of superiors could be appealed in memorials sent to the agent of the railway.[18] A strict hierarchy founded on both military models and a notion of moral obligation for self-governance emerged as the solution for the inadequacies of the Indian and potentially wayward European/Eurasian railway worker.

The Railway Act provided a general framework, but this was added to by local government instructions and the regulations of individual companies. Over time the severity of punishments increased in order to counteract the innate weaknesses of Indian employees that were seen as the cause of accidents. For example, following a series of accidents on the East Indian Railway in 1859, the government ordered magistrates to make prompt and careful inquiry into all accidents that might occur in their jurisdictions and to prosecute railway workers in the Supreme Court whenever they were shown to be responsible. This was necessary because of the "heedlessness and apathy of the natives" that could not be prevented by the issuing of regulations alone.[19] The regulations had to be backed up by strict enforcement. The heedlessness made it important to prosecute European employees who had Indians in their charge as well. This was the only way to ensure that the Europeans kept as tight supervision over Indians as was possible. A further spate of accidents, in 1860, led Captain Beadle, the consulting engineer to the Railway Department, to suggest that magisterial authority with limited powers of caning and imprisonment should be instituted along railway lines. He felt that district engineers for the railways might be vested with these powers or a special railway magistrate should be created. If work gangs were involved in these accidents, then the *sirdars* (foremen) of the gangs should be imprisoned, the actual offenders caned, and any women involved should be imprisoned too. Lieutenant Governor J. P. Grant added that the *sirdars* of the gangs should be taken from the railway company's police establishment. They would be carefully drilled and instructed in their duties and should make sure that workers would be criminally prosecuted if found at fault. These discussions reveal how the hierarchy of the railways increasingly took on the qualities of judicial and policing institutions in attempts to counteract the moral and physical inadequacy of employees. Special magistrates were not created for the railways; instead, employees all along the chain of command gained aspects of magisterial and police authority.

The work environment that emerged from these concerns caused increasing dissatisfaction and led to a high turnover of staff at all levels. This was of particular concern to the administration when these staff members were skilled European drivers, guards, and stationmasters. In the 1850s and 1860s each monthly packet of letters sent home to the board by the agent of the East Indian Railway included news of at least three men who had absconded or been dismissed for drunkenness, indolence, disgraceful conduct, or insubordination.[20] By 1862 desertions by imported workers had become so frequent that Agent Edward Palmer called for the original agreements with workers to be forwarded to him regularly from London so that he could prosecute absconding workers in the Supreme Court.[21] Yet in 1863, in the process of an attempt to create a more attractive working environment, the pattern of infusing the hierarchy of the railway with punitive powers was extended. Palmer suggested that valuable European staff might be retained if direct magisterial inquiries were confined only to cases of serious personal injury, with minor offences judged by a committee of executive officers of the railway. This committee would have the power of fining and dismissing with the discretion of handing over serious cases to a magistrate. This procedure was adopted, creating a judicial institution within the railways. Yet this measure did not replace magisterial powers; it added to them. Grant, the lieutenant governor of Bengal, objected strongly to any curtailment of the authority of magistrates where public safety and the carelessness of railway employees were concerned.

As the railway establishment grew the internal procedures for dealing with failures of duty by staff became more formalized. The severity of this regime did not go without protests. In 1876 a group of covenanted European railway men on the East Indian Railway and Great Indian Penninsula Railway formed the Amalgamated Society of Railway Servants in India with W. Atkins as its secretary. This society was intended to represent their interests to the bureaucracy. The guards and drivers at Allahabad, Asansol, Tundla, and Gaziabad had particular complaints. These all related to the unquestioned authority of their superior officers to decide their fates. They protested against the suspension of men simply for declining to sign fine sheets if they disagreed with the decision of the locomotive foreman on their responsibility for specific mistakes. They suggested that before men were punished there should be an open investigation into the charge made against them, with one official of the railway and one engine driver as investigators. Any loco foreman who treated men under his charge badly should be taken before a commission of inquiry of a certain number of East Indian Railway officials and the same number of drivers. The rules of the provident fund should be modified so that men dismissed for the vague crime of misconduct would still be entitled to payments from the fund. Traffic Manager Campbell and the agent decided that it was not appropriate to alter the existing system. Instead, all complaints should be referred to Campbell as head of the department concerned.

In the 1900s the administration responded to the continuing discontent over its procedures by making them more like those of a court of inquiry. The employee was presented with a charge sheet listing his offences, to which he was required to submit a written explanation. He then was brought before the officer competent to dismiss him, and if this officer thought a case existed then a departmental inquiry was ordered.[22] The proceedings partook of all the language of guilt, innocence, and proof that one would expect in a courtroom, and cases of inefficiency and misconduct became translated from issues of economy to those of moral governance. This metonymy of morality and efficiency became acute in cases of dismissal for immoral conduct in which decisions were passed, for example, on stationmasters for seducing colleagues' wives. In these cases the machinery of the Watch and Ward Department, introduced for the purposes of guarding railway property, and of the government's Railway Police, introduced to enforce the Railway Acts, were deployed against the employees themselves. Even in cases in which these agencies failed to gain proof of misdemeanors or crimes, if they were "convinced" that a man through slackness or connivance was responsible for illegitimate acts, they could inform the divisional superintendent, who could discharge the employee.[23] The category of discharge did not require the process of departmental inquiry unless the employee had completed ten years of service. If the employee could not be found guilty of or be suspected of a specific offence, he could be discharged at the discretion of the divisional superintendent on general grounds for being inefficient and lazy, persistently troublesome, or a confirmed drunkard without actually being drunk on duty.[24] By the early 1900s an essential function of the railway bureaucracy was to act as a machinery for monitoring, punishing, and convicting its employees. Workers carried out their jobs under the imminent threat of either magisterial or departmental authority. Even more importantly, there was apparently little distinction between the obligations to one's job and moral obligations to one's self, community, nation, or family. These inquiries and workplace rules all used a moralized form of judicial language that made matters of ethics into issues of obedience to rules, conformity to duty, and resistance to temptation.

Railway bureaucrats did not rely on workplace discipline and racial hierarchies alone in order to secure the safety of the traveling public in the context of the dangerous environment of India. From the 1860s, they also began to introduce paternalist policies for European and Eurasian employees that would guarantee their physical and moral ability to keep charge of the men and machines under their control. They were the essential linchpin in the chain of command that prevented terrible accidents from happening. Under prevailing ethnoclimatological theories this danger could be prevented only by measures that intervened in the domestic life and self-governance of these employees. The systems of racial hierarchy and punitive discipline that suffused the railways relied on a notion of biomoral somatically realized capacity and incapacity. Therefore, as we will see in the next section, the East Indian Railway began to introduce measures to guard the morals and physical welfare of its European and Eurasian employees.

## THE RAILWAY COLONY AND THE DOMESTICATION OF THE RAJ

In the period from 1854 to 1859 railway bureaucrats showed constant concern about the physical health and morals of the imported workers brought in to hold key positions in the mechanical, locomotive, and traffic departments. In spite of the indifference of the government, the chief engineer of the East Indian Railway, George Turnbull, and various district railway doctors campaigned for the provision of salubrious housing far from native bazaars, cottage accommodations, and recreational facilities. They suggested that these facilities were the only means of preventing the insobriety and degeneration of these men. In addition, they might encourage the employees to stay on after their initial period of service with the railway. Overall, such measures might prevent the frequent desertions and dismissals that occurred. Initially, the government insisted that such expenditure for the sake of keeping imported workers on the straight and narrow might be avoided by training up local labor. The East Indian Railway therefore began to recruit domiciled European and Eurasian workers, mainly from military orphanages such as the Lawrence Asylum, to replace imported labor, which created "constant anxiety and trouble."[25] The railway companies could more satisfactorily bind these trainees to their service by the 1850 Apprentices Act. This had given employers the rights to take on all the responsibilities of a parent to a child. This act had been designed to provide legislative means for European and Eurasian child vagrants and orphans to be provided with training in duty and habits by their employers.[26] It was seen as appropriate to India, despite its repeal in Britain (apart from the City of London), where it was seen as inhibiting the free circulation of workers, because it would prevent the growth of a community of Indianized poor whites.[27] The government and railway companies were equally enthusiastic about its use in the railways because it not only solved the problem of expensive imported labor, but it also meant that railway employment could provide a place of reform for Eurasians and domiciled Europeans. The gradual growth of this workforce with mixed affinities of pedigree alongside the continuing importation of European labor had an effect opposite to that originally wished by the government. It forced the government to change its position on the provision of facilities for employees.

From 1859 onward, the companies and government, increasingly concerned about the morality and physical health of their upper subordinate employees, set about planning and building railway colonies. These places combined the paternalist impulse of the Apprentices Act with measures designed to check the degeneration of European and part-European workers. From now on, the railway companies would not just take on the responsibilities of parents to children in relation to their European and Eurasian employees; instead, they would attempt to change the very nature of family ties and private life. The personal and public conduct of employees should ideally follow the logic of the management of the economy by railway bureaucrats writ small. Self-governance and family life should be addressed toward the preservation of the physical life of individuals and the transmission of moral obligations that would secure the healthy reproduction of empire and nation. The continuing prosperity of both capitalist enterprise and British rule in India demanded such measures. If they were not undertaken, both the imperial nation-state and the efficiency of the railways would be at risk.

From the earliest discussions of these colonies, railway officials were equally concerned about the physical and moral health of their employees. In 1859 Agent Palmer sent a request to the government for funds and land to form a new settlement for engine drivers at Buxar. This was necessary because the current site was now near a "large bazaar" that "materially interfered with ventilation," and Palmer argued that "the health of those who had to reside in the station must suffer from these causes while the habits of the engine drivers etc. were likely to be injured by the neighborhood of a large bazaar."[28] The new site chosen was "situated in a fine open maidan [park] without any native building near it" and was far from the new constructions by the raja of Buxar around which another village had sprung up.[29] Similar sites were chosen for large settlements of drivers along the lines of the railways, such as Jamalpur (1864) and Connagar (1867), that were located far from cities and Indian settlements because these provided similar "temptations to vice and excess" and would place workers under the scrutiny of their superiors.[30] Sites were always chosen so that they would be "healthy and unobjectionable on moral grounds."[31] The architecture of these railway colonies was designed to reproduce British forms. A journal for engineers (largely read and contributed to by Indian railway engineers) in 1858 described the colony at Kanpur in the following terms: "There is no conciliation policy about the designs, no assimilations to Hindoo or Mahommedan styles. It is a good bold English architecture, something firm and solid that it does your heart good to look at."[32] A European space was emerging that would physically secure the separation of workers from the temptations of Indian habits and associations and would also preserve their natural biomoral substances.

In these railway colonies the workers were provided with cottages rather than barracks, which were "very demoralising," because, in these all-male spaces, "Good men if they are not corrupted by the bad are dissatisfied at being so closely associated with them."[33] The cottages were designed for two single men or one married man. The higher rent for these facilities than that which had to be paid for residence in the earlier system of barracks was subsidized by payments from the government. The architecture of the cottages was designed to provide the particular facility of ventilation.[34] As is shown by a lecture given in the Railway Mechanics Institute in Howrah in 1863, this theory of ventilation was a strategy designed to maintain European character. The lecturer argued that "governments may stamp the manners, but it is to a great extent the air we breath [*sic*] which moulds the form, temper and genius of a people" and proceeded to enumerate the sanitary measures necessary for preserving British genius.[35] In this theory a naturalized essence of the nation exists within the body. Yet this substance can only be preserved in inhospitable climes by the intervention of science so as to reproduce the qualities of the land of the nation-state that will then nurture the physical life of its natural citizens. The report on the sanitary situation of stations in Bengal and the Punjab in 1865 reflected this vision, which demanded that buildings not be crowded, native bazaars be removed, and vegetation cut back.[36] Employees were encouraged to remove all traces of Indian vegetation around their houses and to plant British seeds imported specially by the company, literally reproducing the natural attributes of the land back home in order to sustain their own life and morals.

In 1874 Sanitary Police were introduced in the East Indian Railway colonies "for the proper enforcement of sanitary regulations and for the security of the settlement."[37] Whenever settlements of Indian workers or bazaars encroached on the railway colony, measures were taken to remove them. In 1875 the agent reported to the board of the East Indian Railway: "It has been found that a great many natives were living within the station bounds at Sutna, who were not employed by the company, but were relatives and friends of the menial staff and that they built huts for their own accommodation . . . as to affect the sanitary condition of the station. All these people have now been removed."[38] When bazaars came too close to the colonies, land was purchased to create a "sanitary zone" around the settlements.[39] The threat of bazaars was partly that of disease, but, after the discussions around the 1868 Contagious Disease Acts, the bazaars had also been watched and regulated as the place of prostitution and residence of Eurasian women of dubious morals. European and domiciled European workers had to be kept safe from such associations that might adversely affect their physical and moral integrity.

As we might expect from the alliance of clergymen and doctors in the discussions of ethnoclimatology in the Committee on Colonisation, the measures for the reform of workers combined both spiritual and medical advice on correct forms of asceticism. In 1860 the government sanctioned the provision of clergymen at large stations on the East Indian Railway "for the good order, better morality and improved discipline of the European employees of the railway," giving them "a most beneficial influence on their lives and habits."[40] From 1860 onward, "rational entertainment" was provided for workers in the form of railway institutes and swimming baths. These were provided on the medical advice of the civil surgeon at Allahabad that they would prevent the vices of drinking that led to other immoral associations and caused degeneration in European physiques.[41] In fact liquor acted as a key danger that linked together the moral and medical discourses on the preservation of life. For religious professionals it was a temptation that led to further sins. For medical professionals it had measurable deleterious effects on the body and apparently worsened the physical degeneration caused by the Indian climate. Leisure facilities in the colonies were designed to draw workers away from environments where liquor and other moral dangers were easily available. In 1865 institutes began to be built at all large stations along the line on the model of the Lahore Railway Mechanics Institute, which had the functions of keeping "the subordinates of the staff in health and amusement and weaning them from those habits of idleness, intemperance and self-indulgence, which seemed before the Institute was thought of to deaden and debase as soon as they were off duty."[42] These institutes also kept them out of colonial public spaces. They prevented the growth of European "idlers on platforms, who created an undisciplined "nuisance."[43] The regulations of the institutes emphasized practices of civility, courtesy, and sobriety. They provided rational entertainment in the form of journals and newspapers imported from Britain and concerts and lectures.

It was not only the individual worker who was the target of these measures to improve the quality of biomoral life. Their families were increasingly seen as relevant to the company policies. Measures that sought to promote domestic relationships that would reproduce in the present and through generations the European and British character of railway families were developed from the 1860s. In 1867, a hill sanitarium was established for the subordinate servants of the East Indian Railway at Landour, following the logic of theories of ethnoclimatology that insisted on the necessity for a regular revival of British qualities in salubrious climates. But this was not the only aim of this scheme. The locomotive foreman at Allahabad urged this measure to the board (his letter was passed on to government officials to persuade them this measure was necessary) as a means of encouraging railway subordinates to bring their wives and children to India with them. He suggested that only this would prevent the degeneration of the drivers and guards, who, even if they were uxorious, often sank into dissolute habits because their wives were unfaithful to them, giving detailed examples of such workers' despair.[44] The sanitarium would thus preserve not only the morality of the working classes in India, but those in Britain as well. The government duly sanctioned the sanitarium.

In 1868 the railways and government raised the issue once more of the utility of British wives as a prophylactic against the loss of European habits that residence in India might produce. They discussed the possibility of granting railway mechanics the cost of half the passage of their wives and children to India and if necessary to advance them the other half. This was a measure designed to prevent the following progress of the mechanic:

> A man who has been married a few years and becomes steady and domesticated, if he leaves here for India and leaves his wife behind him, when he reaches his destination he finds everything different to what he had known here, and he sighs for his home, his wife, and his little ones; he gets disheartened and loses energy in his occupation, or seeks for a change in debauch leading to destruction. If he has his wife with him, they both get acclimatized, and intend to make India their home.[45]

The concerns of railway officials and of government officials (who had just passed the 1868 Vagrancy Act that had focused on the railways as the source of European vagrants who wandered from British affiliations) coincided, and the measure was sanctioned.

By 1876 the *Annual Report on Railways in India* described with satisfaction the British spaces of capitalism founded on middle-class domestic arrangements that its policies had produced:

> On approaching these places they present quite an imposing appearance. Large square brick houses are seen placed in compounds or gardens bearing a resemblance to the villas and mansions occupied by the wealthy citizens of a London suburb. . . . In connection with this colony there are generally Institutes, libraries, swimming baths, billiard rooms, churches, schools, cooperative stores, hospitals, recreation grounds—everything in fact that can be thought of to afford occupation for the mind and body. It is very desirable to attend to the health, comfort, and amusement of European mechanics in India as well as to the education of their children. There are great temptations to indulgence and excess and it is obviously expedient to secure well behaved, steady and intelligent European communities of this class in the heart of India.[46]

This pleasing order of the railway colony as it appears here and in Kipling's account of Jamalpur as a place of "holy calm" that heads this chapter comes from its naturalization of the connections between race, nation, and capitalism in the domestic order of families. Here we have the British nation in microcosm guiding the economic progress of those it rules and bound together by Christian values of sobriety. The railway colony appeared to represent the utopian realization of the legitimizing dreams of the colonial state and its middle-class bureaucracy.

Here mechanical expertise, qualities of command, bourgeois forms of domestic life, and rational entertainment were produced as inherent racial and national characteristics of particular pedigrees unconnected to the space of India in which the railway colony stood. Indian workers were kept beyond the boundaries of this society in a manner that reinforced the idea that they were inherently incapable of becoming like Europeans.

The separation of the colony and its inhabitants from either "degenerate" Europeans or other Indians was, of course, imaginary. It was a space through which people circulated, often acquiring and losing again the British identifications that were apparently so fixed and distinct from Indian ones. Its boundaries were profoundly permeable. For example, the "disreputable" vagrants removed to workhouses under the Vagrancy Act were often former railway employees. The list of vagrants sent to the commissioner of police, Calcutta, to be placed in workhouses in 1871 from Monghyr district included George Smith, fireman East Indian Railway, Jamalpur, discharged on reduction of establishment; A. Emken, discharged by railway for breach of duty; Francis Anderson, worker on Jubalpur line, unemployed for a year; Peter Thomas, telegraph signaler, unemployed since 1869; William Maclaughlin and George Payes, assistant stationmasters on the Bombay and Baroda line, discharged on reduction of establishment.[47] Railway workers often also ended up in the slums of Calcutta living with Indian Christians in arrangements that did not fit the models of respectability in the colony. When a committee was set up by the government in 1890 to inquire into pauperism among Europeans and Eurasians, railway workers appeared often in its evidence. The superintendent of the District Charitable Society Alms House in Calcutta reported that half the male inmates were European and Eurasian railway men.[48] The inspector of police of Lilotollah district informed the committee that there was a large colony of native Christians in the Bow Bazar section who "live in huts like natives and sleep on the ground."[49] Living among them were discharged soldiers who had taken up appointments on the railways, but who had lost them. They had children with the women, but they did not send the children to school. This "kinthal" class contracted "paper marriages." These were certificates attested by witnesses that the parties were man and wife, which were often temporary legal arrangements.[50] Most of the Eurasian paupers who gave evidence had been employed at some point on the railways. A characteristic story is that of A. B., who gave the following description of his life:

> I am 32 years old. My father was a European soldier and my mother was a Eurasian. I was born at Vizagapatnam. My father died when I was 3 months old. I was educated at Moorgehatta orphanage and then at Calcutta free school. I left school at 18. The school got me into the fitting shop of the

East Bengal Railway. . . . After 3 months the workshop was abolished. I
then obtained work in the Entally workshops. I stayed three months after
which I resigned as I received no pay. During these 6 months my mother
supplied me with clothes. My mother allowed me Rs 15 per month until
she died. . . . After the railways I was a barman at a native liquor shop in
Chowringhee. I then joined Wilson's Circus. . . . Then I was appointed on
Tirhoot State Railway as a second guard. . . . I was discharged on reduction of establishment. I then came down to Calcutta. Since then I have
had no regular work. I support myself by selling cigars on commission
and by playing in the "foo-foo" band. . . . The bands play chiefly at native
weddings. . . . I get food from the tiffin ground where gentlemen's servants
bring leavings of their masters' tiffins.[51]

The racial exclusivity and respectability of the railway colony masked the fact
that many of the employees housed there had mobile lives like the one described
above. Domiciled Europeans and Eurasians often lived crossing the boundaries
the colony attempted to produce.

In addition, the families housed in railway colonies apparently because they
were in part European in origin often had acquired this identity as a result of
their work on the railways. Whenever railway officials sought verifications of the
statistical accounts of the percentages of Europeans and Eurasians in their employ, they ran into problems. For example, in 1875, when the East Indian Railway
wanted to set up a school for children at Jamalpur, they asked for a statistical
return of families of European origins. They received an unexpected reply from
the commissioner of Bhagulpur:

As regards the case of Jamalpore there are a few families claiming to be
European or Eurasian which are in truth Eurasian or pure Native only.
As these, however, are accepted at their own estimate both in and outside
the workshops and having raised themselves by good behavior and stead
application are found desirous of maintaining their children in a position
equally good if not better by giving them the benefit of education. They are
returned in the tables *at their own price* [emphasis added].[52]

Here the fiction of colonial political economy that there were certain kinds of
people with particular pedigrees and forms of moral life who were suited for the
command of mechanical enterprises such as the railways meets its limits. Families
acquired a higher social standing along with a different racial and national identity through work and residence in the railway colony. Similar evidence of this
process can be found in the response in 1902 from the Imperial Anglo-Indian As-

sociation to an attempt by the government to estimate the numbers of Eurasians in different positions on the railways:

> The comparison of statistics tabulated in your reports fail to furnish any true indication of the racial facts which the government seeks to arrive at, for many reasons, but chiefly because men of mixed parentage—conscious that the stigma of mixed race, though it may be hidden by a non-swarthy complexion has been a very tangible barrier to the better salaries and allowances given to men of pure European parentage—endeavor to pass themselves off as pure Europeans, while natives because of the higher salaries paid to persons of mixed parentage, assume European names and pass themselves off as members of the Domiciled community, thus rendering a true estimate of the community an impossibility.[53]

Sometimes people made a transition to a different racial status by adoption into the railway colony. From oral accounts of the 1930s, it seems that often when an Indian Christian woman married a Eurasian or European railway worker their sisters and brothers would join them in their new family.[54] The railway worker would adopt them and they would be entitled to education in the colony. They would effectively acquire for themselves and their whole family of birth retrospectively the status of Eurasian or European identity.

Yet this permeability of the railway colony coupled with the racial work hierarchy produced an atmosphere in which racial distinctions and respectability were a matter of intense social scrutiny in the domestic realm. In the railway colony private behavior was open to question as a potential sign of less than pure racial origins. To misbehave was potentially to betray not just yourself, but the status of your whole family as being of a racial or community category. Distinctions between people, when they could be made, were also strongly marked. Eurasians were not allowed to drink with European drivers in the running rooms or the refreshment rooms at stations. Indian Christian wives were excluded from the railway institutes, even if their children by Eurasian or European husbands could attend events. At railway institute dances people passed comments about the skin color and pretensions of Eurasian employees.[55] Goanese Christians and south Indian Christians did not socialize with Eurasians and vice versa. In church, whether Anglican or Catholic, different racial groups and communities had assigned pews. People who were further up the hierarchy, living in the "types" cottage-style houses, were seen as a "different tribe" from people who lived in the blocks. Yet for Eurasians to move up the job hierarchy was seen as an increase in financial *and* racial status. People described their relatives as becoming "almost European" when they were promoted to positions as district traffic superintendents or traveling ticket inspectors. The railway colony was a place of reform that in enforcing the boundaries between races and communities unintentionally enabled the transubstantiation of "essences."

In addition to the instability of the racial distinctions in the railway colony, its domestic respectability was also breached. Evidence of this is hard to trace, but in the prosecutions under the Contagious Diseases Act some material has survived. In 1876 the magistrates of Patna and Dinapur became concerned about the spread of disease from unregistered prostitutes to the soldiers in the cantonment at Dinapur. When they carried out their investigations into this they discovered that the Eurasian wives of soldiers were contracting liaisons and probably prostituting themselves to both Indians and Europeans. Some of these relationships involved men in the railway colony at Dinapur. The magistrate of Dinapur reported that the provost sergeant of the regiment had informed him in a recent case that an Indian man who was seen with two traveling prostitutes from Patna also had the reputation of being the barrack women's leading pimp. The sergeant said, "I have from inquiries learnt that he comes to our married quarters and to those of the artillery and takes the women away to the railway and other places for no good purpose." The magistrate continued that this statement was supported by that of several Indian witnesses who added that the man helped soldiers and railway employees to procure drink and prostitutes.[56] The sanitary boundary set up between the colony and the bazaar was transgressed by such people. In some cases the servants of railway workers supplied them with women. Dr. Jameson, who ran the lock hospital at Dinapur, reported that Indian and Eurasian women were brought down by rail from Patna every three months, providing a fresh supply. These women were claimed as wives by the servants of men in the barracks and railway colony so they would not have to be registered as prostitutes under the Contagious Disease Act. These men then supplied the women to the Europeans and Eurasians they served.[57] Sometimes soldiers and railway workers claimed women who lived in the bazaar as their own wives, contracting *nika* (temporary) marriages with them.[58] In these reports it is hard to determine whether prostitution was actually taking place. The distaste colonial officials had for unorthodox relationships led them to stamp all bazaar liaisons with the dishonorable mark of prostitution even when they could find no evidence of money having changed hands. Yet what is certain is that railway workers were not always conforming to the respectability required of them in the colony. And sometimes women must have permanently passed through the boundary from bazaar to railway colony as the legal partners of railway employees.

These personal transgressions did little to disrupt the hierarchical and moral separation of Indians, Europeans, and Eurasians in the policies and workplaces of the railway. As far as railway bureaucrats were concerned, Indian workers were a separate category of employees who did not require housing or other facilities. Instead, they would remain embedded in their own domestic milieus and opaque traditional patterns of sociability. Until the 1900s the Indian railway worker lived on the outskirts of the railway colony. In 1872, the housing of Indian menial staff first surfaces in the records as a matter of the management of criminal populations. The Judicial Department informed the agent of the East Indian Railway that there were strong grounds for believing that the coolies employed along the railway line in the Hooghly district sheltered *dacoits* (thieves) and "many bad characters" in the guise of railway workers.[59] The remedy suggested was to arrange for the lines of huts to be made accessible from the nearest road so that they could be inspected by the police day and night, and that they should be built in the vicinity of the railway stations to enable supervision by superiors. Next, Indian workers appeared as the vectors of disease. The chief commissioner of railways in 1876 laid down a ruling that placed Indian workers outside the housing policies of the companies, stating that only native staff who had to be kept on the railway premises so that they could be reached at short notice, such as pointsmen and signalers, should be provided with barracks. The carriage and wagon superintendent of the East Indian Railway protested against this exclusion because it meant that Indian *khalasies*, who had close contact with European railway drivers, lived in cramped conditions in the bazaars and carried cholera from there into the European settlement. The board of the East Indian Railway decided that the solution was to provide such workers with land on which they could erect their own huts.[60] In 1877 this policy was standardized at the Annual Railway Conference. The agents of the railways agreed that Indian workmen should be allowed to erect temporary huts near their place of work as long as the presence of women and children was discouraged because they were of "doubtful respectability."[61] If housing was provided it took the form of barracks, which were seen as inappropriate for Europeans. Indian workers were expected to reside apart from their families. Even the skilled native drivers were given this kind of minimal provision that split them from family members. The East Indian Railway provided two unused coal sheds for the newly trained native drivers and firemen to live in at Jubalpur in 1878. There was no exception to these practices, even for stationmasters who had greater responsibilities and were from a higher status background. In 1878 the traffic manager urged the board of the East Indian Railway to construct some kind of accommodation for native stationmasters, preferably with courtyards and screen walls, which would provide "that entire seclusion for their females, which custom requires their class," thus enabling them to bring their wives to live with them.[62] But his requests received no response apart from the construction of a few barracks and the reiteration of the policy of providing land.

By 1887 the unplanned growth of villages of huts at the stations that resulted from this lack of provision of housing had become a problem. It was criticized by the chief government engineer for the railways in his *Annual Inspection Report of the East Indian Railway*. He complained about the "unsightly mud and mat erections still generally existing along the line" and suggested that enclosure walls and screens should be built around them. These would provide "natives" with the privacy they required by custom to allow their families to live with them and to prevent their huts being viewed from the tracks. He rejected the idea of providing a standard structure built by the company on the grounds that "where so many castes and creeds exist it is difficult to build a type of native quarter acceptable to every class of employee."[63] The East Indian Railway responded by building the required screens and providing land further from the stations on which workers could build their own huts. It wasn't until 1901 that there was any change in this policy, and even this was only a slight alteration. In the interests of sanitation the board decided that "in certain areas where men have to live in close proximity to a station or other important buildings it is advisable that quarters should be neatly built and in general keeping with the surroundings, but where such close residence is not necessary I consider that cheaply constructed blocks of menial lines, built more in conformity with native ideas would be found suitable."[64] In these measures Indian workers were dealt with as populations composed of criminals, vectors of disease, as governed by their own opaque customs, and as unsightly bodies to be hidden.

Because statistics were not kept on Indian employees and their lives were not of concern to the bureaucracy, it is difficult to trace their origins and the effects of railway policies on their domestic life. On the East Indian Railway by 1900, the majority of posts held by Indians were as assistant stationmasters, signalers, pointsmen, ticket collectors, *khalasies*, drivers of slow goods trains, and workmen in the repairing shops and on the line. A quarter of the locomotive department employees were Muslims. By contrast, Muslims were a tiny minority in the traffic department in roles as stationmasters, signalers, and the like. Instead, these positions were largely held by Hindus and a quarter of those were Brahmins. The workshops at Jamalpur, Howrah, and Liluah were staffed by a mixture of local and migrant labor. In urban areas the railway often relied on labor contractors to supply these workers, but in Jamalpur they recruited from surrounding towns, in particular Monghyr, which was described as a place in which for centuries there had been iron-working castes.[65] In the Kharagpur workshops different migrant labor clustered around particular tasks for which they were seen as having a natural aptitude. Punjabis built the carriages, specializing in the fine carpentry necessary for this task. Biharis and West Bengal Muslims worked on the boilers. Members of north Indian hill tribes were put to work in the foundry making the components for the carriages. The measures that were introduced for their housing left all of these workers, whatever their origins and position, squatting beyond the boundaries of the railway colony. In this respect their domestic and recreational life was marked as different from that of Europeans and Eurasians in a manner, which further justified their exclusion from positions of responsibility. In a self-fulfilling prophecy they appeared to be not European enough to command because they were not admitted to the colony. They worked on the railways but could never acquire the domestic and personal characteristics that would make them fully part of its European modernity. Instead, a plethora of community and caste affiliations nested within the railway hierarchy with some jobs broadly associated with particular kinds of Indians. Housing policies, or the lack of them, meant that domestic arrangements built on already existing patterns of caste and community affiliation. By the closing decades of the nineteenth century the contradictions and exclusions that underlay these policies were becoming increasingly unmanageable. Yet it wasn't until the 1930s that the railway administration altered them significantly. The years from 1875 to 1900 were marked by increasingly elaborate efforts by the railways to maintain the separation between Europeans, Eurasians, and Indians. The most important of these involved the bureaucracy in a project of providing education for the children of Eurasian and European employees. This was designed not simply to revive and protect biomoral inherited essences as the railway colony had been. This was a state- and company-implemented project intended to guarantee the existence of national sentiments founded on Christian ethics. It attempted to intervene in the reproduction of the invisible bonds of the nation among the young.

## THE RAILWAY SCHOOL AND NATIONAL SENTIMENT

In the period from 1876 to 1890, political organizations such as the Indian Association, and later the Indian National Congress, protested against the taxonomies of race that excluded them from the civil service, Public Works Department, and railways. They also attacked the "unBritishness" of British rule in India in both abstract and specific terms. Individual colonial officials and the agents of British rule were also faulted for their failures to live up to the high principles portrayed as being inherently British. The whole system of governance was also demonstrated as not conforming to the fair principles of metropolitan political rights. From the 1890s, press campaigns directly questioned the fitness of working class Europeans and Eurasians for positions of responsibility on the railways. In this atmosphere British anxieties about the moral conduct and loyalty of working class Europeans and Eurasians increased. These concerns came together in the discussions around European education in the 1870s. From these emerged a complex and expensive system of educational provision for the children of Eurasian and European railway employees that sought to tie their invisible loyalties to the national imperial endeavor. National sentiment now had to be actively generated through interventions in the attachments of Eurasians and Europeans to the moral standards of their "homeland." The nation was no longer simply understood in these discussions as a quality of biomoral life naturally linked to particular territorial and climatic terrains. Instead, these earlier visions were overlaid by an understanding of the nation as a domain tied together by ethical sentiments modeled on Christian practices. It was these sentiments that would be enforced by education.

Before 1875 the government and railways showed little concern about the issue of European education. In that year they combined their forces with church institutions in order to provide extensive facilities for the education of the working classes. It was the campaign of Archbishop Bayly of Calcutta that publicly raised the issue of the provision of education for poorer Eurasians and Europeans. He envisaged the establishment of elementary schools at a very low cost for the lower-class Eurasian population in large towns and in railway colonies funded by grants-in-aid and inspected on the model of the new English national schools. Higher-level boarding schools would be provided at the principal towns, which would be funded by government aid and private voluntary contributions. In this system all children would pass up at the age of nine or ten to a hill boarding school. This was to prevent a "deterioration in their bodily vigour and mental energy" that would reduce their subsequent productivity and lead them to produce enfeebled children.[66] To this end Bayly suggested that a cheaper range of boarding schools should be created in the hills since the children of the working classes could not go to the same schools as wealthier Europeans. Railway companies, religious organizations, and the government would fund these.

For the lieutenant governor of Bengal, Richard Temple, Bayly's scheme was important because it had alerted him to a scandalous situation in which education was not reaching the poorer classes of Europeans and Eurasians. In Calcutta alone, he reported with shock, one child out of every three children whose parents earned less than 300 rupees per month was not going to school. As a result the children of poor parents were growing up in ignorance in a manner "detrimental to the public interest and [bringing] discredit on the government."[67] This situation existed despite the fact that there were already forty-three schools in Calcutta for the education of Europeans and Eurasians. Now aware of this failure, Temple asked education officials and civil servants to inquire into the situation across Bengal. In particular he wanted to find out whether there was enough educational provision and why these poorer classes were not attending schools.

The answers received reveal an interesting collision between the ideas of bureaucrats that Europeans and Eurasians constituted a discrete, unified community and the variable practices of families according to class position. Government education officers and clergymen reported that the main reason poorer Europeans and Eurasians did not attend schools was that they did not want their children educated alongside Muslims and Hindus in government secular schools by Bengali teachers. Nor did they want their children to study with Indian Christians in missionary schools. These ideas were attributed to an essential difference of sentiment between racially and religiously grounded communities. However, these assertions were contradicted by commentaries from other officials. For example, the commissioner of the Chittagong division reported that the lower class of Feringhees (people of Portuguese-Indian origin) descended from Portuguese settlers around Noakhally did not require a separate school from those of natives. He added:

> The families of Firneys and Andrews are said to be of upper class, the rest are chasas of the lower class. . . . The children of the upper class still adhere to their non-Asiatic dress for out-door wear, but the lower class, which forms a vast majority and the same class of Hindoos and Mahomedans are so much alike that no difference is observable in their appearance, dress, habits and manners.[68]

The malleability of Eurasian identity was reflected in a different way in the report from railway towns mentioned earlier in this chapter that suggested that families acquired identities through their job status on the railways.

This evidence of racial and national affiliation as related to class position did not lead officials to abandon the project of European and Eurasian education. Instead, it led them to assert that it was the fault of parents that children did not live up to their racial and national essence. They blamed parents for domestic subversions of the natural, invisible moral bonds that made up the community of Europeans in India across differences of class and religion. These parents provided bad examples to their children by their drunken habits, improvidence, lack of respectability, and most of all absence of moral sense. They had no concern for their children's education and left them to the mercy of Indian servants. Their children became degraded versions of the European moral self. As a result it seemed vitally important to remove European and Eurasian children from the influence of their parents. Schooling would now be directed to preventing domestic subversions of the natural ties of national/racial community. Government-funded schools would lift children from the influence of their families and return them with a new, more appropriate moral sense. Temple concluded from this dossier of evidence that the blame for the lack of the education of European and Eurasian children should be laid at the door of their parents. His solution included the recommendation that elementary schools for Europeans and Eurasians under the age of nine should be funded by government grants so that they were affordable and accessible for all. But he also insisted that it was important to follow Bayly's scheme in which all children at the age of nine or ten should go to boarding schools in the principal towns or hills. This would create a level of discipline among such children that they would not receive at home.

This new project of education as a program to morally rearm the sentiments of the national community of Europeans was implemented enthusiastically on the railways. Already by 1876 government grants had been given to elementary schools for Europeans and Eurasians at the railway towns of Barrackpur, Rampur Hat, Howrah, Patna, Dinapur, Buxar, and Jamalpur.[69] This new idea of education was most fully realized in the boarding schools set up for the children of railway employees partly funded by the government. From 1875 to 1888, railway companies and churches built eleven hill boarding schools for them in places such as Kurseong, Nainital, and Mussorie. Central boarding schools in the plains, for example at Jamalpur, were also constructed. Temple and officials in the Education Department kept a close watch on these schemes. The central boarding school in Jamalpur was planned for railway employees' sons from eight years old. This was to eliminate the need for dame schools, so named because they were run by unqualified female teachers, or other preparatory schools in which it was felt the discipline and style of education was not sufficiently rigorous. It also meant that children could be removed from parental influence. Pressure would be brought to bear by railway officials and charitable bodies on Europeans and Eurasians to send their children to the schools. In 1876 a Diocesan Anglican school was set up in Nainital for the children of railway employees, warrant officers, civil clerks, and subordinate officers in the Police, Telegraph, and Public Works Departments. In 1879 the East Indian Railway opened the Oak Grove boarding school with the help of government funding at Mussorie. Under the instructions of the new lieutenant governor of Bengal, Ashley Eden, in 1879 the Education Department spent the large sum of Rs 28000 purchasing land in Kurseong and providing bricks for the construction of a school for the children of state railway employees who were of European descent.[70] These hill schools were mainly intended for European children or children who were "nearly" European with a father who was British and a mother who was Eurasian. They, according to ethnoclimatological theories, required the reviving influence of a "British" climate. Eden perceived these schools as particularly vital. He argued that a comparison of the physical appearance of "even Eurasian boys brought up in the hills with that of boys of a similar class brought up in the towns in the plains" would even reveal "the advantage of the hill climate on the physique of the boys."[71] But more important than this, he suggested, was the removal of children from their "home-training" because "the study of nature amidst the splendid and impressive scenery of the Himalayas is likely to have a more elevating effect on the minds of boys than studies of society and nature pursued at Boitakhana and Bow Bazar."[72]

In 1879 the viceroy, Lord Lytton, gave his backing to these projects in his minute on the education of Europeans and Eurasians. He argued that the government of India should spare no efforts to give free elementary education to such children and that the government should bear a substantial amount of the cost for the establishment of industrial boarding schools. These institutions were necessary in order to produce "young Englishmen" "brought up and educated in India itself" who would be equipped with the right British cultural competency to work in upper subordinate positions in industry, replacing imported European labor.[73] These schools would also provide a similar cultural competency to girls, but they would be trained only to an elementary standard and provided with domestic skills. Although previous viceroys and lieutenant governors of Bengal had mentioned the usefulness of Europeans and Eurasians as a source of labor, Lytton particularly emphasized this point. Yet it is important to note that this apparently unequivocal statement of a class-based educational project was not so transparent in its intentions. This concern with the proper training of European and Eurasian laborers has to be seen against the background of the demand by Indian middle-class organizations that Indians should be employed at all levels of the Raj in greater numbers. In the agitation against income tax in 1870 and 1871 and against the new civil service regulations from 1877 to 1879, these organizations specifically attacked the use of Europeans and Eurasians in supervisory positions. The Indian National Congress continued this attack. It is in this context that we must see Lytton's concern with European and Eurasian education. Like other government officials he responded to these challenges to the Raj's biomoral typology of pedigree by stepping up efforts to enforce European habits of life and "higher" moral standards within the national/racial community. Any departure from these standards could potentially be seized upon as proof of the hollowness of British arguments against further employment of Indians in the civil service and railways because of their moral unsuitability to lead.

The syllabus and routines of the schools set up during this period in the plains and hills laid down the form and content of European education up to Independence. Government inspection standardized routines and forms of instruction. Annual holidays were for Good Friday, Easter Monday, the Queen's birthday, and the last week in May and the first in June, with a one-month break at Christmas. This tied pupils to a Christian and state-based calendrical year that had nothing to do with the rhythms of Indian weather or festivals. In year one English-language reading, penmanship, simple arithmetic, and drawing were emphasized. In year two language work continued with more stress on elocution, which was seen as vital to the cultural competence of children. Geography and British history were introduced in the fifth year, as well as geometry and grammar. In the sixth year along with the composition of letters the geography and history of India were added. At this point Urdu also began to be taught.[74] Throughout, military drills were carried out by male children. Often as boys grew older their teams were attached to local volunteer or military battalions. On this basic framework technical education was offered to boys and domestic skills were taught to girls. Catholic schools offered Latin as a second language and some places also offered French to female students. Children were usually educated only to fourteen if they were girls and sixteen if they were boys. Schools did not offer any preparation for university admission exams, as this was seen as unnecessary for the children of subordinate employees.

The primary aim of schooling across all these contexts was "above all to form the character" through exercise and a disciplined British environment.[75] Almost as many girls as boys went to these schools. For example in 1908, 210 boys and 151 girls attended the East Indian Railway's Oak Grove School at Mussorie. The education of girls was seen as necessary because "the future of the domiciled community of this country lies in the hands of its women."[76] As was typical of many of these schools, at Oak Grove there was an annual prize day at which the railway agent gave awards for "womanliness" and "manliness" and the boys performed military drills. So important were these domestic and military elements of education both in the plains and hill schools that in 1884 the Education Department in Bengal made the grants provided to schools partly dependent on whether they taught drill, gymnastics, and needlework.[77] Catholic and Anglican schools followed these same patterns of teaching and the standardized syllabus. In these schools the national and moral rearmament of the bodies and sentiments of working class children were both literally and metaphorically combined.

This project of moral reform of citizens was consciously molded on what were described as "Christian" ethics. Dependence on government grants-in-aid meant that all schools whether they were Anglican, Catholic, or nondenominational had to be secular. Yet this insistence on secularism went hand in hand with an assertion that the education provided in order to transform children into upright citizens through the inculcation of morals should be "Christian" in spirit. In 1881, when the Education Department drew up a specific code for European schools and set up a department for European education, this insistence on the practice of a Christian secularism provided the rationale for a separate system of schooling. It was assumed that parents of European extraction and habits of life would not countenance sending their children to government-funded schools for natives where there would be a non-Christian atmosphere.[78] In this project of education, frontiers within people and the national community were even more rigidly marked with signs of race, habits of life, and religion.

Yet schooling also produced a hierarchy within the community of "Europeans." This hierarchy wove together differences of class and graded differences of race. One of these distinctions could now not be imagined without the other. Which school you attended not only affected your class position but also retrospectively indicated the degree of your European lineage in a complex realization of the ideas of pedigree that were first visible in the Committee on Colonisation. By the 1890s a three-tier system of education had developed that continued until Independence. Elite hill schools such as St. Paul's Darjeeling provided education for children with solely European parentage and middle-class parents. The newer railway and Protestant hill schools provided for children with lower-middle-class parents and more ambiguous backgrounds. These schools were perhaps the least successful in terms of attracting pupils and often suffered from financial deficits.[79] There were several reasons for this. Lower-middle-class parents were not certain that their children needed the distance from their domestic environment and the kind of reform that these schools promised. However, parents who were in favor of such a form of education periodically panicked about the moral atmosphere of particular schools. They feared especially the influence of other pupils "of the lower grade subordinates" on their children.[80] This suggests that the aim of the educational project was somewhat deflected by the agency of children in the schools. It also reveals just how permeable and fluid, dangerously so in the eyes of colonial officials and some parents, the boundary between social and racial groups was in this system of education. It was possible to lose the essential status of pedigree simply by your children associating with children who had come from less prestigious backgrounds.

This anxiety about the malleability of children also reflects a muted awareness that education did not just provide a service for already existing segments of European society, but helped to make the internal boundaries within that society. Education now guaranteed both social privileges and a particular kind of pedigree. It did not simply exist for Europeans; instead, it helped to make them. The children of railway employees were the target of such efforts for several reasons. Despite the prescribed domesticity of the railway colony, as the offspring of working class and often Eurasian parents they were seen as particularly vulnerable to pernicious home influences. Their parents couldn't be trusted to raise them to be loyal and decorous representatives of their race and nation. Second, once they were properly educated, these children could provide a future supply of respectable railway wives and railway workers. They would be a bulwark of loyal and sober employees on the railways in key positions of command. This loyalty was seen as even more important as strikes driven by the racial contradictions and inequalities of railway service spread across the network at the turn of the nineteenth century.

## THE RAILWAY BUREAUCRACY, LEGITIMACY, AND PEDIGREE

In the period from 1860 to 1900 problems of management on the railways were immediately understood by middle-class bureaucrats to be a matter of pedigree—the organization of workers according to their natural, inherited biomoral qualities and forms of ethical life. Technical problems such as the occurrence of accidents were seen as the result of the inadequacies of certain pedigrees and were solved by racial hierarchies of command and strict workplace regulations. Discipline was tight, modeled on judicial practices, and guided by close scrutiny of the moral behavior of employees in order to compensate for the natural inefficiency of Indians, working class Europeans, and Eurasians. Railway colonies were provided for European and Eurasian employees in order to preserve them from their own innate weaknesses and to revive their vulnerable natural qualities of command. The hold of the concept of pedigree over officials was so tight in part because it was the linchpin supporting the idea that Britain had a particular imperial and national destiny. Individual qualities reflected the inheritance of natural national attributes that expressed the distinct destinies of Britain and India—one to rule and spread industry and enterprise, the other to be a subject country tutored by Britain. The notion of pedigree also suggested that the middle classes were naturally suited to command by their inherited characteristics and moral probity. When the legitimacy of this vision was challenged by Indian nationalists, bureaucrats rearmed the boundaries of the nation through projects aimed at reviving the moral vigor of working class Europeans and Eurasians through education. The health of the empire and nation would now be secured and monitored not just through pedigree, but also through the judicious management of the sentiments of natural communities of interest, which were understood as being based on religious principles. The railway bureaucracy and its institutions materialized a theory of the management of populations that was at once about economic, moral, and physical life. It was suffused with practices that linked private morality, natural inheritances, and public efficiency. The next two chapters explore the contradictory impacts of these spaces and practices. In particular they address their effects on the forms of popular nationalism and protest among railway workers.

*Chapter Four*

# Industrial Unrest and the Cultivation of Railway Communities, 1897–1931

I also beg to add that I am not now prepared to take up service under your unjust government. . . . The seriousness of the matter in taking undemocratic attitudes in disposal of Indians . . . is the main cause of so much grumbling against the British justice and government.

—B. R. Misra, former locomotive repairman, to G. H. Colvin, agent, East Indian Railway,
October 25, 1932

Indians probably learnt more about equality from the colonial practice of inequality than from the British theory of equality.

—A. Beteille, "Caste in Contemporary India," 1996

In the period from 1897 onward, railway workers began to protest their conditions of service and the hierarchies that governed their labor. Strikes that often became linked to nationalist aims disturbed the rarefied calm of colonies. Sometimes national-level political movements directly triggered strikes such as those on the railways in the Punjab during the anti–Rowlatt Act agitation in 1919 and the Khilafat movement in 1920. At other times local events such as assaults or mistreatment were scaled up to protests about colonial rule itself. For example, a worried district commissioner wrote the following to his superiors in 1922 about industrial action on the East Indian Railway: "The strike is a challenge to the state. And it would be a serious blow to government if the strikers were to win."[1] By 1931 the Royal Commission on Labour in India singled out railway colonies as "active foci of discontent and disruption."[2] This chapter explores the ways in which the railway bureaucracy responded to these challenges and examines the traces of forms of popular nationalism among strikers. Many histories of the working classes in India have focused on their fragmentation into disparate groups, the ambivalence of Congress toward the cause of labor, and the failures of unions to build long-term solidarities. Explanations for these features of working class action and Congress politics in India vary. Some commentators have stressed the ways in which notions of community disrupted potential solidarities. Others, including Chandavarkar, have followed a more convincing interpretation by focusing on why in certain circumstances it became possible to forge political solidarities between segments of the working class and between them and the cause of Congress. In the account that follows of the strikes that occurred in the railways from the 1890s to 1931, I will follow Chandavarkar's approach by situating the activism and nationalism of railway workers in the context of their direct, daily encounter with the legitimizing practices of the imperial state in their workplaces. As we will see, a scaling up of their immediate grievances to the level of an issue of colonial legitimacy and national self-rule was not difficult to produce.

But the attractions of *swadeshi* and Gandhian nationalism to railway workers cannot be explained by this unequal workplace hierarchy alone. These forms of political language found a resonance with railway workers because of their particular content. These were moral theories of the necessity of national self-determination for the physical and ethical well-being of the people of India. They both contained, as Alter has put it, speaking of Gandhi's politics of the body, a "biomoral imperative of public life and personal health."[3] Using idioms of *jati*, *swadeshi* rhetoric spoke of pollutions of the body politic that necessitated self-rule. Gandhian notions of *satyagraha* (struggle for truth, nonviolent resistence) and *brahmacharya* (pursuit of religious learning, celibacy) linked "biological and moral, impersonal and personal, global and intimate projects" through idioms of individual ascetic renunciation and self-discipline.[4] Gandhi also suggested that a particular family-based code of ethics should order industrial relations. As Chandavarkar has described it, this was a vision of "capitalists serving as trustees for the moral and material welfare of the labouring class." It rested on the idea that capital and labor should be "a great family living in unity and harmony."[5] I will suggest in the account that follows that these nationalist visions had a particular salience to workers because of the forms of workplace discipline founded on ideas of pedigree and morality they experienced in their daily lives.

## SECURITY AND THE CALCULATION OF LOYALTY

In 1897 the skilled guards on the Great Indian Peninsula Railway, who were members of the Amalgamated Society of Railway Servants of India and Burma, stopped work to protest against the system of fining and scrutiny that had first become an issue in the 1870s. This organization was affiliated to the same railway union in Britain and consisted mainly of imported covenanted drivers and guards. Although successful in resolving this strike, the railway bureaucracy began to fear that its European employees in the upper subordinate grades were too militant to provide a reliable workforce. Their concerns increased when Indian signalers carried out a strike for higher wages in 1899 on the same railway. They were supported by nationalist newspapers such as the *Maharatta* and the *Kesari*, and strike funds were collected for them by Pherozeshah Mehta and D. E. Wacha. This agitation occurred at the same time as the execution of the Chapekar brothers for terrorism. The British press and authorities feared that the strike was a sign of further Brahmin conspiracy against the Raj, especially as most signalers on the Great Indian Penninsula Railway were Brahmins from Pune.[6] The railway bureaucracy was thrown into a panic, afraid that politically motivated strikes would make the military and administrative might of the railways grind to a halt. The bureaucrats were even uncertain of the loyalty of Eurasians and domiciled Europeans, as a strike on the Indian Midland Railway in 1900 by the Eurasian drivers and guards was timed to interfere with the movement of supplies and troops to South Africa. These early strikes and the atmosphere of unrest provoked an examination not of conditions of service, but of the military defense of railways and the community composition of railway workforces. In the process, the focus of the bureaucracy on the efficient arrangement of biomoral capacities within the railways was overlaid with an emphasis on evaluating and administering the sentiments of a range of communities. The idioms of nationalism that rested on the concept of the invisible ties binding communities together that had driven the projects of European education in the period from 1870 to 1900 were now transferred onto Indian communities.

In the same year as the signalers strike on the Great Indian Peninsula Railway there had been a series of train-wrecking incidents in the North West Provinces. Both of these forms of unrest led Curzon, the viceroy, to call for the appointment of a railway defense committee. The instructions were that it should consider the defense of important bridges and tunnels; the arrangements to be made for garrisoning these places in times of disturbance and the number of volunteers available to do this from the railways; the arrangements for armored patrol trains; and how railway workers could be deployed at times of internal uprising to defend the lines and stations. The committee, composed of three military men and two civil servants including the head of the railways, reported its findings in 1902. The committee members concluded that in dealing with internal uprisings the services of the Railway Volunteer Corps were essential. The strength and power of all the important garrisons depended on the railways connecting them and speed of movement at times of threat. Rather than setting up a separate railway corps, they suggested that the Railway Volunteers be made more professional. These measures would change them from an amateur infantry that was largely "devoted to parade and ceremonial movements."[7] At times of disturbance they would man and work patrol trains containing columns of troops and guns. They would also defend the railway from attack. They should be instructed in the schemes for defense for each section of the line and drilled in emergency procedures. It was felt that they were already fitted for such a role due to the duties and discipline of railway service. The agents of all the railways set about introducing this new, more rigorous role for the volunteers. This change would have a double effect. European and Eurasian railway workers would be made to feel their duties and loyalties more keenly. They would also act as a line of defense against uprising, whether this took the form of political strikes, external attack, or internal rebellion against British rule. The biomoral work hierarchy that had come into existence to prevent accidents was now changing into a paramilitary mechanism for controlling other railway workers and local populations.

The second inquiry ordered by the government was an investigation into the possibility of employing more Anglo-Indians and of the distribution of "different creeds and castes" among the employees in the locomotive and traffic departments of the railways.[8] When the figures were reported back from the various companies to F. Upcott, the head of the railways in India, he was worried to find out that there were concentrations of particular communities. These, it was assumed, would provide the basis for political agitation along the lines of "family parties" and religion. Brahmins apparently dominated the posts of stationmaster and signaler in the Southern Mahratta; Great Indian Peninsula; Bombay, Baroda, and Central Indian; Rajputana-Malwa; Indian Midland; East Coast; East Indian; Bengal-Nagpur; East Bengal; Oudh and Rohilkund; and South Indian Railways. In addition, Muslims worked in large percentages in the locomotive departments of most railways. The other community bodies it charted as abstract signs in its statistics were those of Sikhs, Christians, and Parsis. Upcott and Curzon recommended that steps be taken to lessen the concentrations of particular communities, to produce "a more even distribution of the different creeds and castes among the employees." They also urged that Eurasians and Indian Christians should be more widely employed beyond their roles as drivers and guards, even though this might incur an "additional expenditure" on wages.[9]

The agents of the railways largely agreed with these recommendations. However, they also pointed out that Eurasians could not act as a "leaven" to break up "family parties" throughout the hierarchy of the railway.[10] The more extended employment of Eurasians beyond their upper subordinate roles was seen as impossible because they could not be employed on lower wages. They required a certain pay in order to maintain a European lifestyle, which in turn made them suitable for positions of command. As the consulting engineer to the government of India for railways, Lucknow suggested, "The fact is that Eurasians require higher pay to enable them to live, marry and educate their children, than is necessary for native competition."[11] The agent of the Southern Mahratta Railway argued that it would be difficult and improper to get the Eurasian worker to live in smaller stations, "even if we did give him higher pay and altered the quarters built for native station masters at roadside stations so as to suit him."[12] "Natives," however, could live on such low wages because of their "Indian" habits and their natural suitability for certain positions. Yet "natives" apparently could not be used as a leaven in the same way as Eurasians. The agents felt that they had too great loyalty to region and place to become a mobile and transferable workforce with a primary allegiance to the company itself. The official consulting engineer for railways in Bombay wrote to the government of India, informing them that although he agreed with their plan to evenly distribute castes and creeds the insuperable barrier to this was that, for example, the Bengali "Babu" "is a plant that will not bear transplanting. He is regarded by the people of the country in which he is transplanted as a noxious weed and is treated as such. The air, the water and what not do not suit his constitution. . . . They feel out of their element and departed as opportunity offered."[13] Similarly, the general traffic manager of the Great Indian Peninsula Railway wrote, "The Bengali will not emigrate to Bombay except for short periods and under caste conditions which no railway can either afford or arrange nor will the Brahmin to Bengal even if higher wages are offered to him."[14] The regional identity and caste practices of Indian populations meant that they could not be turned into interchangeable abstract individuals driven by wages to leave the ties of their community. The only bodies that could do this were the transferable, "rootless" domiciled Europeans and Eurasians, and Indian Christians.[15]

In 1903 a compromise was reached between the wishes of the government and the concerns of the agents at a meeting of the heads of the railways. They agreed to more widely employ Anglo-Indians in positions that paid more than 30 rupees per month.[16] In particular, more Anglo-Indian guards and drivers would be recruited because of their vital strategic role. In addition, attempts would be made to increase the numbers of native Christians throughout the railway. The railways accordingly stepped up their program of preferentially apprenticing Eurasian and domiciled European boys. Following the advice on the cheap loyalty of Indian Christians, railways such as the East Indian Railway also built special hostels for orphans from Bhagalpur Orphanage to train and house them.[17] The employment hierarchy that had originally been based in ideas of the physical and moral capacities of bodies was subtly changing. It was now grounded in calculations of the "natural" political loyalties and disloyalties of different groups, and these were understood to be like the ties of religion. It attempted to reckon the degree of an employee's allegiance to region, caste, place, nation, and empire. Community origins were now a guide to individual skill and political sensibility. In these sums, only Europeans, Eurasians, and native Christians had a rootlessness that made them mobile workers with loyalty to British rule. It is therefore not surprising that the railways remained the only arena of the colonial state that continued to give preference to domiciled Europeans and Eurasians in recruitment from 1870 to 1930.[18] Even in 1923, nearly half of the Anglo-Indian community was employed by or associated with the railways as dependents of employees, and in 1932 almost 100 percent of the upper subordinate positions on the state-managed railways were filled by Anglo-Indians and Europeans.[19]

These commissions of inquiry and the measures taken after them did not remove the inequities of racial distinction in the railways or alter the conditions of service. In fact, they made increasingly stark distinctions between the qualities of British, Anglo-Indian, and Indian employees. They also pushed Anglo-Indian and domiciled European employees through military drilling and economic incentives to more strongly identify with the railways they worked for and their loyalty to British rule. It is therefore not surprising that railway strikes continued to occur with increasing intensity in the early years of the twentieth century. More importantly, these protests that emerged from within the context of the workplace of the railways, which emphasized national and racial distinctions, frequently moved from disputes over specific issues into popular protests against British rule. In 1906 alone there were strikes at Kharagpur, Howrah, Asansol, Jamalpur, and Raniganj. All of these strikes combined specific concerns with political aims. For example, in 1906 at Kharagpur the workers of the carriage building department, especially the daily-paid carpenters from the Punjab, went on strike for better contract rates and grain allowances. Worried members of the political department wrote to the secretary of the government of India that *swadeshi* agitators were present. They found a receptive audience among the strikers. The strike was enforced on more recalcitrant members of the workshop by the use of idioms of pollution for political ends. Those who didn't strike were threatened with being made to eat cow or pig flesh, according to their Hindu or Muslim origins. Baskets full of cow bones were found strategically placed along the roads to the workshops in order to throw at scabs.[20] Ideas of pollution that created distinction between the *jatis* of disparate castes and communities were being used by some workers to enforce an alliance united in its resistance to British rule. Emerging in such action we can see an expansive meaning for the concept of *jati*. Idioms of *jati* began to acquire an association with a *swadeshi* community of common national interests tied together by a moral purity and moral sanctions. In this respect they echo the form, but not the content, of the idioms of race and nation in the railway hierarchy. The railway bureaucracy had made the practices of daily and family life among its European and Eurasian employees an emblem of the moral legitimacy of the Raj. These Indian employees were attempting to forge a counterversion of this moral purity of political communities with a more democratic impulse than the versions of *jati* among Bengali nationalists in the 1890s. In this community, as in the railway's paternalist practices, obligations to a national and political community are of the same kind as those you owe to your family and social community.

In the same month as the Kharagpur strike, the clerks of the traffic and locomotive departments at Asansol and one hundred men on stations along the line struck work. The strike quickly took on a political and moral character framed by idioms of *jati* and pollution of the body politic. A. C. Banarji, a *swadeshi* activist from Calcutta, addressed a strike meeting in Asansol and found a receptive audience. He gave a speech about driving the English out of India and the pollution of sugar by animal fats as a symbol for the corruption of the times. European railway subordinates added to the atmosphere of a political confrontation by turning up at the meeting and shouting "Rule Britannia" at the Indian crowd.[21] Meanwhile the police were posted at various stations along the line and the European subordinates who were afraid of their quarters being attacked were reassured by the establishment of a temporary armory at Asansol. As a result of the strike, 206 men were dismissed under the Railway Act for failure to fulfill their duty and endangering the public. Medals were awarded to the men who didn't strike. The railway colony was no longer a place of calm. Instead, it was on the front lines of the confrontation between, on the one hand, *swadeshi* activists and discontented workers joined together by an expansive political idiom of *jati* and, on the other, British rule. Issues of sovereignty, legitimacy, and national self-determination were profoundly intertwined with industrial disputes in the context of the railways.

In this atmosphere of political agitation, the tension between European, Anglo-Indian, and Indian workers increased. As Jagga has argued in his pioneering work, the engine where Indian firemen worked side-by-side with drivers became a particularly difficult space to negotiate. For example, in 1907 the European drivers on the Howrah to Jahjah division met with a conciliation committee of the East Indian Railway to discuss their concerns and grievances. Their main complaint was about the present friction between European drivers and Indian firemen. They insisted that they needed to have greater control over their subordinates. In particular, all benefits given by the company to Indian firemen, such as increases in salary, promotion, and leave, should depend on the driver's recommendation. They also sought to be distinguished from Indians in their treatment by their superiors: "We are not treated as become men at enquiries or when we are called into office to submit an explanation. We are spoken to as so many coolies and the threat is always held out to us of dismissal."[22] The conciliation committee refused to implement the greater powers over firemen. These were left in the hands of the locomotive superintendent. But this representation captures the mounting tensions of the time. Racial hierarchies were increasingly difficult to implement.

## TRADITIONAL VILLAGES AND RADICAL TRADITIONS

The railway strikes among Indian workers left the agents of the railways searching for new measures with which to subdue the growing militancy of their Indian employees. They focused on alterations in housing policies as a solution. They aimed to design communities that would follow the rhythms and practices of traditional sociability and therefore would not be attracted by union agitation. For example, in 1911, the Railway Board sanctioned the establishment of village settlements for the Indian railway workshop staff in the neighborhood of Kharagpur. This strategy was designed to solve several problems at once. These settlements would be on the outskirts of Kharagpur and therefore would carry no risk of spreading disease, but they would be under the control of the sanitary inspectors of the railway. There, workers could live, cultivating small plots of land, and there "they might live under their own conditions of life," as discrete Punjabi or other communities settled together after their migration from different regions of India.[23] The separation of these communities spatially from each other would also prevent "a coalition amongst them in cases of dissatisfaction."[24] The domestic habits of employees were once more seen as salient to colonial political economy, but in the case of Indian employees this meant the use of traditional ties of community sentiment for the containment of discontent. At one level these measures were successful. They helped to reproduce a domestic separation between different kinds of Indians. Oral histories suggest they prevented the growth of intercaste and intercommunity marriage in this industrial town, where class status might have overcome other markers of distinction. Interviews with the children of workers who went to live in Kharagpur in the 1920s (who had retired themselves from work in the same town) revealed that each community placed great emphasis on its domestic separation from other communities. But in spite of the way housing policies reinforced broad distinctions of community and caste in domestic arrangements, they did not achieve the aim that the administration had intended. They were unsuccessful in preventing the growth of grassroots agitation and union organizations.

Before and after the First World War, various labor organizations sought to represent the interests of railway workers across different regions. In the main these did not control the incidence of strikes nor did they seek to provoke them.

Instead, they attempted to act as brokers between employers and workers. Non-political unions were started by European and Anglo-Indian employees, but some of these expanded to draw in Indian workers. They included the Amalgamated Society of Railway Servants of India and Burma, which was active in south India, and the Railway Workers Association, which spread along the lines of the East Indian Railway and Bengal-Nagpur Railway. These aimed to be organizations that would negotiate over issues of working conditions and pay. As more Indians joined these unions tensions arose because there were increasing demands for the removal of some of the racial inequalities in railway service. In addition, the companies took measures to split the alliance of European and Indian workers. New service agreements were introduced that improved work conditions for covenanted workers. Joining the Indian Auxiliary Force was made compulsory for all European and Anglo-Indian employees, and the Railway Volunteer Force was absorbed into this organization. As a result, male employees were drilled in the spirit of patriotism during the 1914–1918 war. Legislation was also passed that banned European and Anglo-Indian employees from striking, with the penalty of dismissal for dereliction of duty.

As a result of these shifts, by the 1920s, non-politically-affiliated unions were largely led by Indian skilled workers such as stationmasters, drivers, guards and clerical staff. Such organizations affiliated themselves to the All Indian Railway Conference, which first met in 1921. The leadership of this organization consisted of the superior and upper grades of Indians in railway service, who were mainly in clerical positions in the bureaucracy. The Railway Board and agents of the railways agreed to negotiate with this organization and the unions affiliated to it as long as their demands remained nonconfrontational issues of worker welfare and pay. More radical organizations developed on various lines, in particular on the North Western Railway during the Khilafat and anti-Rowlatt agitation from 1919 to 1920 and on the East Indian, Bengal-Nagpur, and East Bengal Railways in 1921 and 1922, just before the arrival of the Prince of Wales on tour to these regions.[25]

In the period from the 1920s to 1940s, at the grassroots level union organizations in the railway towns were run by an eclectic mix of railway workers of different political persuasions. On the East Indian Railway and Bengal-Nagpur Railway these included socialists, quit India activists inspired by Congress politics, radical humanists inspired by M. N. Roy, and communists. Many of the union organizers were the first generation of railway workers in their families, with fathers who had been postmasters, clerks, or teachers. They often were of middle-ranking castes, and a large number of them were Bengalis. They usually had B.A. degrees that had equipped them for positions as guards, stationmasters, or clerks. Railway employment had sometimes been preceded by involvement in anti-British protests or in radical organizations such as the Bengal Volunteers. An example of this is the career of Bimal De, who was involved in the East Indian Railway Employees Union from the 1940s and was its general secretary from 1973 to 1983. In a written account of his life, he claimed that from his childhood he longed to do something for the poor and to remove the British from India. He joined the Bengal Volunteers to achieve this, but he had to go underground in 1942. During this time he joined the Railway Police in order to fight the British from within. He was court-martialed for his activities, but he managed to hide this and get a job as a clerk on the railways in 1945.[26] Most of the union office-holders were inspired to join the unions by specific experiences of racial discrimination. A typical example of this kind of motivation can be found in the account of S. R. Mitra, who became joint general secretary of the East Indian Railway Employees Association in the 1940s, of the first day of his job:

> On 23.03.38 I came to Fairlie Place H.Q. office of E. I. Railway [sic] for joining as a clerk on Rs. 30/-fixed. As I stepped to go up by the main staircase near the lift a watch and ward Sepoy who was sitting near by pointed out to me by finger two signboards by the side of the staircase, one depicting, "Dogs prohibited" below this, "Clerks not allowed." Derogatory indeed. . . . That day I promised to do my best so that the two boards are removed.[27]

Some union officials were not railway workers, but Congress or Communist party members deputed to prevent political takeovers by rival political groups within the unions. This kind of official party activity increased after the mid-1930s. In the wake of further electoral reforms it became clear to all political parties that the membership of unions could be formed into a valuable potential vote bank. This activity provided politicians with a training and power base that led to some prestigious careers. Jyoti Basu, the future chief minister of West Bengal, A. P. Sharma, who was a cabinet minister under Indira Gandhi, and V. V. Giri, who became president of India, are included in this list. The railway workers who made up the membership of the unions were predominantly employed in class III and IV positions in the goods sheds, running departments, and workshops. These were all sites where the work process required coordination and cooperation in labor, yet where people were divided from one another by strict biomoral hierarchies of command. Workers in these contexts would feel the contradictions of their position keenly. They all were part of the same work process governed by the timetable or the engine, and/or were engaged in building the same product. Yet they were simultaneously divided by rigid hierarchies and often by specialized community roles, especially in the workshops. No doubt the contradictions of this situation helped to create the radicalism of these employees. The unions also successfully used some of these hierarchical relationships against the companies. Very often the key to recruiting workers to the union was first to persuade the leader of the gang or head of a section to join. Then, all the workers under him would sign up.[28]

In general, these union organizations provided a means to direct and coordinate the already existing militancy of workers. Rather than following directives from the unions, workers often took spontaneous strike action as a result of their own shared sense of outrage. Usually unions acted as brokers. They mobilized resources to sustain strikes or negotiated with employers. For example, on the East Indian Railway, strike committees inspired by the issue of anticolonial agitation had been formed by workshop men at Allahabad, Jamalpur, Asansol, and Liluah in the period from 1920 to 1921. But it was the tense space of the engine that sparked off protest from December 1921 to April 1922. The Indian drivers, firemen, and menial staff of the locomotive department left work in December after the assault of an Indian fireman by a European driver. The men insisted that the district loco superintendent negotiate with their representative, Swami Darsanand, who led the Central Labour Association. This organization was based in Ranegunj, and it had explicitly noncooperation aims. He demanded that the assault be investigated and that the strikers not be punished. In this heightened atmosphere, the Indian firemen left work at Jhajha on December 19, after hearing a rumor that the European driver of an express train had killed his Indian second fireman. A departmental inquiry was held, which exonerated the driver, but the workers did not accept its findings. The strike spread to locomotive staff members all along the western part of the line, some of whom attempted to derail trains. Workers rejoined in January 1922 on the conditions that the circumstances of the assaults be investigated and that they would receive no penalties for striking.[29] Another assault on a fireman named Ramlal by a European driver at Tundla sparked off a spontaneous strike in February, which lasted until April and spread along the line as far as Allahabad and the Punjab. The assault had been inquired into by a magistrate. The workers had been outraged when he had concluded that the fireman had not been assaulted and the incident had been set up by noncooperation agitators to provoke unrest. This strike had the atmosphere of national confrontation about it with, for example, ten thousand workmen leaving the Jamalpur repair shops, shouting "Gandhi ki jai" (victory to Gandhi), and the army assisting European workmen in running emergency trains. The nationalist intent of the strike preexisted and was independent of any actual political involvement by Congress in the events. Yet Gandhi and his widely publicized biomoral projects had found a resonance with the railway workers.

Congress eventually did intervene in the escalating tension, as a broker rather than instigator of the actions of the workers. C. F. Andrews offered to negotiate with the agent on the issues of racial discrimination and the Tundla assault. A general inquiry into issues of race was rejected by the agent because the skilled European drivers threatened to strike if this was carried out. However, Andrews did manage to institute a second inquiry into the assault on Ramlal and to negotiate for the restoration of forfeited gratuities to all workers who had struck since 1918. The workers had managed to assert their right to strike without penalty for the first time and to make it more difficult for drivers to assault their subordinates. Most workers resumed work, but a group affiliated with Swami Darsanand's organization refused to return until their union was recognized and they would be guaranteed no victimization. They held out until April. A group of 1200 men out of the locomotive staff of 1500 at Tundla continued to stay away, refusing to recognize the authority of Congress, any union, or the agent.[30] As in this example, when railway workers went on strike over specific workplace incidents there was a frequent scaling up to issues of colonial legitimacy and national self-rule. Sometimes, as in the case of these 1200 men at Tundla, workplace experiences produced a sporadic radicalism that led workers to refuse to negotiate with any of the current political brokers, seeing them all as equally illegitimate.

The period from 1926 to 1930 saw further unrest as retrenchment during the economic depression in India was used as an excuse to sack union members from the railways. Vincent Raven was appointed to head a committee that was designed to study surplus labor in railway workshops and to suggest where it could be cut. When the recommendations of the committee were implemented on the Bengal-Nagpur Railway, protests began. The union on this railway and the events around this strike provide an important insight into the resonances of Gandhian political idioms for railway workers, as well as the increasing significance of Congress-linked politicians as brokers with employers and the state. The union was started in 1921 in Kidderpore by a group of employees. In 1922 a group of union members sought a direct alliance with Gandhian Congress politics. When Giri was released from jail, where he had been imprisoned for Congress noncooperation activities, these workers literally asked him at the prison gates if he would become its organizing vice president. Within a few months Giri had opened thirty branches of the union along the railway line, which were staffed by railway workers, and by 1924 he was president of the union. Giri set about regularizing relations with the railway company, reassuring the company that he sought negotiations on issues of wages and conditions rather than confrontation. The agent responded by granting the union recognition, which could, of course, be withdrawn at any time if members acted as more than brokers. Workers also waited to see how effective a broker the union was. More than four thousand men joined the union overnight when it successfully contested issues of pay and privileges in the workshops in December 1925. The political idioms of the union were explicitly Gandhian. Gandhi himself visited the union office in Kharagpur in July 1925 as part of his campaign to propagate *khadi* (the making and wearing of homespun cloth). However, the apparent easy reconciliation of Gandhian politics, company interests, and workers' concerns, which seemed to exist in the activities of the union, broke under the strain of the fallout from the Raven Committee recommendations in December 1926.

The company began to dismiss workers as recommended by the Raven Committee and to harass members of the union, provoking protest from workers, who then approached the union officers. Giri presented their grievances to the agent. These included the dismissal of workers who were members of the Bengal-Nagpur Railway Union; the retrenchment of men who were replaced by men on lower wages; the frequent assaults and insults on workmen by European and Anglo-Indian foremen; and very low wages. He also asked for an inquiry into all these matters. The administration stalled on this and also victimized the secretary of the union by transferring him to work under an unsympathetic superior. A lightning strike began, independently of the union, on February 12, with all the workshop men marching to the Kharagpur railway station. The workers occupied the station and the station yard and took possession of the signal cabin. The line was brought to a halt. The Railway Auxiliary Force was called out, and they opened fire and also used their bayonets and the ends of their rifles to beat back the crowd. The district magistrate ruled the strike illegal under the Indian penal code. In response to this, the union intervened to organize a successful stop of work all along the line. When the Kharagpur workshop was reopened on February 14, the workers occupied the place and simply sat down without doing any work in a *satyagraha*. This was an unprecedented form for a strike action, which shocked the railway administration and the government by its linking of nationalist and labor politics. The agent locked out the workers on February 16 and stated that all those who did not return to work by February 21 would be dismissed. Within a week, 40000 workers along the line to Calcutta had stopped work. The strikers were supported by Joshi and Neogy in the Central Legislative Assembly, who pressured the government to answer questions relating to victimization, retrenchment, and the progress of the strike. The government prohibited meetings, censored the union's telegrams, and arrested its leaders. The railway also issued notice to 1300 workers at the Kharagpur workshop. They intended to retrench the militant workforce and replace it by contracting out work to private firms. When the railway reopened the workshop once again, 8000 workers turned up each day, occupied the place, and sang *bhajans* (hymns). The workshop had to be closed indefinitely.

With the intervention of Congress and negotiations between Giri and the government, a settlement was finally reached. This did not address the issues of discrimination, but it agreed to take back all the retrenched men and to pay full wages for the time during the strike. Gradual redundancies and transfers would replace the mass retrenchment originally planned.[31] This was a strike that had exposed to a broader public the violence that underpinned the railway hierarchy as demonstrated by the actions of the Railway Auxiliary Force.

The measures to create distinct traditional communities of interest in Kharagpur through separate housing had been decidedly unsuccessful. Instead, the spontaneous events of this strike, in particular the novel use of *satyagraha* as part of labor politics, suggest that Gandhian nationalist visions had acquired a particular salience for railway workers. This may well have been because they echoed the paternalist, ascetic, and biomoral projects of their workplace, but in a manner that overturned the moral hierarchies of the railway bureaucracy. A further clue that railway service made such political visions plausible and had created the foundations on which idioms of *jati* and family could be seen as relevant to the public domain comes from another element of this strike. During the strike at Kharagpur, if any of the men wavered in their commitment to the cause, then the wives of other workers would leave *shindoor* (red powder placed in the part of a woman's hair as a sign of her married status) in their houses, implying that they were as weak as women. Notions of masculinity and domestic authority were used as sanctions in order to create a community of political action. Like the earlier strike at Kharagpur, this demonstrates that the novel uses of "tradition" that the communities formed within the context of railway labor were developing in order to forge unities of national sentiment at a local level. These actions escaped the intentions of the railway bureaucracy in its aims to produce pacific enclaves of tradition.

Ironically, in spite of the failure of community housing and domestic traditions to quell activism and nationalism among railway workers, after the strikes of the 1920s the agents again turned to invocations of community and traditional "Indian" sociability to administer solutions. Wherever railway colonies were surrounded by rural areas they argued that the best policy was either to construct villages like those at Kharagpur or to run workmen's trains from already existing villages in order to contain the possibilities of discontent. The agent of the East Indian Railway argued that this was the "ideal condition of life for Indian labor" and that this method had meant that there had been less discontent at Jamalpur than at Liluah, where the workforce did not reside in villages.[32] When colonies were surrounded by urban areas, such as in the case of Liluah, the agents agreed that in order to keep a supervisory hold over men lines of barracks should be constructed and recreation facilities on the lines of the European railway colonies should be supplied. But this was seen as far from an ideal solution. When the Royal Commission on Labour in 1931 singled out railway colonies as problematic in their radicalism, the solution they offered was the domestication of community within the railway colony.[33] The commissioners suggested that Indian employees be given residences in colonies that were in concord with "good local traditions," and that colonies should be built close to tightly knit communities.[34] Indian laboring populations, despite their growing militancy, would ideally be administered according to the bureaucracy's version of their traditional practices. Railway bureaucrats sought to minimize the effects of work on the railways on the lives and identities of workers. The biomoral order of the colonies may have been challenged by the agitation of workers, but the split between a modern, individualized European laboring subject and its Indian double intensified in the policies of the railways.

In contrast to the assumptions underlying the policies of the railways in the period from 1890 to 1929, Indian railway workers had become increasingly politicized by their unequal conditions of service. The attempts of the administration to calculate community loyalties and to distribute different groups equally through the railways in order to prevent cross-group coalitions had been a resounding failure. Similarly, their aim to produce content, self-contained segments of the workforce bound together in village communities had not succeeded, even in the place where it was first tried, at Kharagpur. Instead, railway employment and the space of the railway colony had become key sites for the forging of a popular nationalism among workers. We have clues that this nationalism combined a series of moral idioms based on Gandhian nationalism, concepts of *jati*, and masculine authority over the domestic sphere. By concretizing theories of ethnoclimatology, race, and national distinctions, the railway bureaucracy had created a workplace in which workers felt the daily indignities of being Indian under British rule. In this context, a commonality of interest among workers over wages and conditions could easily translate into ideas of a commonality of national ties. Strikes used the changing ideas of tradition and community for a quite different end than that intended by railway bureaucrats. They used them as sanctions, as in the strikes in 1906 and 1926 at Kharagpur, which would form a united body of Indians who would resist the illegitimate practices of the Raj. Disputes over wages and conditions on the railways were always simultaneously about the legitimacy of the Raj. The sporadic nationalism of railway workers was partly figured through biomoral idioms of *jati*, Gandhian concepts of *satyagraha*, and versions of masculinity that expanded domestic and community idioms to the level of political struggle for the nation.

## RAILWAY CASTES AND NATIONALIST COMMUNITIES

The increasing attempts to tightly tie the hopes and fears of Anglo-Indian and domiciled European workers to the future of the British Raj from 1897 to 1931 were only partially successful. On duty and during strikes they would usually act in the interests of the company. Yet their personal, family, and political loyalties were more complex than those prescribed for them. This divided affiliation was even sometimes shown in the activities and statements of the Anglo-India Association, the elite political organization that claimed to represent the community from the beginning of the nineteenth century. In 1928, the chairman of the Anglo-Indian Association, Henry Gidney, made the case for a reservation of upper subordinate positions on the railways in order to counteract the increasing demands by nationalists that these posts be given over to "Indians." He argued to the Simon Commission for constitutional safeguards for fifty years that would give the community temporary economic protection while it attained the level of education achieved by other Indian communities. He suggested that his community had only been formed as a result of the policies of the government and the railways. He pointed out that the British had created and used his community in key administrative departments and that current moves for Indianization tended to "disown and disinherit" the Anglo-Indian. He suggested that far from being alien to India and hostile to nationalism Anglo-Indians were "sons of the soil, who not only have our roots in the country's past, but will live, work and die here in the pursuit of our avocations."[35] He also urged nationalists to recognize that "a blood relationship exists with almost all the peoples of India," and therefore that "the element of sentimental attachment and racial responsibility should help to reinforce the political pleas for protection."[36] He emphasized the strange exclusion of Anglo-Indians from the category of "Indian" by nationalists and British officials, stating: "If, as an Anglo-Indian, I am a native of India, how can you Indianise an Indian? If I am an Anglo-Indian and a native of India, why should I be replaced by another Indian when I am doing a job well? . . . That is our difficulty; Government themselves create this cleavage."[37] Government too had created their unfair disadvantage and unequal position: "My education has been imposed upon me. My education is a system that has placed me in hostility with the Indian universities, and I am handicapped. . . . That is why I want this grace; that is why I want protection for this time."[38] This period of economic protection would enable the Anglo-Indian to "bring himself into line with the other peoples of India" and would allow Anglo-Indians to be "a valuable asset in the coming 'National' India."[39] In his request, Gidney captured the ways in which a distinct population of Anglo-Indians had been produced by the hierarchies of colonial political economy on the railways. More surprisingly, he suggested that this was not an experience confined to Anglo-Indians alone. Instead, he argued, all communities had been allotted distinct positions in the colonial state, "in India, where every employment tends to develop into a caste, certain communities have grouped . . . for generations into particular services, thereby acquiring a special aptitude in these departments, e.g. Madrasis in finance, Sikhs and Gurkhas in the army, Bengalis in offices and law and Anglo-Indians in the railways."[40] The experience of being Anglo-Indian had made Gidney and the people he represented acutely aware of the daily trading in biomoral signs of blood, belonging, and community that suffused colonial workplaces. This awareness was in part because they had become that most paradoxical of things—a railway caste.

Yet, for nationalist politicians, Anglo-Indians were an alien community that did not share the biomoral characteristics of Indians. In debates in the Legislative Assembly, they were repeatedly perceived as outside the boundaries of the national coalition of Indian communities. For example, in 1928, when K. C. Neogy addressed the Legislative Assembly on the topic of the Indianization of the railway services, he made it clear that he was demanding this only for "the pure-blooded Indians," the "Indian Indians," and "not for those who claim an admixture of other blood."[41] Ironically, in such statements nationalists replayed reifications of race and pedigree as natural expressions of the nation that had been produced in part by the hierarchy and paternalist employment practices of institutions such as the railway. Gidney too argued partly within the frame of pedigree with an attempt to suggest that Anglo-Indians had a natural democracy of blood within them, which made them more fully Indian than other Indians. Yet this naturalization of community was also destabilized by his emphasis on the formation of communities and aptitudes as a result of the actions of colonial bureaucracies.

These political exchanges about the railways leave us with an interesting question. How were the self-perceptions and public moralities of Indian workers altered by labor on the railways? This chapter has shown that they sporadically began to conceive of themselves as a coalition of national interest that would be liberated by the removal of British rule. There is some evidence from the strikes at Kharagpur and Asansol that this national community was bound together by a moral discourse based in notions of purity and pollution and of masculine domestic authority. It seems that some elements of ideas of *jati* and Gandhian notions were being extended metaphorically to the level of the nation. But it is unclear from this material exactly how the form and content of this national and personal sensibility was shaped by service on the railways. The next chapter will show that it was not only Anglo-Indians who became railway castes. Indian workers too became tangled in the moralities, pedigree, and community reckoning of railway paternalism. This, as we will see, affected their imagination of their own selves and of the national community of Indians.

## Chapter Five

# An Economy of Suffering

*The Ethics of Popular Nationalism in Petitions from Railway Workers, 1930–1947*

We are fighting and praying and making known our requests and yet we are out of our calculations.

— Mrs. Packwood, widow of engine driver, writing to agent, East Indian Railway, 1930

Research in the Agent's Record Room at the Eastern Railway risks turning history into a ledger. Endless, minute accounting of indents, tariff rates, wages, leave rules, allowances, and provident funds suggests a railway bureaucracy concerned with the disenchantment of the world. The bureaucracy wrote this mirror of production into reality in minutes of official meetings and letters between the agent and the board, which were directed at an audience of shareholders and civil servants, who always had their eye on the gap between the government-guaranteed profit to shareholders and the actual profit of the commercial concern itself. This archive was also directed at the posterity of railway officials who would build precedent out of individual cases and would carry their logic into the future, giving teleology to contextual decisions. These documents circle around the universal logic of capital inscribing its agency in decisions as diverse as the tariff rates of elephants, compensation for the loss of limb, dismissal for drunkenness, and whether to employ Sikhs or Anglo-Indians.

Yet also filed in this archive are petitions sent by employees and their relatives in the period from 1930 to 1947. These documents seem not to belong to the atmosphere of routinized work discipline present in the rest of the archives of the Indian railways. Instead, they contain a supernatural, royal, and moral language of violence, tyranny, suffering, and despair. They tell of secret conspiracies, physical disfigurement, and brutal beatings, and they also predict riots and warn of impending disasters. For example, a Mrs. Packwood, the widow of a driver on the East Indian Railway, whose sons also worked on the railway, complained to the agent in 1930:

> Regret to address you again, but I find that the cursed low who are aiding and abetting in mischief and crafty black denominations have been cruelly detaining my sons and myself in my welfare. . . . We are fighting and praying and making known our requests and yet we are out of our calculations. . . . My sons and myself have been deliberately persecuted and amazed and riled and vexed and tortured. . . . We have been incessantly disfigured and discoloured.[1]

The petitions, like this one, seem as if they are fragments from a world quite different from that of the railway bureaucracy. Yet, as I will show in this chapter, these petitions were active engagements with the experience of working under the command of this institution. They did not come from outside the procedures of the railway, but from the paradoxes of inhabiting the space of the other body in its disciplinary regime. Perhaps even more importantly, their historical effects, as we will see, could not be contained by the attempts of colonial bureaucrats to read them as examples of native irrationality.[2] They played an important role in the forging of the intimate politics of popular nationalism among railway workers.

## DESPOTISM AND WELFARE

The practice of writing memorials to the agent to protest against one's treatment by superiors had been part of the bureaucracy since the first Railway Act. But in the 1920s and 1930s, it took on a new importance as part of the attempts by the railways to end discontent among workers with measures addressed at their social welfare. The widespread strikes of the 1920s that had paralyzed the railway network threatened recurrent civil disobedience or potential revolution. The first response of the bureaucracy to this was to set up works committees in order to divert the discontent of workers away from unions into regularized institutions. These were designed to reform relations between the staff and the rank and file. They were intended as a measure that would consolidate and expand the older practice on the railways by which disputes were settled by direct discussion between the local representative of the employer and the man concerned. This scheme of committees originally suggested in 1923 by Sir Clement Hindley, the chief commissioner of railways, was designed for the local settlement of disputes. They dealt with issues of the welfare of the staff, quarters, sanitation, recreation, and conditions of work. They were also meant to provide a forum for the ventilation of grievances. Workers' representatives on the committees were expected to explain all its decisions and the general policies of the railways to illiterate employees. Equal numbers of staff members, selected by a vote among various classes of employees, and of railway officers sat in the meetings. Their recommendations could be considered by the agent for implementation and redress.[3]

On the East Indian Railway, "Faidamand Panchayats" (welfare committees) were formed in all divisions in March 1928. They were composed of elected representatives of the staff and railway officers nominated by the divisional superintendent.[4] Matters considered of general interest by all members of these committees could be referred to a higher-level Area Welfare Committee composed of senior subordinates, some of them nominated by the divisional superintendent and others elected by the staff. The Faidamand Panchayat could not consider individual complaints and grievances. This was the responsibility of the upper-level Area Welfare Committees. If a majority of the members of the Area Welfare Committee considered that an individual case had been harshly dealt with, then they could refer it to the divisional superintendent. He could recommend that it be reexamined by the Divisional Advisory Appellate Board, composed of four senior officers selected by the divisional superintendent, including the officer whose order formed the subject of the complaint. The divisional superintendent was not bound by the orders of the board, but his final decision was communicated to the Area Welfare Committee. This system was modeled on *panchayats* and was seen to be "in tune with the immemorial custom of this country."[5] The new system of councils encouraged workers to think that the administration should be interested in their welfare and pushed them to express their discontent in writing to the bureaucracy. Yet the hierarchical system of Area Welfare Committees and the inability of the Faidamand Panchayats to consider individual cases counteracted this impression once the system was put into practice.

Not surprisingly, these measures did not reduce discontent on the railways. As we saw in the previous chapter, another wave of strikes occurred in 1928. In 1929 the railways were challenged by the Royal Commission on Labor to examine their system of employment. The commission was set up in order to inquire into the policies that needed to be introduced to improve the welfare and contentment of workers. It aimed to replace older colonial racial inequalities in the workplace with practices that emphasized principles of Taylorist welfare. A new mass of statistical inquiry began to surround Indian workers in the research carried out for this commission. Their welfare was charted in family budget statistics and labor turnover figures. They were seen also as the subject of new rights and laws such as the Washington and Geneva Conventions and the Trades Union and Trades Disputes Acts passed in 1926. Before this moment what was distinct about India was a refusal of the law to recognize worker welfare as an object of state concern.[6] Earlier legislation and inquiries, such as the Factory Acts of 1881, 1891, and 1911 and the Indian Industrial Commission of 1916 to 1918, were concerned with labor as a commodity of production. However, these measures did not represent a coherent social project, and the railways, the largest employer of labor, were not in the purview of this administrative action. Provoked by the Royal Commission, the railways set about working out how to fundamentally alter their employment policies.

It would seem that there would be much that needed to be altered on the railways. As we saw in chapter 3, the contractual and social space occupied by the railway worker was one in which he was racialized and criminalized. His labor was marked as distinct in an intricate biomoral classification of hierarchies of command, salary, and leave rules. The successive Railway Acts of 1854, 1869, and 1890 made him into an individual with criminal responsibility for his insobriety of habits, not to mention breaches of discipline and failure to prevent accidents. He was not a subject of legal rights; instead, he occupied a space in which once he signed a contract with a railway company he had to give up even his private status as a plaintiff. Personal differences and disputes between the railway police and company employees were settled departmentally, and the prosecution of employees under the Railway Act was at the discretion of the agent. The status of workers as members of civil society was restrained as well. They could not communicate or publish information about the affairs of the company under threat of dismissal.[7] Not surprisingly, when the Railway Board inquired into the sources of discontent among workers for the Royal Commission, it found that these were punitive fining, racial employment hierarchies, instability of service, and arbitrary practices of dismissal. After discovering this, the members of the board set out to discuss the means for a complete reform of the management of workers with the companies. Yet the fundamentally hierarchical and anachronistic practice of petitioning intensified as a result of this liberal impulse. So why and how did the practice of petitioning remain the only legitimate means left to protest against the actions of the bureaucracy?

The Railway Board may have initially been in favor of radical reform, but the individual companies gradually persuaded it that current practices of discipline and command should be retained. They suggested that these represented the best antidote to the spirit of carelessness, idleness, and insubordination that marked the Indian worker, who, unfamiliar by tradition to the new conditions of labor, did not possess the same level of efficiency as the European and American working class with their "inherited skill and dexterity."[8] Despite the Royal Commission's impulse for reform, the Indian worker still found himself in the extralegal and autocratic contractual space of disciplinary measures and dependent on the local, personal decisions of superiors. Alongside the retention of these existing practices, the Railway Board argued that the system of works committees in place on the East Indian Railway should be expanded to all other railways in order to reduce union activity. They also promised the Royal Commission that there would be a gradual end to racial distinctions in service, but that this had to progress very slowly, as at the moment Indian workers could not be found with the requisite skills. Therefore, the outcome of these discussions was a paradoxical work environment that combined older biomoral and criminalizing practices with a rhetoric of worker welfare. In this system, the petition occupied a special place. It was the only legitimate means through which individual workers could question their treatment. It was also a document that was increasingly incited by the promises of the bureaucracy to look after the welfare of its employees and by the system of works councils. Its crucial role in the bureaucracy was the result of the attempt by British railway officials to retain their authority to guide the economic governance of India without fundamentally reforming the unequal disciplinary practices of the bureaucracy. The practice therefore intensified in a space of colonial governmentality that translated Taylorist discourses into idioms seen as appropriate to Indian realities.

What, then, were the rules of exchange between the agent and a worker seeking redress through petitioning? This was intended as a purely individual transaction. No pleaders, union officials, or anyone other than the worker involved could make representations on a case. The agent preserved the sublime authority of the bureaucracy by promising to consider whether facts had been established by his subordinates, whether these provided sufficient grounds for taking action, and whether the penalty was excessive or reasonable. In return, the employee agreed to couch his appeal without disrespectful or improper language. The figure of the agent maintained a fiction of the possibility of justice in a bureaucratic system that removed most possibilities of this. Theoretically, the agent could decide to pass on the petition if it was necessary to the governor-general. Ultimately the highest authority in this chain of decision making was His Majesty the King, Emperor of India.[9] The petitioner had become more akin to a subject addressing a sovereign than to a worker who had rights and was part of an industrial enterprise.

This chain of authority for petitions symbolically linked the ability of railway bureaucrats and of the agent to respond fairly to these petitions to British monarchical idioms of royal pedigree and the figure of the patriot king. The final years of the reign of Queen Victoria had seen a huge commercial, artistic, and political elaboration of her as a "Patriot Architect," in Tennyson's terms, and the "imaginative fulcrum at the centre of an unprecedented global imperial system."[10] Her successors built on this foundation, and the monarchy continued to serve as the symbolic linchpin of the fairness, unity, permanence, and innate superiority of

British laws, institutions, and bodies through the 1930s and 1940s. This continued early modern traditions in which the patriot king guarded the liberty of subjects by standing above party strife, defending the constitution, and promoting trade abroad while acting as an enemy of moral decline, corruption, and materialism.[11] Imperial bureaucrats such as those on the railways symbolically partook of this royal pedigree through the practice of petitioning, becoming patriot architects themselves. The inequalities of this kind of symbolism were made explicit in the role of railway bureaucrats as the audience for petitions. Petitions were directed to them as preservers of the rule of constitutional rights, while, of course, the very act of petitioning showed that colonial subjects were on the contrary not the subjects or agents of the law or rights at all.

But in the act of petitioning, the railway worker was given the seductive possibility of directly demanding justice and of confronting figures of power with their suffering. It is not surprising that railway officials despaired at the quantity of petitions that crossed their desks. Sweepers, workshop laborers, guards, drivers, assistant stationmasters, ticket collectors, clerks, and their relatives seized the opportunity of an encounter, through writing, that might change their fate. They sent dramatic tales of the violent effects of discipline, composed if they were illiterate with the help of literate union members. The bureaucracy seemed to have succeeded more than it could have hoped in capturing the interests and affections of railway workers. But to call this a success is premature. The content of the petitions very often did not match the expectations of railway officials. The scribbled comments on them chart the shocked surprise of the agent and divisional superintendents at the apparent madness of their language. Railway officers often wrote on them "irrelevant, please file" or "this woman is completely crack-brained." For them, these petitions were, as one retired railway official in his memoirs put it, "congestion on the circuits" generated by the misunderstandings of railway employees.[12] British railway officials interpreted the strangeness of the language of the petitions as further evidence of the profound difference of Indians from themselves. It was another example of what the Royal Commission on Labor claimed was the deficiency of reason among Indian workers, which could be improved by their further incorporation into the habits and procedures of the bureaucracy.[13] The content of the petitions did not match the rules laid down by the Railway Board either. Half of the petitions preserved in the record room were requests for a redress of injustice or reinstatement, but a quarter were complaints, often anonymous, about the corruption and immorality of superiors. Therefore, the introduction of the practice of petitioning did not take the shape officials intended. In the next section I will analyze some of the recurrent content and forms of these petitions that so perplexed railway officials.

## VIOLENT DISCIPLINE

In the petitions workers sent to the agent, it is striking how the railway bureau-cracy appears as a place of despotism and potential violence. It is not that peti-tioners complained of actual acts of violence; in fact, as I will discuss later, they rarely did this. Instead, the letters are full of violent metaphors used to describe what officials would have considered regular procedure and of images of the agent as a ruler. The petitions often opened by the workers making it explicit that they did not consider the bureaucracy to be a place of routinized discipline by endow-ing the agent with the power of a sovereign. Workers began their petitions with phrases such as, "We pray to God that you may adorn the high chair of Agent and may God grant you long life so that we the staffs may get pure consolidation and peace and justice from your noble soul."[14] They suggested that the agent's power was not neutral and regularized; "It is only your hand that can feed the hungry and destroy the convicted."[15] The workers wrote in idioms of repentance, pledg-ing, "I faithfully promise never again to commit myself, as it this time means destruction for all eternity."[16] Appearing before the agent in writing was a matter of him releasing you from "shots of trouble unable for bearing," by his "act of kindness."[17] Seeking reemployment was not a matter of ability or of efficiency, but of "forgiveness, I sincerely assure you Sir, that my repentance is greater than my sin."[18] The agent was addressed as an omnipotent sovereign in phrases such as "With your unquestioned authority and immense power at your disposal you can very easily season that justice with mercy, a divine virtue!"[19]

Petitions often used monarchical language to flatter figures of authority, but they equally used it in an attempt to shame the agent by confronting him with the violent justice of the bureaucracy. Many petitions complained that the agent and his officers behaved like a tyrannical king surrounded by corrupt courtiers. One petition described the dismissal of a worker as a "murder of justice."[20] It then continued with the following complaint: "Kind Sir! A murderer even is given a fair chance of defence and demonstration, but myself on the contrary have been disposed of."[21] One petitioner wrote that he could not understand the excessive enactments of punishment against him, since he had "neither beaten with hands, bamboos, sticks, bomb nor shells, nor hanged nor killed, looted or plotted or at-tacked any king or employers nor have my family done so."[22] These petitions with the aim of flattering or shaming the agent into action confronted the bureaucracy with its own despotic procedures of fining, dismissal, and fictions of justice. The everyday practice of colonial discipline on the railways was indicted as a form of violent justice.

Other railway workers tried to draw attention to their cases by issuing threats of violence or by predicting a violent end to the agent's rule over them. Cutting through the pretense that an exchange of evidence presented in good order would help their case, they instead sought to intimidate the agent by using the same violence against him that the bureaucracy had enacted on them. A former guard threatened physical violence against the agent if he didn't respond, writing: "I am not so concerned as to the discharge as I am in the reason of my discharge . . . due to favoritism and to see justice done I am ditermined [sic] if not by EIR then by the Viceroy and perhaps by myself which you know by this what I mean there being no need to make it plain. . . . I am not a man who will tolerate interference and that I am a man that should be well left alone."[23] A group of sweepers who were employed to clean station platforms warned in a petition composed with a union official that if their case wasn't listened to "there will be a day of retribution. The children of Adam are limbs of one another and are all produced from the same substance, when the world gives pain to one member the others also suffer uneasiness. 'Death' is the foe."[24] This image points to the violence of discipline and also rejects the individualizing thrust of such discipline. Other petitioners amplified their threats with supernatural insights. A former ticket collector predicted, "today I have seen dream that your throne will be shifted from Delhi to Calcutta nearly on 13 April 1932 and will not be good and no one will hear your case."[25] In these threats petitioners suggested that the true currency of interaction in the railway was violence and intimidation, but they also warned that the agent's despotic power over them was reversible and dependent on their continuing cooperation.

There are echoes here of older idioms of power that were infused with a new salience by the introduction of the practice of petitioning on the railways. In the images of the agent as a king responsible for the well-being of his subjects at times of crisis there are obvious references to idioms of Shakti, dharmic action, and honor used by peasants in their relationships to zamindars.[26] The assertions about the reversibility of the agent's power can also be linked to an earlier fragility of personal honor and authority, which was based on the devotion of followers and the relative status of other people. Ideas common among the bureaucrats of Mughal successor states in north and east India are given new life in these documents as well. In particular, the image of the employees of the railway as part of the same "body" suffering the same pain reanimates the sense that *nawabi* (Mughal and successor state officials) bureaucrats had of states as human bodies that required all their elements from officials to subjects in order to continue to exist.[27] Yet we must remember that the image of the agent as a despot or king and the reversibility of his power were recurrent in petitions, whether they were written by Anglo-Indian, British, or Indian railway workers. What is significant is the fact that these idioms were given new life in the context of railway labor. The bureaucracy itself crossed the languages and practices of political, moral, and economic authority in its paternalism and biomoral hierarchies. This provided fertile ground for these other political idioms.

In each of the petitions we do not have a simple recurrence of older forms of address; instead, we have a palimpsest of experiments in how to address the agent. In each of them there is an attempt to forge a language, and its features need to be related to the form itself and to the experiences workers had of railway justice. The sense of the reversibility of the agent's power and of its dependence on the cooperation of subjects is evoked by the intimacy of the petition form itself, which offered the promise of a potentially close relationship with a figure of authority. The hope of railway workers was that the agent was really somehow equally dependent on them to maintain this relationship. But the choice of monarchical and violent images reflects the fact that the railway bureaucracy left its workers seeking justice from an agent who with a single autocratic act could change their fortune, and that most of them had been subject to a bureaucracy that was not in fact accountable, even though it promised it was.

Petitions were filled with another kind of metaphor of violence. Workers sent petitions that told scandals of corruption to the agent, which were described as the cause of tyranny and of the "butchering" of the employees.[28] Petitioners sometimes offered themselves as spies and rigorously followed the accounting procedures of proof that were practiced by the railway itself. But they turned these procedures against British officers. For example, a former train examiner wrote to the agent to inform him that he had been on "secret service" and had gone out for the benefit of king and country on a "real pilgrimage" to discover the misdemeanors of his British officers.[29] In these petitions on corruption the language of economics and accounting hovered around the acts of bribery themselves, which were described as having been "enumerated," "recommended," and "accounted" by those who took them.[30] The slipping of this language of bureaucratic procedure into the realm of illicit acts blurred the distinction between legitimate acts of deduction and those driven by the selfish, individual economic interests of superiors. Petitions often suggested that, in fact, "terrorism is the stock in trade of the railway," which possessed a "secret code of conduct" that did not match the conduct rules supplied to employees forbidding bribery.[31] Petitioners addressed the agent showing him that the unequal power given to superiors to frame rules and change them "at their own sweet will" and their greater credibility in the bureaucracy enabled them to practice "tyranny" and to "torture, degrade and humiliate the men . . . to kill their soul."[32] Many of these petitions in fact suggested that bribery was the symptom of the rapacious desires that colonial economics itself produced by its racial hierarchies of command, which meant that the word of British superior officers was always believed over that of Indian workers. These petitioners argued that the perversions of bribery were the product of the inequalities of the railway bureaucracy itself; the bureaucrats had "more by their secret and iron rules than by their service to humanity obtained the hold upon some good people."[33]

Some petitioners argued that economy and efficiency were irrelevant in the context of the enterprise of the colonial railways. For example, a group of ticket examiners in the Howrah division sent a petition, probably composed with the help of a union official, that argued that rumors and networks of bribery undermined the economic forecasts of the bureaucracy itself. Hearing that if they paid bribes they could be promoted to head train examiners, they did not believe the rumor because they thought the railway was under financial difficulties and could not afford to make any new appointments. But they bitterly realized that the railway "does not require competent hands at present" when a junior train examiner was appointed after paying the requisite bribe and the other vacant positions were filled by Anglo-Indians.[34] Protesting against the bureaucracy, they demonstrated that it created superiors with rapacious economic self-interest and a belief in biomoral racial taxonomies that undermined the wise governance of the prosperity of the railway and its workers. In more theoretical terms, petitioners insisted that a kind of foundational violence suffused the disciplinary practices and rules of the railway.

When railway workers sent requests for personal reinstatement or the removal of unjust fines to the agent, they were following the rules for the submission of petitions. These were intended to deal with individual cases of dismissal or punishment. But the accusations of bribery had not been solicited by the organization. Why then did railway workers send these? The carefully itemized lists of railway materials misappropriated and of circuits of corruption represent diverse strategies and understandings of the bureaucracy. Some petitions may have been inspired by simple vindictiveness that sought to disguise personal dislikes in an act of public duty. Sometimes the genuine hope of petitioners was that the agent as a sublime figure of British justice would make superior officers accountable. The petitioners were usually disappointed. The agent, if he found the accusations credible, would refer them to the officer accused, who would reply that they were untrue. But what is interesting is that railway workers, even if they were just pursuing a personal vendetta, thought that the agent would be interested in their information.

This assumption by railway workers grew in part from the fact that the Watch and Ward Department and Railway Police spied on employees in order to sniff out corruption. Some petitions explicitly mimicked the reports of the Watch and Ward Department, even though members of this department had not sent them. The assumption also rests on the long experience of precolonial and colonial bureaucracies as institutions that recruited spies and, later, news writers. Suggestively as well, most of these petitions on bribery hover between simple reports of misdemeanors and personal indictments of the agent himself. There was a long history of Hindi and Bengali histories and pamphleteering that insisted that the selection of unworthy officials represented an absence of merit on the part of a ruler. Good government had long been associated with a bureaucracy whose subjects would be assured swift justice and would be protected from oppression by public officials. These theories of the polity had been used to criticize British rule since the first days of the East India Company.[35] It was, I think, the elective affinity between these versions of just governance and the measures used by the bureaucracy to stamp out corruption among lower railway officials that made sending a petition on bribery an irresistible opportunity to bring the agent himself to account. This combination produced a profoundly new way to critique the foundational violence of the railway bureaucracy, which workers experienced in the daily unequal practice of disciplinary procedures. Both the petitions about bribery and those that addressed the agent as a sovereign held him and the bureaucracy fully accountable for the corporeal well-being of workers and refused to accept the ways in which bureaucratic rules measured legitimate and illegitimate acts of discipline. These rules and railway justice were nothing but violence.

## SUFFERING BODIES: RACE, *JATI*, AND COMMUNITY

The petitions sent to the agent were full of descriptions of bodies as expressive surfaces. The bodies of petitioners appeared as irrefutable evidence of suffering, often with a kind of forensic detail of sickness and the marks of labor. The bodies of other people had a different role. They displayed surface evidence of deeper dishonor or of race or community origins. Overall, the tales told about the physical body reflect the experience employees had of a workplace in which there was a contradictory combination of Taylorist notions of welfare and colonial sociology of difference at work. At times in the petitions we can see the fusing of *jati* moralities with the biomoral hierarchies of the bureaucracy, producing novel languages of social distinction. The mode of critique of superiors and fellow workers demonstrates the ways in which ideas of *jati* were being extended to the employment hierarchies of the railway. This extension disembedded them from caste hierarchy and anchored them in a new series of racial and class-based status markers. In this section I explore the new economy of moral meanings associated with the bodies of workers and their employers that we can see at work in the petitions.

One set of meanings of the body centered on the idea that its well-being was the responsibility of the bureaucracy. Railway workers repeatedly wrote confidential tales of the marks of pain on their bodies to the agent. In this they responded to the claims of the administration that it existed to preserve their lives. For example, a memorandum of the Railway Board to the Royal Commission on Labour surveyed the general health conditions of workers and the extent of medical facilities provided. It concluded: "The preservation of the health of the staff and the prevention of epidemic diseases in railway settlements have a very important bearing on the efficient and economic working of railways and apart from the humanitarian aspect of the question, an efficient medical organization is of direct financial interest to railway administration."[36] The board added that in response to this concern expenditure on medical relief by the principal railways had gone up by nearly 30 percent during the previous five years. They located the inadequacy of the effectiveness of the welfare of the staff not in the medical facilities provided, but in the extent to which they were utilized by the staff, arguing that "there is a certain amount of prejudice against treatment. . . . It is partly due to doubts as to the efficacy of western methods of medicine and partly to the fact that patients prefer the accustomed ministrations and uninstructed nursing of their own relatives to trained attention by others."[37] In the memorandum, the railway companies provided statistical proof that they were fulfilling their duty of sustaining the lives of their workers and of the rational links between workers' welfare and the welfare of their profits. They added, "It does not appear that occupational diseases are incidental to any railway operations either in workshops or elsewhere."[38] They exonerated themselves further by stating that any accidents that occurred were due to "want of caution on the part of staff," who suffer from "pure thoughtlessness."[39] This irrational behavior was located in workers' Indian origins, which led to the administration having to deal with employees of "little imagination" who "contract dangerous habits quicker than those who can visualise the results of carelessness."[40] The commission concluded that, unlike in Europe and the United States, where fatigue study had yielded appreciable results in decreasing the incidence of accidents, in India such studies were irrelevant.

The petitioners to the agent wrote to him in this language of an economy of welfare demanding monetary recompense for their physical collapse. They turned their bodies into the same kind of commodities that the memorandum has transformed them into, linking issues of profit and compensation to their illnesses. They also took the claim of the railway seriously that it had a duty to sustain their welfare. Believing in the intimacy of their relationship with the agent, they sent him long and detailed descriptions of the histories of their family's sicknesses, begging for intervention. These petitions sought to demonstrate how workers had become "sufferers in life, due to life and labour on the railway."[41] They cited examples of how their work had left them "pale and dried up" and "drifting in the vast ocean of woes and miseries in a watery cemetery."[42] A former railway guard, after carefully listing his unfair fines and finally his dismissal from service as a guard, sent to the agent a photograph of his face, demonstrating an injury he had received during his work on the railway. He wrote, "I have an ever-lasting scar on my face. . . . With this disfigured countenance and the inner injury as the annexed photo shall indicate, I am getting discharged . . . and shall have to countenance the severest kind of hardship that one can expect in the world."[43] For the petitioner, this photograph provided the ultimate proof that labor on the railways was all about "punishments coming in torrent losing all proportion and ends of justice."[44] Others directly related their work on the railways and its punitive systems to their declining health. One widow claimed that the paying of fines by her husband, a stationmaster, led to his death, that the health of her husband declined in direct proportion to the deductions from his salary. She wrote: "The shock was too great for him as would be evident from his attendance record to show that with payment of each of the installments of payment he fell ill. So keen was his feeling of injured innocence over this fine."[45] These petitioners refuse the distinction between discipline and violence and argue that labor on the railways is a form of corporeal "wanton punishment" that disfigures the body of the laborer.[46] They insist that the railway has a duty of care for their well-being, challenging it to live up to its promised Taylorist intentions.

Workers directly indicted the administration for its failures to preserve their health in more literal terms as well. They also expressed a different experience of the paternalist care of their bodies provided in the railway network of hospitals and doctors. They often complained that the only purpose that the railway doctors served was to provide certificates that showed that the employees were not malingering in their claims to be sick. The doctors were described as inspectors rather than preservers of life. These petitioners argued that doctors asked for bribes composed of their "blood earned money" in payment for the issuing of sick certificates.[47] These doctors withdrew the life and money of laborers. They were described as hungry ghosts that turned up at the burning ghat and demanded attendance fees from grieving families.[48] The petitioners also argued that their lack of faith in the systems of allopathic medicine were a product of the oppressive nature of this system, which existed only to scrutinize their claims and to extract money from them. For example, the Indian workmen of Jamalpur works wrote that they wanted to be placed "under any doctor where we have faith."[49] They added that the demands by the present doctor for bribes meant that they were treated not "according to our faith and purse."[50] Here, faith has a double meaning that questions the understanding of the reluctance of Indians to resort to modern systems of medicine held by the railway bureaucracy. This faith was not traditional prejudice against allopathic medicine. Instead, workers wanted a doctor who would not exploit their dependence on his certificates. They wanted to escape "the clutches of oppressive doctors."[51] The economy of suffering that workers wrote about in petitions is a product of the colonial welfare practiced by the railway in which doctors became inspectors. Marks of pain on the body were not healed by these agents of the bureaucracy; instead, they were increased by them. Workers in their petitions insisted on the moral responsibility of the bureaucracy to preserve their well-being.

Other kinds of physical manifestations of injustice were presented as evidence in petitions that exposed superior officers for unfairness or corruption. The aspects of the body discussed here reflected a fusing of the railway's hierarchies of pedigree with moralities of *jati*. These petitions provided a litany of moral faults visible in the physical behavior and appearance of senior officers and fellow workers. These workers of "great temptation" took "bribes for fornication" or to provide money for abortions.[52] Many of the petitions offered physical signs of this immorality and betrayal of bureaucratic honor. For example, a group of clerks from Howrah wrote, "what to say of the character of Mr. Jones? It can be proved from the syphilitic eruption of Mr. Jones who always enjoys the sweet company of low sweeper women of Inward and makes amorous gestures with them."[53] They added that the economic misdemeanors of this officer, such as the unfair promotion of one of his friends, were due to the aid this friend gave him in getting treated secretly for syphilis at the Calcutta Hospital of Tropical Medicine. In this list of the faults of Mr. Jones his failings were demonstrated using ideas derived from both *jati* morality and railway respectability. Similarly, some laborers from the Lucknow locomotive works reported that, "Here are two bribe eaters one of them is the chief man i.e. Mr. Hemming Production engineer . . . who remember who has got 3 lady typists, one was pregnant and Mr. Hemming took her to Simla and tried through the Doctors and organized an abortion and brought her back."[54] Some petitioners even more explicitly conveyed the series of condensed associations between race, *jati*, morality, and correct economic behavior that lay behind these accusations. For example, one petitioner, complaining of the actions of a sanitary inspector, states, "please arrange an European Sanitary Inspector instead of the one who by appearance will himself exhibit his face like Negro or 3rd class Anglo Indian of dome breedy."[55] The public ethics of railway workers now combined a racial notion of pedigrees that fitted certain people for command with idioms of *jati*. Bureaucrats who did not preserve their biomoral essence or did not have it in the first place had no right to govern the labor of their subordinates. Ethical obligations and practices relevant in relation to the immediate kinship group and political community were now finding a home within the public life of the railway bureaucracy.

These idioms of bureaucratic honor found a fertile home in the framework of workplace disciplinary hierarchies. Procedures of discipline rested on a moral schema that clothed British officers with a greater aura of respectability and justified their command of what was called "the railway family."[56] In their daily activities the Watch and Ward Department staff and government Railway Police scrutinized the moral habits of railway staff. Guards, drivers, stationmasters, and subordinate staff members were dismissed due to their inability to maintain discipline because they had acquired "very immoral habits," showed "moral turpitude," had "seduced the wife of another."[57] The concern of petitioners with bureaucratic honor and secrets of immorality was an attempt to turn this kind of procedure against fellow workers and superior officers. There were two grounds on which railway workers seem to have based such a reversal. First of all, by taking seriously the opportunity to whisper secrets into the ear of the agent through the private, individualized medium of the petition. Second, on an elective affinity between notions of *jati*, bureaucratic, and kingly honor and the moral hierarchy of the railway. Ideologies of bureaucratic and royal command had long rested on notions of a virtuous honor exhibited externally in physical appearance and behavior. And the use of idioms of *jati* detached from their grounding in caste hierarchy is clearly visible in these petitions. All of these sources of moral outrage combined with the railway's own morality were deployed to question the legitimacy of British and Anglo-Indian officials.

Another mode of address in the petitions attempted to gain the agent's attention by using the other bureaucratic typology of the bodies and sentiments of workers—that of community. From the 1890s, the railways had attempted to balance the numbers of different communities in departments under the assumption that this would prevent corruption and strike action. In the 1930s they began to implement policies in the name of social justice that would balance the percentage of different communities employed in the railways according to the size of their population. Petitioners were supposed to write to the agent as individuals seeking justice for themselves, but often they used their community identity to make their individual case. For example, a discharged punching clerk first listed his family's service to the government during the 1857 rebellion, "saving the lives of many European ladies and gentlemen," dispelling any ideas that he came from a disloyal population. He then suggested that his status as a Muslim had meant that he had not received equal treatment from the railway bureaucracy: "Being a Mohamedan and without any patron I was helpless to ventilate my grievances for redress." He made his final argument for his reinstatement on the grounds of community: "I humbly pray that I may kindly be given a chance in any capacity and anywhere that you may be pleased to put me according to the Government of India orders that the 19 % Muslims should be provided in the railway department."[58] Thus, he sought to exchange his community affiliation for its value in the calculations of governance.

Other discharged workers took another tack and traded in the paranoia about community conspiracies that guided the Railway Board's calculations of the percentages of castes and creeds employed in the railway. They accused their Hindu or Muslim superiors of favoring their own communities. For example, a discharged gunner wrote to the agent that "in seven years time seven gunners Mohammedan have been discharged in Asansol division. None of the Hindu gunners met this fate though offences of a similar nature were committed by them."[59] When his requests for redress were ignored by the agent, he wrote to the viceroy, supplying him with lists of the dismissed guards in his division so that he could compare the numbers of Hindu and Muslim guards dismissed. Thus, like railway bureaucrats, he turned the abstract numbers of administrative lists into politically salient community calculations. He added in his letter that the "indifference of the Railway petty officers . . . is responsible to bring out serious political conveyances," arguing that this indifference meant that "Hindu staff receive every encouragement at the hands of petty officers to commit such offences which might lead to train robbery and collision."[60] He sent back to the bureaucracy its own obsessions with community conspiracy, public safety, criminal coalitions, and the impossibility of producing a neutral public sphere of capitalist efficiency in India. He finally pleaded: "We the Mohammadans as a community have pledged to remain loyal to Your Excellency. . . . It breaks our heart to see that petty Officers as carrying English names hear their [Hindus'] influences so much." Following the railway bureaucracy's own logic of European universalism and objectivity, he questioned the British essence of officers who carry English names but act on behalf of specific communities. He also offered the government signs of his loyalty through the plural of a community identity.

Another petitioner practiced a similar strategy of making the signs of his community count. He advised the agent to trace the marks of conspiracy in the lists of names of men appointed to the crew system, promoted, and dismissed during the previous six months. He wrote that this neutral accounting will, "give you Sir, an exact idea as to how Mahommodens [*sic*] have been treated or are still being treated through a widespread conspiracy of the Chief Operating Superintendent" and will show that "Justice is not possible so long as Robertson is at the head of the affairs of the East Indian Railway." This suggestion shows that to be called into colonial political economy was to take up an individual identity in a list as a Muslim and that this list was not concerned with neutral accounting but with themes of politics and conspiracy. These petitions both questioned and were guided by the railway bureaucracy's own image of itself as a neutral organ for restoring the judicious arrangement of disparate populations in the practice of economics.

However, other petitioners revealed that the trading by the bureaucracy in ideas of communal conspiracies, threats, and calculations only led to injustice and the production of illusory paranoia. A typical example comes in an anonymous letter describing the oppressions of the Patna Junction Goods Shed staff by a Hindu officer who used his high position to circulate communal rumors to cover up his own attempts to extract bribes. The letter writer then revealed that when the workers refused to follow the Hindu officer's instructions to take bribes from merchants, he misinformed the Railway Police, writing:

> The irregularity whatever took place in this good shed is entirely due to communal faction and I thank to the enquiring officers that without thinking on this point and enquiring into the truthfulness of his statement they report the fact to the office and the result of which the innocent Mohammedan staff of Patna junction good shed are swept without any blame. Out of four Mohammedan, two are already transferred and two are in consideration. . . . He oppresses the innocent staff.[61]

This letter circled around the eruption of the communal into the economic and the problematic relationship set up between them by colonial political economy. Here, instead of community operating as a sign of economic efficiency, the trading in signs of community covers up illegitimate economic acts. The radical instability of the railway bureaucracy's typologies and procedures of proof are critiqued and deployed.

The disciplinary measures and workplace practices of the railway bureaucracy in the period up to Independence were contradictory in their production of expressive surfaces on the bodies of employees. Taylorist practices of welfare and notions of economic efficiency individualized the bodies of workers and made them the responsibility of the bureaucracy. The bureaucracy also encouraged workers to see themselves and others as possessing a group essence in their body and sentiments that related them to a community or caste. Alongside these newer measures, older colonial hierarchies of morality and race continued. Petitions to the agent express the paradoxes of trying to reconcile these different logics of the body and of working under these contradictory practices. Workers suggested that the coexistence of these various forms produced an economy of suffering that made their bodies vulnerable to many kinds of violence—illness from labor, oppression from immoral superiors, and communal attack. They spoke in the petitions of the divided selves that the bureaucracy dealt in as a result of its adaptation of Taylorist welfare to a colonial context. They also revealed the new ways in which workers had begun to see themselves and others. They had formed a novel kind of railway morality based on idioms of *jati*, racial concepts, and ideas of respectability that linked private and public ethics.

## VIOLENT WRITING

So far I have described how the petitions reflected the contradictions between the unequal disciplinary practices and universalist claims of the bureaucracy that it existed to protect the economic efficiency of the railways and the welfare of its employees. This gap was rendered in them as a form of violence or as something that led to tyranny, corporeal suffering, and communal violence. To end this section I want to discuss first of all the kinds of violence that could only be hinted at in the lines of these documents and then to discuss the kinds of writing they contained.

There is one kind of evidence of suffering that appeared rarely in the petitions—accounts of physical attacks. From oral histories I have collected, it seems that these were fairly common in the environs of railway colonies, if not in the workplace. This absence is somewhat surprising, as the content of documents was far from restrained in its indictment of superior officials and in its trading of scurrilous information about them. When accounts of physical attacks did appear, they were hidden in long lists of other kinds of misdemeanors. Petitioners began by attempting to attract the interest of the agent using lists of exactly how much money could be reclaimed by the administration if it instituted an inquiry. They placed in the middle of descriptions of furniture, ghee, and uniforms misappropriated secrets that were disparate in their brutality. The fifteenth or twenty-second items of these lists are descriptions of "Laloo Cooly shot in the chest while pig shooting" by a superior or of how the case of "Dilchand's wife beaten by a driver" was hushed up.[62] Petitioners seem to have clothed their outrage in the language of economics, claiming that they have nothing in view but to "save revenue pocketted by so called tin god of the railway."[63] Given the expansive descriptions of other kinds of suffering, the violent threats issued by petitioners to the agent, and the metaphors of violence that suffuse the petitions, this evasive description of actual acts of violence deserves analysis. Petition writing was based on a notion of civil procedure and the free exchange of words between people who occupied very distinct positions in the railway hierarchy. Explicit descriptions of violence would have ruptured the founding fiction of this form that such an exchange was possible by highlighting the extreme inequalities of position between sender and recipient. Such descriptions would have finally ended an exchange and shown that railway justice and paternalism were founded on a lie. This, I think, is why petitioners were so hesitant to report such things to the agent, and it explains why when they did they hid violent acts among lists of economic waste as just another instance of a loss of resources.

The form of the petition, like all the bureaucratic writing on the railways, lived in the illusion that language was a neutral administrative tool, authored by accountable individual agents, which expressed thoughts and through which certain truths could be established. The form of the petition relied on this assumption as well. But railway workers experienced this neutrality differently, and the modes of address of petitions reflect the strains of maintaining the fictions of the expressive agency and neutrality of bureaucratic writing. The only kind of legitimate agency left to railway workers to protest against the bureaucracy was to write a petition. As a result, some petitioners struggled to give their letters as much authority as possible by borrowing the forms of bureaucratic documents and legal memorandums, and even sometimes by using East Indian Railway–headed notepaper. Others adopted even more radical strategies.

Some petitions questioned the idea that bureaucratic language and documents referred to a series of verifiable facts or to an individual responsible author. Placed among the files of appeals from individuals are anonymous petitions that warned of strikes, corruption, and impending violence. A typical example of this form was a petition received and seen by the agent of the East Indian Railway from an unnamed "Friend" who claimed to be part of the Agra Criminal Investigation Department. His petition showed that all spaces of the railway colony could be made to tell secrets, but that these secrets told in anonymous letters ultimately reveal the indeterminacy of the evidence that fuels the agent's rulings. The Friend described with realistic accuracies of time and place a meeting between Muslim conspirators that he attended in disguise as a villager. Their plot was to prevent the transfer of a Muslim office clerk by sending an appeal to the divisional superintendent informing him that there is "communal feeling at the station" and that "Hindus are trying to take all good jobs from Muslims." If this petitioning strategy didn't work, then they planned to send an appeal to the agent stating that the divisional superintendent was favoring the Hindus, and meanwhile they would incite a communal riot by beating up some of the Hindu clerks.[64] The warning to the agent from this Friend was about the dissembling of individual workers, but it was also a warning about the system of representation in petitions and appeals itself. This anonymous petition reveals, by the fact that it reached the eyes of the agent, that such indeterminate rumors made up the evidence of the bureaucracy. It shows that petitions, even when authored by accountable agents and sent to the divisional superintendent as these conspirators planned, did not reflect truth or evidence, but piled up to create the realities of communal threats. The railway bureaucracy incited this kind of written evidence by its procedures, but this did not guarantee their truth. Their truth could only be guaranteed by further procedures of rumor and inquiry. The disguise that was revealed by this petition was that of the bureaucracy that dissembled itself as a place of fair procedure and rational evidence.

Most of the anonymous petitions represented this kind of troubling of the certainties of the railway bureaucracy, complaining of how the superintendents of the Watch and Ward Department ignore lengthy reports from the staff and investigators and higher officials throw complaints into wastepaper baskets or suppress information. They traced the circuits of bribery that made "slurs" on personnel files or "mysteriously effaced" them, or how the possession of papers by individuals showing the guilt of superiors enabled them to blackmail their superiors so they get "double lifts in the teeth of superior others."[65] The petitions showed that the written archive of the bureaucracy guaranteed nothing. Anonymous authors seized the circuits of rumors and investigation for their own purposes, becoming, in the words of one petition, "onlooker[s] from the workshop," rather than the ones surveilled. But more than this, such authors troubled the act of bureaucratic writing itself, showing that appeals and petitions made truths and did not merely refer to truths.[66] The procedures and inquiries of the works councils, inspectors, and divisional superintendents are shown as institutions that did not guarantee representation and the airing of grievances. Instead, they made grievances proliferate, filling the bureaucracy and the lives of railway workers with suspicions, rumors, and inequalities.

The petitions also break with bureaucratic language in another way. They leave behind its neutral accounting of events to take on a language of drama and vivid literary style. The bureaucratic writing procedures of the East Indian Railway and the recommendations of the Railway Board lived in the fiction of fair procedure and the neutrality of orders issued in the name of economic governance. The petitioners expressed a very different kind of modernity, one in which words issued from above had a murdering force. The theatrics of petitioners' statements such as "your hope-killing letter," "at the stroke of his mighty pen," and "the maiden whiteness of whose service sheets has been ruthlessly defiled" were a result of the inequalities of their agency.[67] Some petitioners abandoned neutral, nonliterary forms altogether, sending the agent poems after their "persuasive arguments, unadulterated truths and pathetic statements" failed.[68] A former assistant stationmaster wrote:

> Oh God, Oh Lord! I pray to thee
> Be pleased enough to excuse me
> Please save my kind masters
> D.S. Howrah and the Agent E.I.R.
> I am a poor man got some thing to state
> Before their honor regarding my fate
> After 29 years service in E.I.R.
> Have to beg door to door as a street beggar

This is not desirable at the End of Life
As my sorrows always looked by my children and my wife
Their honor therefore should be pleased
By which my troubles may be ceased.[69]

The inequalities of the agency provided to workers by neutral bureaucratic procedures pushed them to adopt other genres.

The violent hierarchy of bureaucratic language was openly criticized in some petitions, such as that sent to the agent on behalf of sweepers employed at Moghalserai. Accused by the local head sweeper of irregularities, they complained that there was no one to speak on their behalf to the local sanitary inspector. Their petition then became a meditation on the "filthy languages" of those in charge of them.[70] This language, they suggest, turned them into beasts of burden under the control of their superiors, with no hope of redress because they had already been named by the bureaucracy as people who deserve punishment. They write:

We think the story of the fox suits exactly, who on being seen running away and limping someone asked what calamities occasioned him so much tripidation [sic]. He replied, I hear that they are going to press a camel into service (like above quoted supervisors) your honor may observe and like our impudence as to what relationship is there between us the camel and what resemblance have we to that animal, our reply is to be silent, for if the malignant out of evil design should say this is a camel and we should be siezed [sic], who would be so solicitous for our relief as to order an enquiry into our grievances?[71]

It is the hierarchy of bureaucratic naming and its fictitious neutrality that these sweepers suggested turned them from a fox into a camel, a free animal into a beast of burden, and innocent into guilty, and that reduced them to silence in the face of the "false judgment of things."[72]

Overall, all the documents I have described struggle with the inequalities of the agency provided to workers by the fact that their only right in a situation of injustice was to write letters to the agent. Their theatrical, evocative language is provoked by the very poverty of the agency left to them. They all attempt to show suffering in the lines of civility. Ultimately, it is this civility that appears as a kind of violence because it is so difficult to insert their experiences and outrage into its notion of good form and the neutrality of bureaucratic writing.

Most petitions began as an attempt to flatter power or to call it to account, but with the strain of writing the petitions became scandalous literary tales. Railway workers, in their attempts to cross the boundary between the bureaucracy and their everyday experience in the material form of petitions, were forging a language of critique. Some of this language was based on their understanding of the practices of the railways. Other elements were derived from older understandings of power and institutions. But these experiments in addressing the agent on his own terms have one important element in common. They seized the opportunity of petition writing and used its fictions of reciprocity and fair procedure to a very different end than that intended by officials. They used this practice to hold the agent and his officers accountable for the violence of colonial discipline.

## TYRANNY, HONOR, AND PROTEST

The language of critique in the petitions escaped its confinement to the files of failed claims in the Eastern Railway Headquarters. If we examine the union newspapers, memorandums, and flash points for strikes on the railway for the same period, from 1930 to 1940, we find that workers were mobilized by similar attacks on the legitimacy of railway discipline and on British superiors as violent, immoral, rapacious, and despotic. Union newspapers such as the *Mazoor*, published by the East Indian Railwaymen's Union from 1924, were filled with stories of adultery by British railway officers, petty embezzlement as a sign of moral turpitude, and the measurement of the suffering of laboring bodies. The crossover of the modes of address is more than coincidental. Oral histories and personal written accounts of people who were union activists in the 1940s show that one of their important activities was to help workers to compose petitions to the headquarters. As well as dealing with local complaints in the settlements they were based in, such as Lucknow, Dinapur, and Liluah, railway workers who were union officials traveled to all the smaller colonies along the line in order to help write these documents. This was an essential activity for unions because of the very weakness of their position as brokers and as representatives of workers interests. As Chandavarkar has argued, the intolerance of employers, constant repression from the state, and the independence of workers' strike actions all conspired to make unions vulnerable. They could only keep themselves alive as institutions by forging relationships with workers through intervening in their daily disputes with the authorities. As union representatives and workers sat together discussing these disputes they talked through the inequalities of their situation and forged a common public language of the violence of discipline. Petition writing proved to be a successful way of recruiting new union members. S. B. Lahiri, who in the 1940s and 1950s was an officeholder in the Kanchapara branch of the East Indian Railwaymen's Union, describes how this worked. As a store clerk in the railway workshop, he noticed how the union officers, who worked alongside him, had a stream of workshop staff members coming to them to help them draft petitions. Impressed by the help those workers received, he joined the union and began to write requests for people too. Valuing this intervention, they would then join the union.[73]

Petitions were a practice that made the gap between the claims of the bureaucracy to be a neutral guarantor of economic governance and its reality as a punitive system of command all too explicit. Workers, in their efforts to cross the boundary between state and society in the form of the petition, were forced to confront the hollowness of the claims to legitimacy of the bureaucracy. Paradoxically, railway officials had created the space for such an experience of dissonant hiatus by their adaptation of European practices of Taylorist worker welfare into the "Indian" idiom of the petition. The Railway Board had aimed to capture the affections of workers through works councils and petitioning, but they had only succeeded in making witnessing to the scandals of discipline into a public discourse.

Yet the kind of community imagined in the context of union agitation had been affected by the practices and procedures of the railway. The aim of union members was to throw off the *zoolum* (tyranny) of the bureaucracy and to replace it with *swaraj* (self-rule). This project was filled with a moral sensibility and outrage that fused notions of *jati* morality with the notions of pedigree current in the railway bureaucracy. For example, the newspaper *Sadai Mazoom* (Cry of the oppressed), which was produced by the East Indian Railwaymen's Union in the 1930s, was akin to a gossip sheet. It listed the moral faults of specific people in the bureaucracy while clothing the leaders of the union in an aura of purity. A typical edition began with the complaint that "fellow feeling has totally been wiped out from this world. It has come to this condition that brother does not feel for his brother, father for his son and son for his father." The fellow feeling that had been lost in all aspects of public life is conceptually modeled here on the duties and obligations appropriate within families. What appears to be in need of restoration is a sense of both public obligation and obligation to one's lineage group and immediate family. In this manner, expansive concepts of *jati* and kinship underpin the political vision of the union. The newspaper continues to report that, luckily, "God is kind to his creatures" and there are still those that follow "God's way," including the secretary of the East Indian Railwaymen's Union, Babu Harsarup Bhatnagar. This man and his family are described as never shirking the work of the union, because "fellow feeling does not allow him to sit idle. All along he thinks about the welfare of others. . . . God be pleased to keep him engaged in doing these acts and his shadow to fall on the head of the union all along." At the heart of achieving *swaraj* is this morality, which will wipe out "the chain of slavery on the neck of Indians."[74] Bhatnagar can bring liberation about because of the moral purity that makes him an appropriate leader. He is imagined hierarchically blessing the union, like a god or a high-caste person, as a result of his "shadow" falling upon it. We can see in this account a vision of the ideal national political order grounded in an extension of moralities of *jati* and of the immediate kinship group bound together by a common lineage. [75]

In contrast to this hagiography the rest of the newspaper is filled with descriptions of immoral men and their questionable female relatives. There, idioms of *jati* fuse with the ideas of pedigree and public probity current in the railway hierarchy. For example, the paper describes how the wife and sister-in-law of a Mr. Pearce, the head of the locomotive power section, traveled by rail without tickets, "thinking the railway their own," in the same way that Mr. Pearce treated the employees under him, as "slaves like private servants." Equally problematic were the clerks of the locomotive running shed at Moradabad, who were misled by their supervising officers. They took bribes for jobs and leave permissions in order to benefit themselves and their grasping wives, who wanted Western commodities:

> Oh shamelessness you are the only means. The officers are teaching their employees how to make moneys illegally and also instruct them how to kill the helpless and illiterate employees like the cocks are killed. . . . These Babus are the gainers, pockets of them are filled with Rs 50 taken on the plea of giving the remnant to the sahibs, Rs 40 for their own shares, Rs 10 for memsahib either to give her a wrist watch or carpet. [76]

These men even victimized a poor worker in the most extreme of despair. They demanded a bribe from him in return for permission to go off duty when he needed leave to find his wife and jewelry, both of which had been stolen from his house. The "Babus'" immorality therefore prevented a fellow Indian from regaining his own domestic honor.

Other union newspapers such as the *Mazoor* reported regularly in a similar manner on scurrilous court cases involving British and Anglo-Indian employees. The power of this critique must have been immense in the context of a hierarchy that emphasized the moral capacities of superiors and judged employees according to such criteria. More problematic was the manner in which combined idioms of *jati* and respectability could be used at one moment to imagine a united ethical national community and in another to critique the domestic habits and personal demeanor of other Indians. This politics also circulated visions of national honor that relied on fused middle-class British and Indian notions of personal and especially female respectability. The honor of the nation and the private honor of the family were sutured together in this political ethics. The railway bureaucracy in its paternalist measures and moralizing discipline had governmentalized the European and Eurasian family, turning it into a key site for the reproduction of national essences, and had made economic efficiency a matter of biomoral calculations. It had also sought to administer Indian workers by their various biomoral propensities and then community sentiments. The ethical idioms of the railway worker and unions turned this calculus against the bureaucracy. They showed how the British bureaucracy spawned public and private immoralities. *Swaraj* would be brought about by those who governed themselves and their family members according to higher standards of propriety. The project of the railway bureaucracy of creating families in which the relations among state, nation, and economy were writ small met in this politics a project of extending community and *jati* moralities to the level of bureaucratic and national life. British concepts of pedigree and Indian concepts of *jati* and bureaucratic honor combined their idioms in union activism to produce a new version of railway morality that had a radical intent. Yet, as we will see in later chapters, this fusion has had problematic public and private consequences in postcolonial India.


## INTIMATE POLITICS

I began this chapter by quoting from a petition from an Anglo-Indian, Mrs. Packwood, to the agent of the East Indian Railway. I would now like to return to this petition and its particular disorientating effects. Mrs. Packwood writes:

> We cannot get rid of this cursed spirit. I have complied with the desired effect of the church and though my husband is dead the spirit seems always talking a lot of rot to us and though I am praying for my own son's welfare I find that even during the last strike he was entirely forgotten. . . . Now a young man who is honourable and gentle is Mr. Packwood and his family and I find that even against my pray and command we are being horribly neglected . . . while the majority of others Catholics or any other denominations have been encouraged my sons and myself have been deliberately persecuted and amazed and riled and vexed and tortured and . . . we have been incessantly disfigured and discoloured much to our annoyance.[77]

She continues on to describe how the ghost of her dead husband causes railway officials to conspire against the welfare of her family despite the fact that her family has "every authority not only through keeping the laws, but within the law and can prove our identity" as "pure Europeans" and as a family that has "pedigree in the King of England." Her husband's voice also leads her sons to disobey her, and she reports on their moral infirmities that lead them on "the trail of some damned wench" or into the arms of "sluts." She adds that even though she excels in going to communion and in her knowledge of Catholic and Protestant prayers, her son has not even got his right from the cursed Office and the heathen are exercising too much authority. . . . Divisional Superintendent Mr. Hunter knows the truth lawfully and is aiding in waiting for the gods to act and has not acted himself. Mr. Brooks and Davies and several others here have arrowed us and burrowed into our flesh and on top of that instead of being treated as children of light we are being driven by every blast of creation . . . and I have to keep decency going on a paltry pittance of Rs. 140.

She adds that "the issue of promotion seems to be in God's hands and he playing on us for death sentence the while."

Later, not receiving any reply from the agent to her request that her sons' case for employment and promotion should be looked into or their sufferings relieved by a gift of money from the agent, she writes:

Kindly take an interest in my fatherless young ones . . . because they are the real crown princes. I speak as objectionable uncertainties are . . . the times are desperate and there are many errors of creation knocking about and a diversity of flesh which please acknowledge correctly as I am in holy agony about my own son's welfare and the Gods ought never to defraud the truthful. My son has to establish insolvency instead and we need not be denied anything, as false flesh ought not to be in possession.[78]

The disorientating significance of Mrs. Packwood's petition does not come from her madness, but the ways in which her madness follows the lineaments of the railway bureaucracy's own systems of representation and practices. Her apparently mad theology follows the language of many petitions in the archive whether they were from Anglo-Indian or Indian employees. The slippage in her text between the agency of agents and divisional superintendents and that of Gods echoes the supernatural threats and language of justice and theology that we saw was the currency of petitions. Her emphasis on her family's royal, European pedigree and their decency replays the overlapping of economic efficiency, race, and respectability that operated in the petitions that addressed the maintenance of bureaucratic honor and in union newspapers. Her frantic claims that her family's flesh has been burrowed into, disfigured, and discolored by the illegitimate actions of the bureaucracy echo the language of petitions that addressed the sufferings of labor. Her statements link these economic sufferings to a loss of racial identity, a discoloring, that seems not dissimilar to the assumptions of the railway bureaucracy itself that economic efficiency can be linked to pedigrees. What produces Mrs. Packwood's madness is the overdetermined nature of the economic sign in the context of the railway bureaucracy. What sends Mrs. Packwood mad is her lack of comprehension of her economic troubles as simply economic. She hunts for the theological, moral, legal, and racial guilt within her that has reduced her to poverty, and since she cannot find herself lacking in any of these qualifications for prosperity she invents a voice that supernaturally directs these disorders. All the signifiers of the railway bureaucracy of race, respectability, religion, and decency flow into one another in her text once they can no longer be anchored around the economic. She finds herself in a nightmarish realm surrounded by "false flesh" and in a "desperate" time in which "many errors of creation are knocking about." She correctly diagnoses the source of these errors of creation. It is the voice of her dead husband, a railway employee, who first brought her into the realm of the colonial railway bureaucracy in which the universal logic of capital never operated alone.

In the lines of the petitions such as this one we can feel the strains of being the subject of a contradictory combination of Taylorist and colonial practices. We can also follow the entanglement of the personal and political visions of railway families in the typologies of the railway bureaucracy. As railway workers—whether Anglo-Indian or Indian—protested against its practices they also developed a discourse of oppression that had a problematic resemblance to the morality and essentialist logics of the bureaucracy. Bhatnagar and his fellow union members would never have recognized their affinity with the Anglo-Indian Mrs. Packwood. Yet they shared a language of railway morality in which issues of personal and family honor suffused the public sphere of work and politics. It is not surprising that, as became clear in the previous chapter, Gandhian nationalist rhetorics of self-governance and of the necessity of "family" relationships between capital and labor found a fertile ground among railway workers. The foundations for such a politics of scaling up from personal and domestic ethics to biomoral and nationalist idioms had been by the railway bureaucracy. As a result of union agitation, the racial hierarchies of the railway were gradually removed in the period from 1940 onward. Yet, as we will see in the chapters that follow, the typologies of respectability, race, community, and morality were now deeply entangled with the experiences of both Anglo-Indian and Indian railway families. These have proved much harder to displace.

## Chapter Six

# Public Genealogies

*Anglo-Indian Family Histories and the Railway Archive,*
*1927–1950*

Mr. G. Wright states that the original papers in connection to his nationality (there are no copies) are at Ranchi and he has taken leave to procure these papers and show them to you in person.

—Divisional superintendent, Allahabad, to deputy general manager, Calcutta, April 24, 1941

I have shown these papers to Mr. Robertson [deputy general manager] and he pointed out that although it is now clear that Wright's father was a European and that his mother's father was also a European it is not clear whether his mother's mother was also a European. Evidence on this point is necessary in order to deal with the case and unless it can be furnished Mr. Robertson regrets he is unable to give any decision.

—Personnel manager to divisional superintendent, Allahabad, June 16, 1941

## DISEMBEDDING FAMILY HISTORY

In the 1920s the East Indian Railway began to keep an unusual sort of archive for a bureaucracy concerned with running an economic enterprise. This was composed of files on the nationality of its Anglo-Indian, domiciled European, and Indian Christian employees. This archive was generated as much by workers and their families as by the bureaucracy. Workers began to write to the railways in order to protest their classification within it and to request proof of their origins. The East Indian Railway nationality files began to be kept at a time when the old racial distinctions of railway service were formally removed. Since the 1890s the Indian National Congress had campaigned against racial inequalities in pay, conditions, and promotions in all the public services, including the railways. In response to these campaigns, in 1924 the Lee Commission on the Indianization of the Public Services ruled that racial distinctions in pay and privileges should be abolished. All employees would now be classified by domicile, Asiatic and non-Asiatic, rather than by the assigning of a racial or national identity. In the letter of the law these new rights of domicile were apparently based neither on *ius sanguinis* nor on *ius soli*, but on place of education, ownership of property, and the maintenance of kinship links by marriage. These became evidence of the legitimacy of legal rights and the veracity of claimed sentimental relations to a country. National affiliation seemed in this measure to be losing its racial foundations in notions of pedigree and grounding in deep community senti- ments. It appeared to become simply a matter of economic and social ties made or maintained during the course of a person's life. The only inequality left in this system would seem to potentially be that of class position—whether you could afford to maintain links with a homeland through immovable property or paying for certain kinds of education.

On the railways those of non-Asiatic domicile would be eligible for the privi- leges of higher pay, a pound sterling provident fund, and periodic furloughs in Europe and would have their passage back to Europe paid on retirement. The East Indian Railway in 1927 began to implement the recommendations of the Lee Commission. Up until that point, in line with ideas of pedigree, employees had been inspected by a medical officer at the time of employment and their na- tionality—European, Anglo-Indian, Indian Christian, domiciled European—or caste was discerned from their appearance and demeanor and then noted down on their history sheets (personnel records).[1] The agent of the East Indian Railway now decided that the nationality of employees could be accepted according to their own statement of affiliation without any certification on the part of the chief medical officer, although, to make sure that employees told the truth about their nationality, they were threatened with dismissal if they lied about it. Work- ers already on the payroll would still have their nationality fixed on the basis of the original decision of the medical officer at the time of employment. The domicile of workers was to be determined on the basis of forms and support- ing documents in line with the Lee Commission reforms. All new and existing employees filled out these forms. As I will show, this apparently liberal move had three important effects on the relationship between Anglo-Indian railway work- ers and their family histories. First, it intensified investigation into the domestic affiliations of Anglo-Indian workers, with final authority being attributed to doc- umentary evidence of their movement through state institutions. Second, it drew family histories and genealogies into an unequal and inconclusive relationship with documentary archives. The railway bureaucracy made the national affilia- tions of people dependent on the forensic practices of history linked to archives and documents, which proved a certain kind of time depth to their genealogical identifications. Third, it created acute indecision among Anglo-Indian railway workers and bureaucrats about the nature of nationality and identity, whether these rested as visible signs on the body, in sentiments, or in documentary proof. Overall, the practices of this archive disembedded Anglo-Indian family histories, making the bureaucracy and its documents the arbitrator and guardian of their origins. In the 1860s the concepts of pedigree held by railway bureaucrats had tied nationality to the inheritances of the body sustained by certain kinds of ethical practices. From the 1890s, their concepts of community had linked nationality to natural sentiments stimulated by education. Now domicile made national origins a matter of traceable family history. As we will see, this new form of nationality did not simply dissolve the older forms and lead to distinctions purely based on class, but added another layer to the previous inequalities.

The new emphasis on proof of domicile in determining access to European benefits drew Anglo-Indian and domiciled European railway workers into a peculiar and expanded web of criteria that designated national affiliation. The questions on the domicile form that all non-Indian employees were required to fill out were unstinting in their demand for information and emphasis on temporal depth to identity. They went as follows:

> When and where was your paternal grandfather born? What was, or is his profession or occupation? Where was he when your father attained his majority? Is he alive? If not when and where did he die? Was he ever in India? If he was where was he educated? Where was he married? In what capacity did he come to India? How often did he leave or has he left India and for how long? Was his wife ever in Europe? If your grandfather is dead had he retired before his death? If so how long did he remain in India after retiring? Had he ever any immovable property in India? [2]

It asked similar questions about the worker's grandmother, father, and mother and the worker and his wife themselves, adding a question about whether anyone in the family had ever corresponded with any relatives or friends in Europe and whether they intended to retire to Britain. These questions demanded proof of private affiliations ratified by state documents and private correspondence, giving documents a primary material power to prove social relationships and origins. At the bottom of the form was a list of documents that had to be provided in order to confirm the answers to the questions. The responses of workers to these questions reveal the inequalities produced by the demand of the bureaucracy. Questions were repeatedly answered with a simple "not known," "as far as I know," "we cannot yet afford property in Europe, but we intend to buy it," and stories of failed intended trips to Europe that were aborted at the last minute because of lack of funds or sickness.[3] One worker wrote, "In regard to questions 1a, b, c, 2 a, c, d I beg to state that on the death of his mother my father who was very young, was taken over by his grandmother and therefore cannot give the information called for."[4]

These domicile forms traced the circuit of workers through civic and state organizations in India, making personal genealogies, life histories, and kinship a matter of public institutions and records. From these forms railway officials drew up authoritative kinship diagrams tracking nothing but the traces of the state in the lives of railway workers and their antecedents. The family history of Anglo-Indians and domiciled Europeans was being disembedded from a domain of family stories and bodily signs of belonging into a public sphere of records. Simultaneously to this, the Indian ancestors and relatives of Anglo-Indians and domiciled Europeans were rendered irrelevant to this public archive and became a private and disabling secret. In particular, a failure to produce documents, or a silence about the origins of female relatives, was always interpreted by officials as a sign that the worker had disabling kinship connections to India (this was explicitly called a "disability"). Indian railway workers, however, could simply assert when asked by the officer employing them whatever identity or caste they chose to with no requirement for proof. Indian family histories were left in the domain of private, unproblematic links among body, place, and family stories of lineage.[5]

The new regime of documentary proof generated a flow of protests from Anglo-Indian and domiciled European workers. The files on nationality and domicile in the East Indian Railway began to fill with their requests for change of status. If you disputed the decision of local railway officials, then you were referred to the authority of the agent, who issued strict instructions that he be the final arbiter in disputes. If you could win him over with your written requests, then you had the hope of having your private sense of origin and identity ratified. Since the railway administration instructed its employees that the onus of proof rested with the individual worker, the nationality archive at the East Indian Railway grew, expanding in size and authority. It drew into its files not just the decisions of medical officers, but also the private correspondences of deceased grandparents, the testaments of magistrates, the assertions of parish priests, the protests of the Anglo-Indian Association, and the opinions of divisional managers on the nationality and domicile of subordinates. We find in its files from 1929 the following list of documents offered to prove the nationality of Mr. Kennedy, an inspector of works:

Records offered to prove Nationality
1. Extract from parish register books of St. Johns Calcutta, Mr. E. J. Simpson married Miss L. Wyatt on 5/1/1865
2. Burial certificate of Mrs. L. Simpson

3. Letter no. 6 dated 29/9/26 from R. J. Twyford and Co., solicitors to Mrs. S. Kennedy

4. Burial certificate of Mrs. L. Simpson, widow of Captain T. R. Simpson R. N.

5. Death certificate of Mrs. F. A. Wyatt

6. Chart dated 10/12/29 showing the antecedents paternal and maternal of Mr. Kennedy's mother.

7. Letter dated 3/1/1817 from Mr. G. N. Wyatt to Fanny Wyatt

8. Letter dated 4/4/1813 from Mr. G. N. Wyatt to Fanny Wyatt

9. Letter written in 1817 by A. Wyatt to Fanny Wyatt. [6]

The railway bureaucracy replied with its own archive, stating that Mr. Kennedy was declared to be Anglo-Indian at the time of his appointment and that throughout his entire record he was classed as such. The agent added that this file contained no papers relative to the representation Mr. Kennedy's father is said to have made in 1906 protesting against his classification as Anglo-Indian. Therefore, his nationality could not be altered especially on the basis of private correspondence that contained "no relevant facts at all."[7] Mr. Kennedy was asked to produce more evidence of his domicile. In these files a public documentary history of Anglo-Indians, domiciled Europeans, and Indian Christians was coming into being. They all became related to an archive and began chasing documents through all the institutions of the colonial state, trying to prove their right to be part of an archive of nationality.

The inequalities of this hunt for documents become apparent from the efforts in 1934 of Mr. Hampton, a foreman in the wagon repair shop in Ondal. He sent to the agent extracts from the Sind Civil List from 1872, a newspaper cutting from 1863 showing the Commission of the Peace issued and directed to officers serving in the Punjab, and a marriage certificate and death certificate to prove the European credentials of his father. He provided evidence from the Government Directory and Gazette of India that his three brothers were classed as Europeans in the Public Works Department, Burma, Indian Educational Service, Bareilly, and Commissioner's Office, Jullandhar. But he regretted he was unable to obtain any papers for his mother because she was born in 1844 at Calcutta and there were no papers available before 1860. His claims about his brothers were tested by the railway administration, but their requests to the relevant government departments were met with the reply that all the relevant papers had been "weeded out." Mr. Hampton was then asked to prove his mother's nationality. He produced a letter from the senior United Board chaplain in India, Kasauli, certifying that to the best of his knowledge she was the daughter of French parents. Mr. Hampton added to this a promise for a certificate from the doctor who attended his mother in her last illness, but he asked for patience from the authorities because this would take time because he did not know where the doctor was now stationed. The agent then asked him to fill out a domicile questionnaire, and Mr. Hampton continued his finally inconclusive quest for his own history.

By 1949 the size and authority of the railway's archive of Europeans had grown so much that it became the object of requests for proof itself. Mr. Ford, the son of a railway guard, wrote to the general manager of the East Indian Railway, requesting "any information you may have on record in support of my father's status of nationality as a European English subject." He needed these records in order to submit to the United Kingdom Citizens Association in response to their demand for documents supporting his registration as a citizen of the United Kingdom.[8] The administration replied, "at this distant date the records he asks for are unavailable." Mr. Ford was left dispossessed of his "origins," longing for them, referring in his final letter to his father's claim that his status was recorded in the "Minute no. 464 of the Agent dated Friday October 23 1917 that at the request of the General Traffic Manager, endorsed by the Acting Chief Medical Officer that the nationality of guard W.J. Ford had been changed from East Indian to European (vide correspondences ending with Chief Medical officer's letter No: 5786, dated 6th October 1917)." Mr. Ford was finally left with nothing more substantial than this memory of a line from the minutes of a board meeting.[9]

I suggested earlier that the founding of this archive marked a shift from an emphasis on nationality and race as signs on the body to one of domicile proved by state documents. But if you examine in more detail the ways in which decisions were made by railway officers and the claims of workers, it becomes clear that something much more problematic was taking place. Railway officials were working with contradictory ideas of belonging—one based on domicile, one on nationality. The idea of domicile depended on a notion of identity as dependent on your behavior during the course of your life and your class position anchored by the class status and behavior of ancestors. To attain a non-Asiatic domicile, the most important criteria were that you were educated outside India, had married in Britain, owned property in Britain, had visited Britain often, corresponded with relatives there, and had an emotional connection, which meant that you intended to return there at retirement. Important as well was the fact that you were in India merely in the exercise of a profession. A purely economic, unsentimental tie to India disembedded you from belonging in that place. What domicile was about therefore was a class position, whether you could afford to maintain some kind of connection to Britain. As such, it corresponded to the idea of an unbounded seriality of citizenship rights that was dependent only on a ranking of people according to their ownership of property and their economic activity.[10]

Yet railway bureaucrats were still also working simultaneously with the idea of nationality as an essential part of the body, combining a logic of inherited pedigree with that of property and equal citizenship in their vision of rights of abode and political status. When railway workers signed on for employment, they were still required to fill in their nationality/caste. They were placed in different sections of the railway gazette and official lists according to their nationality/caste. Nationality was still something quite different from domicile; it was an inherited feature marked on the body by skin pigmentation and cultural habits that was an unchanging essence. In the setting of the Raj, the ideas of pedigree, blood, and inheritance that had been identified as central to English kinship were applied to the technologies of parsing citizens from noncitizens. Notions of blood and pedigree became articulated in the railway bureaucracy to concepts of racial distinction manifest in skin pigmentation that in turn defined the natural national body from that of internal others. There was also an attempt to make this racial and national pedigree relate to documentary proof, family genealogies, and family histories. Here, on the frontiers of empire, where the nondomiciled and domiciled were divided from each other, one of the historical trajectories of English kinship is made manifest. Pedigree here was irrefutable proof of an unchanging essence that divided citizens from noncitizens. Via ideas of race and nation, social distinction became a permanent feature of bodies, family histories, and genealogies, limiting mobility in new ways. Ideas of pedigree were implicated in and marked by the history of colonial institutions such as the railway bureaucracy that articulated English concepts of kinship to idioms of race and nation.

In practice, when railway officials made their decisions on cases, they veered between these two criteria of nationality and domicile. They tried to bring decisions on nationality (based on inheritance and the body) in line with their decisions on domicile (based on documents and class). Often, when documentary evidence was unclear, the agent would order the railway worker concerned to pay a visit to the chief medical officer, who would decide the matter on the basis of appearance. The railway bureaucracy's contradictory practices in which it was unclear whether bodies or documents guaranteed nationality and domicile made the body simultaneously an indisputable and treacherous witness. This is captured by a memorandum from the chief medical officer to the deputy general manager in 1940, which was sent to try to determine the case of a railway guard who had been designated Anglo-Indian when he was first employed by the railways, but was now challenging the decision thirty years later:

> The physical examination upon which this classification used to be made is a most fallacious one and depends entirely upon the presence, absence and degree of pigment over certain areas of the body. I have known of cases

where dark Europeans and fair Anglo-Indians and Europeans respectively and I am aware of at least one case in which one brother was classified as European and another as Anglo-Indian. After the age of 35–40 physical examination is almost useless, except in extreme cases, as pigmentation increases with age and other factors such as pressure and exposure to temperature have to be reckoned with. Driver Brinkhurst must be between 50 and 55 and unless he is very dark it will be impossible for me to arrive at any conclusion. The Medical Officer who examined him on appointment was in a much better position to arrive at a more accurate conclusion than I can possibly do now and his classification should stand.[11]

This memorandum was used in many other cases as evidence for the uncertainty of physical proof of nationality. Yet agents and railway officers continued to be unsure about the primacy of written or physical evidence as proof of family origins.[12] Despite the assertions of medical officers, they could not let go of their category of physical manifestations of nationality.

For example, two brothers, Mr. C. Stanhope Jones and Mr. V. Stanhope Jones, were inspected by a medical officer at Liluah in 1929, who decided that "from personal appearance and from the examination of their maternal and paternal records I am convinced that both these brothers are Europeans. I am informed that one of their brothers, who is on the Burma railways, is under the European leave rules," and the controller of stores altered their records accordingly.[13] The agent protested this decision taken without his authority and referred the Jones brothers for an interview with the chief medical officer, who in turn argued that the case could be decided just as well by the head of the department as a medical officer. The secretary to the agent insisted that the chief medical officer should certify them, and he decided that they were Anglo-Indian. Similarly, the agent's request for the inspection of a Mr. Whaley's European nationality by the chief medical officer was met by the assertion from the doctor that "there are no particular signs known to medicine which are diagnostic of pure European parentage the chief mechanical engineer is just as competent as I am to decide this question."[14] However, the agent insisted on a decision from him. All requests from employees that started work under the previous medical regime for alterations in their status were greeted with the response that there was no possibility that the doctor's diagnosis of their origins could have been wrong.

This bureaucratic vacillation in which the rules of domicile insisted on documentary proof and bureaucrats insisted on physical proof left employees confused in their representations to railway officials. They supplied documentary proof from private doctors of their mother's or father's domicile, confusing requests for changes of nationality with changes in domicile, demanding that since their domicile had been determined as non-Asiatic they be classified as Europeans. For example, Mr. Newham, an apprentice signal inspector, protested his classification as of Asiatic domicile, stating, "your place of abode may change but it does not alter the blood that flows in the person and hence the nationality is the same." He added:

> I am a European, moreover since both my parents are of European parentage and my mother has relatives now in England—owners of property—her grandfather a military veteran buried in the Residency in Lucknow was European. . . . Regarding my grandfather . . . he was a pure Irish man and people to-day in Dublin will link his name and affairs till he came to India.[15]

The railway authorities responded to his outrage, which combined a logic of blood, family history, nationality, and domicile as indeterminate as their own, by calmly informing him that "a domiciled European is of Asiatic domicile but that this has nothing whatsoever to do with nationality."[16] The confusion of railway workers about what the signs of nationality and identity actually were echoed the railway bureaucracy's own continuing confusion about the relationship between bodies and documents, inherited essences and behavior, racial identity and class position. Here, we have an example of the recurrent and still problematic contradiction between nationality imagined as genealogical belonging and as a civic, political right gained through residence not family origins. Property alone did not divide citizens from one another; notions of blood, genealogy, and race did as well. This division came to the fore rather than retreating with the removal of explicit racial categories. What divides citizens from now on is not just a matter of biomoral substances expressed in present actions and sentiments of loyalty, but also genealogy, the time depth and inheritance through generations of biological and other substances gained through descent.

Given that the process of proving your identity or challenging your assigned domicile and nationality was often invasive and inconclusive, we might ask why railway workers took part in this process at all. Cases would take an average of two years to resolve, and only in a handful of cases did it result in the change that the worker had requested. Railway officers had a simple answer for this question. Workers were seeking to improve their economic position illegitimately and to gain access to non-Asiatic privileges of leave, higher rate of pay, pensions in sterling rather than rupees, and a passage back to Britain on retirement. This economic interpretation works for some of the requests, but not quite in the way railway officials saw it. From the perspective of railway officials, workers who were really Anglo-Indians or Indian Christians were trying to disguise themselves as something quite else, Europeans or Anglo-Indians, that they actually essentially were not. Workers, however, were sometimes willing to strategically abandon an apparently essential identity, understanding that there was nothing vital or essential about this status. Railway officials refused to admit the permeability of the system they were involved in, that it enabled the transubstantiation of apparently essential identities.

But alongside this strategic economic adoption of a past, petitioners had other reasons for challenging their nationality and domicile status as recorded by the railway. They were in part motivated by an alternative view of what guaranteed the identifications of a family and membership of a nation. The letters sent to the agent repeatedly offered proof gathered from church records that they were of a particular nationality. Baptismal and marriage records were carefully transcribed and shown to officials even though these contained no explicit mention of nationality or family origins. For example, baptismal records usually just listed date of birth, place of baptism, the names of parents, their place of residence, and the trade of the father. It would have been possible to distinguish an Indian Christian if the surname and parents' names were not European, and sometimes chaplains wrote "Indian Christian" on these records. But beyond this limit case, a parsed and precise national or racial origin calculated through maternal and paternal lines was not visible on these records. In spite of the telegraphic nature of these records, Anglo-Indians and domiciled Europeans clearly saw them as proof of their family status. They appear to have conceived of membership of Catholic and Protestant churches as providing them with an irrefutable bond to the community of "Europeans." The documentary records of these churches also linked them to their ancestors.

This notion of a divinely underpinned citizenship is not surprising when seen in relation to the general history of Christianity and the colonial state in India. The connection between social identities and religious practices has always been clearly visible in the context of caste practices. Also, in Hindu families records of the generations were often only kept or known precisely by family pandits who performed marriage and death ceremonies. Pandits in pilgrimage centers such as Haridwar also kept books containing records of the visits of family members through the generations. Colonial law and bureaucracies intensified the connection between social and religious identifications, enfolding these into the practices of the state by separating the administration of communities along religious lines. In this context, conversion in India has long produced a dramatic refounding of belonging, community status, kinship networks, and legal rights.[17] Different forms of worship also at times became articulated with local caste rivalries and hierarchies.[18] This long history of an elective affinity between social and religious community is at work in the attempts of workers to prove their nationality through religious documents and institutions. More specifically, their use of church records to prove their nationality and legal citizenship rights reflects the effects of the railway colony and the educational institutions of the railways. Both of these institutions linked ethical obligations to Christian morality to membership of racial and national groups. Schools were designed to be suffused with a spirit of Christianity, which would provide the foundation for the sober observance of secular obligations to race and nation. Railway colonies attempted to tie self-mastery, domesticity, obligation to workplace rules, and loyalty to race and nation through ascetic practical Christian morality. The case I mentioned earlier in which Mr. A. Hampton offered the agent a certificate from the senior United Board chaplain that his mother was European is attributable to this sensibility. This logic can also be seen at work in the cases where workers wrote to the agent asking for the designation of their nationality on their employment records to be changed from Christian to Anglo-Indian. The two terms appeared interchangeable to them. In spite of its provocation in part by their housing and educational policies, Railway bureaucrats did not recognize the legitimacy of this vision of a kind of divine citizenship that motivated the challenges of workers. Officers repeatedly wrote on the files statements such as "this 'evidence' is valueless."[19]

The new precision of the rulings on domicile based on documentary evidence, which proved a temporal depth to identities, also undermined another aspect of Anglo-Indian and domiciled European family identification. They stressed the importance of historically and laterally deep kinship connections to Europe on both paternal and maternal lines proved by documentation. On the basis of the domicile forms, officials set about tracing these connections backward in time and across space in the present. Officials additionally felt that these connections were also somehow, if at times indistinctly, linked with an essence of nationality that was transmitted down the generations, often as a physical marker. Such a model collided with the more fragmented and present-oriented family formation of domiciled European and Anglo-Indian workers. Their representations to the bureaucracy tell a story of broken connections, particularly to European fathers and grandfathers, who moved on to form other families. They also reveal shallow present-oriented family recollections, stretching often only to parents. In addition, they show a lack of concern about the deep reckoning of maternal lines. Workers wrote assuming that if they traced their father's line that would be enough to get them Anglo-Indian or European status. Some of them expressed their lack of comprehension of the deep reckoning of nationality required of them. Characteristically, one mother wrote complaining that her sons "worry her to produce evidence regarding . . . nationality." She added that all the records of her first marriage and birth certificates had been lost since her second marriage and that she was "at a loss to understand why fresh enquiries are necessary." Under the circumstances, she asked that the railway "accept her word to her nationality."[20]

This sense that present claims to family identity should be enough was rein-forced by the regulations surrounding the electoral rolls introduced during the 1930s. These stated that people could go to their local district magistrate and de-clare by their own oath what their nationality was. But this legal regulation is not enough to explain the petitioners' protests at the demands now made of them by the bureaucracy. These protests were also due to the previous form of the bureau-cracy itself, which had emphasized a shallow understanding of a worker's origins tied to the identification that a railway doctor made at the time of employment. There was another source for these protests as well. This was the distinct and more present-oriented vision of family identities at work in domiciled European and Eurasian families, which I will discuss further in the ethnographic sections of the book. This kinship reckoning rested on the practices and sentiments of cur-rent households rather than on deep genealogical ties. A notion of pedigree and past-oriented reckoning of identity was now colliding with the more fluid family formation of domiciled European and Anglo-Indian railway workers.

Workers challenged the rulings of the administration for another reason as well. Many of the unsuccessful claims of workers are permeated with a sense of sadness and frustration about their families being drawn into a documen-tary regime. They protest that their immediate family connections forged in the household were suddenly displaced and made insubstantial. What was at stake in many cases was the possibility of building a continuous public identity and life story for yourself, your close family members, and your children in the present. Many of the requests from workers pointed out that their sons were classified differently from themselves in the public railway lists. Others had been classified as European or Anglo-Indian by other colonial institutions such as the army or in electoral registers because these institutions demanded proof only of European parentage in the male line. The railway's criteria were more rigorous, since one had to prove European parentage in the male and female lines. Other contempo-rary definitions in the Government of India Acts for the purposes of drawing up electoral rolls (1919 and 1935) insisted on European descent only in the male line, as did army regulations during the First and Second World Wars.

Workers protested the fragmenting of their identities by these different defini-tions of "Europeans." For example, a Mr. Brinkhurst wrote in 1939, demanding that his nationality be altered to European, "England and the Allies Sir, are at war to-day only because Germany deprived Poland of her birth right. If we are to take the action of England as sincere then Sir, you as British officers must admit that I have a right to fight for my proper place."[21] He threatened the administration with the withdrawal of his patriotism in light of the insincerity of British officers and their refusal to allow him a "place" of origin. Mr. Pedrick wrote in 1945 that he had been classified as a European British subject in the Regulation for the Registration of Engineering Powers Ordinance, but that he was classified East Indian in the railway lists. He protested this contradictory classification of his identity: "It cannot be European for one purpose and East Indian for another and I wish you to please correct my birth right from East Indian to European and let me here [sic]."[22] After another similar application that cites the Government of India Act of 1935, the agent called for an opinion about the definition of "European Nationality" under this act. When he found out its definition, he wrote incredulously, "Then you might as well call 50% of Anglo Indian[s] Europeans!"[23] Other workers were provoked by the Government of India Act on the Composition of Legislatures (1940), under which magistrates were given the authority to register people as European on the basis of documents proving their male line, to request a change of status in the railway lists. In all of these cases, railway bureaucrats referred to their own archives as definitive and stated categorically that nationality "cannot be altered merely on the basis of the fact that for certain other purposes the man has declared himself to be a European."[24] The workers who wrote to the railway officials never forgot the power of the archive to define their public identities and determine the veracity of their personal stories. They demanded their "birth right" after repeated rejections of their requests; asked how it could be that their brothers were classed as Europeans but they weren't; and asked why their domicile could be changed to European, but their nationality couldn't. By writing to the railway bureaucracy, these workers sought to end the contradictory ways in which their houses were enfolded into colonial archives. They sought a seamless public identity that could verify their private family stories. They wanted a final piece of documentary proof that would stabilize the disjuncture between their private family stories and their public identities. That it had become so important to close this disjuncture shows the degree to which the practices of the railway bureaucracy had disembedded the family stories of Anglo-Indian workers and had brought them into a relationship with documentary proof. But, as I will explain, it also reveals much about the wider historical moment and the shape that community identities were taking in the Indian public sphere during this period. The genealogies of identity in the East Indian Railway nationality files turn out to be relevant for the tracing of the genealogy of the idea and practice of community in Indian politics.

## A GENEALOGY OF COMMUNITY

Although the longing for a public ratification of their private stories by the railway bureaucracy was a particular predicament for Anglo-Indians, it reveals much about the new politics of community rights and entitlement that was emerging in the period from 1919 to 1947. It has long been a truism of historiography that the Montagu-Chelmsford electoral reforms in 1919, which created separate electorates and provincial legislatures, were motivated by a policy of divide and rule. Similarly, the agreement in principle to economic reservation for minority communities in the Simon Commission in 1928 and subsequent implementation of this in the civil services and railways have long been interpreted as a strategy for creating divisions of interest. But what seems equally significant about this historical moment is that some of the measures introduced to calculate electoral eligibility and economic entitlements tied private genealogies to political rights. Genealogies and sometimes documentation were becoming significant in a new way to the arbitrations of the state. They could be used to prove the existence of an inherited substance within individuals, which they shared with other members of a bounded "community" and that entitled them to political and economic rights. The nationality archive of the East Indian Railway was just one of the many and more obviously problematic examples of this process. Most of the community claims, like that of the caste categories of Indian railway workers, appeared to be self-evident and did not generate inquiries or extensive archives. But the protests of Anglo-Indians in the East Indian Railway nationality files, who were caught between these emerging lines and left with inconclusive longings for their transgenerational essences to be ratified by a state institution, remind us that these communities were something new and different that grew in the context of the removal of explicit racial inequalities and democratization of the public sphere in India. This archive also shows that as communities emerged in the calculations of bureaucracies, they were tied to broader national identities—in this case Asiatic/non-Asiatic. The racial categorization of families may have retreated from public life during this period, but its specific history and ideas of origins were increasingly tied to community and national projects. The impoverished and divisive logic of this bureaucratic reckoning assumed that family histories could simply nest within the bounds of communities, which could then potentially ultimately be associated with particular nations and sometimes races. But the objections of Anglo-Indian railway workers and vacillations of railway officers show how inadequate and strange this bureaucratic reckoning was.

The peculiar nature of the political communities that emerged in the public sphere in the context of this bureaucratic reckoning is particularly visible in the shape taken by the elite Anglo-Indian Association from 1928 to 1947. From the late nineteenth century, wealthy Eurasian professionals in Calcutta, Madras, and Bombay had formed organizations to represent their interests to the government on issues of employment and education and to reform their "community" from within. From 1902 to 1910, these organizations became more formalized, with regular meetings, publications, and branches across India in railway centers and major towns. They periodically cooperated in conferences on political and commercial questions with similar associations such as the Marwari Association, Bengal National Chamber of Commerce, Central Mohammedan Association, and Calcutta Trades Association. Despite the acceptance in the president of the Imperial Anglo-Indian Association's annual address in 1902 that they should be politically unified with other Indians in their movement for free electoral representation, this did not mean that members supported Congress politics.[25] Instead, they sought to stall the process of Indianization and objected to what they called the "sometimes unconstitutional" methods of Congress. By 1928 most of these organizations were amalgamated under the leadership of Sir Henry Gidney into the Anglo-Indian Association, with a headquarters in Calcutta. The introduction of limited electoral reforms, the rights given to minority communities in the Simon Commission, and the growing mass nationalist movement had completely changed the nature of the Anglo-Indian Association. In the pages of its journal and local meetings, there was now a self-conscious exploration of how to become a legitimate Indian community with political rights, but which also had greater national loyalties shared with other Indians.[26]

In their explicit experimentation in how to belong to India, middle-class members of the Anglo-Indian Association attempted to counter all claims that they were inauthentic and unpatriotic. The link their arguments made between public political and private legitimacy reveal some of the assumptions that grounded the new natural boundaries of communities in civil society. They asserted first of all that Anglo-Indians were the legitimate offspring of Indian and British ancestors, casting off the common accusation that they were the descendants of illegitimate relationships between low-caste Indian women and low-class British soldiers. Second, they insisted that they had a genealogical tie to India from the inheritance of the Indian bloodline of their ancestral mothers, which linked them to the national motherland. Sometimes they added to this that they were, in fact, the most naturally national Indian community, because their families had their origins in all regions, castes, and creeds. These lines of argument and the objections from other Indian communities that they sought to anticipate reveal the ties being made between genealogical and public identities. These meditations and assertions should not be seen as separate from the efforts of the organization to acquire and guard rights to reserved jobs and voting rights. They were the new kinds of genealogically provable claims that during this period underpinned some forms of political rights.

Members of the association also set about attempting to acquire the elements that Anglo-Indians lacked in comparison with other Indian communities. Local branches compiled Anglo-Indian anthems, histories, and literary collections. They also began to dream of founding an Anglo-Indian agricultural village in

McCluskiegunj. Although this project has been interpreted as an ill-fated uto-pian, separatist dream, it was a scheme that was designed to finally link a mobile labor aristocracy to the soil of India. Anglo-Indians would put down agricultural roots in a cross between a homeland and village home. Becoming a community with political rights now not only required genealogical reckoning of legitimacy, but also some kind of territorial foundation in a *desh*.

All of this might seem to be an interesting improvisation that used bureau-cratic notions of genealogical entitlement for another end or that successfully countered other Indians' delegitimization of Anglo-Indian claims to belong. But the institutional formation of this community turns out to have been as impov-erished as the bureaucratic practices of the railways. From 1933, the Anglo-Indian Association used its local district branches to inspect the genealogical credentials of prospective members, people who asserted they were Anglo-Indian on elector-al rolls and for the purposes of gaining reserved posts in the government services. "Vigilance committees" were set up to police membership of the community, which borrowed the documentary practices of the bureaucracy and enacted these at the local level. The majority of Anglo-Indians did not accept this restricted notion of solidarity based on documentary proof of legitimacy. Once the associa-tion introduced these procedures they had tremendous problems in recruiting members, especially from among railway workers. There was a constant crisis of funds, as subscriptions remained unpaid, members left the organization, and people chose not to join. Fifty-one out of fifty-nine of the district branches of the Anglo-Indian Association were in railway colonies and were staffed by one or two members, mainly railway drivers or traveling track or ticket inspectors. But these branches could not generate an enthusiastic membership among the Anglo-In-dian labor aristocracy. Perhaps they were unwilling to participate in a community that defined its solidarity using the narrow bureaucratic practices of inspection of documentary credentials and kinship relationships. Sometimes doubts about these surfaced even in the pages of the Anglo-Indian Association journal. For example, in 1938 Kenneth Wallace, an inspector of schools, wrote that people who wanted to join the association should just be asked to declare that they were an Anglo-Indian rather than be asked to produce proof of their origins. This way the organization would be filled with "Asil," or genuine Anglo-Indians. He added that it was just a class prejudice that led the association to exclude poor Anglo-Indians as "Indians."[27] But this eloquent plea did not alter the activities of the association, which continued to build an exclusionary, class-inflected form of po-litical community on the basis of genealogical reckoning. In general, the attempt of the Anglo-Indian association to build a community echoed the impoverished notions of community practiced by the colonial bureaucracy in nationality ar-chives such as that of the East Indian Railway. Although political leaders like

Gidney claimed to represent Anglo-Indians and negotiated rights and privileges for them, poorer Anglo-Indians seemed ambivalent about or disinterested in this new politics.

Yet Anglo-Indians who did not subscribe to this class-inflected bureaucratic notion of political community found it difficult to become engaged with other forms of politics. The exclusion of Anglo-Indians from nationalist and union agitation had many causes. One of these was their structural position as defenders of colonial public space, for example, the compulsory enrolling of all Anglo-Indian railway workers in the Auxiliary Defence Force, which as we have seen often brutally suppressed strikes. Another was their economic position as intermediaries who implemented the orders and hard work regimes that Indian workers were protesting against. But Anglo-Indians were by no means the only Indians who enforced the colonial rule of law or economic hierarchies. In fact, many of the Indian middle and lower-middle classes did this in the army and the public and private sectors of the Raj. What made it difficult for Anglo-Indians was the increasing elective affinity among notions of *jati*, community, and nation. One of the great challenges for Indian nationalism during the 1920s was to overcome restricted notions of community and to formulate a common political destiny for a unified Indian "people." Obviously, the forms that solutions took—from communist-inspired strike action to Nehru's vision of communities unified by a developmentalist state—were diverse and had very different kinds of political effects. However common, political action, whether at the local or elite level, was often grounded in metaphorical and analogical leaps built around the term *jati*. Both *jati* and the "community" measurable by the colonial state were by the 1920s operating with a shadowy genealogical imperative. In fact, from the perspective of Anglo-Indians, it is hard to tell the difference between them. The *jati*/community of Nehruvian socialism, Gandhian *swadeshi* utopianism, or railway unions seemed to them merely to operate with the fundamental assumptions of bureaucratic archives such as that of the East Indian Railway nationality archive.

Anglo-Indians had long been a problematic "community" for the Indian middle classes. For example, from the late nineteenth century, in Bengal Eurasians and Indian Christians had been labeled with the term *tash*, which suggested that they were low-class, low-caste, cheap imitations, too Anglicized, rootless, and sexually disreputable.[28] But from the 1920s, as a result of the debates on the Indianization of the public services and general salience of the category of community in politics, Anglo-Indians became visible as an area of inquiry. Articles in the *Modern Review* speculated about the damage that was done to the cultures of both India and Britain by their mingling in the homes of Anglo-Indians.[29] Mahalanobis carried out mathematical calculations on the physical features of Anglo-Indians to try to determine the effects of race mixing.[30] This combination of cultural nationalism, race theory, and class distinction played constantly with the metaphor and multiple meanings of *jati* as a form of physical and cultural inheritance through time. As we have seen, petitions from railway workers during the same period record their protests about being supervised by Anglo-Indians, calling them, for example, "third-class Anglo-Indians of dome breed."[31] As a result of these anxieties about Anglo-Indians, when their political leaders sought alliances with the Indian National Congress, they found out that their community was not quite respectable or Indian enough to be included. For example, Dr. H. W. Moreno, a leader of an Anglo-Indian radical political group, sought a rapprochement in conversations and letters with Gandhi from 1925 to 1926. Gandhi reassured him that Anglo-Indians were as welcome as all other minority communities within the Indian National Congress. However, Gandhi was outraged that Anglo-Indians defined their identity through their inheritance from a European ancestor, saying that as long as they did this they could not be included within the nationalist movement. He also suggested that they lived a false mode of European existence in railway colonies and that their moral and physical tastes showed signs of degeneracy. Moreno wrote back that these attitudes from nationalists were what made it so difficult for Anglo-Indians to feel part of the political movement for independence.[32] From the perspective of working class Anglo-Indians, there was little difference between the disenfranchisement they faced from railway officials, leaders of their political groups, or other Indians. All of these demanded proof of their private affiliations, origins, and family histories that they often could not provide. In particular, they were now faced with an impossible choice. To make their family histories into public identities they had to prove their European affiliations with documents to institutions like the East Indian Railway or the Anglo-Indian Association, but this, according to Indian nationalists, disqualified them from belonging to the Indian nation.

During the 1940s, Anglo-Indian leaders such as Frank Anthony did manage to build a working relationship with Congress. By this period, the notion of India as a conglomeration of competing political communities was firmly entrenched as a natural state of affairs. Nehruvian socialism sought to create a state that would arbitrate between these rights. It was on the basis of this vision that Anthony succeeded in negotiating minority rights for Anglo-Indians, guaranteeing preferential employment on the railways until 1960, reserved places in English-medium schools, and nominated MLAs in the provincial and central legislatures. At Independence, many Anglo-Indians celebrated along with other Indians, and theoretically they have taken their place among the other now naturalized communities of interest in India. Yet, as we will see in later chapters, this has not affected the attitude of other railway workers to Anglo-Indians or their quotidian experience of belonging. The final effect of the railway nationality archive and the historical moment it emerged from was to make Anglo-Indians into a profoundly un-Indian, rootless community. Caught between the genealogical reckoning of the colonial bureaucracy and the imagination of *jati* by other Indians, their predicament reveals much about the genealogy of community and its relationship to nationalism in India. From the 1920s, community emerged as a bridging category in Indian public life that still serves to make personal affiliations, family history, domestic arrangements, and bloodlines relevant to issues of national loyalty.

## POSTCOLONIAL CITIZENSHIP AND GENEALOGIES

Balibar has linked the production of state public archives of descent in France to the dissolving of kinship frontiers and private genealogies.[33] He argues that this move led to the emergence of an all-encompassing sense of belonging to a French national race. Similar processes were at work in the production of a public genealogy in the East Indian Railway nationality files. But what this material shows particularly clearly is that the nationalization of family histories and the emergence of public genealogies does not smoothly produce a new coalescence of bodies, documents, and domestic behavior within the encompassing boundary of the nation. The East Indian Railway archive represents a moment in the history of the troubled relationship between civic entitlement and genealogical community. In this moment, the profound contradiction inherent in the notion of national citizenship as both a civic, political right and as an ethnic or racial and genealogical history grounded in the family and the body comes to the fore and intensifies. The colonial and post-Independence history of communities and nation in India and Britain has not succeeded in overcoming this contradiction. In both places, but with very different entailments, civic entitlement always has the specters of genealogical histories and natural inheritances hovering around it.[34]

Even more strikingly the story of this archive and the forms of genealogical community that emerged in the public sphere during the last decades of British rule in India show that both Indian and English kinship are postcolonial. As this and previous chapters have shown, notions of *jati* and pedigree were in the context of the Raj and its institutions intimately linked to the creation of the boundaries of race and nation. From 1919 to 1947, bureaucrats, politicians, and workers attempted to articulate in their practices a different, more egalitarian idea of the unbound seriality of the nation filled with citizens with equal rights. This utopian vision, however, was not fully realized, but was dragged down by logics of inheritance understood through historically produced nationalized idioms of *jati* and pedigree. British railway bureaucrats set out to distribute rights to citizens on the basis of domicile, but ended up arbitrating between ranked degrees of belonging along the lines of racial inheritance and its manifestation in family histories. Anglo-Indian political organizations sought equal political rights with other Indian citizens. Yet they also parsed their own membership according to discriminatory documentary practices and attempted to prove their rights to be Indian citizens on the basis of their family legitimacy and mingled bloodlines. Indian nationalists and railway workers sought to create an ideal space of the nation, but in attempting to suture together this homogeneous space often used the idioms of *jati*. This raised the specters of legitimacy, family origins, respectability, and bloodlines at the heart of Indian public and political life. As we will see in the second half of this book, for contemporary Anglo-Indians this history has left them feeling both existentially and politically disenfranchised. More generally, I would like to suggest that the life of communities and families in the present continues to be affected by the ranked serialities of belonging that emerged out of attempts under the last decades of British rule in India to create more democratic, egalitarian, and de-racialized forms of citizenship.

# Part II

## Chapter Seven

# Uncertain Origins and the Strategies of Love

*Portraits of Anglo-Indian Railway Families*

To move from the large sweep of history in the first half of this book to the ethnographic encounters with people presented here in the second half involves a dramatic change in scale. Yet this transition is justified by the history previously charted, which showed that nation and race were made part of intimate genealogies and family practices in transactions with the railway bureaucracy. The political legitimacy of the Raj and struggles against it were also played out in a moral register that tied the fate of public institutions to domestic ethics. To be precise, throughout this history there was a politics of scale at work in which intimate practices were linked to transcendent national orders and public practices were fused with microcosmic domestic orders. Through this process railway families have become always more than themselves and have to negotiate not just their economic fortune, but also their place in the national cosmology and moral practices of the bureaucracy. Their relation to history, in particular the history of colonial institutions, has also become particularly fraught because of the ways that the nation and its political communities were embedded in family genealogies in the final years of the Raj. In the chapters that follow the current effects of this history are traced within families that have lived and worked for several generations on the railways. In particular, the ways in which idioms of family, history, kinship, and ethics used by Anglo-Indian and Bengali railway families are a response to interactions with railway institutions is explored. Also revealed are some of the continuities between the moralizing practices of the present bureaucracy and those of the past, which indicate the connections between colonial and postcolonial institutions in India. Finally, the attitudes toward and memories of the colonial past among workers are analyzed. In particular their eerie sense that it is determining or disrupting their lives in the present is explored. At the core of the ethnography, as at the heart of the earlier historical account, are the experiences of Anglo-Indian railway workers and their families. Their situation reveals the entangled history of nation, race, and family, but it also brings to light the diverse family strategies that are difficult to trace from bureaucratic archives and institutional settings alone.

Here I introduce some of the Anglo-Indian families (a later chapter addresses Bengali railway families) that are at the center of my ethnography. My ethnography in Kolkata and Kharagpur began in institutional contexts, but the people I met in these settings drew me into their social networks and domestic spaces. My work began to concentrate on the sentimental and practical life of key families. In this chapter I provide portraits of aspects of their stories of origins, household formation, idioms of affection, notions of relatedness, status anxieties, and material circumstances. From these portraits we gain a sense of a core dynamic within Anglo-Indian railway families shaped by, but using a logic parallel to, the history of pedigree, *jati*, race, and nation within the railway bureaucracy and nationalist movements against it. For these families a strategy of love as the basis for alliances in the present has the potential to found or retrospectively cement genealogical origins. Yet the origins secured by founding marital couples are always subject to the economic fortunes of families. Any loss in income is potentially a sign of the impurity or degeneration of a line. A strategy of self-determining freedom dependent on love alliances and economic fate is underpinned by a fear of choices that will show the essential inadequacies of inherited lineages. In these kinds of strategies Anglo-Indian railway families reveal the particular opportunities and anxieties created by the transformative power of railway employment under the Raj. Economic fortunes, educational opportunities, and domestic arrangements could prove the foundation not just for different class status, but also for a change in the origins of individuals and families. Loss of status could potentially signal a "disfiguring," as Mrs. Packwood put it, a loss of essential being felt in and on the body. The hopes and fears about status that exist in current Anglo-Indian families reflect this history. Yet Anglo-Indians also use idioms and practices that draw on different sources to authenticate their emotional connections and to commemorate their families. In particular they improvise on forms of Catholic worship and concepts of *jati*.

The family portraits of Anglo-Indian families I give here have much in common with the Dutch family portraits and photographs analyzed by Bouquet in that they emerge in part from the self-conscious efforts made by people to make relatedness appear.[1] They are also derived from performances that sought to represent "the family" to me as a place and time of emotion and obligation apart from the public spaces that people move through. But my sketches of families are guided centrally by the specific conventions of Anglo-Indian family portraits that are revealed by the forms of images that are proudly displayed on the walls of their homes.

In Anglo-Indian homes three kinds of images are placed on view. These are pictures of the sacred heart, small statues of the Virgin Mary, and photographs of deceased maternal *and* paternal relatives. These are strung with tuberoses and often placed close together. When incense is lit at dawn and dusk in front of the sacred heart by the wife of the core conjugal couple of the household, portraits of these lost family members become part of the process of devotional worship. One seventy-five-year-old Anglo-Indian woman, Phylis Daniels, expressed this connection in her description of the reason for her devotion to the Virgin Mary: "She is the mother. We all have earthly and heavenly mothers." She was cutting in her judgment of people who changed their religion from Catholicism, because for her this meant that you were abandoning your ancestors and would not meet them once again in heaven. The link between religious and family images in Anglo-Indian families is made explicit in the regular practice of a priest coming into the home on the birthday of recently deceased relatives in order to bless the sacred heart image.

The bilateral nature of these sanctified family portraits is emphasized by a common practice among Anglo-Indians. For Anglo-Indians images of dead parents and grandparents are particularly evocative if they can be rejoined as couples. Single photos of fathers and mothers are given to professional photographers so that they can be manipulated into one image. These images are sometimes startling in their combinations. For example, one woman in her sixties, whose grandmother was Indian Christian and grandfather was in the army and then the railways, had made up an image from her grandfather's military portrait. The final result showed her grandfather on a horse wearing a pith helmet with her grandmother in a sari standing at an awkward angle next to him. In general these family portraits indicate the emphasis among Anglo-Indian families on core conjugal couples who form the origin point of the family with their love and also create the features of the family that mark its boundaries from the world of public and community life. Continuing ties of relatedness within families are made in part around these bilateral and sanctified images, which demand devotion and are manifestations of the idealized devotion of conjugal couples that are seen to be the foundation of kinship connections.

Another kind of portrait hangs on the walls of Anglo-Indian houses, one that is absent from Bengali railway workers' homes. These portraits place living and dead members of the family in the context of institutions. Formal photographs of railway sports teams, work groups, retirement tributes, and most commonly school classes are placed in clusters in living areas. These institutional portraits indicate a common pattern among Anglo-Indians. The participation of bilateral ancestors and relatives in public institutions is produced as evidence of the most intimate essence of kinship and origins. The job status of ancestors and relatives is cited as an indicator of their origins, and people proudly showed me "certificates" from the railways indicating their parents and their own ranks. Similarly, attendance at particular schools is asserted as the sign of the pure Britishness of ancestors and of one's own origins. References to schools attended are used liberally in the context of accounts of pedigree. For example, consider the following conversation I had with Eugene Havilard, a man in his eighties, who had grown up in Jamalpur, where his father was director of stores. I began by asking him about how his family had come to be Anglo-Indian. He replied:

> My father ran away from England to India taking the sea passage because of some family trouble. He ended up working for the GIP [Great Indian Peninsula] in Allahabad. My grandfather's family were descended from Sir William Jones [founder of the Asiatick Society in Calcutta in the 1780s]. My grandfather was not like other domiciled Europeans and he married another domiciled girl. Other Europeans lost contact with their country and married Indian women. My mother's father ran away from England too in just the same way. I was educated in two boarding schools, the Railway School in Kurseong and then Saint Edmunds in Shillong.

He then bent down and took out a cardboard roll from under the bed in which were carefully preserved all his school exam certificates and references from his headmaster and from his early career on the railways as a clerk and, later, as a factory foreman in Bihar. His Indian Christian wife, whose father had worked on the Darjeeling railways and who was listening in on our conversation, added as we looked over the papers, "It's because he learnt Latin at school that he speaks such beautiful English now like a Britisher." In their emphasis on institutions as part of individual and family portraits, Anglo-Indians, unlike other railway families, tangentially acknowledge the role of the railway bureaucracy and its moralities in structuring substances of relatedness and forms of social reproduction.

In Anglo-Indian railway families less formal photographs of living family members are also kept and sometimes collected into albums. These photographs are predominantly of two types: images of family members dispersed abroad and of bilateral grandparents, parents, and the core conjugal couple and their children dressed in style for weddings, dances, and Christmas parties. These are treasured images that people produced as evidence of deep ties of love, and therefore of obligation, that stretched backward in time and horizontally across a range of different contexts, including to other countries. That these images are above all seen as proof of the ties of love that make families was made clear to me by Gavin Jones (40), who was brought up in the railway colonies at Adra and Anara and now works in an English-medium school in Kolkata. When we were looking over his family album he pointed out pictures of old flames of his mother, Marigold, from before her marriage kept among the images. One he turned over and said, "This is one of her beaux—look at what's written on the back." Scrawled in ink was "Yours to the bone." Gavin then said that the real love was between his mother and father. To indicate this, he pointed to an image of them from 1946 dressed to go out, his mother in a wide satin circular skirt and daring short-sleeved top with his father in an army uniform. The ownership of photographs was a source of family disputes. For example, Gavin, while we looked at his album, recounted how a girl who had stayed in his mother's house had been put up to stealing the photos by an Uncle Alvin, who had moved to Australia. When the girl was challenged she said to speak to the uncle on the phone. Alvin then claimed that he had a note from Marigold's dead uncle Spencer (who brought her up) that said all the photos had been bequeathed to him. He swore that they could take the note to a handwriting expert to check and have the paper tested to see what age it was. Under the circumstances they had to give Uncle Alvin some of the photos, but they never felt the same about him again. Photographs of relatives settled outside India (cousins, aunts, and uncles from paternal and maternal lines) were frequently shown to me on first meetings with Anglo-Indian families as evidence of the expansive lateral connections of the household to Australia and Britain. These pictures "proved" the lateral links of the family to places abroad, which retrospectively secured its origin as Anglo-Indian. They also demonstrated the love and, therefore, reciprocal obligation that united it.

The family portraits I offer below reflect the conventions of the presentation of relatedness that are traceable in these photographic practices among railway families. They are also formed in part from my own presence as a particular kind of audience for family stories. I evoked a range of associations for people. For Anglo-Indian families I was a confusing figure. Because I was British I possessed a certainty of origins that was immediately threatening and also attractive. Attractive in the sense that links with me would help them to reconnect to Britain. And yet I had chosen to marry a man from the Ivory Coast, someone who was "of a different *jati*," as they put it. This alliance helped to draw out versions of what it meant to be Anglo-Indian that were less reliant on an idea of a purity of origins. For Anglo-Indian families I did, of course, have an immediate authority due to my access to officers in the railway bureaucracy and my comparative wealth and mobility. In the portraits that follow I describe moments when people signaled the relevance of different aspects of my status to their self-representations of family formation. It is also important to note that in spite of my emphasis so far on the structured presentation of "family," the versions that I give of people's domestic life below are also based on less articulated practices. The time I spent cooking, chatting, and helping with daily routines also meant that I saw other informal aspects of households that are included in these portraits.

## KHARAGPUR: RETROSPECTIVE ORIGINS AND THE OBLIGATIONS OF LOVE

### A Cosmopolitan Family: Abdel and Donna Ahmed

My research in Kharagpur spread along the networks of a railway family, that of Abdel and Donna Ahmed, a Muslim man and an Anglo-Indian woman, who presented themselves as an exemplar of cosmopolitanism in their personal and professional crossing of community boundaries. Abdel was sixty-five when I met him and had retired six months previously from his position as a foreman in the workshops after a lifetime of service. He is the third generation of his family in the railways. Abdel's account of his family focuses on railway work alone as a way of framing his origins. His grandfather started off in the workshops of the Nizam State Railway, moving to Vizak and then the Kharagpur workshop by 1906, where he had a position in the smithing section. Abdel's father was born in Kharagpur and spent his whole life there, rising to the position of superintendent of the tool room. Abdel's extended family had remained a railway family too. Two sisters had arranged marriages outside the colony and moved away to Chennai. His two brothers worked on the South Central Railway; they had both had arranged marriages as well.

Abdel portrayed his father as a great union man, who left work with V. V. Giri in the 1926 strike. He was also a wrestler, and Abdel said that he had inherited his father's strength and love for sports. Abdel loved to describe how as a child he had sneaked into the railway colony and watched the athletic meets from a gully behind the stadium (no non-Europeans were allowed in there). He often joked that the Europeans kept Indians like him out because such Indians were very dangerous fellows; they spit blood—or so the British thought—mistaking *paan* juice for blood. Abdel's nickname among his family and fellow workers, Begum—the honorific name for a Muslim woman, was an ironic take on his extreme sporting prowess and masculinity. Since Abdel is 6 feet tall, well built, and has a dapper black-dyed quiff, the name is obviously funny. Abdel felt that his physical prowess had lifted him out of the boundaries of his community. His skill as a runner and javelin thrower had secured his job in the railways as part of the sports quota, it had led to his meeting and courting his wife Donna (who had been a runner, shot-putter, and hockey player for the railway and other teams), and it now gave him the status to organize the Kharagpur stadium sports club, arranging meets and events. The place that he had stolen glances of as a child was now his own.

Abdel represented himself as an example of the cosmopolitan face of Kharagpur. For him, his own, as he described it, "intercaste marriage," motivated by love, exemplified the modernity of the place. He explained that it took seven years for Donna and him to persuade both of their families that they could marry. Abdel said that his mother had loved Donna from the beginning, liking her long plaits and sweet demeanor but everyone else had to be brought round. Donna had run away from her parents' house in Adra to marry Abdel in a Muslim ceremony, which she described with vivid detail and obvious enjoyment. It wasn't until a year later that her elder sister, a ticket inspector, had brought her to their parents' house for a reconciliation. They had sealed their approval thus: "whatever belonged to me, they gave to me, right from gold, silver, clothes, everything, what is mine is mine." From those possessions Donna had "made her own home." Donna and Abdel's private victory came to symbolize a public triumph as well. Both of them were proud of the fact that they had networks of friends and acquaintances of, as they put it, "all castes and creeds." Abdel was also a skilled "fixer" of jobs in the workshops and helped his subordinates and colleagues to write petitions to appropriate officers. His access to a range of contacts through his management of the sports club also meant that he could arrange all sorts of favors, from securing caretaking jobs in the Railway Institute to smuggling liquor into stadium meets.

Donna was from an equally old railway family and for her part defined her origins through the railway service of her paternal line. As soon as I asked her about her family history she offered to show me the records of her grandfather's and father's jobs, adding that her father and grandfather each got two sets of complimentary passes on the railways. Her paternal grandfather was born in Ambala, worked on the Bengal-Nagpur Railway (named South-Eastern Railway at Independence) as a locomotive foreman in Kharagpur, and then had a stores job on the Eastern Railway in Jamalpur until he retired. Her father was a fireman and then a goods driver in Kharagpur, moving when he was promoted to passenger driver to Adra, from where he retired. Donna was raised in Adra with her five sisters and one brother—Esmarelda, Daisy, Evie, Jonie, Mary, and Lionel. They were all educated in the railway school in Adra. Donna was uncertain about her mother's origins, although she assured me that she went to a good boarding school, Bishop Westcott in Ranchi, run by Protestants and English teachers. She didn't see her mother's parents. Her maternal grandmother died when her mother was very young, and her mother's father, who Donna said was "a pure Englishman, six four in height, massive man, blue eyes," disappeared from her mother's life, leaving her to the care of her maternal aunt. His father had come out to India from Britain, although Donna is not sure how. Donna attributes her own 6-foot frame, pale skin, and brown hair to this lost Englishman. Pointing at my hair, Donna on one occasion insisted, "oof actually the color of my hair is lighter than yours also. Putting coconut oil and all it's turned darker." I asked her if she wanted her hair to turn darker. She said, "No, no. When I was small I had golden brown I was. My sister's children also they are blond and they used to call me straw doll at school."

In addition to asserting vertical originary connections to abroad expressed in physical characteristics, Donna asserted lateral links founded in sentiment. She, like other Anglo-Indians, proudly listed those of her relatives who have settled in Australia and Britain. One of her sisters, Maureen, left for Britain in the 1970s on a "job voucher" gained for her by a sympathetic former boss at British Oxygen. She is settled there now with two sons and an Anglo-Indian husband. Her father's brother, who Donna says had particular affection for her and whose house she was born in, moved to Australia with his wife. Despite her interest in the physical trace of a lost British origin and lateral connections to abroad, Donna also looked for the origin for her own sporting prowess in the qualities of her Bengali maternal grandmother. She said that her grandmother, who was a Ghosh before marriage, was famous for swimming the "gondola," the place where the Hooghly enters the Bay of Bengal. This was the first and only time that an Anglo-Indian mentioned a named Indian relative to me. This perhaps reveals the retrospective effects of Donna's desiring a cosmopolitan foundation for her present life.

Donna worked most of her life in the railway primary school as a teacher. She still tutors students in Bengali, Hindi, and English under the veranda of the railway colony house she and her husband have occupied for the past twenty years. The company showed no signs of turning them out from it, probably because of Abdel's continuing work running the sports club. They had adapted the colonial building to their own needs. The house bulged with a series of ramshackle conversions that overspill the boundaries of the property. Lean-to shacks for chickens, palm-leaf screens, bamboo verandas, and a clay tandoor oven have grown like secretions around its walls. Donna is fluent in Bengali, Hindi, and English and cajoled her students sometimes in a dizzying combination of languages. Even when she speaks in English, Hindi phrases break through repeatedly. Their house had a constant stream of visitors, who greet Donna and Abdel equally with *pranams* (touching their feet in respect), looking for Abdel's help or to catch up on family news. This house has been the home to the two sons of Abdel's brother, Wasim and Manna, who Donna and Abdel have brought up as their own children. Abdel's brother died very young, leaving a wife with three children under ten. In these difficult economic circumstances and because they were childless themselves they unofficially adopted Wasim and Manna. Donna often suggested that their sons have become part English through her influence. Both Donna and Abdel were proud that Wasim was studying for a bachelor's degree in commerce at a provincial college and Manna was working as a secretary in a chemical company for a British boss. Donna, although she hadn't converted to Islam, brought the children up as Muslims in, as she put, respect to their father and mother. Abdel and Donna celebrated both Muslim and Christian festivals. They shared the experience of going on a pilgrimage to Velankanni near Chennai. There, they offered miniature gold discs, a javelin, and a shot put in order to guarantee their continuing athletic success to the image of Our Lady of Health. Both Donna and Abdel explicitly asserted to me that they felt cosmopolitan rather than Indian, Anglo-Indian, or Muslim. Their diverse networks certainly attested to this sentiment, and it was along these links that I moved through Kharagpur. Abdel took it upon himself to drive me on the back of his motorcycle to introduce me to various railway families.

*Family Fortunes and Origins: The Delijahs*

Included among these introductions arranged by Abdel was one to the Delijah family, with whom I stayed during my research in Kharagpur. The eldest member of this family was Harry Delijah, an eighty-year-old retired railway mail driver, who had an English mother and an Armenian father and was born in Iran. He was Donna's brother-in-law through her sister Daisy, who had died eight years before. Now the household was run by another one of her sisters, Esmarelda, who had moved in to help, fulfilling a promise she had made to Daisy that she would take care of the family after her death. Esmarelda had remained unmarried all her life, first assisting her mother in running their household and then after her death working as a matron at Saint Vincent's Technical College in Asansol. The core conjugal couple of this household was now Harvey (55), Daisy and Harry's son, and his wife, Emma (34). They had an eighteen-month-old daughter, Florrie. Also living in the house were Elsie, Daisy and Harry's twenty-five-year-old daughter, and a nephew of Emma's, Carlton. He was just sixteen and hadn't been doing well at school in a smaller railway colony, Anara. As a result he had been sent by his parents to the Delijahs in an attempt to improve him, because they had recently become known as a good, sober, respectable, and successful family.

The large household was supported in some style by Harvey's work as a merchant seaman and by Emma's much smaller salary from teaching in the senior classes of Saint Agnes's Convent School. Harvey was away for six months at a time. He joked bitterly that this was the "progress" with the new generation. His father had been away on runs on the trains for two days at a time, and now he had to be away for six months. But Harvey's salary had bought them all a newly constructed, three-story, grand concrete house with a large walled compound including a vegetable garden. This property loomed above the grassy open ground by Hijli station beyond the southeastern boundary of the railway colony proper. It was near the railway track going south toward Puri, and both Esmarelda and Emma had the habit of breaking off their conversation and naming the timing and destination of the trains that rattled past. Emblematic of the prosperity and respectability of this family was "Emma's Taxi." It was a favorite joke among other Anglo-Indian families that Harvey had bought his wife her own taxi, a dedicated shiny new cycle rickshaw that stood outside the front gate with a permanently hired "driver" for whenever she needed it. This stamped her with a kind of respectability because she didn't have to traffic with the usual rough-mannered rickshaw wallahs.

The economic success of this family gave the members a security about their origins as well. Harry Delijah was the founding figure of the family, and he had had a hard start in life. He was born in 1920 in Iran, where his English mother and Armenian Christian father had a farm and an orchard. His mother and sister died when he was very young, so when he was five years old he was sent with his three brothers to Armenian College in Kolkata as a boarder and then to Saint James's School, where, he proudly told me, the principal was an Englishman. He only saw his father three or four times in his life after that, when he visited India. Harry left school at fourteen to become a grade one apprentice at Kharagpur. He had been offered a post as an apprentice driver because he had been such a good boxer. He was the all-school boxing champion, and his face shows the marks of his bouts with a flattened nose from one fight. His life story centered on his affection for the work of driving trains and the physical bravery it required.

Harry's somewhat obscure origins didn't concern the family at all. His son's prosperity had secured the status of all the household's members. This had been sealed by his marriage to Emma five years previously. Emma was well known as a very respectable girl whose stature was signaled by the fact that she worked with the nuns at Saint Agnes's School and had agreed to marry Harvey on their recommendation. She was from a renowned "pure Anglo-Indian" railway family from Chokradapor and Adra, and her father had been very active in Anglo-Indian Association events in both places. Harvey and Emma's sumptuous wedding in the local Catholic church because of Harvey's good salary had been, as other people put it, "just like a foreign wedding, just like abroad." Other families told me that they regretted that they had not been able to marry off their sons to Emma because of her unimpeachable character and pure Anglo-Indian background. The more gossipy ones among them said that the whole Delijah family's declining fortunes had been reversed because of Harvey's job and his marriage. They suggested that no one would look at him before he started work "on the ships" because of his shady origins and advanced age (he was fifty when he married Emma). The close interconnection of economic fate, reputation, and advantageous family alliances indicates, as the family portraits on the walls of Anglo-Indian homes do, the centrality of conjugal couples in forming the nature of kinship and origins within households. There is a retrospective respectability of origins according to the success of the core couple and what their bilateral union creates as the substance of kinship. Family portraits look different according to their progeny. What is important is less the source of your own, your parents', and your grandparents' birth identity and more the alliances that you can make during the passage of your life. Your acquired connections to institutions also alter your status. The walls of the Delijah family's living room had pictures of Harry in front of his engine, Harvey in front of the railway school at Kharagpur with his classmates, and Emma posed in a photograph outside her school in Adra. However, lineage reckoning of course does not disappear completely in this process. It was, after all, Harvey's ability to draw Emma's unimpeachable background into the family that secured its status.

Although the Delijah family does not figure as largely as some other families in the chapters that follow, the time I spent with them affected my interpretations in many ways. From them I learned the everyday practices of being an Anglo-Indian family. The routines of Catholic worship in the home, the emphasis on food and cooking on the *chillah* (hearth), and the texture of teasing affection inform the interpretations of mine that follow. Esmarelda prided herself on her ability to command the *chillah*, and with no maid's help; like her mother before her she cooked what she called "typical Anglo-Indian" food for the whole family, tutoring me in its finer points while often assuming that dishes I had never heard of were familiar to me from Britain. Esmarelda and Harry joked about things that would be considered inappropriate for elders to talk about in Bengali railway families. For example, they laughed about the scandalous "midnight man," who they insisted used to frequent Adra. He would dress in "full black" and would turn the lights off in the railway houses and sneak in to "play a joke on everybody." Once, a driver left to run the Chennai mail, and the midnight man jumped down from an upper balcony into his house and startled his wife. When wives were in their nighties and dressing gowns he would pass remarks through the windows. Once, when a wife of a driver was getting her husband's tiffin box ready, the midnight man grabbed her and kissed her. He would jump out in front of people when they were making love, but no one could catch him. All the boys in Adra tried to get him but he always disappeared. As demonstrated by the above conversation, all family interactions among the Delijahs were marked by a striking teasing informality, explicit gestures of affection, and lack of hierarchy, although it was obvious that Harvey and Emma determined all financial matters. Everyone insisted that it was ties of compassionate love that united them. Esmarelda and Emma would cajole Florrie in a mixture of English and Hindi, calling her "Buddhu, Buddhuma," meaning "our sweet little silly one." The nursery rhymes and fairy tales they told her had Indian inflections—Jack falling down and "breaking his topee," the three bears that lived in "the jungle," and Ring-a-Ring-a-Roses ending with the phrase "Aasho, Basho, all fall down." These experiences were echoed in other Anglo-Indian homes and inform my overall interpretation.

### The Dilemmas of Love and Vulnerable Status: The Vanjos

Also particularly significant for the chapters that follow is the Vanjo household. Clarence Vanjo, whom I first met with Abdel in the Catholic graveyard crying over his wife's grave, lived in Choto Tangra in a rented three-room flat perched at the top of a precarious external staircase on the third floor of a concrete building. Choto Tangra is halfway between Hijli and the railway colony. Near the Vanjos' flat is the Waldorf Chinese restaurant with its frontage of red dragons. This and the name, little Tangra—the name of the Chinese district of Kolkata, preserve the memory of the 1930s, when the railway imported Chinese workers from the city to work during strikes at the workshops. Clarence said that his flat was owned by a landlord who, unlike many others, wasn't fussy about renting to a Christian family that eats beef. He had moved there on his retirement as a railway guard five years previously from his railway colony flat with his wife, Milly, three daughters, Mavis (28) Marcie (25), and Paula (23), Paula's son, Johnny (4), and his mother, Lotte (80). In the year previous to when I met him his wife and his mother had died in quick succession. The family supported themselves on Paula's work as a secretary at the Tata Ball Bearings factory north of the colony and Clarence's pension. Mavis and Marcie had worked as teachers in Saint Agnes's Convent, but they had left their jobs because they were both recently married and were waiting to join their husbands, Samuel and Julian, who lived in London. For the moment they stayed at home with their father and helped look after Johnny. Clarence's son, Leo (38), had moved away to Kolkata, where he was doing well in a junior marketing job for Dunlop. He was unmarried and committed to leaving behind his Anglo-Indian status. I once traveled on the local train to Kolkata with him, and he told me that he never told anyone he was Anglo-Indian. He had made a point of studying all the works of Vivekananda and Ramakrishna and reading the literature of great nationalists so that he could become as Indian as possible.

Clarence, in contrast to his son, insisted on his Anglo-Indian status and made sure that the domestic rules followed what he said was a British pattern. No one took off their shoes at the door, they served as mild food as possible, and his daughters, unlike Donna, for example, never wore *salwar kameez*. Mavis and

Marcie also made every effort to respond to me in the same clipped English accent I used, which they said they had picked up on their trip to Southall in London, where they met their husbands at an Anglo-Indian dance. They gave Bible readings regularly in the services at the Catholic Church, and their accents became even more pronounced in this formal setting. Clarence founded his family in his grandfather, who he said was Dutch, and his father's mother, who was Portuguese Goan. None of the current family members had ever met the grandfather, but they had met Clarence's grandmother, who was a "lady doctor" in the military. She worked in Rawalpindi, but after partition she was stuck there and it was hard for them to see her. Clarence insisted that although people think that his name is a Goan name, it isn't; it is spelled differently and is a "rare name." He proudly added that you can't find any other Vanjos in Kolkata, you can only find relatives of his in England. One of them, he claimed, was a famous opera singer from Kolkata, Kenneth Vanjo, who is now settled in London. He argued that it was obvious to anyone that he was different from a Goan because of the way he spoke English. Whenever we talked about his family he said that his grandmother used to have all the family papers. Every time she visited she brought them in a roll, but she took them back to Pakistan; Clarence mourned the fact that these were now lost like his grandmother's fortune in property and diamonds. She used to bring diamonds for his mother whenever she visited. Clarence would say sadly that the papers and property were all somewhere in Pakistan, along with his grandmother's grave. which they couldn't even see.

Clarence grew up in Kharagpur with his six brothers and two sisters, and they all went to the railway school. His father had founded the family in this place, working as a guard all his life. Clarence was silent about his mother's family. In compensation for these silences and the Goan associations of his name he emphasized his lateral connections to abroad. Two of his brothers left in the 1960s for Britain, and one for Australia. His daughters had cemented these overseas connections by their recent marriages. Clarence said that he couldn't leave when his brothers did because someone had to take care of his mother, and she didn't want to see the family broken up by migration. In fact, both he and his sister Loretta said that the great love within the family was a kind of hindrance. It would have broken their mother's heart if they had all left, and now Mavis and Marcie were ambivalent about leaving to join their husbands because they loved their father, sister, and aunt so much. Mavis and Marcie both pointed out that they had only married their husbands once their mother had died. Like the Delijahs they insisted on the ties of love between conjugal couples and between parents and children as the foundation of kinship ties. This compassion could draw waifs and strays into it, incorporating them into the family. Clarence told of how his mother at one point rescued an old man who had been abandoned by his family, welcoming him into their circle; he had even lived with them too. Donna and Esmarelda told me similar stories about their mother, who had taken in unrelated people when they had hit hard times. This act was an ideal because it exhibited the same kind of compassionate love that was at the foundation of the notion of relatedness in Anglo-Indian families. It had primacy over any other kind of "biological" or "natural" connection of blood. However, the love for parents was consistently strained by love between newly formed conjugal couples, which would found new kinship units and points of origin. Mavis and Marcie were caught in the crux of this problem in an extreme manner. Their moving to Britain would bring them economic opportunities, potentially give them a new, less ambiguous identity, and would retrospectively cement their family of birth's origins. However, it would also stretch the ties of affection within their family of birth to the breaking point because they would move far away from this family. The emphasis on love as the substance of relatedness, which made social mobility and fluidity of status possible for Anglo-Indians, would always be haunted by the potential severing of ties with families of birth.

Importantly, both Clarence and his daughters' accounts of their affiliations to abroad and "caste" identity became more complex once they knew of my marriage to a man from the Ivory Coast. When I finally plucked up the courage to tell them about my husband, Clarence laughed and said, "Oh now you've joined our coloured caste. He's black almost like us, we're black. You should have told us before." This blackness had some positive associations for Clarence because he was a great jazz enthusiast and a skilled clarinet player who practiced two hours a day trying to emulate great African American artists. This fact about my marriage also drew out a new line of conversation with Mavis and Marcie. Mavis described the range of relationships that she had considered before marrying her Anglo-Indian husband, Samuel. Her first relationship was with a Goan, who was "too fast for her liking." Then she moved to an Anglo-Indian, Jonathan Hall, who was "too handsome for her to trust him." She was then engaged to a Keralite Christian, "one of those dark types," as she put it. She said that she had always wanted to have children like those you would have with a "West Indian cricketer with tiny plaits and ribbons in their hair." But his family objected, and she didn't want to marry without the family's approval. Keralans, she added, were very strict about arranged marriages and dowry. She also went out with an Iranian boy from the Indian Institute of Technology in Kharagpur, who was now in the United States. He had wanted to marry her too, but she was nervous about it. She didn't want to go to the United States and leave her family and India. Finally, she had fixed on Samuel, whom she met at the Anglo-Indian dance in Southall, but who unfortunately had been married to her mother's sister thirteen years previously. This marriage had broken down many years ago. Mavis emphasized that Samuel had pursued her to India after she refused to marry him, showing the depth of his love. Mavis's descriptions of her options show both the range of alliances that are possible for Anglo-Indian women and the constraints on her "choice" placed by other families and her own fears of breaking her ties to her immediate family. Alliances involved a complex weighing of the value of old and new ties of sentiment, their potential permanence, and their impact on one's past and future sense of self.

After Marcie had heard about my marriage, she wanted to tell me about the complexity of her husband's nature and of the traditions that graced her wedding. She described how Julian's father had moved to Kenya from Goa in order to escape caste prejudices and high dowries in Goa. He didn't want his children to grow up in Goan society so he took his wife to Africa. Julian was born in Kenya, but just before Independence his father was determined to leave and moved to England. There, Marcie said that they were brought up in "a nice colony full of only Britishers." Julian now says to her that the only thing Goan about him is his name, although when "he went to Goa he couldn't stop eating the Goan food—this in inborn." Marcie joked that Julian had now become too British—he is "too liberal." Yet Marcie added that Julian had married her in the "African way" at the registry office in Kolkata, putting the wedding ring first on her thumb, then her middle finger, and then on her marriage finger, reciting "in the name of the father, son, and the holy ghost." Both Mavis and Marcie, after they had heard about my own, to them, dramatic alliance through marriage, told stories that expressed the complexity of identities formed by affiliation and the passage of one's life. These were meditations on how much would be altered through these processes, what would be lost and gained, and the limits also placed on this passage by other people, essential natures, and the ties of love to families of birth. They revealed the complex calculations of affiliation and sense of potential becoming that structure Anglo-Indian marriage choices. Once again lineage and essential natures do not disappear from these calculations, but they are foregrounded and made material by present actions and choices rather than guaranteed as preexisting qualities. This makes the process of choice and daily mode of living full of heightened consequences.

## Wild Men and Holy Women: The Campbells

The Vanjo family was linked by marriage to Colt and Loretta Campbell's household. Loretta (58) was Clarence's sister, and they had a close and affectionate relationship. Colt (65) was retired when I met him. He had worked the trains with Clarence, as a guard and then as a loco inspector who scrutinized the safety of the trains along the line. He also knew Abdel well, and it was Abdel who first took me to meet the Vanjos in their rented bungalow, named Dolly Villa, close to Hijli station. This was a rather grand title for the whitewashed single-story building with three rooms, but the Anglo railway family that had built and christened it had ambitions of having a peaceful retirement there. There are ten such villas in the area built since the Second World War for similar reasons by Anglo families. Loretta and Colt loved to sit outside the cramped rooms of the bungalow on charpoys under the veranda with their pet parrot, Polly, squawking in a cage above their heads. Often at the house was a quiet boy of seventeen, Terence, who never spoke to me other than to greet me. The gossip in Hijli claimed that this boy was Colt's son by his Telugu maid, and that Colt and Loretta had taken him in because the Telugu community had forced them to in the courts. Loretta and Colt never explained his intermittent presence. Colt usually wore a Stetson-like hat. This was one in a long line of hats that he had worn since his youth in Kharagpur. When I asked him how he got his name Colt, he answered: "from CKP [Chokradapur]. I was very fond of Western books and I always would wear my hat. I used to have a Stetson you know. Now I couldn't get one from Australia when I visited my sister there, so I've got this one. Normally I had a straw one. One of the Anglo-Indian girls there in CKP christened me with the name, used to call me Colt." Colt consciously founded his rabble-rousing masculinity in the frontier, outlaw identity of cowboys. It was this rather than his family's origins that shaped his account of his life. He briefly told me that he thought that his mother's family was Dutch, the Van Aftens, and that his father's grandfather was an Englishman who came out to India in the war. He didn't know which war this was. His father was a head train examiner in Kharagpur. But Colt spoke more about his "wild days" and the trouble he had caused Loretta, his "holy woman." The complimentarity of holy women and wild men that both Colt and Loretta placed at the heart of their bond to each other was a recurrent idiom in Anglo-Indian marriages.

At the Bengal-Nagpur Railway European school, as he called it, Colt described how he was: "a bit of a rough fellow, stealing their tiffin, hiding up their books, always trying to get into a mix up. I was always fighting; I was always aggressive. I always used to walk about with a chip on my shoulder. I got into scraps always at dances—take a little extra [drink], have a little extra and you're looking for someone to fight with." As he grew up he continued in this vein. He boarded with Donna and Esmarelda's family in Adra and eloped with their sister Jonie to Bankura. He sneaked her into the guard's van, but the family had "put the word out," and he was arrested at Bankura and put in jail. He also killed his best friend in a fight when they were drinking and was almost convicted for murder. Colt spent a Christmas in jail in Midnapur, but he was eventually acquitted by a judge. When I met him he had given up all drink because his wife had gradually become ill and he wanted to be in a fit state to look after her. She had been off her work as a teacher at Saint Agnes's Convent for a year due to her diabetes and high blood pressure.

Loretta defined herself in relation to her husband's cowboy persona as a counterbalance to it. Unlike her brother Clarence, she appeared uninterested in telling stories about her father's origins. More important to her was her Catholic faith and the way it linked her to her mother's compassion. For Loretta, Catholicism provided the medium and the idiom for healing ties of love in families and wider communities. Loretta claimed that it was her faith and love that had helped reform Colt. In this she followed the pattern of many railway wives. She also felt that the saints, especially Our Lady of Velankanni, and her daily prayers to the sacred heart had helped her get better during her recent time in hospital. When her mother died, Loretta held a special mass at her house for the family and friends. This was because her illness had become worse when her mother died: "I couldn't go to the cemetery. I took very bad. I felt worse than ever." A huge crowd turned up and showed how much her mother was "loved." Loretta said, "I was shocked when I saw the crowd, didn't expect so many, a whole crowd full of Anglos. After that I began to feel much better, after the mass. Oh yes she was loved." The expression of this love in the form of a Catholic ritual had a healing effect on Loretta, just as she had healed Colt with her holy love. Loretta felt that her faith made her just like her mother. Her mother above all had this quality of overflowing affection. When one of her sons died at twenty-one she spent the rest of her life grieving for him. She wouldn't send any of her children away to boarding school and was heartbroken when two of her sons moved to England. Loretta said that her mother "would never part with us. She didn't want to part with any of her children." For Loretta this sanctified, healing love connected to the religious community of Catholicism is the substance that underpins and makes families.

## Scandals at the Margins: Santa Barbara

Close to Loretta and Colt's house, along a winding mud path through an *adivasi* village, was another cluster of Anglo-Indian homes, known as Santa Barbara. The name comes from the American soap opera and signaled the fact that the goings-on there were as scandalous and steamy as in this TV show. It was also known as a mini-Australia for its reputed loose morality. Santa Barbara was a mud-brick compound with burnt-umber walls streaked with yellow clay. There was no nameplate or number labeling the gateless entrance, just a break in the curving facade that opens on to a wide, undefined courtyard shared by the five families and three elderly single men who lived here. Abdel was hesitant to take me there at first because it has a dubious reputation. He and Colt warned, or perhaps teased me, that a Bengali girl from a Kolkata university had gone with a clutch of surveys to the compound. They told me that all the Anglos had been drunk on a mixture of country and foreign liquor. According to them, once you give Anglos this then they get all "mixed up" too, like *kichuri* (a Bengali dish of rice and vegetables), and they "mixed the Bengali girl up too."

Santa Barbara was owned by Hamish Thomas (32), a local passenger-train driver. Hamish's grandmother had bought the land in the 1930s and built the compound for Anglo-Indians to live in. There was a small open air chapel at one corner of it where his family worshiped. Clarence Vanjo described Hamish to me ironically as "a new British species, with his long hair and strange ways." Hamish organized dances and Christmas Trees (children's Christmas parties) for Anglo-Indians in the compound, which are renowned for the fact that alcohol is allowed, unlike in the Railway Institute dances. He lived in his part of the compound, a small three-room hut, with two young women, both of whom were rumored to be his wives, but I never confirmed this. He rented the other huts with lean-tos to Anglo-Indian and Indian Christian families. He proudly claimed that he is the one who is attracting all the Anglo-Indians back to Hijli from all round the world, including the elderly man, Jigger, who lived in two rooms in the compound. Everyone loved to tell the story of how Jigger used to live in Australia but never did a stroke of work in his life, even there. Hamish planned to build a dance hall at Santa Barbara so that the community has a center for socials. He called himself "the Don, the good Samaritan, the Godfather," but he also knew that people told all sorts of "bad stories" about him. All the inhabitants of Santa Barbara knew that the place was called that and seemed unperturbed by the seamy reputation produced by the rural environment and relative poverty of some of the inhabitants.

When Colt and Abdel did take me to Santa Barbara I was greeted at the entrance by Hamish Thomas, Gracie and Freddie Dover (in their 60s), and Celia Junshon (30) and her brother Tony (25). Hamish, Freddie, Celia, and Tony were noticeably drunk. Celia immediately complained about the Bengali girl who had turned up with all her forms asking them about their antecedents, and she added proudly that her grandfather was of French descent. Each time I went to the compound Celia and Tony challenged me, asking what I was going to do for the Christians. Celia joked several times that the only thing I could do for them was to have a marriage of convenience and take her brother back to England with me. The family from Santa Barbara that is particularly important for the following chapters is the Dover family. Gracie and Freddie lived in a four-room mud house with their son Joseph (30), who is a goods driver, and his wife, Maggie (28), who teaches at Sacred Heart School at primary level, and their six-month-old granddaughter, Violet. Freddie retired as a mail driver five years previously, and Gracie made a little money from sewing and tutoring. They had brought up their son and daughter during an itinerant career in Chokradapur, Rourkela, and Kharagpur. Gracie identified herself as an old-fashioned up-country railway girl brought up in Chokradapur who is just "a country bumpkin." She said that she was brought up strictly by her parents, who made sure that she was home before the "street lights burnt." Gracie was happy to reckon her lineage as an Anglo-Indian along matrilineal lines. She told me soon after we met that her father was a Goan mail guard, and his grandfather was famous for being the oldest living Goan. Her mother she described as an Irish Piggot. Her strikingly fair skin, she suggested, showed this lineage clearly, although she was unsure how any of her Irish ancestors had come to India. Freddie was born in Mumbai, and his Anglo-Indian father wrote dance music. His mother died when he was six, and he and his three brothers were taken over by her sister and sent to boarding school in Asansol. Freddie, rather like Colt, defined himself by his rebellious streak and the pleasure he took in his work. He told me of his schooling at Asansol, describing it as a place full of Irish priests. They were very strict, and he was a naughty boy. There, he learned "all British history and Latin." When he reached twenty years old, in 1952, he joined the railway at Chokradapur. He said that his work was his pleasure. This family, as we will see in chapter 10, like other Anglo-Indian families, defined itself around practices of Catholic worship and supernatural tales of ghosts, which gave the family members roots wherever they lived.

### The Dangers of Love and Origins Under Threat: The Dovers

The family of Freddie and Gracie was linked to another household that is central to the chapters that follow. One of Freddie's brothers, Clive, was married to Hope until his death two years previously. His death had left Hope (41) and her four children who still live with her, Roger/Raja (19), Henry (17), Joycie (9), and Tarzan (7), in a very difficult financial situation. They eked out a living from Freddie's pension and the intermittent income of Henry. He worked sometimes as a driver's assistant on long-distance trucks and occasionally as a waiter. Hope's eldest daughter, Serina (25), had escaped this household by her marriage to an Indian Christian, Sam, who is a traveling ticket collector. I first met Hope in the Kharagpur railway offices while she was attempting, as she put it, to "petition" Mr. Bal, the head of personnel, for jobs for Roger/Raja and Henry. I had been talking to Mr. Bal about everything from the value of magical rather than social-ist realism in literature, on which he claimed to be an expert, to the benefits of railway jobs. Periodically he had picked up the phone and barked orders in Hindi and English to various subordinates. One of the peons had knocked on the door and hovered by it once Mr. Bal asked him to enter. The peon told Mr. Bal that Hope Dover had come again. There was marked irritation and impatience on Mr. Bal's face. He called Hope inside, and she explained her case in pleading phrases while she stood by the door. She wanted her sons to be granted jobs through the family quota on compassionate grounds because their father had died. She looked like an ancient schoolgirl in a short, flowery frock with her thin, curly hair cascading to her shoulders partly hiding her wrinkled face. Mr. Bal instructed her in a condescending tone to come back in a couple of days, adding that he doubted anything could be done because her husband had been retired when he died. As soon as Hope left I made my excuses and went into the corridor to look for her. She reminded me vividly of Mrs. Packwood, and I wanted to speak to her. Hope immediately offered an invitation to her house in Hijli for lunch the next day. No doubt my access to Mr. Bal and my Britishness both led to this, and her consciousness of my status affected all of our conversations.

Hope lived in a four-room shack by Hijli station beyond where the electric poles go and where local villagers pick over piles of coal looking for scraps to burn. A rusted iron girder propped up one of the leaning yellow mud walls, but there was a painted metal sign on the shack that proclaimed proudly in white paint, "Mr. Clive Dover, ex-Railway Driver." The interior whitewashed walls were stained from the leaking roof and kerosene stove. The furniture was makeshift, with cushions and cloths thrown over metal trunks to serve as tables and chairs. Above the bed that Clarence and Henry slept on in the living room was a shelf on which a small statue of Jesus offering his sacred heart stood. The only photos on the walls were Hindi film posters of heroines. Hope, when I first visited her, did show me a collection of photos of her paternal relatives abroad in Australia and a studio portrait of her daughter Joycie dressed in Western clothes and holding a handbag, which she said made her look "just like a European." Joycie slept in the next room with Hope, and Tarzan joined them between terms at Saint Thomas's Kidderpore in Kolkata. The loss of Clive and the general insecurity of income in the family had created emotional and financial chaos for Hope, Serina, Clarence, and Henry. In their accounts of their situation they reversed the forms of Anglo-Indian relatedness. Marriages, rather than founding families, were described as prisons, as full of conspiracies over resources, as marred by violence, and as full of threats. The love that ties families together was seen by this family to be potentially damaging as well. In the context of the ambiguity of the love between the core conjugal couple, Hope and Clive, and the loss of Clive, the "good" origins of children were no longer automatically guaranteed. Instead, negative as well as positive traits could be inherited "naturally," and children could threaten the purity of their blood by their behavior. Economic instability in the family and emotional conflict within it led the Dovers to unravel the forms of relatedness that underpinned other Anglo-Indian families. This can be described as an unraveling because it left them feeling surrounded by an immoral, predatory chaos.

Hope was unflinching in her descriptions of her marriage to Clive. She told me that she was married to him when she was fourteen. She didn't want to marry him, but her brother who worked with him was in favor of the match as were her mother and father. Clive first tried to court her sister, but she married another man. Hope claimed that he kept returning to their family to find a bride because he wanted to "marry some good Irish blood, the McCoy family, not bad like this Indian blood." Clive pursued her for five years, but, not surprisingly since she was so young, all she wanted to do was go out and play "with her *chota* [little] Bengali girls" in Kidderpore, where she lived with her parents. At the wedding ceremony she threw the ring back at her husband and said that she didn't want to go with him. She refused to go to his house for six months, but she was forced in the end to join him in a small railway colony at Waltair that was "full of Oriyas," as she put it. She felt very isolated there. At that time her Hindi was bad, because she had attended Saint Thomas's Kidderpore, where students were taught only English. She and her husband moved after a year to Kharagpur. She said that the railway colony was "like a prison—I was serving a sentence there. I couldn't roam about freely like in Kolkata." She left the colony as much as possible, going back to the freedom of Kolkata where she could "roam the streets and have something to watch, even just the trams." Hope described her marriage as being founded on coercion rather than complimentarity. She also felt that her "Irish blood," rather than being a founding attribute of a productive relationship in the present, had trapped her in an unhappy union. Thus, she reversed the usual image of the core founding couple.

Clive was twenty-two years older than Hope and a widower. He had given up his children by the previous marriage to his parents. Hope's relationship to this abandoned family and to her in-laws she described as a drain on the family's resources and as full of threats to her and her husband's physical integrity. She said that Clive's parents tried to "conjure" her when she went to live with them when she was first married. She said that they took "one mometer [*sic*] for taking temperature" and fed her mercury from it three times. She claimed that they had in fact killed Clive's first wife. She was going to have a third child and they fed her something to get rid of it and she went into the hospital and died. Clive's children had turned out to be a different kind of threat because of their immoral behavior and financial demands. Clive used to give them handouts. He gave his daughter money for a trip to Canada and to leave the "useless" men she took up with. Hope described this daughter as "a low person who lived with a Mr. Ghosh on Ripon Street and then with an Anglo chap." The son was a "topper," or waster, who drank, smoked, and swore. These stepchildren still bothered her.

Clive had left her without any papers for the house or land, and the stepchildren were mounting a court case to make a claim to the property. They also had all of Clive's bank account papers. Hope felt that they were just waiting for her to die. At times she also suggested at times that her son Roger was in league with them and they all wanted her to sell the house.

In Hope's account of marriage and family all the substances that are supposed to guarantee the foundation of an Anglo-Indian family had proved unreliable. Her Irish blood had only brought the prison of a marriage against her will. The integrity and financial well-being of the family founded by a core conjugal couple was threatened by previous, abandoned families. Ties to affines had become difficult to negotiate. Hope saw her parents-in-law as actively hostile because they succored this abandoned family rather than supporting the newly founded one. It is not surprising, therefore, that Hope reversed the usual values and insisted on the dangers of too much sentiment between husband and wife. She often congratulated her daughter Selina for not noticing when her husband went away on line duty, saying that was just how she and Clive had behaved. Hope also liked to suggest that Clive's death wasn't so hard on her because they used to go their own way and do their own things, although, as we will see in a later chapter, the family's stories about Clive, his death, and his ghost suggest that this lack of sentiment was not the whole story. However, at an explicit level Hope regularly contrasted her family to the De Souza's. She would then describe how one day this couple was at home when the wife died in the bathroom of a heart attack; the husband, seeing this, died as well. This was for Hope an example of the lethal consequences of too much sentiment. For Hope, if there was a sentiment that bound the family together, it was her love for her children. She constantly said that she was motivated by "love for my babies" alone and that she would do anything for them. She explained that this was why she was so thin, from denying herself food, and why she would never touch drink and go astray. She would sacrifice everything for the respectability of her children. For example, she said she often went hungry so that her daughter Joycie could have good new clothes, because otherwise some man would tempt her with offers of them.

For Hope the general chaos of the family's fortunes and sentiments led to ambiguous inheritances and left individual family members open to pollution. In her accounts she made explicit the links within Anglo-Indian families between ideas of origins and notions of *jati* that I later followed in other contexts. She was very proud of her youngest son and granddaughter. Tarzan had received his name because he was so like a European. According to Hope he was very fair and only liked to eat bread. Her granddaughter she proudly described as calling her and Clive "father" and "mother" in spite of her actual origins in the union between Serina and Sam. She also described happily that when they called her granddaughter a black baby, meaning a black sheep, she always crossly replied by pointing at her "fair" hands and saying "No, I'm not black, I'm fair, see," adding "I'm English—don't call me Oriya." Hope said this caused problems with Sam and his parents because they felt that somehow she was making her granddaughter, as Hope put it, "ashamed of her *jati*." But other members of the family were imperiling everyone's reputation. Roger, in particular, had inherited, according to Hope, all his father's violent temper. This led to him hitting her for money and accusing her of "eating up daddy until he died." Not only this, but Roger was threatening the purity of the family's blood by his behavior. He had, according to Hope, all sorts of bad habits. On one occasion she characteristically described these as follows: "He only studied to class eight. He goes round to an eighty-year-old woman's house. She is known as 'Alice in her palace,' and she entertains all the young boys with music and cigarettes. She blackens up her eyes and has a good figure bloated from drink." Hope was most worried that Roger would catch leprosy from Alice's son-in-law who lives with her, whom he helped to bathe. Hope feared that if Roger got infected everyone would think that it was due to something "bad in his parent's blood," and it would affect all of them. Leprosy as a disease particularly frightened Hope because it implied a moral infirmity rather than a physical one in the family's blood. Overall, her and her family's few claims to status and origins are under severe threat. Their present circumstances threaten to undermine the reality of any of these and might lead through Roger's actions to a disfiguring of their reputation.

Roger, Henry, and Selina offered an equally bleak image of their circumstances and of the ties of sentiment. When I asked Selina to write down an account of her life, she gave me a third-person account of the degeneration of the Anglo-Indian community in which she described how husbands beat wives, wives had affairs, and sons beat mothers. Henry said little to me, but one day I arrived at Hope's house to find him lying on the small bed in the living room looking ill. Hope began to explain that he had "shot his liver" by taking a blue stone in one of the stores in Gol bazaar. She added that she thought it must be because of some girl that doesn't want him, that was what the rumors were saying. Roger said that was wrong and that Henry took batteries because he was experimenting to see what would happen if he ate them. Henry quietly said that wasn't why he did it either, he just got to thinking too much without any work to do. Roger confided in me and a male friend who accompanied me on some trips his rejection of sentiment and frustrations that someone who was descended from *sahebs* couldn't get any work. Roger told my friend that he had given up on girls and love. There was one he had liked, but she had turned him down, and he had decided not to have girlfriends, only to go to prostitutes. He then described how in Sonagachi in Kolkata you could have a woman do everything for only 45 rupees. He also said that he and Alice got drunk together and had fun looking at pornography. He was scornful of Hope, suggesting that since she couldn't even show affection to the family dog she could never have shown affection to her husband. He claimed with bravado to my friend that he had been interviewed by the local *goondas* (criminal bosses), who asked him if he wanted to trade in blue films or drugs with them. Roger complained that it was impossible for him to get any other job because as an Anglo-Indian he didn't have any backing. Yet Roger would always try to claim back some status of origins by asserting proudly that his father always told him that he should remember that "we used to rule this place and we were *sahebs*." The nickname that he had given himself of "Raja," which was used by all his young Indian friends, reflected this sense of entitlement. Each of the children sought in their different ways to escape their fragmenting family, which was splitting apart as a result of the ambiguous sentiment of the core conjugal couple and economic difficulties. Selina had done this by marrying an Indian Christian, Henry by attempting suicide, and Roger by seeking an "unrespectable" life opposed to familial sentiments. It is perhaps not surprising that in the Dover home there were no family portraits proudly displayed on the walls.

## KOLKATA: SOCIAL MOBILITY AND THE RAILWAY COLONY *DESH*

In Kolkata I followed the extended networks of Anglo-Indian railway families by looking for people who had left the colony behind. I often found railway families by tracing them through the circuits of institutions that were set up for them under the Raj: the Anglo-Indian Association, the English-medium schools, and old people's homes created to solve problems of "pauperism." It is only these colonial institutions that Anglo-Indians feel are "their" public spaces and in which they collect. These institutions are also important for an analysis of Anglo-Indian railway families because they are and have been intimately connected to the broader process of family formation and kinship among Anglo-Indians. Boarding schools, "orphanages," and old people's homes are as central to the life cycle, notions of relatedness, and creation of Anglo-Indian families as the railway colony domestic unit. My research in Kolkata was initially an attempt to learn as much history as possible and to locate railway Anglo-Indians within a broader community of Anglo-Indians, but my conversations led me to pursue it for other reasons. On the one hand the families in the railway colony could not be understood without tracing their connections to their relatives and to these institutions in Kolkata. On the other, it emerged that for Anglo-Indian families in Kolkata the railway colony as a place of memory and conceptual space gave families a kind of foundational point of origin, a *desh*. Anglo-Indian accounts of railway colonies were equivalent to the stories of the family *desh* told by other urban groups in the city, such as Marwaris and Bengalis. These specific associations with rural places are the foundations for the regionalized forms of nationalism that are characteristic of many lower-middle-class and middle-class Indians.[2]

The profoundly industrial space of a railway colony was associated with a rustic simplicity. A teenage Anglo-Indian girl told me she visited her aunt there because it was lovely and peaceful. Railway colonies were known as places filled with "up-country girls" in particular, who were homely, respectable, and simple in their habits, and who didn't have to take jobs outside the home but knew how to stand beside the kitchen fire and work hard. When I visited the railway colony at Adra with the Jones family from Kolkata, they were shocked by the changes, but they immediately started to think up schemes for buying land on the outskirts of the colony to build a home. When we visited their old servant in a compound just outside the boundary of the colony, Gary Jones (the forty-year-old father of the family) was silent with emotion for a while. Then he said with regret and longing, "At least they have this. What do we have? Nothing."

Ironically, stories about Hijli pushed all of these associations up a notch, and all railway families seemed to have heard of it. I was told that in Hijli there was a true Anglo-Indian *para* (neighborhood) of about forty families, who lived among *adivasi* villagers. People would add with wonder that they were not only people who still worked on the railways or had retired from them, but also that there were Anglo-Indians who had chosen to return from Australia, New Zealand, and Britain to settle there. Given the general desire to seek greater economic and educational possibilities abroad common among the lower-middle and middle classes in Kolkata, this was truly astounding for people. It stood as proof not only of the attractions of the place, but somehow also of Anglo-Indians' ultimate attachment to a peculiarly Indian mini-England. Here was evidence that there was a way to root Anglo-Indians in the landscape of India among *adivasi* villagers. Most of all, Hijli was described as a place where there would finally be a point of rest encompassing a neighborhood, a community, Anglo-Indian culture, and an Indian place. Here was an extraordinary thing, an Anglo-Indian *desh*.

Yet Kolkata railway families also argued that the railway colony was now in inevitable decline. They had to escape it because if they had stayed there they would have been at risk of degeneration. This threat reached out to them in the city in the form of obligations to family "left behind" in or retiring from the colony. These relatives jeopardized the status and economic well-being of the family members in Kolkata, often turning up at their houses in the city asking for support. As a real place in the present, rather than as a site of nostalgia, the colony had to be escaped. Strikingly for my research, even though these families had attempted to leave the colony behind, their forms of genealogy, notions of sentiment, and anxieties about origins are marked by railway morality.

The Kolkata railway family that appears most often in the chapters that follow is the Jones family. They and their extended set of friends and relatives became central to my research. The oldest member of the family was Marigold Jones (60), the widow of Gerald, an Anglo-Burmese railway driver. She had her home in a six-room flat on the outskirts of an old Anglo-Indian neighborhood near Park Circus, which is now predominantly Muslim. The flat was arranged as a long corridor with rooms leading off it. It was crammed with heavy sofas and a dining table and was scattered with what Marigold called the "all-English" toys of her grandchildren. Presiding over the corridor was a large image of the sacred heart with a small shelf for incense underneath it. Marigold spent most of her time at home looking after her youngest grandchild, Getrin, singing him nursery rhymes such as "Here we go on a frosty morning" and telling him stories about the three bears that got lost in the jungle. She frequently scolded him, saying, "Baby Jesus is angry with you. Yes, he is crying. Don't be dirty." Marigold shared the cramped flat with one of her two daughters, Paula (45), who was unmarried, two of her five sons, Ronnie (35) and Charlton (25), their wives, Gail (30) and Diana (21), and their three children who were all under seven. She brought up Paula, Ronnie, Charlton, Neil (32), Gary (42), Gavin (40), and Shila (28) in railway colonies at Adra and Anara. They all went to the local railway schools at primary level and then on to Catholic boarding schools in Jamshedpur and Entally.

All of the family, apart from Gary and Gavin, had gone to Kolkata on Gerald's retirement fifteen years ago. Neil had immigrated to London six years previously. Shila had married a Bengali man. Gavin and Gary moved to Kolkata before the rest of the family, to work as teachers first in Frank Anthony School and then Saint James's School (both English-medium schools), when they were in their twenties. They had trained to be teachers at Mount Hermon College. They had separate flats near their mother's home. Although there had been a split between Ronnie and these two brothers (which I never found out the cause of), family members, including Shila, were frequently in one another's homes. Marigold's household ran on the income of her pension, remittances from Neil, Ronnie's job as a computer-booking reservations clerk in the railways, and Paula's job as a school secretary in the Jewish School. Although all of these members of the family as well as its extended network are important to the interpretations that follow in the rest of the book, here I will concentrate on Marigold, Gavin, and Gary as exemplary of their general approach to origins, relatedness, and the railway colony.

Marigold began the story of her origins from the point at which she was adopted by her father's younger sister and her domiciled European husband, Spencer, when she was six years old. They had settled in Adra, where Spencer worked as a loco inspector. Each time her aunt went home to Secunderabad, where her father worked in the railway workshop, she took back one of her brother's many children. First came Joseph, then James, then Marigold, and finally her younger brother, George. Marigold never told me her parents' names or those of her two sisters who remained with them. Nor did she give me their genealogy, preferring to emphasize the fact that Spencer was a pure Britisher who came out from England during the First World War with his brother in the Cheshire regiment. She said that the love of Spencer and her aunt Gloria for her and her brothers made no distinction between them and their own daughter, Josephine. Marigold said, they "treated me the same as Josephine, just like we were twin sisters. My uncle would dress us in the same material made into the same dresses." This identical clothing and quality of love bound her into the household. As I discuss in the next chapter, these things also began to affect aspects of her origins as an Indian Christian. Marigold proudly told me that she and her siblings were legally "fostered" by her uncle and aunt, so they "were given all facilities, could go to the railway school, get traveling allowances." Marigold brought this adoption to the fore when trying to assert her origins. She never explicitly told me that she was Indian Christian, but I inferred it from things she omitted and other people told me.

This same quality of love bound her to her husband, Gerald. She had met him at Adra at a social evening during the Second World War. He had been evacuated from Burma with one of his aunts and joined the Air Force of India. As a result, he was posted from "station to station just like a sailor" and went to Adra. One of Marigold's girlfriends brought her a message from him that "he gave his love to me. He kept haunting and haunting me." This persistent love paid off, but her reputation had to be endorsed before they could get married. Gerald's auntie was against the match because Marigold had a reputation for being a flirt. She took a character reference from the local Catholic priest. Marigold also gave me another kind of character reference by telling me that before Gerald, a Scottish boy named MacIntyre who was in the Royal Artillery wanted to marry her. She underlined the fact that he was a "foreigner" who felt "true love" for her. She had kept a memento of this potential, verifying connection to abroad all her life. It was the photo that Gavin had shown me of one of her "beaux" in the album with "Yours to the bone" written on it. Marigold also suggested that her marriage to Gerald was bound by a complimentarity. Marigold described how she soothed Gerald's bad temper and kept the family together with her love. Gavin, her son, emphasized how their educational success and mobility had been achieved by the moral example of their mother, who had loved them all so much she had scrimped and saved to send them all to boarding schools. His mother, he suggested, also stopped his father from drinking.

For Marigold, Catholicism had played a much greater role than just certifying her reputation. It underpinned the bonds of family life and allowed an acknowledgement of relatedness that was in shadow in other contexts. She described how Spencer converted to Roman Catholicism so that they could be "all one family," and she said that the "family was very religious, saying grace and doing their religious duties." This practice had continued in her alliance with Gerald, and the family would all get together without fail on Sundays. Religion was so important as the foundation for family sentiment that her daughter Shila had kept her tie to her family of birth within her new Bengali family of marriage. Marigold recounted proudly how, "when Shila was pregnant and couldn't go out to church, her Bengali mother-in-law told her to make a Christian altar in the *puja* [worship] room." Significantly as well, Marigold's only remaining link to her Indian Christian parents until they died was that she returned to Chennai for the feast day on September 8 of Our Lady of Health at Velankanni. She described with joy how she and all her brothers and sisters would be reunited with their parents in the nine days of prayer before the feast. Her children continued the association of Catholicism and family ties. For example, Gary said, "My family's not, what shall I say, a family that always carries the rope or shows people seeing the rosary. What I mean to say is that a family that stays together prays together. If you want happiness to remain, mother and father have to be ideal examples, and we have been given a proper religious background by our parents, and my mother is very holy." Like for Marigold, for Gavin Catholicism cemented the family, authentically sealing its sentiments and connections, rather than being part of an outward show of status.

Marigold's sons were less comfortable with their mother's life story, with its two beginnings, a barely acknowledged one in Secunderabad with her Indian Christian parents and another one foregrounded in Adra with her domiciled European uncle. They strongly emphasized their paternal line, alliances by marriage, appearance, and links to a railway colony *desh* in order to assert an essential "Anglo-Indianness." Gavin (38) lived with his wife, Carol (35), and their three children, Isolde (16), Lorissa (10), and Theodore (7) in a crowded four-room flat (the children sleep on a converted veranda). It was at the top of a precipitous staircase in a concrete building near to Beck Bagan and Park Circus. The tiny living room was full of heavy sofas impractical in the heat and a giant dining table. The heat in the flat increased when Carol cooked for the family on three roaring gas stoves hidden behind a thin wooden partition with a giant dresser wedged against it. On the wall above the dining table was a photo strung with tuberoses of Carol's father, Robert, holding a gun with a dead panther at his feet. Above the doorway was a sculpture of Jesus' head and shoulders with his heart bleeding and exposed. In the next-door room, where Carol and Gavin slept, there was a small house-shaped shrine with clay images of Jesus and Mary. The household is supported by Gavin's income as a schoolteacher of the senior classes at Saint James and Carol's job as a secretary at Dunlop.

All of the family members were meticulous about their appearance, tailoring their clothes according to the latest fashions on Sky TV and in imported magazines. I only once saw a family member in Indian clothes. This was when Christine dressed for a work colleague's wedding in a bright red chiffon sari and giant paste earrings. They also treasured any food that was obtained from abroad and hunted for recipes for making their own versions of foreign products unavailable domestically, such as Bailey's Irish Cream. Gavin was extremely proud of Carol's strikingly beautiful appearance and her fair skin, long dark hair, and green eyes. He loved to tell stories of how Carol was mistaken for a foreigner by taxi drivers and the touts at New Market. He teased her affectionately, saying that her face is his fortune, or maybe his misfortune: fortune because it inspired his love and increases his status; misfortune because it led her to aspire to the expensive tastes of Europeans. He especially made this comment when she returned from extravagant shopping trips. Carol mourned the fact that Theodore's blue eyes, which he had been born with, turned brown later. She proudly told me that her grandfather was a German diamond merchant who settled in Gorakpur in a grand house with lots of land. She added that he married a fourteen-year-old Armenian girl in an arranged marriage. This was why her father was very fair with blue eyes; she added, "I don't know where all this fairness has gone in my children, but their children might be fair in the next generation." However, her unimpeachable "Anglo-Indian" background and appearance bathed the family in reflected status. This is the reason a photo of her father had pride of place above their dining table. This connection to abroad was also asserted in their emphasis on following foreign fashions; this continued a family tradition. Marigold described how when she was a teenager she used to get the local tailor in Adra to make dresses from saris in the latest magazine styles. Gerald, according to Gavin, also used to get all his smart clothes sent to him from his grandmother in England.

Gary and Gavin both maintained a silence about their mother's parental line. Each time I asked Gavin about his family history he offered to write a family tree for his father, but he claimed that he didn't know anything about his mother's background. He then recounted that his grandfather, whom he had never met, had a British passport, that his father's brother lived in Baltimore, and that his father's sister married a Britisher. He obviously felt uncertain about this origin point as well, becoming quite stiff when I asked if he knew how his grandfather had gone to Burma because he couldn't answer the question. He also insisted that he could prove this line, but he didn't have access to the documents far away in a Somerset House in London. This uncertainty was counterbalanced by his nostalgia for the old Anglo-Indian community in Adra and Anara and his assertion that this was a place where origins couldn't be "bluffed." He recalled a childhood of summer holidays spent in the colony playing sports, celebrating Anglo-Indian Association events, and going to dances and on picnics. In the colony also, he insisted:

> You couldn't bluff in those days because families were so close knit. Like in a place like Calcutta you can bluff and then later on only start checking. But in a railway colony you couldn't do that, because each one knows who your grandparents were. Now my mother grew up there for forty years or fifty years so she definitely knew who the father was and who the grandfather was and who the great-grandfather was. Also the railways asked for your baptismal certificate so they checked who you were.

Gary expressed similar sentiments of nostalgia for the railway colony. Gary lived in a small three-room flat with his wife, Sandra (35), daughter, Ranya (16), and son, Randolph (18). Ranya and Randolph slept in the small living room over which a new TV with a cable connection as well as a sacred heart presided. Sandra had previously worked as a secretary but now stayed at home because of her periodic bouts of "depression." Randolph worked for a travel agency picking up tourists from the airport and making sure they got to their destinations. The household was mainly supported by Gary's work as an English teacher at Saint James. Gary's nostalgia for Adra was intense. He rhapsodized about the freedom he had as a child to run about in the open spaces of the loco section of the colony, hunting with slingshots and riding the train into villages, spotting the "Colgate girls," or women who brushed their teeth with sticks at the side of the tracks. This last image was an important and funny one for him that drew a stark distinction between the consumption habits of Anglo-Indians living in an industrial context and those of Indian villagers. Even the graveyard was a place of fun for Gary. There, the boys would crouch behind gravestones to watch the "courting couples"; these were often their own railway school teachers, so they "couldn't take them seriously after that."

Despite these happy recollections, Gary and Gavin shared a sense that the contemporary railway colony and the Anglo-Indians who had remained in it were in inevitable decline. For example, Gavin insisted that

> the ones that have left, like me, have done better. Their childhood was spent in the railway colony—ethics, habits, work habits were much better and now they can easily adjust. But the ones that have stayed on there have become relaxed because I feel they have nothing to live for. . . . If I had stayed on in Adra I would have been the same as them. They can't see a future. They can't see a future for their children.

This ambivalence had its source in the fate of their relatives "left back" in Adra. Marigold's brother, George, who had married an Indian Christian woman, Sonya, had been a worry and financial drain for the family. Until the time that all the family had left Adra and the nearby Anara for Kolkata the family, according to Gavin, "kept an eye on his drinking." But once they had all left George had no one to, as Gavin put it, "keep him in check," although they still sent him money. His health steadily declined, and he had died the previous year. They still as a family contributed to the upkeep of Sonya and her son, Bastian. Another relative from Adra provoked similar anxieties. Leslie (65), a divorced and recently retired mail driver who was Sandra's mother's brother, often joined Gary's household. Gary and Sandra told me that they had to go to Adra and "rescue" Leslie from a death from drink when he retired from the railways. They pointed out that his two brothers had died on the job from liquor. Yet Leslie was a direct encroachment on their space and resources. Often I would turn up to find that they had sent Leslie back to relatives in Adra or to his friends in Kharagpur after quarrels over his behavior and drinking. They did, however, always take him back because of their love for Sandra's mother. Both Gary's and Gavin's stories of decline in the railway colony were linked to their ambivalence about these poor relations, who would encroach on their respectability and family resources.

Marigold's family was attempting to remain on the path of social mobility she started when she was adopted into her domiciled European uncle's family. Gary and Gavin were in particular trying to leave behind her origins in an Indian Christian family. To be Anglo-Indian meant access to places kept on a quota for the community in Catholic and English-medium schools. Gary had also become the education officer of the Anglo-Indian Association. Both Gary and Gavin accrued tremendous amounts of respect and status through their work as teachers in Saint James, where they were well known and popular. But their attempt as a family to become increasingly Anglo-Indian through education, appearance, and marriage was more than a strategy for economic gain. This was a desire for a comparative certainty of origins and respectability learned in part from the experiences of their mother and father in railway contexts and their own childhood spent in the railway. This strategy of mobility now had an added feature; they wanted to escape the degeneration of the contemporary railway colony experienced as the decline of relatives who drew on their resources. As later chapters show, the anxieties that motivated Marigold and her family are both specifically their own and related to the wider public institutions and history of the railways.

Marigold's old age was being spent at the heart of her family, but some elderly Anglo-Indian women from railway families found their last home in the charitable institutions set up under the Raj to end pauperism. One such woman was Phylis Daniels, who was seventy-five when I met her in the Tolly Homes.

I frequently visited her either in her partitioned cubicle decorated with family photographs or in a three-room house in the grounds, designed for married couples, where Phylis was staying to help look after a friend who was dying of breast cancer. Phylis had moved into the Tolly Homes four years earlier after her husband, Horace, had died and her adopted daughter (her maternal cousin's daughter), Clare (25), had married a Muslim man and joined his extended family. Phylis had been born in Jamalpur, where her father worked in the loco workshop, and she had lived much of her life there. When her father had retired the whole family had moved to Entally, in Kolkata. Shortly afterward, Phylis had married Horace, who was a clerk in the stores department, and had gone back to Jamalpur with him. They had lived in Kharagpur, Liluah, and Howrah as well. Once Horace had retired, they had returned again to Kolkata, this time to Tiljoya. She described the colonies she had lived in as completely "European," and she mourned having to move finally to Tiljoya: "Tiljoya is wild—the Indians were very bad there. I had to be very strict with my daughter. If she had been from another caste she could have gone wrong. We weren't badly off, though—my daughter didn't turn bad. But other Anglo-Indians couldn't cope when they moved from the colonies. They would throw themselves on the tracks near the houses in Tiljoya."

Compensating for the circuit of movements in and out of various railway colonies that characterized her life, Phylis anchored herself and her family origins in a continuity of Catholicism transmitted through the generations. She explained to me that her father's name was Flury, that his family was French, and that he had come out from France to India. She added that her mother was already out in India, her name was Murray, and her father was European. Quickly, she insisted that "because of my father's and husband's certificates from the railway, that's why I can hold my head up." She continued by saying that her husband's people were "Irishmen," and their name was Hancock. But Phylis smoothed over these varied series of origins and the passage of her life by arguing that she and her family shared a permanent quality of Catholic faith. Phylis insisted that she had wanted to become a nun when she went to school in Entally Convent. This statement linked her to her father's uncles and aunts, most of whom had become nuns and priests. This plan was thwarted by the man who became her husband, but as we will see she still anchored her family in Catholicism:

> I was that holy type, you know what I mean . . . I would never get married to a man, but what to say, I was thinking that. Then my beautiful . . . my husband . . . I saw him on the top of a bridge near Entally Convent and from that I loved him. So I got married to another man's son instead of God's son. I loved him and still I love him. . . . From Tiljoya I had to go

that way and he had to go this way, so I said the devil and the angel are going. . . . I'd say cheerio devil and he'd say cheerio angel.

The only quarrel in her marriage had come when her husband had converted
to the Assembly of God Protestant Church in order to get educational, medical, and other financial benefits. This was an enormous breach for Phylis. She
explained:

> I used to go to the services, but I did not join and my daughter did not
> join. I suppose it's because of the ancestors none of us went another road
> and we were all Roman Catholics. I won't change because that is what my
> ancestors worshipped. . . . We dote on Mother Mary. We have our sacred
> heart and pictures of Mary. She is the mother. We all have earthly and
> heavenly mothers.

Later, a further breach in this family linked by Catholic worship occurred when
Clare converted to Islam, married her Muslim boyfriend, and threatened to raise
her children outside Catholicism:

> I am very hurt with my daughter. . . . The Priest has said that he is going
> to stand and let the children become Catholics now. They are going to be
> Catholics—that's good enough. How many years I've prayed with tears in
> my eyes, yes, darling. I was so worried because our link would have been
> broken among us, like my mother, my father, we would like to be wherever
> we are going all together. Whether we go to heaven or hell, that's the thing
> you see. When it's another caste and another religion, no, no, it breaks the
> ties.

Now in her old age, Phylis revived the presence of her dead family members by
a regular routine of worship, punctuated by offerings to the statue of Mary that
has been set up in the Tolly Homes and by various prayers for certain times of day.
As we will see in the chapters that follow, in her insistence on the connections between family ties and Catholic practices she was far from alone. Phylis made plain
the centrality of Catholic idioms to Anglo-Indian concepts of relatedness.

## SUBSTANCES OF ANGLO-INDIAN KINSHIP

Overall, the substance of love as an emotion, in particular the affections of the
core matrimonial couple, has primacy in defining Anglo-Indian railway families

and their intimate space. This love is both a sentiment and a strategy. It is a strategy because it demands obligations, as in the Vanjo home and Hope Dover's unwanted marriage to Clifford. It is also a strategy because the ties made by love between members of core conjugal couples can retrospectively reshape family origins and status, as we saw in the Ahmed, Delijah, Vanjo, and Jones households. When it is experienced as a sentiment, love is often sanctified by association with the healing love of the Catholic community and seen as emanating from women, as we saw in particular in the Vanjo and Delijah homes. This focus on the female generation of bonds that create families is also reflected in a bilateral reckoning of origins.

What is striking too in all of these family portraits is how origins and essences are constantly at risk in the daily life of families. There is an acute awareness of the necessity of "proving," maintaining, and cultivating these through economic means and personal performances. These performances include a straightforward guarding of respectability as in Hope's account, assertions of affiliations to guaranteeing institutions as in all the families described here, and the use of clothes and consumption as signals of affiliations to foreign origins as in the Jones family. When economic life becomes hard and sentiments are unclear, as in Hope Dover's family, origins are at dire risk from the behavior of all the family members. On the margins, in environments that appear profoundly non-British and nonindustrial, such as Santa Barbara, everyone assumes that the people who stay there are marked by an impurity and unrespectability. Yet this equivocal moral status too helps to partially associate them with the loose morals of "abroad" and is sometimes celebrated as confirming their origins in another less respectable manner. These tensions in Anglo-Indian families between desires for certain origins with time depth and more fluid strategies of love and performance have developed in relation to the practices of pedigree, domesticity, and education in the Raj railway bureaucracy. In particular, they have grown out of the conflict between the class mobility offered by railway employment and the limitation of this by the management of labor along lines of race and community. We can see the anxieties and hopes manifested in Anglo-Indian railway families as a historical outgrowth of the railway colony, railway schools, and employment hierarchy described in previous chapters. Yet the authentification and emotional grounding of family bonds relies on an improvisation on Catholic concepts and idioms of *jati*, which were not part of the railway's taxonomies. The following chapters explore these themes further in relation to family histories and the local micropolitics of belonging in the railway colony and bureaucracy. These discussions focus more centrally on tracing the impact of the politics of scale in which the moralities and origins of families have been brought into relation to the past and future fate of the nation.

*Chapter Eight*

# Traces of the Archive

*Documents, Bodies, and Nations in Anglo-Indian*
*Family Histories*

Icelight. It's that slippery, spermy light that comes just before dawn. . . . But what good is it, you may ask; does it pay the rent? It does in a way. It freezes time, or rather, it traps it at that tremulous point just short of freezing, when time is neither solid nor liquid but simply a quality of light. It comes at the edge of sleep, when all those vivid fragments from the past float up to the surface hard and real but running away like lumps of ice. It allows you to get the past down, to copy it, after it's actually melted away. And the past alone is true. It's my livelihood anyway. Sans Souci for instance—that's our ancestral home—I rebuilt it by icelight.

—Allan Sealy, *The Trotter-Nama*

Anglo-Indian author Allan Sealy begins his novel about the history of an Anglo-Indian family with a narrator, Eugene Aloysius Trotter, who earns his living making convincing copies of eighteenth- and nineteenth-century miniatures. Trotter has invented an authentic school of his own invention, the Kirani School. His pieces end up in museums with authoritative labels and high price tags. The Kirani School we later learn is that of Indo-Portuguese clerks, "miserable scribes, mere copyist . . . pen-pusher . . . member of a caste neither here nor there; country-born Christian . . . all of the above applied to Anglo-Indians generally."[1] The art of the modern miniaturist, we are told, is that of endless repetition, but never the imitation of the world or rendering of reality.[2] Sealy's novel is a kind of literary archive in which we encounter a series of "documents" from precolonial and colonial history. Examples include "Lines in Praise of Nakhlau (*from Qaiym*)," "Entry in Jarman Begam's Diary for June 21, 1799," "Extract from *Gypsy General: The Life and Adventures of Michael Trotter, Irregular Soldier,* by Maj-Genl. Victor Cholmondley, V.C., London, John Eames, 1911," and "Forecast of a Plague of Dust (Proceedings of the All-India Pantheosophical Society, Nakhlau Chapter,

1873)." Seductive in the authenticity of their historically appropriate language, these documents refer to nothing but the fictional reality of an imaginary family's history. They provide proof for a plot that is revealed at the end of the novel as nothing but a tale of an "Agent-and-guide." The authorial voice says in exasperation, "What to do. People want to hear stories about places so you make them up. . . . So if they want all that bloody past-fast rigmarole I give it to them. All the monuments Imambaras Big and Small . . . tell you the truth I made up the whole line—I mean joining up all those Trotters like that. Funny bloody story, more holes than cheese in it."[3] Included in this novelistic archive of fake but "authentic" documents are real colonial documents that are rendered untrue by the narrative. The "Extract from the Minutes of Evidence Taken Before the Select Committee on the Government of Indian Territories," with its essentialist account of the racial characteristics of Indo-Britains, is met by disbelief from the imaginary audience for the chronicle, the Cup-Bearer.[4] Sealy's literary history of an Anglo-Indian family plays with an instability between history and fiction.

As we will see in this chapter, this atmosphere of instability surrounding an Anglo-Indian family history is not a general tale about the duplicity of records or of archives as a technical prosthesis of an always elusive memory.[5] It is formed from the particular Anglo-Indian experience of loss and of longing for a documentary past. Anglo-Indians, especially those from railway families, desire an archive and feel a sense of mourning when it is not present. They hunt for documents or other kinds of evidence in the body that will physically anchor their accounts of the past and of their own origins. They are anxious about the possibility that others will think them inauthentic. They are also surrounded by a sense of uncertainty about their own existential connections to Britain and India. These dispositions have been shaped by the historical moment described in chapter 6 in which a time depth of family origins proved by documentary evidence began to be used by bureaucracies and political organizations to parse citizens from noncitizens and to trace the boundaries of communities. This process has, I will argue, made it difficult for Anglo-Indian family histories to be rendered in anything other than "icelight." Anglo-Indians remain in an unequal relationship with an elusive past and point of origin, both of which seem to melt away and to become unanchored in the present.

## PRESENT-ORIENTED HOUSEHOLDS AND THE DESIRE FOR DOCUMENTS

In the previous chapter we traced in Anglo-Indian households a fluid reckoning of family relatedness based on core conjugal couples and a strategy of love infused with Catholic idioms. This fluidity is linked to another feature of Anglo-Indian households; they are primarily focused around present-oriented ties of sentiment and nurture rather than ideas of deep lineage duties of care toward certain defined relatives. In fact, we might be tempted to see Anglo-Indians as another example of the fluid concepts of relatedness described by Carsten for Lankawi Malays or Lambert for Rajasthan.[6]

This present-oriented logic contrasts dramatically with the legal constitutional definition of Anglo-Indians, which employs a restrictive genealogical and patrilineal logic. Following the colonial ruling made in 1919 in the context of defining separate electorates, Anglo-Indians are classified as those with a European relative in the male line. Within Anglo-Indian marriage practices, there is an idea that echoes this legal logic that lineages of "Irish," "French," "German," or "British" blood make certain spouses, especially female spouses, attractive. This no doubt reflects the advantageous life chances that have been available to the offspring of such marriages since the 1870s in India. Although it was not until 1919 that the legal lines of the community were strictly defined, the children of such marriages would have had easier access to the European educational institutions that were founded in the 1870s. The idea of preserving bloodlines has taken on some *jati*-like features too, with marriages sometimes being semiarranged between friendly railway families through introductions at dances or other social occasions. However, railway Anglo-Indians do maintain a present-oriented emphasis even in the calculation of bloodlines. The desired match is not, and has not been in the past, with a foreigner, but with someone of known background. Friendships between families led them to try to make matches between their offspring. Parents also let it be known within the community of railway families across several colonies that their child was seeking a partner. Priests and nuns acted as matchmakers across colonies as well. The ideal marriage occurred with someone who had an element of European "blood" in his or her lineage, but the current characteristics of their family had primacy in these decisions. This restores a present-oriented emphasis to the calculation of potential ties of affinity. Marriage alliances were and are ideally built on the basis of relationships and family position in the present. A substitute for this could be marriage to a female ward or orphan of a reputable convent school. The institutional origins and membership of the community of the church would counteract any fears about or deep reckoning of such a woman's origins. The most risky kind of marriage was and is that to foreigners or unknown strangers. Despite their apparent purity in terms of bloodlines, the current nature of their family was not known. In the past, this fear extended to marrying British workers in the railway colony or British soldiers met at dances. For example, Marigold expressed this risk to me in the following terms: "To tell you the truth I was afraid to marry a foreigner because you don't know what his background was. My sister-in-law was in the WACI [Women's Auxiliary Corps India] and married a man from Liverpool and they went to live there. But he had a stroke and she was left looking after him and one Mongoloid child that they had together." So even though Anglo-Indians do talk of a reckoning of or continuation of bloodlines in the formation of ideal marriages and of biological risks, their primary emphasis is on a fluid notion of households founded in the present. As we will see, in other areas too Anglo-Indian family structure and kinship links reflect an expansive bilateral definition of relatedness formed from the sharing of food and sentimental ties in households.

For Anglo-Indians food is both a visceral and emblematic sign of their cultural identity that can be transmitted between generations and is a medium that creates relationships. Male and female family members nurture an Anglo-Indian culinary repertoire of typical dishes that includes Marie Rose biscuits, fruitcake, and spiced dried ham at Christmas and rice and ball curry. Women, including Esmarelda and Donna, often showed me their family recipe books in which secret dishes are passed from generation to generation. Anglo-Indians often joke, saying that we are "spicy like our food." Food is used to distinguish Anglo-Indians from other groups. For example, Marigold described how her British uncle, Spencer, "would only eat stew, but we used to eat pungent food because we are Anglo-Indians. To look at his food only we would get sick. His roast had to be uncooked—how dirty it was." Other Indians were distinguished by their dislike of Anglo-Indian eating habits, especially the consumption of beef, and by their distinct regional cuisines. All of the families I met in Kharagpur recounted how difficult it was for them to rent outside the railway colony or to find playmates for their children because landlords and neighbors didn't like "beef eaters." Freddie Dover even argued that the reason Anglo-Indians were chosen for railway drivers was because they were willing to eat beef and therefore wouldn't care when they ran over cows on the track. This would mean that the trains could keep running. Leslie also insisted that the physical superiority of Anglo-Indians and their fitness for engine work was based on their culinary habits. He asserted that Anglo-Indians had always been chosen as drivers because Indians did not have as much stamina: "Look what they eat. Bhaji, bhat, and dal, like the Indian flag, only." Leslie made food, referring to the colors of the various dishes—fried vegetables, rice, and dal—as echoing the orange, white, and green of the flag, into a medium that produced physique and national identity. The distinct features of various regional communities were also seen as a result of their food habits. Clarence Vanjo and his daughters had extensive discussions about the various mortalities and progressive characteristics of communities. For them, Marwaris were fat because of all their rich food laced with ghee, and the Vanjos suggested that they died young as a result of these food habits. However, they argued that Bengalis were more progressive because they were fish eaters and they were healthier. Overall, the Anglo-Indian culinary repertoire is one that defines their cultural and family essence.

Food also makes bonds between people in households, ties dispersed families together, and changes the essences of people. Even in wealthier households, women prided themselves on doing the cooking themselves rather than leaving it to maids, because this act of caring unified the family. Anglo-Indian women, such as Donna, Esmarelda, and Carol, often distinguished themselves from other Indian women by their ability to stand by a chillah and cook. Maids were employed by better-off households, but only for washing, sweeping, and occasionally chopping vegetables. For example, Donna related how she grew up in Adra:

> We never depended on servants, Laura. We had our own portion of work. No servants. My mummy was a very good cook. Then Esmi took over when mummy was taken ill. Everything my mummy prepared—sweetmeats, food, everything—nothing that my mother didn't know. Outside food we never ever bought from outside, prepared everything. We all sat together at the dinner table; dinnertime we must all be present.

Extended families, who live in different households, are bound by eating together on Sundays after church. Reflecting this sensibility, Marigold charted the decline of her family's closeness since Gavin and Gary quarreled with Ronald in terms of the fact that they no longer ate Sunday lunch in unity. People expressed their continuing relationships with relatives living abroad by sending them elaborate food parcels. Colt and Loretta described to me in great detail the masalas and dry items that they sent regularly to Colt's two brothers in Australia. They implied that these were necessary to their relatives' well-being. Nonrelated individuals were incorporated into households through the medium of food. I was absorbed into families in Kharagpur by both eating with them and later cooking with and for them. Adopted children became like their adopted parents through sharing food. Donna, for example, told me how Wasim (her husband's brother's son who she and Abdel had brought up) had a British boss, "a pure Englishman from London, and when he heard my son talk and saw his ways and habits he thought he was just like him. So my son told him his mother's name was Donna." Donna went on to say that this recognition of British-likeness in her son on the part of his employer was because of her "training and food."

This logic of essences and ties created through food could be used to assert connections between people and places. Many Anglo-Indians told me that they would not settle abroad because they could not eat the food there. For example, Colt and Loretta insisted that they couldn't settle in Australia because they couldn't stomach the food. Colt explained that when he visited his two brothers, who have settled there: "I couldn't eat. There's no taste. I lived on chocolate and baked beans. The bread, the rice had a funny smell. Everything had that smell. I told my brother I couldn't live there because of this." For Colt, it was food that tied him to a particular national location. In all my conversations with him the only context in which he expressed a sense of belonging to the territory of India was in relation to this idiom of food. Others reversed the same logic to suggest that they could only eat British food. For example, Eugene Havilard, describing a trip to London in the 1920s, said, "I picked up English food habits, though I ate curry and rice before I left. The ship on the way back stopped in Sri Lanka; I tried the curry and somehow didn't like the taste. Even once I got back to Calcutta I didn't like it. I'm now a mince-and-mash man—no rice, no dal." This, like other people's use of food to bind families and to connect themselves to Kharagpur, transformed his temporary connection to Britain into a permanent link manifested in personal taste. In the settlement of Anglo-Indians in Hijli, on the outskirts of Kharagpur, people attributed their essential nature to drinking the water of the place. Wells in that area were polluted with diesel from the refueling of trains next to the settlement. Although richer people used water delivered by the *bhisti* (water carrier) from outside, poorer families cooked with the local water and everyone bathed in it. This gave the food a distinct flavor, and washing felt like dousing oneself in diesel. People there suggested that this water gave them particular characteristics. For example, Hope Dover suggested that consumption of the well water made all the Anglos roundabout "full of steam." For Anglo-Indian families, identifications, links to family members, and connections to places are forged through the visceral medium of food.

This fluid and present-oriented logic of connection, like the sentiment of love and idealization of core conjugal couples described in the previous chapter, gives structural priority to the emotional ties formed in particular households rather than to some abstract moral duty of care to particular categories of relatives. The ties that are made in childhood houses to the people in residence there are those that ideally persist through life.[7] On the railways these households center on the conjugal couple. Newly married people, if they have railway jobs, can immediately form an independent couple and live apart from their in-laws. Yet often when the husband's or wife's parents retire or one of them dies, they join one of their children in railway accommodation, or, if this residence is not large enough, they all form a household in private accommodation on the outskirts of the colony. As we have seen in the family portraits in the previous chapter, the constellation of relatives around this core couple varies immensely according to sentimental ties formed in childhood households. Both maternal and paternal unmarried, widowed, or divorced relatives often join this core couple for periods of time when they are financially insecure or can help with the family chores. People are likely to provide a home for any relatives from either side that they have developed close relationships with in childhood. Sometimes this extends to any Anglo-Indian in need. As we saw in the previous chapter, people recounted taking in unrelated Anglo-Indians who had fallen on hard times. Shelter was also provided for children of both the wife's and husband's brothers, sisters, and cousins. This occurred if they lost their parents but also happened often as a means to advance the education or life chances of the children. This expansive bilateral reckoning based on affective household ties gives particular weight to fraternal and sororal connections. These provide networks that crosscut families of marriage and link them to families of birth. Married women adopt their sister's children. Brothers and sisters of the wife in a family go to live with her. A woman's uncles or aunts from both her paternal and maternal side may join her family of marriage. Brothers and sisters of both husband and wife are regular social visitors to houses and take part in Sunday lunches, sacred heart celebrations, and All Souls' Day visits to graveyards.

This bilateral reckoning complicates inheritance, leading to many different people asserting rights to property and goods. Carol, Gary's wife, was involved in a complicated family dispute of this kind. Her grandfather's property in Gorakpur had been taken by the government, and she was busy trying to mount a case against them to reclaim it. She had also been told that she was related to a person called Major Cranfield and should be entitled to his property as well. But the missing pieces for making her case were family documents and birth records, in particular, she said, the baptismal certificate of her father's brother. But unfortunately, all of these records were in the possession of her mother's sister who lives in London. She would only release the information to her mother's side of the family, not to the children of her marriage. Carol said that this was because she was intending to mount a rival case for ownership of the property.

Bilateral reckoning also makes affinal relationships and mother-in-law and daughter-in-law relationships tense, as such connections do not have automatic priority.[8] A typical example of this friction is the account of Phylis Daniels, the seventy-five-year-old woman I met in the Tolly Homes, of her relationship with her mother-in-law. She and her family had lived most of their lives in the railway colony at Jamalpur, where her husband was a locomotive inspector. She had been educated there and in Loretto Convent, Entally:

My husband was very attached to his mother. My husband, I couldn't say a word about it. My mother-in-law made a lot of mischief, Laura. When he came from work she used to start with him. Different things what she didn't like. I didn't do anything for her. We lived in the railway quarters with her and my mother and father. Even about them there used to be terrible rows,

darling. . . . I knew she couldn't stay with us, because there would be hell-
ish things, so she moved to Saint Vincent's [an old people's charity home]
and she lived to 104 years; she had 21 children. When she died that hurt my
husband. . . . I can't forget. Aren't you coming to the funeral? he said. I said
no. I won't show that loving to her.

Phylis had ended up in the Tolly Homes because of the structural weakness of
the position of mother-in-laws too, in this case maternal ones. Her daughter
had married a Muslim and Phylis had decided to go to a home rather than cause
trouble for her daughter in her new family by staying with her.

The flexibility of this bilateral kin reckoning, sanctification of the core couple,
and gendered emphasis on love and food as substances of relatedness produced by
women has emerged in relation to the particular colonial history of Anglo-Indian
railway families. The long practice of allocating railway housing to employees
has helped to make the conjugal couple socially and economically central. The
emphasis on the production of substances of relatedness in the present can also
be seen as a more tangential product of the colonial history of Anglo-Indians. The
present-orientation and bilateral reckoning of family ties has made them highly
flexible in a historical context of abandonment, institutionalization, and fluctuat-
ing socioeconomic fortunes. The ancestors of Anglo-Indian families were often
people who had been abandoned by British men and/or absorbed into institutions such as orphanages. A flexible system of kinship meant that the "origins"
of conjugal families could and can be remade instantly in the present even if one
member of the core couple, historically often the wife, had previously been in an
orphanage and had unknown origins. Its bilateral form also reflects the frequent
historical experience of children being abandoned by fathers to the care of their
mother or to their mother's relatives. It allows homes to be formed that do not
rely on absent and often illegitimate or unacknowledged paternal connections.
The expansive and present-oriented reckoning of family has also allowed and allows Anglo-Indians to strategically make and break connections to kin in order
to better their social and economic status. Older women such as Marigold who
had been adopted into their sisters' marital homes described how they acquired
new racial status as Anglo-Indians or Europeans through such movement. Kin
who have done well often stop attending their less-fortunate relatives' key social
events.[9] Now this severing of ties is in order to claim a higher-class status, but in
the past it was a route to "racial" mobility as well.

Yet, paradoxically, within these present-oriented households with rich idioms
of fluid relatedness there was a sense that they lack something. Anglo-Indians were
haunted by a feeling that they lacked a documentary archive that could confirm
the solidity and legitimacy of their families. Sealy's description of attempting to

reconstruct a written history of his ancestral home by "slippery, spermy" "icelight" captures this perfectly. As Anglo-Indians attempted to turn toward the certainties of deep patrilineal genealogical reckoning and family history, these certainties dissolve and melt away. In addition, Anglo-Indians expressed a sense of discomfort and shame around the whole terrain of family history, the lack of records of it, and the relationship of family pasts to family present. The difficult relationship between Anglo-Indians and the archived and family past in general was tangible as soon as I started conversations with them in the railway colony in Kharagpur and in Kolkata. Immediately I found that talk about family history had a particular series of associations for them, none of which were liberating or benign.

When I asked Anglo-Indians to describe their past, two kinds of responses were generated. The first one was an atmosphere of tension and embarrassed silence. This was so marked that I gave up asking direct questions such as, so, tell me where your family originated, where your grandfather worked, and so forth, because these questions seemed to be a profound breach of potential friendship or even the possibility of conversation. I didn't understand this tension at first. Then Gary and Gavin Jones told me a series of jokes. I had just met the brothers for the first time. We were sitting around a broad, polished table in the staff room of Saint James's School with a group of Anglo-Indian teachers. I was explaining my research and that I wanted to find out about their family histories. This had provoked a lot of teasing banter. One teacher repeated the common joke that all Anglos were spicy like their food, and Gary added that I better make sure that my book about them had a lot of spice in it. Gary then said colonies were full of scandals. To pursue this theme he told a joke that all the time Mrs. X's were turning up on the Mumbai express and everyone in the colonies would exclaim, "Watch out! Here comes the Southern femail." Everybody laughed with enthusiasm. The joke sought to capture the double tension of sexual scandal and the dangers of "infiltration" of the Anglo-Indian community by Indian Christians. Gavin then made the joking more personal. He turned to me and said, "Oh, so you've come to prove that we are British and to get us all passports." Everyone laughed again, but with even more tension in the air. The unspoken frisson that made this joke funny was that I might, however, as a British archivist, prove that they weren't all British. Thereby I would reveal the true scandal of the colonies. Questions about family history were immediately associated with the threatening approach of bureaucracies and the discovery of the scandal of inauthenticity. When I asked these questions I took on the guise of an official coming to check their credentials.

The second revealing kind of common response was to general questions about people's lives. As soon as I asked people to tell me about their life and work, they would respond immediately with statements like, "I have the certificates and passes to prove it," adding quickly, "or I used to—they're lost now." Not only was I a bureaucrat, but I was someone who could only be interested in the verifications of official documents. I will discuss these conversations in more detail later, but all I want to express now is how much family history in this context was permeated with a documentary logic and a tense sense of bureaucratic authority. Of course it is part of the general human condition to seek a way of anchoring a sense of self and family within the twin poles of being and becoming, a point of origin and a process of self and relational construction.[10] Similarly, we could see Anglo-Indian dilemmas as a particularly acute version of the anxieties of choice produced by the emphasis in English kinship on individuals creating connections by combining biological inheritances and social strategies. Yet Anglo-Indian anxieties about origins take a specific form related to the verifications of colonial railway archives and the shame these provoked about absent documents.[11] In the ethnographic accounts that follow I explore these issues in relation to the Anglo-Indian family histories I listened to, which often seemed to be haunted by the procedures of the East Indian Railway archive and the historical moment this grew out of, that I described in chapter 6. I will also use Sealy's novel as a kind of literary metacommentary that has emerged from the experience of being Anglo-Indian and will use it to link together the accounts of Anglo-Indian railway families.

## DISAPPEARING DOCUMENTS AND ANGLO-INDIAN ORIGINS

That's the prime mover—the garnering of the past. And the result, for the chronicler, a paper-chase. . . . Someone's got to do it, or it'll blow away like half those old chronicles that came apart and were sold page by page, so that when you ask for them in any of the world's libraries your request slip comes back stamped, in violet, UNBOUND. And so we forget. Past masters in the art of forgetting, my people. My people! I could have laughed up a storm when the words first struck me. Let my people go! Go where Trotterland? But one of the rules of the place where I sat said: Documents the paper of which is brittle shall not be consulted under a fan. So I just sat there and shook.

Allan Sealy, *The Trotter-Nama*

Subject to "History" as a prime mover, the narrator of *The Trotter-Nama* sits in the National Library in Kolkata.[12] This is an archive where the absence of documents leaves him unbound from its colonial and postcolonial repository of nationality, but not a free individual or a political member of a community that can seek liberty or self-determination. So, he shakes like a brittle document under a fan. In my interviews with Anglo-Indian railway families, this disconnection from an archive, which was nevertheless felt to be important, provoked anxiety and, less commonly, a sense of freedom. Documentary evidence of the past was frequently mentioned and even more often longed for and mourned. This sensibility is historically related to the East Indian Railway archive, but it is also given continuing life by the current documentary practices that surround Anglo-Indians. The anxieties of the generation of Anglo-Indians who were adults in the period from 1928 to 1950, some of whom wrote to the railway protesting their assigned status, have been passed within families to succeeding generations. This is because the practices of the railways, the Anglo-Indian Association, and governments to whom Anglo-Indians apply for migration institutionally continue the emphasis on documents as proof of ties of sentiment and of community origin. The railways no longer seek to assign workers racial or community origins, but they do continue to preferentially recruit people from scheduled castes and scheduled tribes backgrounds on the basis of documentation of their origins. This perpetuates the idea among Anglo-Indians that one of the most important guarantees of personal and community origin is paperwork. The Anglo-Indian Association, which remains active in railway colonies, requires that people provide proof that they have a connection to Europe in their male line. The immigration authorities in Britain, Canada, and Australia continue the practices surrounding domicile by asking for documentation in order to prove sentimental ties between family members in different locations that would make migration legitimate.

In my conversations with Anglo-Indian railway families, constant references to documents and certificates made the traces of the archive ever present in their absence from the actual possessions of the family. Whenever I asked Anglo-Indian railway families to tell me the story of their family histories, they always began by mentioning these certificates, adding quickly and sadly that they didn't know where they were now. Even more strikingly than this, the whole form that the telling of family or biographical history took was structured by the procedures associated with the railway's bureaucratic archive. To provide a sense of this I will describe the accounts given to me by two Anglo-Indian women, Antoinette Fanthome and Marigold Jones, in response to the request: Tell me about your life.

I met Antoinette at Saint Vincent's, a Catholic house of charity and orphanage set up in the 1890s to cater to paupers, which is now an old people's home. On the recommendation of Marigold, who knew some of the people who lived here, I made regular visits to Saint Vincent's searching for accounts of the Raj-era railways. Antoinette was one of the more prosperous of the Anglo-Indian and Indian Christian occupants. From her pension she can afford a partitioned space of her own filled with heavy wardrobes, trunks, dressing tables, and photographs of an old Scottish boyfriend in uniform and her friends who now live in Australia and England. She never married and was an only child, so at the end of her life, after retiring from secretarial jobs on the Eastern Railway and then in private companies, she ended up at Saint Vincent's. When I asked her about her life, she gave me the following account, which is paraphrased in the order she told it and with some of the terms and phrases verbatim:

Antoinette said she was born in Lucknow in 1922 and educated at Saint Mary's Convent, Nainital. She said that her father was Irish, but they weren't like those "glorified Anglo-Indians who were fair and looked European and tried to pass themselves off as domiciled Europeans." Her mother's father had family connections to the Middle East. She proudly added that her "family tree, all of it, is in the Lucknow library at Kaiser Bagh." She said that she used to have a copy of this but she tore it up at Independence because she is "the last in my family and I had no use for it." Next, she explained that both her father and herself worked on the East Indian then Eastern Railways. Her father had a British Indian passport and could get "assisted passage to England under the Lee Commission." Her parents sold their house three times planning to go to England, but she "took fright" each time and persuaded her parents not to leave. She explained that this fear was due to the fact that she knew that in England they "treat 'colored' Anglo-Indians very badly," and she could "never belong properly there." When her family was in the railway colony at Waltair, Antoinette even sold her prized grand piano and booked passages, but she lost all of this because she decided at the last minute not to go, afraid that she was not "white enough" to be accepted in Britain.

Antoinette then continued with a description of her marriage prospects through the course of her life. She said that she had offers of marriage in her life, but if she had taken them she couldn't have looked after her parents. Also, she always fell in love with "bad types, wicked people." She once went out with a Ghanaian. Another fellow was married and a drunk. He was happily married, but his wife was having an affair. Antoinette then added that she was really in love with a Scottish police officer. He was married, but his wife was "giving him a treat," and he and his wife didn't "understand each other." Antoinette didn't want to marry him because he wasn't a Catholic. If she couldn't take the sacraments, then she would be very unhappy. She described him as "dead ugly, but some people can be black but you still like them." Her daddy treated her like a baby; he used to say to her, "Baccha, we have you, but who have you got? You should marry." She added that she was spoiled as a child; all her toys were from Oxendales and she had only Barrett's shoes. Her Scottish boyfriend used to write her letters at work, calling her "his paper doll, but it's God's will that I didn't marry him," she said. Her father was quite strict; he wouldn't let her go to dances at first, but when she went to her first dance her shoes were painted in the workshops with silver paint. She ended by recounting how they used to sit outside at the dances and just listen to the music. Her favorite song was "A Sentimental Journey."

In her account, Antoinette simultaneously pointed to the importance and irrelevance of the traces of colonial bureaucratic history on her life. She outlined her marriage options, which might have founded quite various origins for her according to her own volition, taking her on a kind of "sentimental journey." There were limits placed on this malleability as a result of her loyalty to the community of Catholicism. But her sense of life as a series of personal choices and potential origins was crosscut by verifying references to bureaucratic history. This bureaucratic history appeared in the form of genealogies, passage concessions, "Irish" origins, and the names of educational institutions and archives. This history appeared as what I should know about her, what the railway knew about her family, and what the archive in Lucknow could verify. But this history she also saw now as the irrelevant imprint of the colonial state on her life. She destroyed her family genealogy when India achieved Independence. She also felt that these documents were irrelevant because they could not return her to a "home" in England, however many documents she possessed. Antoinette attempted to rebuild an ancestral home by referring to the railways' documentation that imprinted British identity on her male relatives. Yet she also felt that her own female, dark body betrayed such attempts, preventing her from claiming her connection to Britain. She remained surrounded by an inconsistency among the forms of evidence of her family history provided by her private memories, her body, and public forms of history.

Although as we have seen in the previous chapter, Marigold's account of her family life drew on fluid idioms of love and present-oriented reckonings of origins, when I asked her to tell me her life history it too was haunted by lost documents and a sense of the inadequacy of her body to witness to her identity. Marigold began her account with her adoption into Adra, saying that "I was almost as good as born there." She then continued with the description of her life paraphrased below.

Marigold said that when she went back to Secunderabad to visit her parents, her mother would say, "Oh Marigold, she's a lady now. She won't do any work." This was because she had been changed very much by her attendance at Loretto Entally Convent School and railway colony life with Spencer Fletcher, her domiciled European uncle. Sometimes, she said, she "lets the cat out of the bag" that she can speak Tamil fluently, which was her language in her parent's home. She added that she is out of touch with her sisters. She said it is "like partition between them." Continuing, she asserted that Spencer's brother went back to England to live in Kentish town. She then confided that Keith Fletcher, a cricketer who she said was listed in that "biography of cricketers which came out recently must be a relative because he is from there too." She used to correspond with the brother's two daughters, but they lost touch. And now, because she only "thought selfishly of herself" and not her "children's future," she has never managed to get any evidence of adoption. Even Gerald's father, she added, immigrated to London in

1948 and asked them to come along after they had settled down, but she selfishly didn't want to leave her people, her family. She even could have had the chance to go to Britain when her uncle went on his six months' privilege leave as a domiciled European, but she always refused, saying, "Oh, no, I'm too black, even you will look down on me and treat me differently there. I don't want to go." Because she had "no proof of adoption, all the property in Britain went to the brother when her uncle died." If she had her husband's documents from the regiment, she says, she could "come to the rescue" of her children because he was in the AFI during the Second World War.

Marigold self-censored her potential movement away from India because of the evidence of her body, which meant she could never become a British citizen or be at home there. She also sees herself as having profoundly destroyed the possibility of any future for her children without the possession of documentary traces of the archive. Her body's nonreference to Britishness disenfranchised her from possession of the archive, but she constantly referred to the existence of this institution and its teleological entailments. She referred to the criteria of domicile forms (which her uncle and husband would have had to fill out), correspondence, property, army service, and adoption documents as absent presences in her archive of her life and the future of her family. Her conversation also circled around the disjuncture introduced into her homeliness with her parents and sisters by her adoption by her domiciled European uncle, residence in the railway colony, and English-medium education. This made her knowledge of Tamil a secret and introduced the national boundary of partition in her family.

Both Antoinette and Marigold recounted to me life stories suffused with the nonreferentiality between their bodies and the contents of archives. The presence of vanished documents left them unbound from the national narratives of Britain and India, alternately seeking and rejecting the possibilities for home and origins provided by the archives that produced such narratives. Sometimes they rebuilt a paternal ancestral home and origin by references to documents that imprinted British or European identity on their male relatives, but they suggested that their female, dark bodies betray them.

The sensibility of this generation of Anglo-Indians has passed within families, giving a heightened importance to the collection and exchange of letters between people based in India and extended family members abroad. At a first or second meeting, people would often produce bundles of letters in their foreign-stamped envelopes from their relatives who lived in Australia or Britain and would urge me to read them. These letters both proved a past link and provided the substance of a living kinship relationship to another country. For example, when I, a British woman, sent a letter to Hope from Kolkata, she was delighted. She told me that she had said to everyone that her niece, Laura, had written. When I went to say goodbye to Phylis Daniels before a long trip back to the United States, she presented me with a letter that would bind together our relation with overflowing love and remembrance. It went as follows:

> To dearest Laura sealed with a kiss
>
> Accept this token of love and devotion to you and grateful of our friend-ship with each other also God grant you joy happiness health and wealth in all your undertakings in life come what may with all blessings for the future. This wish is for you from an old lady who loves you and care for you from her heart never to be forgotten think of me when you are far away you will always be remembered and never forgotten always in my prayers and thoughts.
>
> Love and kisses<br>Phylis
>
> Feeling very sad and bad that you have to leave me God Bless you.

This was a letter that sought, like the treasured collections of letters from rela-tives, to cement and materialize relations of sentiment in written tokens.


## SPECTERS OF HISTORY

I tell you sometimes I have a dream. . . . A funny city, could be here, could be there, could be both. Narrow crooked mixed-up lanes on one side and on the other side long broad new straight roads. On the old side of the city there are ruins, old-old buildings you know with domes and things like that and plaster coming off. Brown-ish walls, bit overgrown, jungly like, thick grass. A graveyard with graves, some small, some big like houses. One big one has funny foreign words on one side. . . . Other side is blank. I say, tomorrow I'll see whose grave it was. . . . Bus keeps going, keeps going till it comes to the other side, the old side of the city. Suddenly it stops and there's the same big tomb. I get off and see a lady standing there with her parcels try-ing to read the stone. I say, can't you see its blank, men? And she turns to me and my god her face is also blank.

Allan Sealy, The Trotter-Nama

The narrator of *The Trotter-Nama*, Eugene Aloysius Trotter, is haunted by a dream of an indeterminate place that is simultaneously Europe and India, the past and the future. In this place there is a grave as big as a *house*, covered in foreign words, which have no translation. This memorial of the past, rather than giving substance to the present, leaves a nomadic Anglo-Indian woman without physical embodiment. This dream conveys all the domestic violences of the railway's archive and of the historical moment that it grew out of in which communities and nations crystallized in new ways. Trotter's dream conveys the nontranslatability of the imprints of documents into complete living substrates. It also suggests the centrality of the archive's foreign words to domestic spaces. The archive sent Anglo-Indians, like Trotter, to the graveyards of "History" to determine their pasts and futures. It left them in a position where it was impossible for a community to emerge from conversations between them about a shared past, as this past only existed in the form of blank and destroyed documents. Ghosts and graveyards recurred in Anglo-Indian railway family stories, particularly in the railway colony at Kharagpur. I will discuss these in detail in a later chapter, but here I want to concentrate on ghosts provoked by the dynamics of the railway archive, ghosts who are a specific kind of restless and disturbing apparition quite distinct from the homely ghosts I describe later on. The themes of these stories emphasize that people from the past can't rest either because they are troubled by unresolved disputes about rights guaranteed by documents or because other Anglo-Indians have abandoned them. They are specters of intimate connections that can't be made real in documents and of family histories that are untranslatable into the present.

I first met Clarence Vanjo in the Catholic graveyard in Kharagpur when I was on my tour with Ahmed. He was washing the grave of his wife, Milly, and he was beginning to burn candles and incense on it. He told me that he went there to "talk to her everyday," that he might be "mad," but he does it. He added that his mother and brother were buried there too, and he mourned the desecration of the graveyard by Indians. This visit was part of his daily routine. He dressed in his best clothes, including a leather jacket sent to him by relatives in Australia, and climbed on his motorbike to spend two hours there so that "she won't get lonely." Several months after our first meeting, as I was sitting in Clarence's flat, he, Mavis, and Marcie, began to talk about Milly's ghost. Clarence said that she calls to him from the graveyard, drawing him on his daily visits. As he approaches the graveyard on his scooter he hears her voice saying, "Come to me, come to me," and speeds on his scooter "up to fifty" and "almost commits suicide." Clarence then added that Milly appeared to his mother on the day she died. She had heard a knock on the door and suddenly said, "Milly's come home." Clarence continued, adding that Milly also appeared to his grandson, Johnny, on his birthday. He was playing outside, alone. His solitary play was, according to his grandfather, due to the fact that he is "a lonely chap" because there are so few children who speak English in the neighborhood. Suddenly, Johnny called out: "Look! Milly is smiling from the clouds to me." Later, Johnny looked out of the window and said, "Milly's come." That night he dreamed that he was playing with his grandmother all night. Mavis then joined the conversation, saying that she tells Johnny that Milly has gone to England, and he replies, "When you go to England take me with you or else you'll forget me like Milly has."

Clarence added that Milly comes to him at night and watches him in his bed. He then explained that "she can't rest"—she haunts the family because of the controversy over Mavis's marriage. The Anglo-Indian community in Kharagpur is scandalized by Mavis's choice of Samuel, who was married to her sister until thirteen years previously. They accuse her of both an arranged marriage for the purpose of a visa and of being in an "incestuous" relationship. Because of the protests, the priest at the local church in Kharagpur, where she had been baptized and confirmed, initially refused to perform a wedding ceremony. She wrote to the bishop in Kolkata, and the family finally got permission. Mavis has been trying to get a visa for two years to join her husband, but the situation has been complicated by what she called the "evil wishers" who sent a letter to the British authorities saying Samuel and Mavis's marriage was arranged, which caused the authorities to investigate everything. She protested that it is so unfair that the British government even asks them for all their private correspondences and cross-questioned her in a preliminary visa interview, leafing through their love letters. Clarence added, "if they have no honor, just like the railways, no discretion, you might as well just show them to them."

The Vanjo family's web of private relationships and personal history was suffused by the violences of the public spaces of community, neighborhood, church, graveyard, and nation, inherited from the colonial and postcolonial state. These recurrently demand proof of Indianness and Britishness and that there is no dissembling of intimate relationships. Milly may be in Britain, but she only got there through death and the potential forgetting of her family. But she cannot rest; she travels through the family's lives disturbed by the nontranslatability of emotions into the documentary verifications of the state and the divided Anglo-Indian "community." This community, like the Anglo-Indian Association in the past, only makes its presence felt in the scrutiny of private relationships.

A similar restless ghost haunted Loretta and Colt Campbell. They told me about the ghost at a party of the two families at the Vanjo house to celebrate the consecration of the sacred heart picture by the priest on Milly's birthday. Loretta said that she had started seeing and hearing things and no one believed her at first. At first she saw someone walking past the window. Then once, she tried to get up in the night, and she was thrown down three times. Then one night she felt someone pressing down on her chest. Paula added to the conversation that she "saw a woman, an Anglo-Indian woman, in a short-sleeve dress by the window." Colt then diagnosed the origins of this ghost. He explained that it was the ghost of a woman whose family left her behind when they went to Britain at Independence in the care of some other Anglo-Indians. She was handicapped.

They mistreated her, beat her, and shut her up in a room with no food, and she starved to death. Colt added that "her evil presence is still there. She was locked up in the room next to our bedroom. It is all shut up now, no one uses it." Loretta then explained that she kept the spirit away by having a mass said in their bedroom by the local priest and by putting holy water all round the room. But, she added, they were trying to move since they had only had bad luck since they moved into the house.

The ghost at the Campbell house is the trace of a history that because of the unequal procedures of the railway archive can never be turned into Indian or British national history. The family that left a disabled relative behind are representative of the ways in which Anglo-Indians pushed by the railway bureaucracy to long for British origins have abandoned and betrayed a handicapping Indian past. Along with this they have abandoned their responsibilities to specific relatives, causing their decline and death. But this ghost of the abandoned and now impossible to assert Indianness of Anglo-Indians cannot be completely exorcised or "shut up" by Indian and British national archives; it returns to press down on Loretta and Colt.

## ARCHIVING BODIES

I wish to shew how History is made. Understand first, good adept, that there are no sides to it. Front and back there be, certainly, which the vulgar call past and future (the one with buttons and the other not) and also top and bottom, which some call class (the one with epaulettes, the other not). But sides no. No circumventing it, sharp adept: the fabric extends endlessly, defying the lateral cut.

Allan Sealy, *The Trotter-Nama*

In *The Trotter-Nama*, one character, Thomas Henry Trotter, enters the pages of "History" during the 1857 rebellion by dressing in the "costume" of an Indian and blackening his face. He carries news to a beseiged British regiment of a safe route of escape. He is subsequently awarded a Victoria Cross, writes his memoirs, and is known "to the world" as the Guide of Nakhlau. This moment, which reproduces the common disguise fantasies of British writings about the 1857 rebellion, is disturbed by the farcical intermingling of costume drama and history. But this rendering of "History" as costume is a metaphor that is more than just a comic rewriting of one of the most "serious" events of colonial history. It reveals the particular significance of the archiving of bodies and appearance for Anglo-Indians. It also shows how Anglo-Indians have been made to carry the past and future on their bodies in a peculiar way that makes it difficult for them to cut themselves off from the endlessly extending presence of the fabric of colonial history. As we saw in the nationality files from the East Indian Railway, their bodies have been made simultaneously treacherous and indisputable witnesses to an archive of origins. As objects in the railway nationality files, their skin and dress was made to refer to an "accumulation of sedimented archives," "some of which were written on the epidermis of a body proper, others on the substrate of an exterior body. Each layer here seems to gape slightly . . . permitting glimpses of the abyssal possibility of another depth destined for archaeological excavation."[13] In the present as well, Anglo-Indians live in the middle of a dizzying vertigo of uncertainty about what it is about their bodies and habits that makes them connected to their family past or to other members of their community.

The East Indian Railway nationality archive was constantly troubled by the duplicity of bodies. Railway officials were chronically uncertain about whether documents actually referred to nationality and domicile. Anglo-Indian railway workers writing to it and trying to meet its criteria were also unsure about what it was about their bodies, behavior, memories, and histories that could prove their origins. This instability intensified the already existing anxieties about the performance and essence of identity that suffused the railway colony. The colony, as we have seen, was a place of reform and potential transubstantiation of identities that underpinned a racial employment hierarchy. Therefore, the scrutiny of and nervousness about the links between appearance, behavior, and their relationship to origins was intense. In addition to this pressure from above and between workers in the upper subordinate ranks, Anglo-Indians were the targets of the moral critique of Indian workers below them in the hierarchy. As we have seen, this took the form of notions of *jati* fused with the racial and moral hierarchies of the railways. The identities and status of Anglo-Indians were always in doubt. This was even more so as the boundaries between nations and communities hardened along newly framed genealogical lines of *jati*, pedigree, and domicile in the 1920s.

After Independence this intense scrutiny of bodily signs of identity continued within the Anglo-Indian community, especially at its boundaries. This came out most clearly in an account that Charles Loyola (47) gave me of his life in Adra and Kharagpur from the 1940s to the 1970s. I met him through his work as a teacher in the senior school at Saint James. He lived in a three-room flat with his wife, Lolla (30), who was an Indian Christian who grew up in Kharagpur. She spent her time looking after their four-year-old son. Since I came to know him in 1992 he has moved with his family to work in a school in Dubai, continuing an ambition to leave the railway colony as far behind as possible. He was born at Adra, where his Anglo-Indian father, who was a driver, and his south Indian Christian mother lived. He explained that he knew his father was Anglo-Indian because that's what it said on his army papers and that was how he proved his own status now. Shortly after his birth the family moved to Kharagpur. Charles described how his mother, who spoke only Tamil, suffered from the hierarchies of race within the Anglo-Indian community in the railway colony. His experience was profoundly different from that of Gavin and Gary, for example, whose mother had been brought up by a British man. Charles's mother was not allowed in the Railway Institute for Anglo-Indian Association events. To compensate for this, Charles said, as a child, "in a very Indian way," he would smuggle sweets away from events at the institute to give to his mother. The other children would sneer at him about this, and in general the Anglo-Indian children despised him for his darkness and his Indian mother. So, he would play with the village children rather than those from the railway settlement. In the 1960s, at the railway school in Adra his British teacher would mutter "bloody wogs" under her breath whenever Charles pelted her with unripe mango seeds in class when her back was turned. She beat him severely when she discovered he had thrown them. The teacher would prompt the fairer children when they forgot their tables, but she would severely rap his knuckles if he slipped up once.

As Charles grew up into a teenager in the 1960s he came to deeply resent the hierarchy of Railway Institute dances organized by the Anglo-Indian Association. At these the domiciled Europeans would stand at one end, the fair Anglo-Indians at the other, and the dark ones in the middle. They were all supposed to dance with their "type." Charles rebelled by asking the "fair ones" to dance, annoying their husbands. Charles desperately wanted to leave the railway colony and to escape his father, who used to get drunk and beat him. He was offered a job on the railways after the 1974 strike against Indira Gandhi. This was because he and a friend manned the signals, playing songs on his guitar while they waited for the next train. Charles refused the job because of his hatred of the colony. His older brother lost his job in the same strike because of running off into the "jungle" with the strikers. It was his education by Jesuit priests at Loyola School and Saint Xavier's College and teacher training at Don Bosco that eventually saved him from the colony. But it was also the remark of a Jesuit priest that sent him into a spiral of drug taking that led to his dropping out of education for three years, during which he worked on construction sites and in the docks in Kolkata. Charles had spent a year walking for an hour to the college and starving apart from the food that his friends had smuggled to him from the college canteen and managed an 80 percent attendance record. In spite of his commitment, the priest had with derision told Charles that he would rather help Hindus than Christians who throw away and waste all their opportunities. This resurgence of racism at the heart of an institution that he had thought was rescuing him from the hierarchies of the railway colony had led to his "despair."

Given this layered history of hierarchies and intense scrutiny of the body as a bearer and spectacle of origins, it is not surprising that Anglo-Indian railway families constantly worry about the archiving power of appearance, costume, and behavior. Similarly, the absence of caste designation among Anglo-Indians means that the quotidian performance of identifications becomes all-important in order to assert status in relationship to other Indian railway workers. It seems that Anglo-Indians have entered an unstable state in which there is nothing to fix their origins and status apart from their own daily behavior and physical appearance. It is as if they were condemned to a world where only the transactional features of *jati* operated. In contrast to this, everyone around them has some more definitive marker of origins, whether this is based on a substantialized notion of *jati* or a status as part of one of India's communities.

In Kharagpur anxieties about what makes someone an Anglo-Indian leads to a fascination with the dangers of and liberating potential of disguise. Anglo-Indians regularly hold a fancy-dress party called a *pagal gymkhana* (the club gone mad) in the Railway Institutes at Kharagpur and elsewhere. During the *pagal gymkhana* Anglo-Indians take on the costumes of cowboys, nabobs, Muslim rulers, and British gentlemen. Men dress as women. Children go as "Daddy's sins," wearing packs of cards and alcohol bottles. People dress up as typical Anglo-Indian dishes such as rice and ball curry in yellow *pagri* and *lunghi*, their skin representing the balls of beef and the yellow clothes saffron-colored rice. This is a particularly funny image because it plays with the contrasts of Anglo-Indian's pretensions to be British, their typical dish, and the "Indianness" of their skin color and dress. Everyday jokes about the *pagal gymkhana* are common. These jokes emphasize that this apparently exceptional event of dressing up according to your desire for a public performance is not the exception but the rule of all Anglo-Indians' and other communities' claims to identity.

Yet these *pagal gymkhanas* are a source of anxiety too. For example, Hope told me that she doesn't let her sixteen-year-old daughter, Joycie, go to them because she would be tricked into associating with people who have disguised their real origins, adding, "The bottler caste, the one that trades in old liquor bottles, and the fruit-seller castes dress themselves up. Joycie wouldn't know they were just fruit sellers from their looks and they would take her outside and make trouble with her." This anxiety about a lack of fit between appearance and real identity reappeared as a constant refrain in conversations. In particular, people worried about whether I was talking to real Anglo-Indians, adding that many so-called Anglo-Indians were Indian Christians who had just stumbled across a name in the graveyard and started wearing frocks. But the habits of these people might give them away as merely *Upma* (a south Indian dish)

Anglo-Indians, who betrayed their south Indian Christian origins through their enthusiasm for "non-British" food. The fascination with disguise plays with the instabilities between appearance, family history, habits, and identity that obsessed the railway nationality archive. It reflects a concern too that essential substances can be dissolved by inappropriate performances. This relates to the fears of Anglo-Indians about their status in relation to other Indians. Ultimately, this obsession emphasizes the treacherousness of appearance in order to reassert the boundaries between different kinds of people. For example, a common saying among Anglo-Indians is "Desi murgi ban beya Blighty ka saheb." This is a ridiculous image of a common, cheap, local chicken pretending to be a British *saheb*. It cuts down the pretensions of the disguises that other people have put on.

In Kharagpur the archiving power of bodies as the repository of family history is also problematic. It is constantly interrupted by the instability among habits, origins, and appearance. For example, when I asked Clarence about his family's origins, he told me that his father's father was Dutch and his father's mother was Portuguese Goan, but that his family were "really British"; they just came out in "mixed-up combinations" in the same family. He added, "Look at my own family, myself and Mavis and my other son have nice-colored eyes and look British, but my other daughters Marcie and Paula are all dark and swarthy." His assertion of his essential Britishness, archived selectively in his eyes, continued, and he explained that he only ate British food, just rice and dal for lunch and in the evenings bread, "*paratha* as they call it." As an attempt to offer proof of the essential Britishness of the community despite its diverse appearances, he gave another physical sign. This was that Anglo-Indians die off young now because they eat only Indian food. He added that previously they had acquired pure British food from England that suited them better, wasn't adulterated, and meant that they lived to a ripe old age. Clarence was hunting for some form of embodied sign of his family and community origins in a quest for an inheritance of pedigree and *jati* that can never be resolved.

Hope Dover archived her family selectively as well. She, as we have seen in the previous chapter, said that her eight-year-old son named Tarzan hardly looked like her son, adding:

> He's so fair, just like a European. He looks like my aunts and cousins who live in London and Canada. He doesn't like rice and dal. He will only eat bread. We tell him when he is naughty that he's not really our son, that I found him on the Maidan [central park in Kolkata] and brought him home. We tease him that he is really a foreigner and we should send him abroad and we will if he continues this way!

Later she suggested that I take Tarzan back with me to Britain, where he belonged. But this essential foreignness of some members of the family is not a lasting quality; habits and behavior interrupt it. Hope told me after several months that I was becoming too Indian, looking "all thin and black," questioning my ability to retain an essence archived at the heart of my body. Donna and other women warned me not to use coconut hair oil because it would make my hair dark like an Indian's. All these comments show the chronically uncertain relationship among habits, bodies, and costume and the family history and kinship to which they are supposed to refer.

Anglo-Indians attempt to end this slipperiness between bodies and archives of identity in several ways. In some families there is great emphasis on the performance of appropriate "British" behavior. Sitting at a table, not eating with your hands, and not sitting on the floor are all emphasized. For example, one woman told me that often when she took her children around to her mother-in-law's house, her husband would beat her when they got home because their children had not behaved with proper etiquette. When I first met Leslie at Gary and Sandra's house, he sharply told his nephew, Randolph, to get up from the floor and sit on a chair in my presence. Then Randolph teased him, "What are you worried about this for? What are you, the last British gentleman left a little too long in the sun?" These habits are, of course, markers of class status as well. They make lower-middle-class Anglo-Indian families more like those of the cosmopolitan Indian middle classes.

A more usual means of asserting a bodily connection with Britain is through the consumption of contemporary foreign fashions. Dances and weddings in the railway colony are a particular point of display for these foreign fashions. People would pepper their accounts of their youth with vividly remembered descriptions of the clothes they would wear to dances. In some memories these directly assert a connection to abroad. For example, Phylis Daniels told me of a coronation dance she went to in Jamalpur when she was young: "It was supposed to resemble the coronation. My mummy bought dress material in red, white, and blue. I won the dress competition. I took home a big box of chocolates." In others it is the reference of the fashion to the latest trends that marked its wearers. Marigold, for example, related:

We used to wear dresses only, tailored by a tailor from the latest catalogues from Whiteleys. . . . Maybe not as modern now as way back, but they were good. I loved pleats and skirts and blouses. To the dances we wore long gowns and the boys were in dress suits. They didn't allow loafers [badly dressed layabouts] in the dance hall. We used to make saris into dresses, and *lunghis* made lovely skirts.

Photographs of dances and weddings kept by families showed startling high fashion from the 1950s, 1960s, and 1970s in the unlikely setting of railway colonies. The first time I met Coral and Philip Rozario, friends of Carol and Gary's, who grew up and married in Kharagpur, they showed me their wedding photos from 1972. They told me that Coral sang "To Sir with Love" and "My Girl" at their wedding, and they had a three-tiered wedding cake from Kolkata. Her mother, typical of the fashionable crowd in the photos, wore a white miniskirt and matching jacket with a leopard-skin trim. Gary recounted the progression of styles of fashion as a way of marking the stages of his childhood: "When I was small we had those tight pants . . . drainpipes, then we had the bell-shaped pants, but the tight-fitting ones we had skintight. The bell bottoms then the flares. Flared pants came into fashion. My father had the flared pants. Big hats, people used to wear fashionable hats to church. Beatle boots, pointed Beatle boots." Young Anglo-Indians showed an enthusiasm equal to their parents', copying the styles of foreign fashion magazines and VJs on MTV. For example, whenever Hamish, Hope Dover's son, made a little extra money from his waitering job, he would go to Kolkata to buy special, preferably imported fabric that was unavailable in Kharagpur, to have clothes tailored. One of the more striking outfits was a pair of white, extravagantly flared trousers with a shirt made with material emblazoned with all the royal cards in the pack. The sheer shiny newness and flamboyance of the outfit stood out in Hijli and Kharagpur, but Hamish said he had chosen it because this was the latest style abroad.

Dances organized by the Anglo-Indian Association at the Kharagpur Railway Institute dramatically lifted all the participants out of the provincial atmosphere of the town, connecting them to international tastes in dress and music while also evoking past times. One of the Christmas dances I attended displayed this mixture of nostalgia and self-conscious attempts to be fashionable. These dances are now confined to the top floor of the institute because the old ballroom is a Hindi cinema, as many Anglo-Indians told me with sadness. At the top of the stairs was an antechamber with lines of plastic chairs in which cross-generational family groups with young children sat socializing (no sign of the segregation by skin color described by Charles for the 1960s). Older men wore suits, but younger ones were dressed like Hamish in versions of current fashion. Women and girls of all ages chose either nostalgic or fashionable dress. Some wore bright satin replicas of 1930s drop-waisted dresses, complete with pearls. Others wore the floral printed circular skirts with halter tops and wedged shoes fashionable globally at the time. None of them were in the *salwar kameez* and saris that they would sometimes wear to work or if they attended other communities events. Inside the main dance hall a band with electric guitars, synthesizer, and drum kit played an eclectic range of songs, from Hendrix and Motorhead to more current Europop. Everyone proudly told me that the band consisted of boys from IIT Kharagpur who were winning all the local college festivals at the moment. This reputation marked the band with a kind of class status as well as contemporary edge. Couples of all ages danced with linked arms to this pounding music in formal style more appropriate to a waltz. These couples, also in the style of older dances, were fixed before the event. I danced with my allotted partner, Desmond Mitson, all night, for example. The only thing that broke up these pairings was when men disappeared off to drink liquor in the shadows under the colonnade of the institute outside the view of the women.

Pride in fashion as an archiving of links to abroad on the body was also expressed outside of these occasions of display at dances. People, in particular women, insisted that it was their right to wear Western styles on the streets and in the workplaces of Kolkata and Kharagpur. This was despite the fact that for women this kind of clothing attracts unwanted attention. One man told me that his sister in the 1970s had stones thrown at her on the street as she walked in a miniskirt to a wedding. The atmosphere has hardly changed in Kolkata and Kharagpur since then. Anglo-Indian women and young girls told me stories of "eve teasing" that particularly targeted them because of their dress. Yet despite this, women insisted that it was their birthright to wear such clothes. Carol expressed this in the following terms: "Why should Indians make us wear saris? Why shouldn't we wear our own national dress?"

Fashion and clothing, however, cannot bring a resolution to the instability of the archiving power of Anglo-Indian bodies. Instead, as we have seen, it leads to a sense that people can take on disguises and that appearances are treacherous. In Anglo-Indian railway families, the imprints of the bureaucratic archive and the history of the railway colony render bodies the most definitive and most unstable referents to a family and national origin. Anglo-Indians use all the metaphorical resonances of *jati* deployed by other Indians in an attempt to assert signs of genealogical origin. But, unlike other Indians, they can never finally fix their claims in either their bodies or in a caste identity or documented point of origin.

## OTHER ARCHIVES

Given the sense that Anglo-Indian railway families have that their claims to origins and family histories are unstable, it is not surprising that they seek out public institutions that can offer verifications of their genealogies. These organizations seem to offer an alternative source of material evidence from that of the lost documents of the East Indian Railway archive or unreliable bodies. In particular, schools and the Catholic Church provide other ways of tracing and proving their domestic histories.

## Schools and Public Origins

As I carried out research with Anglo-Indian railway families in Kharagpur and Kolkata I was struck by how often people returned to accounts of schooling in order to verify genealogical origins. Education was never described as simply a process of the acquisition of skills and knowledge. It was perceived as a dramatic field for the creation or denial of emotional attachments to families, communities, and political entities. Take, for instance, the account given by Phylis, whose daughter, Clare, had married a Muslim man. In explaining Clare's decision, Phylis told the following story:

> The bringing up is the main thing—a tree must grow straight . . . but you get children, you bring them up, then they are gone. See, my Clare, I have brought her up, not dragged her up. I'm very fond of her. She was a very good actress in school in all the plays. I remember she took the part of Peter denied Christ at school and how funny that she did that. It was foretold to me in that school play that later she would change and become a Muslim. But in the school they just all clapped and said how attractive. Now the link is broken between us.

Later in the same conversation, Phylis added, "I feel sad Clare has left us. Now she won't meet up with her aunts and uncles and grandparents in heaven."

In Phylis's story school becomes the public domain in which her daughter undermines her inherited ties and upbringing. Her performance there heralded her adult decision to transfer her allegiances to another kind of community of Indians and the sealing off of her future identity from her past domestic life and genealogical inheritance. The particular shock of this event would not be immediately clear to someone unfamiliar with Anglo-Indian ideas about education. For Phylis it was startling because Anglo-Indians generally see schools as places in which their genealogical family connections and the links of these to Britain are retrospectively confirmed. Yet Clare challenged this presupposition with her own act of self-determination. For railway Anglo-Indians the *most intimate* aspects of family origins and domestic life cannot be fully imagined as separate from the public institution of the school. This reflects the history of railway education, which I charted in chapter 3, in which schools were designed to purify and reform origins. In the present schooling provides, as we will see, a kind of verification of these origins, but this has troubling consequences. People puzzled over the ways in which education forms and breaks domestic and community ties. At other points they indicated the ways in which schools enable immoral acts and the false appearance of domestic respectability. At times they collapsed the space of the school entirely into the domestic space—making the home almost indistinguishable from the school. The stories people told about education started as attempts to anchor origins, but they soon turned into anxious comments on the ways in which schools produce the interior frontiers of the home and community.

Education appears in the context of life histories as a guarantee of a particular family origin. Schooling is liberally used in conversation as an indication of European or specifically British origins. For example, note the following exchange I had with Esmarelda when I asked her to tell me about her family history:

> My mummy was an orphan. . . . Her father was a pure Englishman, six four in height, blue eyes. She studied in Stuart School in Cuttack. Protestant school. Then it was run by a pure Englishman. Even Bishop Westcott School Ranchi, husband and wife, English family was running the school. My brother had an opportunity; he was in that school. Eldest studied at Saint Vincent's Asansol. My other sisters studied in Saint Helen's Darjeeling and myself, Cuttack.

Esmarelda is offering proof of her family origin through the medium of the public institutions at which she and her relatives studied.

So close is this relationship between schooling and domestic origins that some Anglo-Indians completely collapse the space of the school into the domestic space. They seek to secure the affiliation of families to Anglo-Indian origins by sealing together domestic and school practices. In those cases there is no separation between family honor and reputation and that of the school. The effort required to achieve this fusion is great and often relies on the use of strict discipline within the home. This strategy of attempting to fuse home and school is frequently fueled by a lingering doubt about whether the family can live up to the standards set for being a member of the community of Anglo-Indians. Although there were many examples of this in Kharagpur and Kolkata, this strategy was particularly intense in Gary's home.

Gary saw his education in Loyola Jamshedpur and Mount Hermon with Jesuit priests as the means through which he escaped the railway colony, where Anglo-Indians, he said, have only sunk into poverty and bad habits. He was highly critical of other Anglo-Indians who he felt were letting down the community by not bothering to educate their children properly. But this simple story of self-improvement is not the only way Gary understood education. He was very concerned that he and his family lived up to the standards of dress, demeanor, and self-discipline he learned at Loyola and that he now teaches by example. He enforced these standards quite rigidly, using a belt regularly on his children to punish them if they defied his authority. His need to do this was fueled in part by his own sense that his mother's Indian Christian identity compromised in some way the Anglo-Indianness of himself and his family. This fusing of the spaces of the school, home, and personal identity came out particularly dramatically one evening. Gary had invited family members to celebrate Lorissa's birthday. These included John, an Indian Christian, who is married to Carol's sister, who grew up in Kharagpur and is now head of a Jewish school in Kolkata. Gary and his family members had joked that John had become Jewish himself ever since working there. In one remark they revealed their sense of the fusion of private and public identities associated with a school. As the party wore on into the night everyone began to discuss the different English-medium schools in Kolkata. John said that Saint James was a hypocritical place because they said they gave preference to Christian and Anglo-Indian children, but they didn't; for example, when he asked Gary to get a place for his eldest son in Saint James he couldn't do this. In response, Gary exploded in anger, saying that he had told John never to mention this in his house or to criticize the school in the house. Gary added that he wouldn't have his school insulted, that he would defend its honor to all comers. He completed his outburst with the statement that the school's honor was his family honor. This is a particularly intense example of the collapsing of the school into family and personal identity. So intimate are these public spaces for Gary that their honor is his family's honor. This is, of course, in part because he is a teacher, but it also reflects a more common sense of the relevance of schools to domestic genealogies.

This close relationship between education and genealogy is problematic, however. Colt Campbell insisted at one point in a discussion about what makes an Anglo-Indian:

> They speak English as a mother tongue. No matter how much education an Indian has he cannot talk English to you. I'll tell you straight. You can recognize an Anglo-Indian from an Indian anytime only by the way he talks. It's simple no matter how, no matter what qualifications. He may be a professor, he may have any academic qualification, but they can never talk English like us.

Yet in response to my next question, "Were your parents very particular about the way you spoke?" Colt replied, "Oh, yes, we were taught by English people. I went to the Bengal-Nagpur Railway European School. Very proud it was and all the teachers and masters were from England. They were all English teachers and our certificate was from England, Cambridge, but they abolished it. Now you can buy any certificate." In one breath a mother tongue that indicates origins becomes a facility learned in the space of a school in a way that retrospectively guarantees your origin.

Colt's story reveals another quality of these stories of origin verified by educational institutions—they are full of uncertainties about whether mother tongues and other qualities of being Anglo-Indian are learned or essential characteristics. People fear that far from guaranteeing origins schools can turn anyone into an Anglo-Indian. This anxiety appears clearly in stories of "infiltration." Whenever I discussed education Anglo-Indians of all ages would complain about the permeability of their community to infiltration by people pretending to be Anglo-Indians. Their greatest fear about this was not that it stopped them from getting the places reserved for Anglo-Indians and Christians at some English-medium schools, but that these fake Anglo-Indians were indistinguishable from real Anglo-Indians to other Indians and that they lowered the tone and respectability of the community. In the more elaborate versions of these fears, Muslims in particular intentionally contract second or third marriages with Anglo-Indian women solely in order to guarantee places for all of their children by all of their wives in English-medium schools. This is seen as outrageous because these children have no lineage right to these places nor do they live an Anglo-Indian lifestyle. These accounts reflect a desire to assert that there is such a thing as an essential Anglo-Indian who deserves a particular kind of community right. Yet they also suggest that once people have been schooled to be Anglo-Indians they are almost indistinguishable from real ones.

The centrality of schools in forming relatedness is also puzzled over in another fashion. People tell stories about how boarding schools in particular enable the formation of immoral or false families. Hope Dover told a characteristic version of this kind of school story to me. She wanted to warn me about the character of other Anglo-Indians I knew. She began by telling me about Hamish Thomas, who she said lives with his two wives in Santa Barbara. His second wife was originally an orphan in Saint Thomas's boarding school in Kolkata. He convinced the nuns that her uncle had died and that he was now her legal guardian. They didn't bother to check his claim and he took the girl home with him to be his wife. Hope went on to tell me about another immoral family. She suggested that Emma Delijah's family was not as respectable and European as it seemed. Her sister had married a Bengali and then left him. Their daughter was abandoned in Saint Thomas's Kidderpore. When Hope asks Emma about her niece she denies all connections with her. In these stories boarding schools, rather than being morally reforming institutions set apart from the domestic life of families, are an intimate part of family arrangements. Their existence helps to facilitate immoral behavior and to create the false appearance of family respectability and European identities. Hope's accounts reflected, as do the other examples I have given here, the intimate power of educational institutions for Anglo-Indians as places that can seal and unseal personal and family origins. Once again, as with the East Indian Railway archive, bureaucratic public institutions seem to offer a guarantee of the most intimate substances of relatedness, yet rather than confirming these they destabilize the authenticity of these claims to origins.

## A Divine Verification: Catholicism and Origins

As we saw in chapter 6, church records or affidavits from priests were often produced by Anglo-Indians and Indian Christians as evidence of national origins to the East Indian Railway. Railway bureaucrats rejected these outright. Railway families in Kharagpur and Kolkata still see baptismal certificates and marriage certificates as irrefutable proof of their family history. They would mention these alongside their references to railway documentation when seeking to assert the truth of their accounts. One scandal that was frequently discussed conveys the special qualities of these documents. This was the election of an apparently "inauthentic" candidate to the post of the community's MLA in the Legislative Assembly in Delhi. People always told the story as follows. When Janata Dal came to power after Indira Gandhi's state of emergency, the party was looking around for a non-Congress MLA. Somehow a man named Paul Mantosh from Kolkata was chosen for this role. In response to this a group of Anglo-Indians (including Gary) mounted a case against his nomination in the Kolkata High Court. They argued that Mantosh was a Muslim adopted by an Anglo-Indian man, but that did not make him an Anglo-Indian and therefore he shouldn't represent the community. Whenever this tale was told by people in Kharagpur and Kolkata the element that provoked the most comment was that Mantosh allegedly dragged an old priest out of a nursing home and got him to fake the identity of his father on the birth certificate records of the church. This was the greatest scandal of this story, that someone would contemplate altering a church document.

The importance of church documents to Anglo-Indian families has a strategic strain running through it. Membership of Catholic churches and proof of this membership has in the past and still does in the present create the possibility of social mobility. This is clearly visible in the lives of Charles Loyola and Gary and Gavin. Priests have long acted as the guardians of coveted educational scholarships for Christians and Anglo-Indians. It is through their efforts that talented children in the congregation are spotted and encouraged to go to Catholic boarding schools and colleges. The reserved places for Christians and Anglo-Indians as pupils and teachers at institutions also make priests vital referees and brokers. In a very direct sense, therefore, being a member of the church can translate into access to resources and to particular status groups.

However, it is not strategic interests alone that have led to the importance of church documents and priests' verifications to Anglo-Indian railway families. Instead, these documents are particularly potent because they are linked to performative events in which the authenticity of family history and substances of relatedness are made. Take, for example, the wedding certificate. I was puzzled by Anglo-Indian railway families' emphasis on birth and marriage certificates, until the significance of such documents became clear to me through the events of one particular wedding in Adra.

I traveled with the Jones family to Adra for the wedding of Marigold's brother George's son, Bastian (21), to an Anglo-Indian girl, Michelle (17). Bastian worked as a ticket clerk in the station and lived with his mother, Sonya, in a tiny two-room railway house on the eastern edge of Adra in the traffic section. Sonya kept two goats, Sipali and Dipali, who wandered in and out of the house, and the kitchen was a series of mud hearths in the garden. In the main living room a picture of George sporting a short back and sides and a leather jacket was hung next to a silver foil house with statues of Jesus and Mary in it. Over the door were photographs of Sonya's father and mother, her three sons, Tyrone, Carlton, and Bastian, and a recently added one of Michelle. With the help of the Jones family Sonya was paying for everything in the wedding, and a huge purple and yellow *pandal* (awning) had been erected on the front of the quarters. Michelle's parents refused to contribute and were not expected to attend the wedding because Michelle was four months' pregnant. Her father had thrown her out of the house, and she was staying with her mother's sister, who had taken her in. Sonya was very happy about the marriage, according to Carol, because Michelle was a hard worker who would be able to help her in the home.

Carol and I were called by Michelle's aunt to dress Michelle for the ceremony because, as Carol put it, "We would know the latest fashions in makeup, dress, and everything." When we arrived, Michelle was sitting and looking terrified and stiff in a white satin sari with a blouse with long sleeves and puffed shoulders. The sari, Carol confided, was because she wouldn't have been able to hide her pregnancy in a wedding dress. But Carol set about making Michelle look as much like a "Western bride" as possible. She painted her lips a lurid pink. I helped her to arrange an extravagant net veil draped from a small pillbox hat, which Michelle's aunt said had been "got from abroad, because you can't get such things here." The final touch was a pair of net gloves sent by another relative, from Australia. Just before Michelle set off for the church in a white Ambassador rented for two hours, her parents unexpectedly appeared, and they reluctantly posed with her for a photograph, which I was urged to take by Carol, so there was a "proper record."

Inside the church the pews were packed with the groom's relatives from far and wide and members of the Anglo-Indian community in Adra. The church ceiling was painted in bright diamonds of pink, green, and blue. On the altar were three images of Christ, one with him standing with a crusader's flag unfurled, behind this one of him carrying the cross, and another with him on the cross framed by an arch of red electric light bulbs. Saint Anthony and the Virgin flanked the aisles. In the absence of Michelle's father, the priest, dressed in shining gold lurex robes, led Michelle down the aisle to the strains of "Here Comes the Bride." This was played on a synthesizer by Bunty, a traveling ticket collector, who I knew to be famed for his picking up of all the latest tunes. During the ceremony the priest gave a sermon along the following lines. He first described how "our everyday lives" and the lives of "this community" went unrecorded. However, he said, "we had all come together to celebrate a moment of recorded history willed by God. Recorded in the church register it would be found by generations to come, who would recognize the significance of this day and its holy bond even if they found the names strange and antiquated." He added that even if this couple had not intended to come together in marriage four or five months ago, they had been "brought together by God and were part of his larger plan." The congregation audibly murmured their appreciation of his words. After the vows Bunty played Cliff Richard's song "Congratulations" as the bride and groom left the church.

The three hundred guests then moved on to the *pandal* outside Sonya's house from which Europop and Hindi film music blared. Men of all ages were dressed in their best suits. A few women wore *salwar kameez* and saris, but the majority were in tailored versions of current fashions. The celebrations began with Bastian and Michelle sitting on the "Raja-Rani" chairs of wrought iron filigree with red velvet cushions at the center of the *pandal*. Above them was a white crepe and lace paper wedding bell, and in front of them was a wedding cake. Their union and its sentiment were then celebrated. As the couple cut the cake the bell was rung, and a cascade of silver tinsel showered out. Small pieces of the cake and raisin wine were handed round. Gary toasted the couple. Maurice, the husband of Bastian's paternal cousin, who is a driver in Adra and was good friends with George, then followed this with a speech. He offered, he said, a "bit of biblical geography." He described how "the River Jordan flows into the Sea of Galilee and ends in the Dead Sea. In the Sea of Galilee the water gives out all its sweetness. In the Dead Sea it's stagnant and no water flows out. So it becomes salt and bitter." This, he said, was "just like marriage." If you don't "give to your spouse then the bitterness creeps in. It is always better to give than to receive." Everyone cheered the speech and its advice on the qualities of conjugal love imagined through the fluid metaphor of biblical rivers. After several hours of chatting while people waited for their turn at the three sittings of food, the music was turned up louder. Michelle's parents had made a quiet but conspicuous exit without eating anything, and everyone was sad about their snub. The mood changed, however, and everyone began to dance. Isolde and Ranya ran about flirting and giving out favors, bright ribbon bows attached to safety pins, to all the young men.

In this wedding, as in others that I attended, the wedding certificate recorded an event that celebrates the union of a couple as a founding act of sentiment and a ceremony that visually demonstrates links to abroad. This document acquires a peculiar resonance for Anglo-Indian railway families because it is quite different in kind from the documents of the East Indian Railway archive and those requested by contemporary institutions. It is a document that gives archival weight and the transcendent seal of God to the fluid reckonings of origins among Anglo-Indians founded on sentiment, consumption, and conjugal couples. It is also carries with it memories of specific weddings in which hoped-for origins and the qualities of conjugal love are spectacularly demonstrated through material performances. Church documents are of particular value to Anglo-Indians, as they offer a transcendent and permanent verification of lateral origins, material performances, and family sentiments.

## BEYOND THE ARCHIVE

Someone who once read a version of this chapter referred me to Borges's story of the library of Babel. Once I read the story I understood why I had been given the reference. Borges describes how outside the library, which is seen as the universe, epidemics and suicides decimate the population and young people prostrate themselves before books and kiss their pages even when they can't read them, all of the people rendered phantasmal by the knowledge that everything real is inside the library. So to end this chapter I will discuss the ways Anglo-Indian railway families exceed the imprint of the railway archives.

One way in which Anglo-Indian railway families move beyond the logics of the railway archive is by interpreting caste and national origins as merely related to economic status and patterns of consumption. Although this notion is at times a source of insecurity for Anglo-Indians because it means that bodies cannot be trustworthy archives, at others it creates a sense of liberty. The best way of conveying this is to provide the words of a song that Gary and Carol Jones sang to me. It was written by their Uncle Alvin, Carol's father's brother, who was a driver on the railways, and it goes to the tune of Harry Belafonte's "Oh to Be in England":

> Oh to be in England now the spring is here
> Oh to be in England drinking English beer
> Boiled potatoes, roast beef, and Yorkshire pudding too
> That is what you always find upon a set menu

> They don't know that I could work an Anglo English fry
> Tell me have you ever heard of snake and kidney pie
> British people watching television every day
> When the kiddies go to sleep they show the sexy play
> They don't know that washing powder selling on the screen
> Changes garments, clothings, skin into white like you've never seen

What this song suggests is those who guard the archives of nationality and community don't know what Gary and Carol know, that skin turns white through certain patterns of consumption and behavior. Garments, clothing, and skin are just commodities made to signify certain things, not essential guarantees of origins whatever certain documentary regimes say about them. Gary and Carol as they sang this song were for a short while beyond the archive's logic of blood, belonging, and history. They turned the economic accusations of British colonial railway officials against British whiteness itself. Rather than suggesting that it is Anglo-Indians who were driven by an economic rationale to claim British identity, they sang of a Britain in which white skin is something that can be bought.

Perhaps even more so than this economic critique of nationality and identity, the ways in which Anglo-Indians who have married outside their community refound their origins expresses a refusal of the logic of the railway's archive. These marriages to Muslims and Hindus have always taken place, despite the Indian middle class's resistance to such matches and the legal and archival indifference of colonial officials to them. Without romanticizing such marriages, I simply want to highlight how Begum and Donna Ahmed located themselves anew in the alliance between their Muslim and Anglo-Indian families with the aid of a certificate. Begum and Donna insisted from the first time I met them that a certificate was important in their lives. After a while they showed it to me, hanging up on their bedroom wall. It was from the local Bengali railway workers association and went as follows:

> Shri. Abdel Ahmed is widely known as Begum. It is not a strange exception that one such as Begum has sprung from nowhere, on the contrary, he has been born and brought up among all the people of India and knowing them all, shares sympathies and works for their greater benefit. An exemplary citizen, Begum has got free access to Church, Mosque, Gurdwara and Temple only due to his superb human friendships and his true temperament. Although he is from an Orthodox Muslim family he is married to a Christian lady. His life is an example of cosmopolitanism. Half India's problems would have been solved if the politicians, administrators, religious supremos could follow Begum's radical humanism.

Begum and Donna had refounded their origins on a very different kind of certificate from that provided by the colonial archive. It was a document that celebrated the present-oriented origins and sentimental ties of their household as a public victory over political intolerance.

This chapter has, like these Anglo-Indian families, attempted to push beyond the enclosed universe of the archive. It has explored how documents as material artifacts and archives as bureaucratic institutions have spread their effects into the apparently most private domains of family histories. It shows that the manufacturing of citizens by archives does not merely involve the production of national myths and representations through the medium of historical accounts. Public genealogies as produced by some archives have very material effects on the creation of links between nations, bodies, and belonging within families. When families, in this case Anglo-Indian families, attempt to prove the materiality of their origins and histories, they attempt to draw in part on the techniques of these institutions. They also seek other kinds of archives, such as physical signs in the body, proof of religious community, or evidence of schooling, to verify their origins. They attempt to use these archival practices in a manner that makes their family life into a natural repository of nationality or community. The whole world does not exist inside the library, as in Borges's story, but instead families and bodies become like archives that must reveal evidence of some form of past, usually a national past, or else they will become problematic and insubstantial. This hunt for family pasts in the present would not occur with such intensity if archival practices and documentary evidence of time depth to origins had not first become so important for the parsing of political rights in India and Britain in the 1920s, as described in chapter 6. Nor would they be so intense if the thematics of *jati* and pedigree had not been so central to the politics of colonialism and nationalism both inside and outside the Indian railways. This specific experience suggests that we need to chart in a wider range of contexts when and how family histories became entangled in colonial and national archives, from which they have often like Anglo-Indians been turned away, but from whose practices they have not been liberated.

## Chapter Nine

# Railway Morality

*Status and Authority in the Postcolonial Railway Bureaucracy*

We need a critique of moral values . . . and for that there is needed a knowledge of the conditions and circumstances in which they grew, under which they evolved and changed (morality as consequence, as symptom, as mask, as tartufferie, as illness, as misunderstanding; but also morality as cause, as remedy, as stimulant, as restraint, as poison).

—F. Nietzsche, *On the Genealogy of Morals*

When I first began my research in Kolkata in the Eastern Railway Headquarters and I informed railway officers of my plan to carry out research in Kharagpur, they strongly advised me otherwise. They suggested that a proper object of study would be the town of Chittaranjan. This is a colony that finally fulfilled the *swadeshi* dreams of nationalists in that it was founded to produce home-manufactured engines. As its naming after a famous Indian freedom fighter would suggest, the new town with a locomotive manufacturing plant at its heart was planned in the 1940s as a practical and symbolic end to colonial dependence. A site was selected in Asansol subdivision in 1947, construction began in 1948, and the first locomotive was produced in 1950. The new industrial town had two institutes, named the Srilata and Basanti. Its streets were designed to incorporate different ranks of housing within one neighborhood. It also acted as a place that would absorb refugees from East Bengal into a new Indian future. Those with railway and technological skills were relocated there, so that by 1963 60.2 percent of the population was displaced people from East Bengal.[1] Citing the phrase used widely for the technological projects of the 1950s, railway officers claimed that Nehru had christened it one of the temples of modernity. Railway officers, in contrast to their enthusiasm for Chittaranjan, suggested that there was little point in studying colonies such as Kharagpur. So great was their excitement that they began to make phone calls in order to organize trips to Chittaranjan for me. This attempt to alter my project was very interesting, especially since all of these officers themselves had lived and worked their way up the ranks in a circuit of Raj-era colonies. They could not or did not want to see these places as part of the present of India. Kharagpur was an inappropriate remnant.

In Kharagpur I was presented with an official account of the place that sought to counteract this impression and to relocate it in the present. This suggested that the railways had transcended the hierarchies of the colonial period and that they were now suffused by a spirit of democratic egalitarianism. The sign of this was that all castes, creeds, and communities were equal. For example, one morning the additional division manager called me to his office so that I could meet some recently retired workers. He began by pointing out the past of the colony preserved in his room as a series of Raj-era sports trophies and list of the names of previous additional division managers on the wall. The names on the list slowly changed from British to Indian as one read down it. Quickly he added that even though they had these traditions from British times preserved in these artifacts, everything had altered since then. He told me that he had chosen some people from the Kharagpur sports club, longtime workers now retired, who could tell me about these changes. He said that he would introduce me to a Sikh, an Indian Christian, and a Muslim so that I could see how the colony had now become, as he put it, a "mini-India" where all communities coexisted with equal rights. His presence silently represented the majority community of Hindus, who gave equal space to the minorities he was about to call in. He asked the former workers to come in and introduced them again as representatives of their respective communities.

Mr. Singh, the Sikh, who had retired as a carriage foreman supervisor, spoke first. He recounted that there is a large Sikh colony near the railway workshop gates on the north side of the colony. It grew up in the 1900s and was built by the Sikh workshop workers themselves with no help from the company. His father went there in 1926 after returning from Nairobi, where he worked with a relative. During the strike of 1926 he was discharged and went to the Punjab for a while, but then he returned and settled in Kharagpur. He added that the Sikh colony was a world of its own during the British time. No non-European was allowed inside the railway colony proper. In fact, he did not see inside it until after Independence. The Sikhs formed a self-contained group, and when they wanted to marry they would send to the Punjab or to the Tatanagar *sidaris* (Sikhs) for wives. Before Independence different communities would not mix together, and if non-Europeans went into the colony they would be beaten up or chased out. He added that all of this had changed now and the colony was a mini-India.

The Muslim man was Abdel Ahmed; this was my first meeting with him. His account emphasized his family's long connections to the railways. He insisted that Kharagpur was now totally cosmopolitan and that there were "intercaste" marriages like his own to an Anglo-Indian woman.

The Indian Christian, Mr. Gomes, who retired as a chief supervisor of goods, told a similar story. He said that his life had started badly under British rule and that his family couldn't have had the chance to live in the colony like he did now. But now everything had completely changed. He added as proof of this that here they were, sitting in front of the additional divisional manager. Before Independence they couldn't even have come into the presence of such an officer, but now they could speak freely in front of him. These accounts of Kharagpur presented it as a place of industrial egalitarianism that united previously discrete communities, including minority groups, in an equal space of endeavor. There is no sign here of remnants of colonial hierarchy or of the railway morality that emerged from it.

As I spent more time in the Eastern Railway Headquarters and Kharagpur I realized that neither of these accounts of the effects of the transitions of Independence on the railways was the full story. Kharagpur and the railway bureaucracy were not merely remnants of the past, nor were they made anew at Independence. The railway bureaucracy has become comparatively egalitarian in the sense that biomoral and genealogical differences of community, religion, and race are no longer relevant to its employment practices. However, the present is not completely cut off from the colonial past. Some contemporary forms of personal and public life in the railway colony and bureaucracy have their provenance in the exchanges of colonial history. These accounts of transition and remnants are in fact attempts by railway workers and bureaucrats to locate their experiences in a temporal-moral frame and to relate them to a national project.

This chapter explores this temporal-moral frame in the present-day railway colony and bureaucracy and its relationship to the railway morality that emerged under colonial rule. It examines which elements of railway morality persist, why they do so, their relation to domestic life, and their effect on the self-formation of railway workers. Given that railway morality emerged in the context of workplace discipline, my discussion begins with an account of the continuities and changes in the hierarchies of the railway bureaucracy since Independence. It then moves on to a short ethnographic discussion of managerial practices in the railway colony. Finally, it explores the entailments of both of these for the current forms of railway morality and temporal idioms within the families of Bengali railway workers who have worked for several generations on the railways.

## A DESPOTIC DEMOCRACY

In the years leading up to and immediately after Independence, the problem of how to alter colonial practices on the railways was a matter of increasing concern to the Congress leadership. Their interest was provoked by the militancy of railway labor. It was also inspired by the centrality of railway unions to communist and socialist political activity, which made them a potential threat to Congress power. A narrowly averted national strike of all the unions affiliated with the All-India Railway Federation (AIRF) in May 1946 on issues of pay and service regulations concentrated the interim government's attention on the railways. In 1946 the government appointed a Pay Commission under Srinivasa Varadachariar and also appointed Justice Rajadhyaksha to adjudicate on hours of employment, periodic rest, and leave. In the same year an Indian Railway Inquiry Committee was appointed to find ways to reform the railway bureaucracy in an effort to remove colonial work practices. In particular, it attempted to alter workplace regulations that led to frequent demotion, fining, and an overall instability of service for employees. A Running Staff Pay and Allowance Committee was set up in 1948 in order to reform the mode of recruitment, training facilities, and leave and working hours of drivers, guards, and traveling ticket collectors. Workshop and Running staff were also covered by the Railway Worker's Classification Tribunal set up in 1948. This standardized the status of employees as skilled or semi-skilled and prescribed trade tests for them.

At first glance these inquiries into the reform of railway practices appear to conform to the promised spirit of cooperation between government and labor that characterized the years just before and after Independence. This spirit of cooperation was most clearly and polemically expressed in the Industrial Truce Resolution between Congress and the main labor organizations passed at the Industrial Conference held in December 1947. This asserted that

> the industrial production which is so vital to the economy of the country cannot be achieved without the fullest co-operation between labour and management, and stable and friendly relations between them. The employer must recognize the proper role of labour in industry and the need to secure for labour fair wages and working conditions; labor for its part must give equal recognition to its duty in contributing to the increase of the national income without which a permanent rise in the general standard of living cannot be achieved.[2]

This goal of an industrial peace would be achieved by three means. First, by the setting up and use of statutory machinery for the resolution of disputes. Second, by the establishment of machinery to determine fair wages and conditions for labor and methods to involve labor in unit production committees. Third, by the provision of housing for industrial labor provided at a reasonable rent to workers. Yet, in spite of all the committees set up to inquire into reforming the railways, the government and railway bureaucrats did not adhere to the terms of this truce in this sector. Railway officers consistently resisted alterations of the structures of fining, demotion, and dismissal. For example, the railway officers who were consulted by the Railway Inquiry Committee complained of recent legislation that had made it more difficult to summarily dismiss and fine subordinate workers. They argued that the railways should not be subject to the recent Payment of Wages Act, which protected workers from reductions to lower posts, fines, and dismissal and that "supervisors should be vested with a power to inflict prompt punishment for minor offences."[3] Their wishes were respected. There was great resistance within the bureaucracy to the dismantling of the colonial punitive work hierarchy based on moral judgments and procedures that echoed criminal prosecutions.

Similarly, the government did not live up to its promises. The introduction of forums for negotiation was slow and sometimes acted to reduce existing mechanisms for consultation. Reforms of pay conditions did occur, but very gradually. For example, on the Eastern Railway (renamed from the East Indian Railway) it wasn't until 1959 that consultative machinery between unions and the railway officials was made active. This actually decreased the amount of contact union leaders had with high officials from once a month to once every three months. As in the 1930s, individual cases and accusations against railway officers could not be discussed in these meetings because this was seen as detrimental to the authority of superiors. Joint consultative machinery between the Railway Board and the AIRF did not function until 1966. Measures to decasualize and offer opportunities for the promotion of the lowest level staff members in workshops were implemented slowly. It wasn't until 1959 that rules were passed that specified that 50 percent of the posts of class IV workshop staff had to be recruited from casual labor in the workshops and 25 to 33 percent of class III staff from class IV staff. This was an important, but again a limited change that shifted the proportion of class IV staff in the railways, who had no security of service or any other rights, from between 68 and 70 percent to 50 percent in the present.

Even more problematic than this slow implementation of promises made in the industrial truce was the consistent attempt of railway bureaucrats and of successive Congress governments to circumscribe union activity and the growth in the popular base of unions affiliated to the AIRF. In fact, the terms of the industrial truce meant that strike action could be called against the national interest and illegitimate. Railway officials and members of the government were equally worried about the rise of union activity associated with socialist and communist parties. Politicians from all parties had long understood the importance of the popular base of railway unions. After Independence they became even more important as potential vote banks and sources of resistance or support for government policies. Their membership numbers were quite impressive; for example, the Eastern Railwaymen's Union alone had more than 70,000 members in the 1950s.[4] It is not surprising that local branches of unions became factionalized battlegrounds for political influence and that different political parties sometimes opened their "own" unions. Communist influence was somewhat attenuated when communist-affiliated unions were driven underground by the actions of the government and AIRF in 1949. These unions had continued to take strike action after the AIRF had withdrawn its strike notice. The AIRF expelled all communist-linked unions and union members for this disobedience. The government arrested 7000 railway men, and 2000 were dismissed from service under the newly issued act, "Safeguarding National Security (Railways) 1949." Many communist party members, in spite of this move to suppress their activities, rejoined the remaining legal unions later on in their private capacity as railway workers. By 1951 the communist party made it official policy that their party members should join already existing unions and work within them. So, communist party influence on the actions of unions remained important. The influence of socialist and anti-Congress political parties on the unions, even though there never was an explicit official affiliation between them, was even stronger than that of the communist party. Jayaprakash Narayan was president of the AIRF from 1947 to 1953. Like other presidents, he achieved this post first by being parachuted in to election as president of the Eastern Railwaymen's Union. A tradition of opposition to Congress was continued by subsequent presidents of the AIRF, including Peter Alvares (1968–1973), George Fernandez (1973–1976), and Priya Gupta (1976–1979).

Given these political realities, it is not surprising that both the government and railway bureaucracy feared the radicalization of railway employees and the influence of unions. The mobilization of railway employees could provide a huge base of opposition. The Congress Party attempted to counter the reach of the AIRF through the agency of the rival Indian National Railway Workers' Federation and its affiliated pro-Congress unions. The INRWF was sponsored by the party and encouraged by the Railway Board and successive railway ministers. However, the INRWF never succeeded in reducing the influence of the AIRF or in cutting deeply into its local base. This was in spite of an attempt in the 1950s to unite the AIRF and INRWF into one National Federation of Indian Railwaymen. It was also in spite of unorthodox local recruitment policies. In collusion with the bureaucracy, these reportedly involved Congress-affiliated union officers offering employees who had been accused of misdemeanors help in getting disciplinary proceedings dropped if they joined the union. These techniques of political persuasion were, however, not the only response of the bureaucracy and government to the fear of the potential radicalism of employees. As we will see, this fear led to retention and, in some cases, extension of colonial forms of discipline and command on the railways. In tandem to this there was an attempt to continue the punitive moral authority of railway bureaucrats and supervisory staff. Railway morality was given new inflections by these processes.

As we saw in chapter 5, in the 1930s the Railway Board had justified the need for wide-ranging powers of dismissal of employees without having to assign reasons. This ultimate sanction against workers continued to be used often after Independence. In part it was used in order to remove active union members from railway employment or to discourage and break strike action. Yet it was also deployed more widely as a disciplinary threat. Rule 148 of the State Railway Establishment Code gave the general managers of the railway the power to terminate the services of an employee without giving any reason under the president's prerogative (a replacement for the king's prerogative under British rule). Rule 1708 gave the bureaucracy the power to remove any employee on the grounds of disciplinary action for any reason. Unions such as the Eastern Railwaymen's Union consistently campaigned against these regulations because they argued that it was "unjust . . . and unfair too to remove an ordinary railway employee on grounds or charges which cannot be disclosed because they cannot be substantiated."[5] They argued that these rules gave all officers in the organization, from high-level ones to lower gazette officers, the power to terminate the service of employees at their pleasure without assigning or recording the reasons or circumstances. They also showed that the use of these rules to terminate employees' contracts had actually increased since Independence. Before Independence, for example, rule 1708 was only applicable to nonpensionable railway servants, but post-Independence it had been made applicable to pensionable ones. Not surprisingly, these rules were used liberally during the strike by the AIRF-affiliated unions in 1960. For example, on the Eastern Railway alone 4132 employees were placed on suspension. At times of normal relations the rule was used to get rid of troublesome employees and union members. The legality of this rule was challenged and overturned in a Supreme Court ruling in 1964, but the rule was immediately replaced by a substitute, rule 14ii of the Discipline and Appeal Rules. This was used to dismiss 30,000 railway employees during the 1974 strike led by George Fernandez. More recently, 700 men were dismissed under this regulation during the 1981 strike of the locomotive running staff on the Western Railway. Various national governments have promised to remove this power but have not done so. Outside times of strike activity, these rules are used in a less spectacular fashion to remove uncooperative union members or unwanted employees.

As workers' rights have grown since Independence, this arbitrary power granted by the rules has given the railway bureaucracy an ultimate sanction against its employees. This can only be questioned by lengthy court action or by a government fiat such as the one when the Janata Dal came to power after the Emergency and reinstated all of the employees dismissed for striking in 1974. This colonial invention has continued alongside the internal disciplinary sanctions and hearings that have the same structure they did under British rule. These are still organized on the model of police and judicial procedures. Workers are presented with a "charge sheet" listing their faults. The accused has a "defence counsel," usually a union official, who interviews the witnesses for the prosecution and defense. The ultimate decision on appropriate punishment, whether demotion, dismissal, stop of increment, fining, or the like, or acquittal is made by a committee of railway officers. Despite the impulse for reform expressed in the 1940s, little has changed in terms of disciplinary procedure on the railways. This remains a hierarchical organization in which one's immediate superior is given an absolute authority to determine one's career and moral probity for employment. When one's behavior is questioned one has to defend oneself in a situation analogous to a courtroom, raising associations of innocence, guilt, and ethical rectitude. The moralizing system of workplace rules and autocratic relationships set in place during the 1860s continues in the present.

In addition to this continuation of forms of colonial discipline there have been reforms that have expanded their reach. These reforms have also made the railway morality that developed under the Raj relevant to the present and have fused them with a Gandhian ethics. This is an ironic end for Gandhi's biomoral nationalism and the radical uses of it in the 1920s and 1930s by railway workers. Yet it illustrates further the unintended elective affinities between these radical moral projects and that of the colonial railways. One could be easily translated into the other because they shared a sense that public probity, efficiency and fairness depended on individual and domestic self-governance. Similarly, they both used familial idioms for economic endeavors. From 1953 to 1955 the Ministry of Railways carried out an investigation into corruption on the railways with "a view to promoting efficiency and introducing a healthy moral tone to the administration." This tone was unabashedly based on a version of Gandhian ethics, with liberal quotes from his writings and examples from his life in the investigation's final report. The report insisted that "effective administrative and other measures calculated to root out or mitigate the evil of corruption are vital to our national life."[6] It sought to suffuse the railways with a spirit of "a kind of socialism which is ethical in quality. . . . Whatever is against the fundamentals of morality cannot be good economics or politics, conceived as they ought to be in human terms and not merely in terms of material goods, possessions or success."[7] To fall in line with this new spirit, railway officers were urged in line with the Gandhian example to stop emulating their colonial forbears in terms of the luxury of their lives and to take on habits of life of a more simpler and democratic turn. This self-sacrifice would set an austere example to their subordinates. Lower-level workers were encouraged to realize that their rights stemmed only from the performance of duties to the national organization they served. However, railway officers and employees saw the problem differently. In their evidence to the committee, railway officers stayed true to form, arguing that all they needed to stamp out corruption was an increase in their powers to take prompt and drastic action against erring and suspect subordinates. Unions and lower staff interviewed suggested that in order to satisfy the illegal demands of higher officials they had to take bribes and that if they protested they were victimized. The committee concluded nothing would change unless the whole railway "cleanses its own house."[8] To bring about this new moral purity they recommended that the investigative and punitive organizations that were set up during the Second World War to check corruption be strengthened.

The teeth to enforce this socialist ethical vision with distinct resemblances to older projects of railway morality were provided by an adaptation of two wartime organizations, the Special Police Establishment set up in 1941 and the Railway Anti-Corruption Organizations set up in 1948. Both of these were created to prevent illegal transactions in relation to government supplies, especially those related to the Defense Department. Most of the cases dealt with by the Special Police Establishment were in the context of railway transport, and the Special Police had teams of informers and set traps for employees. By 1953 there were just thirty-six railway section officers and section inspectors employed by this organization, and it had a poor track record in prosecuting cases. This was in part because the railway bureaucracy would not cooperate in cases involving officers.

The Railway Anti-Corruption Organizations were located at the divisional headquarters of each railway. They provided a public face for the informal practice of the railway Watch and Ward Department, which had long collected information on employees. They dealt with more minor cases than the Special Police Establishment or with those in which there was insufficient evidence to take to court. These organizations were found wanting by the Committee of Enquiry in 1953 as well. This was because they mainly prosecuted low-ranking employees and investigated only a small amount of cases. The committee therefore called for a shake-up in these existing structures, suggesting more coordination between the Anti-Corruption Organizations and the Special Police Establishment. The committee members felt that a greater level of protection of the identity of informers would help as well. Most importantly, they urged an expansion of the Anti-Corruption Organizations. These would be placed under two officers of senior rank, the chief investigating officer and anti-corruption officer. They would preside over an increased number of anticorruption inspectors and a new detective force. The organization would no longer depend on complaints but would carry out active investigations into the probity of the employees. The committee suggested that since corruption was so difficult to prove investigations should be set in motion solely on the basis of the "reputation" of employees, arguing, "When a strong aroma of corruption has gathered around an officer, very rarely will it be wrong."[9] It also argued that in the service of stamping out corruption the power to impose swift punishments on employees should be delegated as widely as possible within the organization. The committee reported, "In Assam, in several places, we saw ludicrous demonstrations with black flags staged against the Enquiry Committee . . . raising slogans of 'Go Back.' Other slogans raised were that higher officials alone were responsible for corruption on the Railways." It added that these union protests were misguided, because railway workers must understand that "their rights must flow from duties faithfully and conscientiously performed. They must also understand that any action of theirs which injures national interest is sure, in the long run, to injure their class interest."[10]

As a result of the report, vigilance departments, secret cells, and networks of spies were set up to report on the personal wealth, habits, and suspect practices of railway staff and their families. These were also used widely in combination with other sources of information to report on union officers, disrupt the unity of unions, and bring false cases against active members. One union official, Ram Chakravarty, who was general secretary of the Eastern Railwaymen's Union and treasurer of the AIRF in the 1960s, explains how this worked on the Eastern Railway:

> M.A. Ashraff a shrewd Chief Personnel Officer was on the Chair. He had an efficient set of staff to man his secret cell. Although the Chief Security Officer had a regular Intelligence Service and had informers amongst Union workers and leaders, Ashraff depended more on his informers of Secret Cell and Union. When the Railway Board was much purterbed [sic] with the solidarity and strength of the Eastern Railwaymen's Union, Ashraff undertook the responsibility of creating division and breaking the union.[11]

Chakravarty also describes how corruption cases were launched by rivals in the union and railway officers in order to discredit him. The vigilance departments gave a new form to railway morality and simultaneously expanded colonial workplace hierarchies. In fact, they institutionalized hierarchies *and* made them more dispersed throughout the bureaucracy. Vigilance departments took over the limited role of the anti-corruption committees in order to actively scrutinize the private and public behavior of employees. In addition, each railway officer was also given the power to summarily dismiss and judge the fitness of employees under him. On the railways the growth of political and democratic rights was accompanied by the institutionalization and dispersal of autocratic management practices. Railway morality was infused with a new life as well, as part of nationalist programs designed to produce economically efficient citizens. Even though workers and unions have become less militant since the early 1980s in a large part as a result of their continually constrained role as brokers between political parties, workers, and the administration, the structures and procedures that were developed in an attempt to contain them are active in the railways today. In the next section I will briefly explore the impact of those structures and procedures on the management style of railway officers.


## RAILWAY OFFICERS AND THE COLONIAL PRESENT

Although railway officers in the Eastern Railway Headquarters and in Kharagpur were quite insistent in their official accounts of the history of the railways that colonial hierarchies had been abandoned, their demeanor, the material culture that surrounded them, and their admiration for colonial precedents suggested otherwise.

The railway offices in Kharagpur and Kolkata were filled with artifacts from the Raj. Well-dusted old sepia photographs of engines, bridges, and stations lined the corridors in both places. Polished name boards of previous officeholders hung in each manager's room; these records often stretched back to the 1890s. The divisional manager in Kharagpur had arranged in cabinets all around his desk shining silver sports trophies won in railway tournaments since the 1900s. He had placed his favorites directly on his desk so that they could be admired by anyone entering the room. These mementos were quite deliberately preserved. It was clear that offices had at various points been modernized with the addition of new carpets, partitions, air conditioners, and Formica paneling, yet these older keepsakes had not been abandoned. The technology of authority had also been repaired and updated rather than removed. The elaborate screens and heavy doors that muffled sound remained, and peons were summoned using light bulbs and buzzers activated by hidden buttons under the desks of officers.

Most striking of all was the manner in which the management style of officers dramatically marked distinctions of rank and powers of command. Every action in the railway offices served to impress relations of authority on all the participants. People sit in lines in corridors waiting their turn for hours. Once summoned to the room of an official, they are not allowed to sit down, unless, very rarely if they are subordinate, they are invited to take a chair. They present their case or business while officers engage in elaborate displays of authority. This involves barking orders down the phone so the other people in the room can overhear them, signing papers brought in by peons while a person is speaking to them about another matter, and shouting at juniors. The impression is given that the official is at the center of a technological and informational web to which he controls access at his whim. This continues all the while subordinates try to present their case. The atmosphere is fraught with social distinctions that are marked by body language, explicit rudeness, and different abilities of operating in English. Officers enact physically and linguistically the hierarchical power they have been given by railway regulations over subordinates. My presence as a foreign, British visitor was often used to increase the frisson of this space. Officials found reasons to make me wait for long periods in their offices and to have me return almost daily. The sight of a foreigner subject to their whims increased their authority over other railway employees. They shouted abuse at people if they walked in on our conversation unannounced. At other times they used my research as an opportunity to tell stories of ruthless, if slightly comic, authority and to directly reference the colonial past. Take, for example, an encounter that I had with the deputy general manager in the Eastern Railway Headquarters, described as follows.

I waited on the veranda, my eyes blinking from the bright light outside. The burning sunlight poured down on an endless vista of weary faces waiting on benches below signs leading to the air-conditioned offices of officials. By the doors, peons distributed slips of paper hanging from strings to the waiting people, on which to write their requests. I filled out my slip of paper and waited on a bench. The red light above a door turned green, and I went inside. There, the crowds were inaudible, only the metallic ring of one of the three telephones on the deputy general manager's desk and the clink of a teacup broke the silence. The manager was wearing a heavy grey suit insulated by the air-conditioning. There were five people already in the room standing to attention, peons and petitioners. The deputy manager ignored me. A clerk handed him a letter. He read it and then brusquely ordered the clerk: "File this somewhere out of my sight." Above the deputy manager hung a list of all the previous managers stretching back to 1900 under the heraldic shield of the Eastern Railway. The deputy manager, now on the phone, nodded his head and indicated with his hand that I could sit down. He snapped into the telephone, and his Hindi was cracked by the repetitive shouting of the English phrase "It's bloody well not good enough." Replacing the receiver, he asked me curt questions about my reasons for being there. He told me that they don't have any records anywhere, and besides he couldn't just let me wander around in the archives because they have maps and other information stored away that could be used by foreign agents. Then he picked up the phone and in the space of a few minutes called Dhanbad, Howrah, Jamalpur, and the personnel librarian. Then he told me that I would have to return many times to find out anything. He turned his attention to the story of the railways, telling me that the railways were a nation-building lifeline and that Muslims, Hindus, low castes, and high castes all sit together with no distinctions. He then went on to relate how the railway colonies inspired the formation of a brotherly community with no caste distinction. He then told a story about where he used to live in the Chief Mechanical Engineers Bungalow in Ondal. It used to be occupied by a Mr. Timms, who had a horse and a car. He used to come home from work each day in the car and the horse would open the gate for him because it was so loyal and properly trained. One day the horse didn't open the gate. So, he shot it. He then laughed, and the clerks in the room shuffled awkwardly. He ended my visit by telling me to come again next Friday.

Despite the lightness of the tale of Mr. Timms, it did convey the idea that disobedience brings immediate summary action of one kind or the other. This is an experience that is not unfamiliar to railway workers. The bodily demeanor of managers is a product of the great power they actually possess to determine the future of their employees as a result of the regulations of the bureaucracy. This is given weight by the presence of Raj-era artifacts arranged around them. A colonial physical practice of authority has been sustained within railway offices, backed up by extensions of colonial disciplinary rules.[12]

The accounts officers give of the management of the railway colony in more informal settings contain the uneasy combination of welfare ethics and paranoia about employees that was present in the Railway Corruption Inquiry Committee Report. Social welfare appeared in these accounts as a story of how colonies had a beneficial effect on the workforce and their relationship to the management. They were described as places of unity bound together by plays, get-togethers, and an annual feast at which the railway gave away awards for good work. Yet this welfare function immediately switched in conversations into a measure for monitoring employees. All managers suggested that the colony prevented corruption. Concerns for the welfare and equal treatment of employees therefore quickly turned into an account of how to supervise their private behavior. Social welfare and authority also combined in contradictory ways in managerial accounts of the effects of railway colonies on railway families. Managers suggested that colonies helped to preserve the ethics and unity of families as well as the unity between workers and management. One organization that had been introduced since Independence was seen as key to this. This was the Railway Women's Welfare Club, run by officers' wives. This organization collects money and uses it to help railway employees and their families with their education and financial situation. It also inspects the *mahila samhiti* (women's society) groups formed among the wives of subordinates. These are social groups designed to create a sense of community among railway women. The groups also provide them with a small source of income, as they stitch the uniforms for railway employees. Officers agreed that the Railway Women's Welfare Club helped to bind the railway together as one big family. To give a fuller sense of the self-conscious management ethics of railway officers and their temporal-moral schemas of the colonial past, I'll describe my visits to the homes of the works manager at Liluah and the divisional manager at Kharagpur.

Mr. Upadhyay, the works manager at Liluah, was in his forties, recently widowed with a young son (12) when I met him. I interviewed him in his huge office next to the workshops that was decorated with immaculately polished arts-and-crafts wooden carvings. He was sitting behind a giant semicircular desk that filled the room. Arranged on the wall behind him were pre-Independence regalia: the insignia of the Raj-era railways, old models of the railway wagons repaired in the workshops, and ancient charts of productivity. He had been in his present post for eight years, had worked for the railway for ten, and before that had been an engineer in a mining settlement in Zambia. He was eager to tell me about the special qualities of railway colonies. He said that they were an enclave from the corruption flooding the rest of Indian society because each worker of each grade lived in identical facilities. Therefore, envy and discord could not develop. In this environment it was difficult for employees to take bribes and conceal it because everyone would know if something new or expensive turned up in someone's house and that person would be informed on to the vigilance department. He suggested that these identical facilities also made distinctions of caste and religion irrelevant. After a tour of the workshops, Railway Institute, and Queen Mary block of houses, a huge red-brick edifice named, Mr. Uphadhyay said, after the ship the Queen Mary that brought the king through the Gateway of India in Mumbai on his royal visit, we arrived for lunch at his allotted house. It was set at the center of a garden at the end of a gravel driveway, both of which would not have been out of place in Surrey. The stepped porch lined with hooks for topees and coats, which were now unused, led to a hall of oak paneling. The balustrade on the staircase emulated the details of Norman church windows and arches. The living room and dining room were dominated by huge, art nouveau, tiled fireplaces that were still immaculate from disuse. As we ate at a vast polished dining table, served by a bearer, Mr. Uphadhyay continued his conversation. He argued that Victorian values were preserved within the railway colony in the sense that "families were kept together by the provision of liberal facilities." He told me of his admiration for Margaret Thatcher, and this reference to Victorian values was an explicit invocation of her and her preservation of such ethics in British society. This insulation of the colony, as he put it, was a great British achievement that prevented corruption. He added that his work in Zambia had convinced him of the value of colonies for worker discipline from his observation of mining settlements there. But he added that Africa and India suffered from different problems of development: Africans had "only been in the trees a generation back; they had no culture, no artistic works of merit," so they had "enormous strides" to make before they reached India's level. For Mr. Uphadhyay, the colony and his place in it were a valuable remnant of the Raj that created a mixture of equality and ethical probity and helped to place India on a scale of progress.

Mr. Khanna (51), the divisional manager in Kharagpur, who had risen to this position through thirty years of work as an officer in the railways, had a similar sense that colonies were places where valuable Raj traditions and a kind of progress that stemmed from them were preserved. In his office he signaled this with his collection of Raj-era sports trophies. In his railway colony residence, an enormous bungalow set in a manicured garden with a vast sloping thatched roof, he had also lovingly preserved the old wrought iron bandstand that had stood next to the Railway Institute. When I went to visit him, this was the first thing he showed me, telling me of his plans to restore it and reinstate it in pride of place next to the institute. He also mourned the spoiling of the railway colony with new buildings after Independence. He described these as "more functional" and "not architecturally in keeping with the surroundings." With enthusiasm he added that there was now an attempt to harmonize the architecture of the colonies with local traditions, because now design functions had been decentralized. Buildings used to be designed from Lucknow, but now they could employ "local architects who lived and worked in the area" and could bring the designs into "harmony with the local colony" as a whole—or, in other words, with the *late Victorian design* of the colony. Over lunch, in the enormous dining room decorated with stone replicas of carvings from south Indian temples, Mr. Khanna described the "social harmony" that he said was characteristic of the railway colony. He said that it had been designed to produce social interaction; all children play together and in the school you meet everybody and shop in the same place. As a result, labor relations were very "harmonious." These were also made pacific by the Railway Women's Welfare Club and *mahila samhiti*, which worked for the welfare of all railway staff and gave them a sense of belonging in the colony. He added that the work of these groups and the atmosphere of the colonies meant that, generally, "all the entire families belong to one family and there are forums for the families to get united." This morality, he suggested, had been laid down by the British in the railway colonies "one hundred years back." Overall, he argued that the women's organizations and colonies all contributed to an atmosphere in which "some of the social problems that might act as an irritant come to officers first, and this stops labor acting because all of this agitation starts first in the house." Through the women's organizations problems come to light and are dealt with informally before they become points of public conflict. Mr. Khanna ended his description with the conclusion that "people feel that the bulk of the best initiatives were created at the time of the British and that our politicians have messed them up." For Mr. Khanna these valuable Raj traditions and the colony are also associated with a schema of progress. He was extremely proud to be in charge of Kharagpur because it was "one of the most industrialized places in West Bengal. That's why they decided to set up IIT Kharagpur here. . . . Also, on the airstrip here in the Second World War the plane that was carrying the first atomic bomb to Hiroshima was refueled."

The managerial practices and self-conscious ethics of railway officers therefore do not simply reflect a Nehruvian or Congress-inflected national project in which all communities combine to work together for the material good of the nation. Social welfare and management in the colony are self-consciously modeled on an image of ethics and industrial progress associated with imperial British rule. Most strikingly, however, it is at the level of the bodily demeanor of railway officers and their preservation of regalia of the Raj that they make present the paternalism and practices of humiliation of their forebears. For railway officers being public servants working for the nation-state offers the tempting promise of complete authority over subordinates and an association with an imperial grandeur and technological progress. The authority they enact is suffused by images of the colonial past, not the democratic present. It gains its aura from the use of English swearwords and material emblems of the Raj. Of course the management strategies of the railways do not permeate the behavior and lives of their employees as much as officers imagine they do. Yet these strategies do make the colonial past present not only as a set of rules and regulations descended from the Raj, but also as a materially realized hierarchical management style.

## BENGALI RAILWAY FAMILIES: *JATI* AND PUBLIC POLLUTIONS

In this section I explore the impact of the railway management style and of workplace practices in general on the domestic life and temporal-moral schema of railway families. In order to examine what has happened to the railway morality that emerged under colonial rule I focus in the ethnography that follows on Bengali families of middle-ranking castes whose members have worked for several generations on the railway. Although my research in Kharagpur centered on Anglo-Indian families in Hijli, I was able to follow networks of Bengali railway families through the professional and private connections of Satish Bose. Satish was a personnel librarian in the Eastern Railway Headquarters, and he had been instructed by the deputy general manager to help with my research. He seized on this as an opportunity not only to develop a friendship but also to advance his status in the offices. When everyone else insisted that there were no records in the building and I had almost given up looking, Satish told me he was sure there were some and set about hunting for them. It was by chatting with him and his fellow clerks on hidden stairways and verandas (built for peons to move round the building without being observed) that I learned about the texture of railway morality. He also began to introduce me to other Bengali railway families.

Satish's father and grandfather had both been accounts clerks, and he had grown up in a circuit of colonies—Liluah, Jamalpur, and Kharagpur. He was educated outside the colonies in a Bengali medium school in Kolkata, but he returned to wherever his parents were during the holidays. He now lived with his mother and father in a small three-room flat in North Kolkata. His brother was also employed as a clerk on the railways, but he was posted far away in Delhi. It was a great relief to Satish and his family that they no longer had to live in a colony. He and his mother hated railway colonies as materialistic, uncultured places. Satish spoke of them in the following terms:

> Railway colonies are bad places. I have a very bad impression of railway colonies. No one is interested in anything outside the colony. . . . If you are the son of a clerk and your friend is the son of an officer then you go to their house and see a grand bungalow and you live in a two-room flat. Then how do you feel? Why do you have to show this difference? It's from the pre-Independence time and we haven't changed from that. The relationship in families there is that of a master to the child, who is a servant and must do what you want. This is also the relation between officers and subordinates in the railway and railway colony. My father wouldn't let me play with anybody in the colony, and I went to school in Kolkata. I had no friends, but my diary was written in English so my parents couldn't read it. The problem with the colony and the railways is there is no culture and the culture is alien, different from India. Just see the plays they put on—inward looking and no modern drama, no Bengali drama.

This dislike of the railway colony was a recurrent theme among Bengali railway families, as we will see. Such workers and their families, during private conversations, expressed anxiety about living in the railway colony. This concern centered on how residence in the colonies would produce a dissolution of their community values. In particular, they worried that it would affect the behavior of wives and children. The image of Anglo-Indians often emerged as the symbol of the potential pollution that might occur. The partners and children of these workers described the results of this anxiety as being a rigid emphasis on the performance of "Indian" values marked by female respectability. We will see that this anxiety has its origins in the failures to fully transform the practices of the colonial railway bureaucracy and in the forms of *jati* that emerged in relationship with the colonial bureaucracy.[13]

As these Bengali railway families told stories about the transition from colonial rule to Independence one of the sources of their anxieties about the railway colony became clear. This was the continuation of colonial hierarchy in the workplace, which appears to be so lovingly preserved by railway officers. The act of becoming a railway worker leads employees to take on the heritage of their colonial forebears in their demeanor in the workplace. This in turn leads to an attempt to separate themselves from this inheritance in their personal lives. They attempt to assert their essential Indianness in the domestic and personal realm in a reaction against this process. The failure to fully rid the railway hierarchy of its colonial practices and the fantasy of colonial power and progress that structures the behavior of railway managers leads some workers into an emphasis on "Indian" practices of respectability within their families.

This process of adoption of colonial techniques of work discipline and then personal separation from them is clear in Ratin Ghosh's account of his life. I first met Ratin (65) in the Liluah workshop. Satish had taken me to Liluah, where he and his parents had lived at one time, to show me what colonies were like. Ratin, who was well known locally, had been chosen by the works manager, Mr. Upadhyay, to talk to me. He told me about his life as we sat in the workshop, quiet because of a lunch break, surrounded by the hulks of blackened carriages. As we had walked toward the workshop he had pointed out to me a vast sculpture of the god Jagannath wrought from scraps and placed on top of an old railway carriage that had been built by a fellow retired worker and placed on display at the entrance. Ratin had traveled to the workshop from his home in a nearby village, where he lived with his son and daughter-in-law. His son commuted to the workshop as he had done; Ratin had recently retired as a manager in the workshop.

Ratin gave me an account of his life working on the railways in the following terms. First, he emphasized the long-standing connection between his family and the railways. His grandfather was a clerk in the headquarters of the railway in the 1890s. His father was a stationmaster at Monghyr from 1912 to 1942. Ratin was educated in the local Bengali-language village school. On graduation he heard that apprentices were being recruited for positions in the railway workshops. So, he joined the workshops after training as an apprentice at Jamalpur. He carefully reproduced the statistical figures of community composition at the training school. 78 percent of the class were Anglo-Indians, 6 percent were Hindus, and 12 percent Muslim. According to Ratin, the Anglo-Indians always stood at the bottom of the class, with the Hindus standing first. All the apprentices had to wear topees and uniforms. From the age of seventeen he worked in the workshops under Anglo-Indian foremen. This he described as a time of order and discipline, when you could not evade the hours of work because there was a token system rather than a time clock in operation. They treated their Anglo-Indian supervisors as god men. No one dared cross or speak back to the supervisors. If someone saw a supervisor coming, then the cry would go up, "A topee is coming, a topee is coming!" Then the workers would either run back to position or, outside work hours, run in the other direction. He regretted that this order was now lost and said that part of his philosophy of management was the use of "Anglo-Indian slang" to scold his workmen, saying "you bloody fool" or using animal terms. He also used the threat of physical violence, like Anglo-Indians did.

Ratin said that the Anglo-Indian foremen left after Independence and he became the most senior worker very fast. In 1947 he was made a chargeman, and in 1962 he was a foreman supervising 1800 people. He said he ruled his workers like a father treated his children, scolding them when necessary.

When I asked Ratin about the railway colony before and after Independence, he gave me the following account. He said that before Independence it was where British and Anglo-Indians lived and he was afraid to walk through it. Hindus like him lived in their villages in their extended families, but for Anglo-Indians wherever they worked was their *desh*. There were no temples in the colony. There was no school in the colony for the workshop children. The Railway Institute was off-limits for Indians. Before Independence the European Railway Institute used to be a hive of dancing, drinking and singing, roller-skating, whist drives, housie, and billiards. After Independence these activities were replaced by theater and badminton. Badminton he described as being quite the opposite of dancing. The drinking in the railway colonies, the large amount of alcoholism, made Indian workers scared to go in to the colony out of working hours. The colony and the village were two different cultures, he said. In the village ladies stayed inside. He added that the difference in culture was shown by the fact that village women wore saris and the railway colony women wore the opposite, frocks. With the movement of Indians into the railway colony after Independence, there was a disintegration of values and extended family life. After 1947, for fifteen years he traveled to the railway colony from his home in the village rather than live in the colony. He finally moved there when he married, but he did not become part of railway colony life because he had such affection for the workshop and would stay there until late at night.

What is striking about Ratin's account is the power he grants to the space of the railway colony to dissolve the essence of his values and self and how far he wants to disassociate his own "culture" from it. When I first heard his account, I thought that this was simply a commentary on the colonial past of the railway colony and, of course, it is such. But his account is also full of an anxious tracking between the assertion that there is an essential community identity and culture that he possesses and a sense that this is perhaps not essential at all. Instead, it is tremendously malleable, deeply embedded in practices. The problem with this is that Ratin, with his love for the workshop and use of Anglo-Indian management techniques, is in danger of becoming that profoundly un-Indian creature—an

Anglo-Indian—wielding all the techniques of colonial authority in the post-Independence period. This is why he emphasizes the essential distinction between the domestic habits of Indians and Anglo-Indians. And this is why he fears the dissolution of Indian values within the spaces of the railway colony. The home is the only arena in which he can continue to assert a distinction between himself and his colonial forebears. A long time ago he first physically and then symbolically began to wear the topee that subordinates feared as a sign of authority.

Ironically, Ratin's emphasis on respectability and domesticity actually reinvokes the original purpose of railway colonies, to prescribe a certain kind of sobriety on railway workers. Yet now, rather than this being a process external to workers imposed on them by the company, it has become a personal project. This focus on personal probity is related to the emphasis that we saw in previous chapters in union discourse and petitions from workers under British rule on Indian forms of respectability and morality. Ratin, who started his career under British rule and who is from a family with three generations of railway employees, bears the accumulated weight of the history of this moralizing discourse. Under the Raj, Indian employees defined the signposts of their distinct Indian identity through an emphasis on the difference between their morality and that of their British and Anglo-Indian supervisors. The transfer of institutional power is supposed to have remade environments such as the railway workplace, making it free of the hierarchies practiced by such supervisors. But Ratin in his physical actions and habits of command in the workplace has mnemonically become indistinguishable from them. His anxiety about this leads him into an emphasis on the preservation of a timeless culture in the domestic sphere.

For railway wives the emphasis on domestic respectability produced by these anxieties about enacting versions of colonial hierarchies in the workplace is often felt as oppressive. Satish introduced me to a friend of his mother's, Supriya Bharat, who lives close to their North Kolkata home in another tiny three-room flat. She was also happy to have left the railway colony. She is the fifty-nine-year-old wife of a clerk in the railway accounts department and the daughter of a railway personnel officer. She was educated in Kolkata at Suniti Shikalya, a Bengali medium school, and was married as soon as she had completed her intermediate exam. A marriage was arranged through her parents to her husband, who they knew because his uncle had already married her elder sister. Since her marriage in 1958 she has lived in a series of railway colonies that includes Bilaspur, Kharagpur, Jamalpur, and Liluah. Unlike Ratin, she described the problematic effects of the concerns of male railway workers with domestic purity within the space of the home. She characterized the railway colony as a mechanical life, all rigid and fixed like a crossword puzzle. Her husband, seeking to retain her honor in this Western environment, didn't let her have friends other than fellow Bengalis of a similar rank in the colony. He said to her once when she went outside the railway quarters and stood on the street, "Why are you standing outside? Are you a prostitute that you do this?" She added, "In this way he is like all the Indian men in the railway colony. Didn't I see that in Kharagpur there were no women on the street?"

Supriya's son Sarat (25), who was listening in on our conversation and also works as a clerk on the railway, added that his father never let them go to the Railway Institute because he said that his son and daughter would pick up bad habits. Sarat said that his father thought that "there, morality was not good and ideals were not good. If we went there we would not maintain a good life in the future. We would be cruel to our parents and shame them. We would end up choosing a wife just for lust like Westerners and Anglo-Indians. We would not maintain culture and tradition." Sarat then argued that the railway colony produced a tyrannical insularity. This enabled his father to practice the hierarchies he experienced in his office in his own family, turning it into what Sarat called a "prison" over which he had command. Sarat said, "my father maintains the railway culture. And his bad behavior to his family is railway culture because it is a tyrannical culture. He is habituated to maintain this culture from the office." Supriya suggested that before and after Independence the culture of the railway colony remained the same: "male candidates order to female candidates you have to do this and that for me. . . . This is not the story of one person it is a story of all railway officers. Inside offices they are officers and outside the office they are giants, or so they think." Once again, as in Ratin's account, Bengali community identity both in terms of "culture" and lineage appears under threat in the railway colony, producing an oppressive reinvocation of its boundaries within the Bharat family. But what is made explicit in this account is that what Supriya calls railway culture is not the opposite of, but the source of, her husband's attempts to maintain the purity of his Bengali identity. In her account, her husband transfers the colonial hierarchies of the office to the home in his insistence on a kind of domestic purity. This undermines the separations between the space of work, suffused with alien forms of humiliation and authority, and the space of the "Indian" home that are important in the accounts of male workers.

So, in short, one source of the moral anxiety about the railway colony is that the colonial past is too present in workplace disciplinary hierarchies. A second source of the anxiety stems not from continuity with colonial times, but from discontinuity. As we saw in the official account of Kharagpur in the additional divisional manager's office, community, religious, and caste distinctions no longer matter in the railway colony. All that counts in its workplaces and social spaces are distinctions of rank. These are no longer linked to special community aptitudes or to specific "racial" groups. In other words, since Independence some of the complex expansive uses of *jati* to mark not only caste, but also community, race, and religious distinctions that developed on the railways have been rendered illegitimate. As we have seen in chapters 3 and 4, these distinctions nested within the railway's policies of separate housing and ideas of special aptitudes and natural communities of interest. This is the situation captured by the account of the Sikh, Muslim, and Christian workers given in the additional divisional manager's office. They described the apparently independent development of distinct communities who reproduced themselves through arranged marriages and endogamy. This separate development, as they point out, has changed after Independence. The extreme example of this process is Abdel, who has made a cosmopolitan "intercaste" marriage to an Anglo-Indian woman. Some Bengali railway families complain in a coded fashion about the undermining of this separation of groups of Indians. They do this by emphasizing the uncultured, materialistic nature of the railway colony. It is indicted as a place where nothing but the company and its ranking of people matters. As we will see, this comparative egalitarianism leads these railway families once again to self-consciously cultivate cultural distinctions within the home, which is marked as a distinct, private arena.

Both men and women in Bengali railway families complained about the materialism of the colony and countered this with descriptions of their own aesthetic and cultural ambitions. Satish introduced me to a Mr. Chatterjee, a friend of his father, who had worked all his life in railway colonies but had now been posted to Kolkata. He was a fifty-year-old personnel clerk, whose father also served on the railways. He lived in North Kolkata in a three-room flat piled high with Bengali literature, which he shared with his wife. Mr. Chatterjee described his time living in Jamalpur in the following terms: "I felt like a fish out of water. . . . I wanted the *adda* [literary and political discussions] and cultural activities of Calcutta. I felt that if I continued to live there I would just live an animal existence just like in a pond. I prayed for a transfer and also wrote to higher officials." Everyone in the colony, he added, cared only about rank, so he and his family socialized only with a school friend from the Anglo-Bengali school in Benares, who was head of the workshop, and another such friend in the audit department. He was transferred eventually to Kolkata, where he had never lived before, but he was soon sent to Dhanbad. When this happened he sent his children, a son and a daughter, to be educated in Kolkata, fearing the influence of the railway colony on their values. Mr. Chatterjee added, "my office life and my personal life have always been very separate. I studied for a BA in Bengali literature, and I always wanted to continue my studies and become a lecturer in a university in Calcutta." His emphasis on his distinct Bengali heritage, educational ambitions, and personal aestheticism in contrast with the materialism of the colony is a coded way of maintaining distinctions of *jati* in spite of the egalitarianism of the workplaces of the railway. For him, these characteristics made him profoundly different from other Indians in the colony and, in particular, distinct from Anglo-Indians. These he described as representing the apex of a pointless and destructive materialism characteristic of the colony as a whole. He suggested that "most of them drink a lot; their lifestyle is different. They spent all their money on dresses and drink so they were very hard pressed for money. They tried on their meager salary to live a Westernized lifetsyle."

Railway wives also shared this sense that it was important to build bulwarks of culture around themselves. For example, Supriya, despite her questioning of her husband's demands for a kind of domestic purity, longed for a kind of culture that existed beyond spurious railway culture. She told me that throughout her life in colonies she had maintained her culture by writing Bengali poetry, keeping up with literary magazines, and stitching dolls of great nationalist figures. She began to write poems at fifteen, but she really took it seriously once she was a housewife in Liluah after the birth of Sarat. She wrote about nature, religion, and the iconic figures of Bengali middle-class religiosity—Vivekananda and Ramakrishna. As she spoke she sat surrounded by glass-fronted cabinets of proudly displayed cloth dolls she had made. These were all images of nationalist figures, including carefully crafted images of Gandhi and Vivekananda. She contrasted her own interest in the aesthetic and in creating patriotic domestic miniatures with the sensibility of other wives and of Anglo-Indians. Railway wives in general she suggested were "not well educated and they are uncultured." She, in contrast to this, "maintained her own culture. Other wives were always concerned to maintain their husband's position and only talk about his increments." She added that the real problem with Anglo-Indians was that they had only a materialistic culture. Overall, the problem was that people in the colony "have no outside culture, no good skills, no artistic skills. . . . They maintain only one culture, office culture. In the railway colony there is nothing but office culture. This is why it is such a bad place." Supriya, despite her dislike of her husband's insistence on maintaining family honor and tradition, also seeks to suppress the effect of railway colony life on her own being. But for her this is a romantic project of developing individual artistic sensibilities and of miniaturizing national heroes so that they are part of the domestic scene.[14] This in a covert way marks the superiority of her *jati* understood in the broad sense of her regional, national, "racial-like," and community identity as well as by ultimate implication her lineage or caste origins. This is clear in her insistence that it is Bengali culture that she cultivates and that she is distinct not only from other types of Indians but also from mixed-race Anglo-Indians. Her covert meanings were made even plainer by her linguistic usage of the Bengali word *sanskriti* for her own culture and the English word "culture" to indicate railway or office culture. *Sanskriti*, of course, conveys a notion of more orthodox and purer qualities of learning that

indicate a higher social status. The English "culture" does not have these orthodox associations and is immediately marked as an alien externality. Overall, in
her account Supriya asserts the continuing relevance of the broad social distinctions of *jati* that emerged under colonial rule and seeks in cultivating culture to
maintain her own essential status.

At times other railway workers I met through Satish in his office or via his
family networks more explicitly described the moral dangers of the social egalitarianism of the colony. For example, a thirty-five-year-old Bengali man, who
worked as a clerk in the workshops at Kharagpur, described how his parents
would not let him or his siblings go to the Railway Institute because this would
lead them into love marriages with inappropriate partners and alcoholism. They
would end up like "Indian Christians, who are dirty." He continued:

> Anglo-Indians and Christians drink wine, and if you go to any bar, 55 to 60
> percent are Indian Christians and Anglo-Indians. Thirty percent are from
> Uttar Pradesh and Bihar, but very few Bengali Hindus go to bars. Seventy-
> five percent of people in railway colonies are drunkards. You can tell a
> drunkard—they have a thick neck the same as their head and dark circles
> under their eyes, like the assistant personnel officer [who was Bihari].

In his statement he condenses anxieties about the absence of distinctions of *jati*
from the public spaces of the railways with a moral attack on low-status north
Indians, Anglo-Indians, Indian Christians, and one of his superior officers. Notions of *jati* are being deployed in a segmentary fashion against other Indians
within the colony in a defense of the potential erosion of distinctions. Similarly,
a forty-year-old Bengali Hindu woman described how the children of a relative
who worked in Kharagpur were shunned by her mother-in-law because they had
become too "crude" and "Anglicized," with "free manners mixing with everybody." Anxieties about the potential free mixing of communities in the present
surfaced in accounts by older people of the effects of the movement from colonial
rule to Independence on social behavior in the colony. For example, one woman,
the wife of a railway driver, in her sixties, suggested that there was no problem of
immorality in the past because communities did not mix.

The continuing colonial hierarchy and new comparative egalitarianism of the
public spaces of the railway give a particular cast to the contemporary forms of
railway morality in Bengali families. They produce an anxiety about the potential dissolution of *jati* either through the process of acting in the workplace like
one's Anglo-Indian and British forbears or through indiscriminate social mixing.
This anxiety in turn leads to a self-conscious emphasis on the reproduction of
cultural identity in the domestic sphere. This can be characterized as a culture of

culture that seeks to produce transcendent essences that are reproduced outside of the flow of historical time. The entanglements of family and community life in colonial history and the connections of the present to this past are suppressed by a metacommentary focused on preserving and transmitting Bengali culture. Although the cultural language of social distinction used by such families and their anxieties emerge from colonial history, the relevance of this history to their personal identities and present situation is suppressed. Anxieties about the dissolution of *jati* also lead to an insistence on the strict separation and independent development of domestic, private life from the public spaces of the railway. Finally, they also sustain the idea that Anglo-Indians are an alien, dangerously egalitarian, materialistic, and polluted other who condense in their behavior all the problems of *jatis* mixing and of the failure of their families to be rooted in a particular regional and national tradition.

Railway workers' concern to distance themselves from Anglo-Indians often produced non sequiters in my conversations in which issues of morality were raised. For example, Satish took me to meet a railway driver, Mr. Roy, in the railway running room at Howrah station. Satish had got to know him because he had gone to the personnel library seeking help with sorting out a dispute with one of his supervisors. As we sat on chairs wedged between the steel bunks on which the drivers rest between runs Mr. Roy told me about his life as a driver. Mr. Roy had been on the line since 1954, and I asked him about the changes he had seen since Independence. He told me that he was trained by a "pure European driver." This man returned to Britain, after which he would write Mr. Roy letters saying how he was treated like nothing there and wanted to return to India. He then said since I had asked him so many questions he wanted to ask me one. That was, "Why did people of my kind have affairs and divorce so much?" He added that he had seen this with the Europeans and Anglo-Indians in the colony. I was lost for words, but the question was answered for me by Satish. He said it was because they didn't choose their spouses as life companions, but only as bed companions. The "faults" of Anglo-Indians are often naturalized as a pseudobiological handicap. Bengali railway employees frequently asserted that the combination of races in Anglo-Indians meant that they had none of the good qualities and all of the bad qualities of each race.

Overall, in Bengali railway employees' accounts of their families, culture, and essential natures we can trace the contemporary constellations of the idioms of nationalism, railway morality, and *jati* that emerged under the Raj. Families in these accounts are the site for transmission of *jati*, understood as a biomoral substance that marks the boundaries of class, regional, and ultimately national identities. This version of *jati* echoes the idioms that originated in the moralizing rules, workplace hierarchies, and racial categories of the early paternalist railway bureaucracy. *Jati* within these contemporary families often ties people to particular locations, to a territorial *desh*, that ultimately is anchored by the broader boundaries of the nation. This *jati* also contains a series of aesthetic, cultural, and ascetic moral values that are transmitted through time in the specific genealogical connections of families. This transmission is safeguarded within the daily cultural practices of the home. In these temporal-moral schemas we can find the traces of the history of the responses of railway workers, unions, and nationalists to the moralities of the railway bureaucracy. Political communities of resistance to colonial rule were rallied and formed around such idioms of masculinity, sexuality, and morality. In these concepts we can also track the effects of the community-based housing policies of the colonial railways, which helped to produce a notion of distinct and often territorially localized identities sustained by intermarriage. The insistence among these Bengali railway families that their domestic values are ahistorical and located in a separate domain from the wider practices of the railway bureaucracy represents an attempt to forget the origins of their moralities in colonial history and in contemporary workplace interactions.

To be Bengali, for these railway families, is to practice an ethics of self-formation that is profoundly marked by the traces of historical interactions between the railway bureaucracy and workers. It consists of possessing a form of *jati* that is at once given in your being as a biological inheritance and is made in forms of cultural becoming. This cultural becoming often has a restricted meaning of the practice of a particular moral code of respectability and domesticity and forms of nonmaterialistic aesthetic endeavor. It is phrased in terms of obligations, duties, and self-control, as well as a search for self-realization. The success or failure in realizing *jati* or of an inadequate *jati* is marked by signs of physical degeneration and ill health in the body. Being Bengali in this manner signals the simultaneous marking out of a regional identity and a class distinction but also often scales up to the level of national and racial categories. This process becomes clear in the definition of this quality of Bengali *jati* as anchored in a link to a territorial *desh* and as opposed to the qualities of departed British and Anglo-Indian superior officers. The image of Anglo-Indians as the ultimate other to the Bengali *jati* makes this scaling up between family practices and inheritances and notions of race and nation particularly explicit. On the one hand, some of the biomoral content of this ethics of being Bengali draws on long-standing idioms of *jati*. As Parry has shown, the insistence on the performance of correct social and ascetic practices that will sustain an internal essence has long been inherent to notions of caste. The fear of becoming other than your essence as a result of inappropriate practices that appears in Ratin's, Supriya's, and Mr. Chatterjee's accounts is connected to this idea. On the other hand, many aspects of this project arise from the historical exchanges between railway workers and the Raj bureaucracy. The emphasis on biological substances that are linked to moral qualities comes from such encounters. So does the emphasis on deep continuities of culture transmitted through genealogies and family practices that are microcosms of communities. Above all, the scaling up from family to nation reflects this history. The insistence on the permanence of culture preserved in the home and through time denies this historical emergence of the ethics of being Bengali. Yet as we will see in the following section, this separation between private, domestic identities and publicly and historically produced ones is hard to sustain. The illusion that private identities are distinct from public reputation in the bureaucracy is often fragile and difficult to maintain. It is frequently breached by the moral judgments made on employees by the railway bureaucracy, which is operating with its own version of railway morality derived from colonial precedents.

## BUREAUCRATIC HONOR

In Bengali railway families there is an attempt to assert the existence of a private moral and cultural status that is outside of the influence of the bureaucracy. However, it often becomes impossible for railway workers to sustain this perspective. The separation between public and private life is breached by the fact that the railway bureaucracy claims to make promotion and demotion partly dependent on the moral qualities of its employees. This is especially true for jobs in railway offices and for posts as stationmasters and guards. The bureaucracy also uses a language of morality in disciplinary hearings and procedures. As we have seen, this colonial practice was extended and given greater reach and Gandhian inflections by the introduction of vigilance departments in the 1950s. In practice this means that everyday life in railway offices is suffused with a language of respectability and monitoring in terms of moralizing rules. As under the Raj, ideally employment rank reflects a kind of moral, and essential, purity. This purity is still marked as much by domestic and personal affiliations as by public demeanor. This claim sets loose a discourse of moral accusation and critique as part of everyday life in railway offices. People keep tabs on one another's demeanor and personal life quite simply because these can be tokens of power in the struggle for influence, promotion, or increments. Notions of purity and pollution borrowed from ideas of *jati* suffuse these discussions. This continuation of railway morality into the present often creates difficult existential dilemmas for employees. In this section I will give an example this from the experiences of Satish and my involvement in his bureaucratic reputation. The confusion and despair felt by Satish as his private and public reputation became entangled was even greater than that of other railway workers because he was from a Bengali railway family.

When I was first introduced to Satish by the deputy general manager, he took me to his library in a small cabin built out from the wall of a vast room like a warehouse. In this room, hundreds of clerks sat in front of tiny wooden school desks, in attitudes of bored inactivity, occasionally turning over the papers in front of them. Against the walls were steel *almirahs* (cupboards) piled high with black files. On the wall, placards lectured the clerks with sayings from Vivekananda, and others such as "Civilisation is man's call to do his duty" and "Cleanliness is next to Godliness." Once we were inside, Satish sat down in front of an open window through which I could see a contraption that funneled water into the officers' air-conditioned rooms above. He promised to help me, saying that there were definitely records somewhere in the building and he would enable me to find them, but that it would take time. He added that he was a great classical violinist, but that he had to give it up because his fiancée's family thought all that performance would lead to bad morals. He also slipped in to the conversation that he had had a chance for a scholarship in London, but that his fiancée could not live without him, so he couldn't go. Abruptly, at one point, he picked up the phone and said, "Is that the head of personnel? Yes, hello sir. I have a friend, a hardworking fellow. He is sitting the exam for promotion. Please make sure he passes. You owe me a favor." Over the next few months I returned many times to the Personnel Library and, as promised, old documents materialized in the Agent's Record Room in the forgotten basement of the building. My relationship with Satish also developed. It turned out that his office was an informal center where workers from all over Bengal and Bihar went to find out the laws relating to their employment and to seek Satish's help in making their case to their superior officers. He was sometimes effective, if only in straightening out their English in petitioning letters, introducing them to other minor officials, who could help them, or pointing them to the important regulations. He was keen that I sit in his library as often as possible because the novel presence of a foreign scholar increased his authority.

As I got to know Satish better he began to tell me his personal troubles. His father and grandfather had both worked in the railways as clerks, and he had grown up in several railway colonies before moving to Kolkata. His present job, he claimed, had not been one that he had sought. He had been demoted to it after having worked as a clerk in the vigilance department. One of his fellow workers there had accused him of taking bribes. Nothing was actually proved so he was let off lightly and given the less important job of being a librarian. Satish was bitter about this experience, insisting that the vigilance department existed merely to persecute the poor who could not pay its investigators off. For Satish the railway headquarters was filled with many examples of this injustice. One day, he pointed to the man who served tea under one of the back stairs. He insisted that this man had been a clerk who, falsely accused of bribery, had begged the authorities for at least the position of serving tea. Conspiratorially, as we walked back to his office through one of the back corridors he added that in the evening no one wanted to work near there, because a man falsely accused of corruption had shot himself in that place, and at night you could still hear the shot ringing out.

Satish was in love with one of his fellow clerks, Lolita, but lived in fear of jealous workers finding out. He would only meet and talk with her outside of the offices. He feared that other workers would spread rumors of his immorality, more specifically that he took bribes that he spent on prostitutes, in order to sabotage his relationship with his fiancée and to bring him to the attention of the vigilance department again. All three of us spent time together outside of the offices, and I often visited both of their homes. I began to do small favors for them, buying Lolita books for her distance BA exam in English that would enable her to gain promotion. I also wrote essays for her on "Travel Broadens the Mind" and "Duty is the Highest Calling" that would help her prepare for her promotion exams. I gave Satish small sums of money to buy saris and gifts for Lolita. As I got to know Satish and Lolita over a year problems in their relationship developed. Her parents disapproved of Satish because he had been demoted, and people started spreading rumors about him in the offices. Lolita's father was a retired Bengali railway clerk who had many old friends in the headquarters. No doubt my friendship with Satish added to these rumors, especially as he had told several people that I was helping him to get a better position in the railway and was living in a flat he owned. I was approached by other clerks who offered to do anything for me since I had managed to get Satish so many opportunities. When I asked Satish about what he had been saying to them, he said that he only told them this because it increased my own influence in the bureaucracy. Yet, of course, I had become a minor token in workplace hierarchies of morality and influence. I was a counter that could point both ways. As a foreign woman with Anglo-Indian friends I carried a hint of immorality, but of potential influence as well. My dubious moral status was probed in many conversations with clerks. They asked me about my marital situation (my husband at that time was far away, in the United States). They advised me on how to dress and behave in public spaces in Kolkata, congratulating me when I wore a *salwar kameez* and *shakha pola* indicating my married status. They told me not to spend too much time with Anglo-Indians. They lectured me on the lack of morals of people "abroad." They also pointedly asked me why I spent so much time drinking tea with Satish on the back stairwells where usually only male employees congregated. My power was signaled by the fact that I had access to the deputy general manager's office and had also visited his family at home in their company flat in Howrah.

As the disapproval of Lolita's parents increased, according to Satish in proportion to the rumors carried to them from the workplace, the strain on him began to show. He lost his temper with Lolita and shouted at her if she appeared in his office during the day, using the alibi of work to see him. He visited me at home in a desperate state to tell me dramatic stories of his troubles. He attributed the stress he felt and his own erratic behavior to his work environment. One day I happened to show him an old document, and he linked his present situation to the despotic nature of the bureaucracy. I was working in the Agent's Record Room and gave Satish one of the petitions from railway workers written in the 1930s to read because I was so amazed by it. It was a particularly "mad" one. The Bengali author, who had been a clerk in the railways, had been driven to his wit's end from years of writing to the agent. He presented himself as Prince Albert and had enclosed poems that he said Queen Victoria had written to him. Satish laughed and said that soon he too would be writing petitions like this to the deputy general manager. He then told me a ghost story, which I had heard from other clerks. He said that at night the Railway Protection Force guarding the building heard the sound of *ghazals* and the laughter of women coming from the Mughal dome that covered the deputy general manager's office at the top of the building. He added that this was the ghost of the Mughal *darbars* (courtly displays) that used to take place on the site on which the railway headquarters was built. He said that the railway officers had planned to knock down this dome, but that if they did the whole building would collapse. In this story the colonial image of the despotism of previous Muslim rulers, the Raj past, and the present of national economics as practiced in the railway bureaucracy all collapsed into one condensed image. The temporal separations between them were erased as Satish related his present entanglement in railway morality to the hierarchical practices of the bureaucracy.

In my friendship with Satish I became a token in attempts to build and break his reputation. But my significance was double edged; I was important because of my apparent ease of access to high-level officers, but I was also morally questionable. Indeed, our friendship may have made Satish's position with his colleagues and fiancée's family more difficult and ambiguous. His story reveals the difficulties of maintaining the separation between railway culture and the domestic domain in Bengali railway families. Although such families attempt to distance their domestic "culture" from workplace practices and events, these often intrude on their personal reputations. These workplaces are also suffused with discussions of the moral life of fellow employees. When the attempt to maintain a boundary between the two domains became impossible for Satish, it led him to draw an intuitive connection between the historical past of the bureaucracy and his situation in the present. Yet he could only imagine the influence of this past as an eerie, uncontrollable presence.

This chapter has been an attempt to supplement Satish's intuitive sense of the relations between the past and present with an exploration of how and why the moralities and idioms of status that emerged in the context of the Raj continue to develop within the contemporary bureaucracy. They have prospered within the structural innovations of administrative forms of discipline introduced since Independence, which built on colonial forms of command. They have also continued in more private attempts among Bengali railway families to maintain "culture" or *jati* in an increasingly socially mixed environment. This chapter has explored this dual process and its implications for the domestic life of Bengali railway families and their ethical projects. Overall, it has been a more wide-ranging exploration of the varieties of temporal-moral schemas that have emerged from the colonial history of railway morality and that structure railway workers' dispositions toward the colonial past. The next chapter explores the dispositions toward space among railway colony inhabitants. In particular, it focuses on the eeriness of public spaces in Kharagpur and on the ways in which Anglo-Indians come to be perceived as inappropriate remnants of the past. As we will see, Satish is not the only railway employee who feels surrounded by ghosts and under the malign influence of the past.

## Chapter Ten

# Ruins and Ghosts

*The Uncanny and the Topography of the Colonial Past in the Railway Colony*

I'm not afraid of ghosts; I am one.

—Freddie Dover, former railway driver, Kharagpur

I opened this book with a description of a guided tour that Abdel Ahmed gave me of the railway colony at Kharagpur. I suggested that this tour offered a series of puzzling sentiments, moral dilemmas, and fears that could only be understood through an exploration of the history and contemporary reality of the railway bureaucracy. In this last chapter I return to this tour and explain the emergence of this uncanny topography as a precipitate of the past in the present. So, as a reminder of this landscape of Kharagpur, I will repeat the itinerary of this tour below.

First, we crossed the bridge over the railway tracks to the old, Indian, north side of the colony. Abdel chose to take me to the freshly painted Ram Mandir. Its head priest sat with us inside the temple and told us his version of its history. He said that the temple was built in 1902 by a local contractor, Mr. Rao, in penance for constructing a butcher's shop for the railway colony. The priest said that this act had made his family issueless. His service to the railway had polluted his lineage. The priest added as an afterthought that the land for the temple had been granted by the railways. Ironically, the railway authorities had helped Mr. Rao to regain his purity. He eventually had a son, but this son remained without children; as the priest said, the curse continued. This was in spite of the fact that the son extended the temple. The priest added with some force that after Independence the son had become a grand master of the Masonic Lodge, implying that this was connected to his infertility. As we were leaving the temple Abdel pointed out a series of European faces carved onto the arch above the door of the temple.

The priest looked irritated that Abdel had drawn attention to them. The priest quickly said that these had been painted over in the recent renovations, and that they had needed "Indianizing" like the railways had after Independence. Next, Abdel took me to the Kali Mandir, where there was an image of the powerful and fearsome Shamshan Kali, the incarnation of the goddess associated with burning ghats. The priest there told us that Kharagpur was one of the few railway colonies where temples were officially encouraged by the railway. The land for this temple had been given in the 1920s by the agent, who had visited it on its opening. The funds for the building were provided by Mr. Nath, an Indian railway officer, who had given up his whole provident fund on retirement to construct it. He had turned his wages into spiritual currency. He also served his duty to the civil society of the railway colony by building an institute for Indian officers in the 1930s on the north side of the tracks. The priest told us that in spite of all his good deeds and respectability, still Mr. Nath's son had turned out to be a waster. In this oblique manner he hinted at a similar problem for the lineage of railway employees as that mentioned by the priest in the Ram Mandir.

Next, Abdel took me to the Catholic graveyard, between the railway station and the old Indian barrack lines. There, we met Clarence Vanjo, a retired Anglo-Indian guard, who was crying by his wife's grave. He told us that every day he goes to the cemetery. He washes the grave, decorates it with flowers, and then burns candles and incense on it. He repeats daily the practice associated with All Souls' Day when Anglo-Indians and Indian Catholics commemorate their ances-tors. He told us that he has to go each day because his wife's ghost calls him there. Mr. Vanjo complained about the state of the graveyard, saying that it was hatred that had made the Indians smash the faces off the angels and take the iron crosses away to make supports for *paan* stalls. His public space of grief and memory, and his intimate past, was disappearing into fragments in the streets of the bazaar.

Finally, Abdel took me back toward the south, into the old European side of the railway colony, to show me the Masonic Lodge. Mr. D'Souza, the caretaker of the lodge, said that he and his family were old railway people. He agreed to let me look into the secret room upstairs where he told me railway officers go for their ceremonies. He added that they go there to conjure up spirits of the dead. Abdel said that the Masonic Lodge was known as the *jadu bari* or *bhut bari* by railway workers. There, the railway officers are said to call up the spirits of the past to control the present and future. He added that all the local railway people say that when you walk past it at night you lose the sense of where you are going and what your destination is. You are controlled by the spirit of the house and wake up hours later not knowing where you have been. At the top of the stairs was an antechamber with an ancient Egyptian–style arch guarding the secret room. Inside the room were two wooden thrones and plinths with mason's hammers. On tables were whips, a skull with measuring calipers next to it, and a copy each of the Koran, the Bhagavad Gita, and the Bible. Against the wall was a picture showing a railway line with cross-shaped signal arms next to it leading up to heaven.

Abdel's tour had taken me to the heart of the uncanniness that suffuses the spaces of the railway colony. This uncanniness is of two kinds and is associated with different sorts of anxiety. First, we have stories about the supernatural influence of the public spaces of the railway and of railway service. In the temples on the north side of the colony, priests present the temples and their practices as being a bulwark against the supernaturally polluting influence of railway service. This apparently brings threats to the purity of individuals and to the fertility and integrity of lineages. The stories about the Masonic Lodge are similar to the accounts of the priests in that they also emphasize the powerful and inexplicable influence that railway spaces and railway officers can have over individual behavior. These stories relate this influence to the return of a past that is seen as too present and determining. Fears about the influence of this past were shared by the priest at the Ram Mandir, who hoped that in the renovations of the temple the European faces would be made invisible. So, one kind of uncanniness in Kharagpur is associated with anxieties about the power of the public spaces of the railway bureaucracy to corrupt lineages, to make the generic colonial past unbearably present, and to inexplicably alter individual conduct. The other kind of uncanniness, associated with Anglo-Indian accounts of Kharagpur, is connected to private spaces and individualized ghostly presences that are often regarded with affection. The uncanny experienced by Clarence Vanjo is intimate, familiar, and domestic. It is associated with an anxiety about the insubstantiality of the public spaces and colonial past of the railway colony rather than with their overpowering influence. These appear as disintegrating ruins, which cannot support the weight of memory. Clarence Vanjo feels that the public spaces of the colony are so ephemeral that they cannot guarantee the continuation of a connection between him and his wife. This has to be maintained through his daily vigils and his wife's entreaties to him.

In the rest of this chapter I relate these two different experiences of the spaces of the colony to dilemmas of ethical self-fashioning that have emerged in relation to the railway bureaucracy.[1] I argue that the presence or absence of the colonial past in particular kinds of spaces is experienced as a function of attempts to form a coherent sense of self in the present. The personal experience of the nearness or farness of the past does not necessarily illustrate its direct causal significance or absence of significance.[2] Instead, the influence of the colonial past can be found at a second analytical level. It is found in the ways that contemporary social relationships, the sentiments that inform them, and the institutions that help to structure them recreate its historical forms in the present.

## THE *JADU* HOUSE AND THE ETERNAL COLONIAL PAST

As I spent more time in Kharagpur I came to find that the stories that Ahmed and Mr. D'Souza told about the Masonic Lodge were widely known. Most people found the lodge mysterious and interesting. They were usually certain that spirits were raised there. They also made the suggestion, based on other people's reports, that the building had a powerful influence at night. These statements were, of course, like rumors—experiments in plausibility—designed to elicit a response of credulity or incredulity on the part of the listener. They were intended as a starting point for speculation. It was not that everyone was convinced of the veracity of the stories, but the uncanny influence of the *jadu* house was an intriguing idea. Different people added their own twists to the tale. For example, one man suggested that it was like the rotary club, but that the officers went in naked and raised spirits as well. Another thought it was a sinister secret society like the Ku Klux Klan. Others said that it had existed to help poor whites with charitable acts, but they weren't sure what it did now. Why did this place provoke such uncanny stories and general speculation across a range of railway families?

One of the reasons for this speculation can be found in the hierarchical management style of railway officers. As we have seen in the previous chapter, the structures of discipline on the railways build on an expansion of colonial forms and enable officers to enact colonial forms of physical authority. Many employees complained to me about the autocratic manner of their superiors and of the railway bureaucracy in general, adding that little had changed since British times. The secret meetings of railway officers in the Raj-era Masonic Lodge provide an opportunity to imaginatively link them to the colonial past that they appear to embody in the workplace. The idea that railway officers conjure up the spirits of the past is engaging because of these hierarchical practices. In this respect, the tales of the *jadu* house are similar to Satish Bose's story of the Mughal palace hidden inside the Raj-era dome of the Eastern Railway Headquarters. They make an intuitive connection between the present practices of the railway bureaucracy and its colonial, "despotic" past. Yet, like Satish's story, they do this by imagining a general overpowering influence of "the past" that distracts from contemporary practices and structures that reproduce its features in the present.

What makes the Masonic Lodge stories even more interesting as a ground for speculation for railway colony families, in particular Bengali railway colony families, is that they express a feeling of a lack of agency *and* remove any responsibility for changing social relationships in the colony. According to these stories, architecture and buildings can exert an irresistible influence over behavior. This resonates with a more general sense among Bengali railway families that the architecture and spatial arrangements of the colony have a determining effect on behavior. In conversations, people repeated the assertion that the physical spaces of Kharagpur and other railway colonies meant that their superior officers behaved like imperial rulers. They added to this that in the colonies and workplaces of the railways it felt like they weren't in India at all and that the colonial past was still continuing in a nightmare of repetition. For example, Sarat Bharat, the clerk we first met in the previous chapter who denounced the tyrannical behavior of his father learned from the workplace, felt that the railway colony buildings deeply affected people's demeanor. He said:

> I hate the distinctions between officers and nonofficers. Office culture is people's whole life. The railway buildings have this effect. Living in the railway colony is not really like being in India. Before Independence, nobody was allowed to go inside the railway colony, and we have maintained this insular British culture. It is a low-minded not a high-minded place.

In the accounts of Indian railway families a tremendous power is given to the Raj-era architecture of the colony. This, it seems, is the source of the extremes of hierarchy that permeate the workplace. For example, Mr. Chakrabarty, whom I met through Abdel and who had worked as an accounts clerk beginning in 1945, eventually rising to a lower officer rank after which he gave up his involvement in a communist-leaning union, expressed this in the following terms:

> In the railway colony the distinctions between different ranks is very categorical. . . . People from the *babu* colony would hardly come over to our place. This is a legacy of the British. The difference has persisted since the British time because the surroundings, quarters maintain the divisions. . . . When I was a junior accounts clerk at Jamalpur I had a bad back problem and was bent over with pain. When I went to the officer's room I was not allowed to sit. The officer discussed a topic with me for half an hour even though it was clear I was in pain. All the administration still works in the British way.

Mr. Chakrabarty added that ultimately when he was promoted to officer rank he couldn't fight these practices himself, as he would have been ostracized by his fellow officers. The tales of the *jadu bari*, or Masonic Lodge, provide a condensation of these notions of the efficacy of architecture and the lack of agency of individuals. It is merely by walking past this structure that people become possessed by the spirits of the past and lose their agency. The evocativeness of this building is perhaps not surprising because of its location and opaque purpose. It is difficult to travel from one side of the colony to the other without passing it, and it stands apart in the middle of a vast open space of grass. It is impossible to see inside as the windows are high up and narrow. The stories that are provoked suggest that railway workers have no agency of their own that can prevent the mnemonic traces of the colonial past invading the behavior of people in the present. In these rumors and in the broader assertions that architecture affects behavior, railway families alienate their own ability to alter social relationships in the present. Spaces take on an occult and uncanny power of their own.

The stories of the *jadu* house invite speculation and are sustained for another reason as well. They resonate with the fears about the dissolution of *jati* in the public spaces of the colony that exist among some railway families. In the previous chapter I described how in Bengali railway families there is an attempt to found their identities in an ahistorical sense of essential cultural difference. They seek to imagine a quality of *jati* within themselves that remains unaffected by the workplace, history, or the railway bureaucracy in general. These attempts at self-fashioning beyond the influence of the railway bureaucracy and its workplaces are supported by the attitudes of the two priests at the Ram and Kali temples where Hindu railway families worship. These priests shared the sense that the spaces of the railways and working for them could have a supernaturally polluting effect on respectability, and by implication on "*jati*," that had to be kept at bay. The stories of the uncanny influence of the *jadu* house and the power of the architecture of the colony involve the return of elements that are suppressed in this attempt to create an ahistorical sense of self. The past is described as a force that suddenly and shockingly determines the actions of people. Raj-era buildings and the magical acts that occur within them penetrate the innermost will. Similarly, railway officers acquire a magical ability to alter behavior. In other words, history and the influence of the bureaucracy over people quite literally erupts, acting on them as a supernatural presence. This uncanny return of the influence of environment and history over essence is made more likely due to the sense inherent to ideas of *jati* that behavior and social interactions have the potential to pollute internal essences. Notions of *jati* contain a dynamic that oscillates between the assertion of an essential substance and fears of the implication of transactions with others for the purity of this substance.[3] In part, the stories of the *jadu* house represent a resurgence of the sense that essences are vulnerable and malleable through time and in the flow of social life. The accounts of the supernatural influence of the *jadu* house are also attempts to grapple with the relationships between the colonial past and the present of the railway colony. They involve speculation about continuities in the public spaces of the colony and their potential effect on people. Yet the uncanny elements of the tales ultimately reify the influence of this past as an external effect of a place and remove the responsibility for social relationships in the colony from people in the present.

It is not surprising given this general sense of the colonial past as uncanny that Anglo-Indians are sometimes associated with *shaitan* (devils) and *djinns* (ghosts). In the previous chapter I showed how for Bengali railway families Anglo-Indians emerge as an alien, egalitarian, materialistic, and polluted other who condense in their behavior all the problems of *jatis* mixing. Bengali railway families, and railway workers more generally, cannot seem to disassociate Anglo-Indians from the colonial past and find it hard to see them as fully Indian. Anglo-Indians in Kharagpur report various examples of the exclusion that results from this. A twenty-five-year-old man, Jacob, who worked in the workshops at Kharagpur as a welder, gave the following account. When he started out in the shops he was given other people's jobs to do and is still given dirty work because he is an Anglo-Indian. His supervisors and fellow workers say to him that he had it good during the Raj and that now he can feel what they felt during those days. Joseph Dover, who works as a driver, told me that his fellow workers kept on accusing him of not being Indian. He retorted by asking them how truly Indian they were since they made such distinctions between different kinds of Indians on the grounds of their being Bihari or Bengali. Anglo-Indian parents complained that their children could not find Indian friends to play with, even though the children went to the same schools. Indians wouldn't let their children play with them or go to their houses because they eat beef. Anglo-Indians also said that it was hard to find places to rent if they lived outside the railway colony because people didn't want to rent to beef eaters, or the landlords asked them to promise not to leave bones lying around.

The moral anxieties and fears about the dissolution of *jati* that these accounts reflect are condensed into a saying that Abdel told me was common in the railway workshops in Kharagpur: "Tikri pa Tikri Loha ka maidan. Adra ki chokari bhooth se be Shaitan." This translates as "Plate by plate making a field of iron. The girl from Adra [a railway colony in Bihar] is more wicked than a devil-spirit." By implication the dangerous female named in this phrase is an Anglo-Indian, as it is only women from this community who "belong" to railway colonies. Abdel reported that his grandfather and work colleagues warned him off Donna with this saying when he first started courting her. This phrase condenses the sense that Anglo-Indian women are amoral predators seeking to entrap, that they are irrevocably associated with the industrial processes of the railway colony, and that they are akin to spirits. Their similarity to spirits works on several different levels. It reflects the sense that Anglo-Indians are remnants of the Raj who do not belong to contemporary India. It also invokes the popular imagination of spirits as predatory beings who are attracted by the moral weaknesses of those they appear to and sometimes possess. *Bhuts* (ghosts) and *shaitans* in general are understood to be drawn by the wearing of inappropriate clothes and improper behavior. The phrase about the girl from Adra therefore warns about the importance of maintaining proper conduct on the part of the people to whom the devil-spirit might appear if they behaved inappropriately. The similarity of Anglo-Indians to spirits also emerges from their uncanniness. Anglo-Indians represent everything that is suppressed in the attempt to preserve an ahistorical sense of an identity based on *jati*. They are born from indiscriminate mixing between castes and communities, practice a casteless egalitarianism, their identities cannot be separated from the industrial spaces of the railways, and their existence recalls the intimate effects of the colonial past. Their reification as an external, uncanny other matches the reification of "the past" and of architecture in the tales of the *jadu* house.

These accounts of the uncanniness of the railway colony and of Anglo-Indians express a sense that the colonial past is strangely near and that it exerts a tempting, powerful influence. They also help to reify this past, representing it as an inexplicable, eerie influence that acts through places and specific kinds of people. Ultimately, this helps to reproduce the sensibilities that had their origins in the transactions of colonial history. In particular, it means that some railway employees do not attempt to alter workplace hierarchies in the present and that they continue to recreate specific sensibilities associated with *jati* that emerged under the Raj. The colonial past is therefore present in Kharagpur, but not through the independent agency of physical spaces and material culture.[4] It is present in mutable human relationships that some families in Kharagpur represent as eternal manifestations of architectural forms, as spaces, and as "other" people.

## "WE ARE NOWHERE"

Railway families in general feel that the colonial past is strangely near and the influence of its spaces is potent. However, Anglo-Indian railway families in Kharagpur have a quite different sense of the spaces of the railway colony. For them, the railway colony is a place of ruins and degeneration rather than of potent, enduring presences. It is haunted, but not by ominous general influences. Instead, as Mr. Vanjo's account indicated, it is filled by domestic, familiar, and intimate ghosts. As we will see, this different sense of the topography of Kharagpur arises from two sources. First, from the particular dilemmas of ethical self-fashioning that arise for Anglo-Indians. Second, from their attempts to connect themselves to their family histories and to the spaces of Kharagpur.

Anglo-Indians in Kharagpur have a clear sense of what an Anglo-India is. An Anglo-Indian is a person who has a British, Irish, Scottish, or otherwise European ancestor in either the male or female line, practices Christianity, and has English as a first language. Originating ancestors are always described as a man who came from abroad and married an Indian woman. However, Anglo-Indians find it difficult to trace contemporary markers, physical proof, or any other sign of continuity to demonstrate the origins of their families and of their identity. In chapter 8 I explored how hard it is for Anglo-Indians to build a narrative of continuity for their families and themselves. Their historical experience of the railway bureaucracy and of their interactions with fellow Indians mean that it is difficult to found a sense of connection between the past and the present on the basis of their bodies or through documentation. They long for what they do not possess—documentation and proof of an essential bodily quality handed down through generations. This specific longing among Anglo-Indians is a subset of their more general longing for a foundation for their selves equivalent to that of the *jati* and *desh* possessed by some of their fellow Indian railway families. Their inability to fashion their selves according to the principles of *jati* and *desh* constituted in the history of railway labor and related to popular nationalisms has a curious effect. It leads to Anglo-Indians experiencing a dematerialization of their memories, histories, and family inheritances. In tandem with this, the physical space of the railway colony appears to be a place of ruins. Unable to assert continuities between the past and the present, Anglo-Indians are left with a sense of the invisibility of their own selves, of the chaotic degeneration of their community, and of the insubstantiality of their surroundings. A permanent substance and place for family and kinship eludes Anglo-Indians in Kharagpur. They long for the sense of a past and a future in the present that such continuity of family would give them.

What, then, are the effects of this absence of *jati* and *desh* on Anglo-Indian railway families' senses of selfhood, place, and time? One effect is an overwhelming sense among Anglo-Indians in Kharagpur that they are a community filled with signs of degeneration and decline. For example, Colt Campbell repeatedly said that Anglo-Indians' existence in Kharagpur is impossible: they "have no future here." He suggested that young people, including his own children, had become "worse than *chamars* [*dalits*, or commonly "untouchables"]." When I asked Serina Dover to write down an account of Anglo-Indian life in Kharagpur, she presented me with a depressing tale of degeneration. It began with "We Anglo-Indians don't think of the future" and told stories of sons beating their mothers, young girls going astray, and husbands drinking themselves to death. It ended with the following statements: "most of our young girls know we have to get married in our own caste and have to face the same problems. So they think why don't we enjoy our lives after marriage. Some girls enjoy herself when her husband is away at railway work. This is the life of our community." Although this despair was born in part from the failures of love in her own family, it is important that she saw this not as an individual dilemma, but projected it into the nature of Anglo-Indians as a whole, who are without any "future." Serina had, of course, escaped the fate of her caste by marrying an Indian Christian. She thereby founded a different genealogical origin for herself.

Tales of moral and physical decline came together most clearly in Hope Dover's account of the moral chaos of the colony. The failures of her marriage and the uncertain economic position of her family gave her a sense, like her daughter's, of a chaotic present. But, importantly, these problems are attributed to the wider predatory nature and immorality of the Anglo-Indian community. For Hope, her community, rather than giving her a secure sense of self, was full of potential dangers of pollution and threats to physical integrity. She told me that when her husband died, none of the doctors could figure out what had been wrong with him. But she knew that her husband "caught his death" at the Jensen's house, where women will "force themselves on young boys for money." There, she said, they "swap wives and husbands and sons and daughters too." Her husband, she added, got his death from a blue stone they put in his drink one night. It was this that killed him, and this was "why the doctors couldn't find anything despite all their scans and tests." She suggested that the Anglo-Indian village compound called mini-Australia or Santa Barbara was also a place where these kinds of things happen. The wives there took, according to Hope, "country liquor before their food." They offered it to her, but she was afraid to take it. She added that "they drink so much—that's why they look so fat and plump." Hope also warned me that the people I was meeting, although they seemed so nice, weren't. Colt was "a bad man who took a knuckle-duster and killed one man and was in prison for it." Then she added that Colt and Loretta's son, "the one who lives with them, is really his servant's child by him. The Telugu community took him to court and made him adopt the son so they took him in." She continued by warning me that I should be careful not to eat in anybody's house. She "never eats anything at people's homes." Her sister said she is "proud that way, but it's not pride"; she "is afraid." Hope sees her community in the railway colony as a site of decline and pollution that threatens her own integrity and that killed her husband. Her vision was obviously extreme, born of personal and economic losses, but it was characteristic of other Anglo-Indians in its sense of the chaos of the present.

Anglo-Indian railway families find it equally difficult to ground themselves and a family history in the spaces of the railway colony. The Anglo-Indians who live in Kharagpur have no sense that it provides a solid foundation for their family and community identities. Instead, they suggest that it is a place of ruins. At times they even feel that Kharagpur is insubstantial and unreal, too fragile and evanescent to mold memories or to be a repository for them. This sense of the insubstantiality of Kharagpur was most clearly expressed by Colt. His locality, even after thirty years of work in Kharagpur, offers him no sense of place. The railway colony, for him, has lost its reality since Independence. He described how it used to be as follows: "We had avenues, we had streets, all numbered and named with gates" that guarded the entrance to beautiful gardens full of roses and dahlias. These streets and avenues still exist, but for him they have disappeared, lost in the application of "cow-dung cakes" and disguised by "saris hanging out to dry." He said that for him and all the Anglo-Indians in England all their memories were in Kharagpur. When they return to it they just sit outside their old houses and recite the names of everybody who used to live in the blocks. He added that that was why they return, in order to "find their memories." He suggested that he and these returning people "remember the old place, so they have affection for it," but that the next generation, including his sons, "don't have this." Kharagpur lost its power as a place for memory with Independence. It has no substance, no reality to mold a future nostalgia. Colt added that the Anglo-Indians in Kharagpur were actually without an embeddedness in place at all: now, "We are nowhere." This sense of the insubstantiality of place as a foundation for memory, family history, and selfhood was echoed in many of my conversations. For Anglo-Indians who still live in railway colonies such as Kharagpur, the transition of Independence and their loss of economic privileges have meant the loss of a home territory. They are painfully aware that especially since the 1960s, when their right to reserved posts expired, the railway colony homeland has ceased to exist. They are also less likely to romanticize their ownership of this space in the past, remembering scenes of late-colonial humiliation. The railway colony quite patently is not "their" space and perhaps never has been. Their desire for a *desh* equivalent to that of other Indians in the colony and other urban spaces cannot be fulfilled. Therefore, the spaces of the colony feel increasingly insubstantial and like ruins.

If the present is a time of degeneration and if space is too insubstantial to offer an anchor for Anglo-Indian family histories, then historical narratives are equally problematic. As Carsten, following Lambek and Antze, has suggested, when identities are in question then memories are also placed in doubt.[5] As we have seen, Anglo-Indian identities are constantly questioned by their fellow workers in the railway colony. Anglo-Indians lacking the crucial qualities of *jati* and *desh* find it hard to place their memories into a continuous historical narrative that could act as an origin story of who they are. Especially problematic are accounts and memories related to events of colonial history. When I first asked Anglo-Indians in Kharagpur about the colonial past and the events of Independence, they talked about an unspecified "then" that was elusive and fragmentary. A typical response was that I received from Colt. He and Loretta told me they couldn't remember when Independence came, and Colt added, "I don't want to remember also."

The only colonial event that emerged in his conversations was "the Mutiny." However, this was a free-floating conventional signifier that according to Colt explained why Muslims and Hindus didn't bother his family during partition riots in Kharagpur. He said they knew that the Anglo-Indians were positioned very high above them after the Mutiny so they didn't touch them. This historical event in 1857 only served to explain Anglo-Indians' lack of visibility in the events of Independence. It was not an origin point for an engagement with the present, nor was it a foundation for Colt's current sense of self or of his family. It explained, according to Colt, why Anglo-Indians were, as he put it, "nowhere to be seen," not part of the transitions of Independence. Anglo-Indians in general evaded discussions of the details of late-colonial events and of the impact of them on their families.

People's uneven recollection and evasion of the Raj-era colony and Independence was sometimes broken through by their dramatic recall of specific events. Gracie Dover, for example, described how as a ten-year-old child she was very excited by the preparations in school for Independence. The schoolchildren made flags and sang a song that included the line "Everyone will have *pan supari*, *gulab jamun*, and *jalebis* when India gets home rule," celebrating with a song about the distribution of Indian sweets. Phylis Daniels recounted how she had saved a Muslim family from death in Liluah during the partition riots there. Christians in the colony put crosses on their doors so that the rioters wouldn't touch them. Phylis, who had lived in Jamalpur and Liluah before settling after her husband's retirement in Kolkata, told me:

> About ten o'clock in night a family came to me. They turned and told me whatever you do, Jesus, three children they had, whatever you do save our lives. . . . I locked them up in the bathroom. . . . What they were doing down the road and on the street, they were taking little five-month-old baby, three-month-old baby, had a knife like that, up like that, the baby on the knife.

These events broke through the general atmosphere of evasion. However, their sudden eruption remained fragments of emotion unconnected to the contemporary life of Anglo-Indian families.

The inability to weave colonial memories into continuous narratives of identity is due in part to the sense of humiliation Anglo-Indians experienced in the Raj-era railway colony. Women described how during the war English soldiers stationed at Kharagpur and imported English train drivers looked down on Anglo-Indians. They, in Marigold Jones's words, thought that Anglo-Indians were "jungly and uneducated." They were shocked that Anglo-Indians could speak

English well. Women described how Englishmen would have relationships with them and then turn out to be married. They also recounted sexual harassment; Phylis erupted unexpectedly into a tirade about the "bloody British" when relating her experiences in the Women's Auxiliary Corps, India. Men recounted their exclusion from workplace leisure spaces such as the tearooms. Quite simply, the colonial past of the railway colony cannot provide continuous ground for narratives of Anglo-Indian families because it was an ambivalent—and sometimes painful—experience. But more importantly, memories of this past cannot become narratives of legitimate selfhood. If Anglo-Indians cite their links to the Raj, then this only serves to confirm their illegitimacy in the eyes of other Indian railway families. As we have seen, Anglo-Indians are irrevocably associated with the past by their fellow workers, even appearing sometimes as devil-spirits. If they made colonial history part of the metalanguage of the origins of their families and an explicit historical narrative in which to anchor their memories, it would only further prove the irrelevance of Anglo-Indians to the Indian present. It would also make them too fatally embedded in the events of history to possess *jati*, which, as we have seen in the example of Bengali railway families, has become associated with an ahistorical property.

In this atmosphere of insubstantiality and degeneration, some Anglo-Indians abandon a search for *jati* and *desh* altogether. Instead, they celebrate their individual lack of responsibility to family or community and envisage a kind of liberty to cross boundaries. Hope, for example, in her optimistic moments told me that she loved to travel to Kolkata. She joked that her friends ask her, "What do you go to Calcutta for, don't you like those up-country [Anglo-Indian] boys? She said that she replies to them, "No, I've tried all sorts now, Oriya, Tamil, Anglo castes, and now I want some Bengali boys." Freedom, for Hope, meant the double escape from the space of the colony and the logic of blood that placed her in an arranged marriage. It is imagined as a mobility in which she mixes with all castes, "trying all sorts," losing respectability in a taste for all types, defying Indian and European bloodlines and community boundaries.

This image of mobility was much more common among Anglo-Indian men than women. Not surprisingly, this was particularly so among those who were or had been engine drivers. Drivers described themselves as "Kings of the Road." Particularly characteristic of this kind of narrative of mobility is that of Leslie Francis. His whole account of his life was built around a kind of restlessness. At seventeen he began work on the engines as a *khalasi* because he constantly ran away from his boarding school in Bangalore. He hated the regular routine there, and he would get bored and then just take to the tracks with four of five other truants. Once he started driving he used to love hurtling from station to station with his best clothes in his driver's box ready for the local dance. He had no attachment to one place; he proudly described how his home could be a blanket on the station platform or a running room. He said that this life had left him unable to sit still. He always has to be on the move, walking around the house. He added that if he closes his eyes now he can still see every detail of the track along his regular routes. He dreams every other night about driving trains. This mobility he said led him to hate being at home with his Anglo-Indian wife. They divorced thirty years ago and ever since, he said, he had tried all types of women. As a driver on his runs he met all sorts, taking up with them all—Oriya women, Bihari women, low-caste, high-caste, and Bengali women. Once, he lived in the village outside the railway colony at Anara with an *adivasi* woman. He loved her very much, but he went off on pilgrimage to Our Lady of Health at Velankanni to cure his liver, and when he returned she had taken up with someone else. In one sense, as we have seen, he presently continues his mobile life as he lives in a circuit of relatives' homes between Kolkata and Adra. In the railway colony, Anglo-Indians suggested that restlessness was an essential quality of their community. They often cite the saying "Muslim ka hari, Bengali ka bari, Anglo-Indian ka gari" (Muslims are all for cooking, Bengalis are all for houses, and the Anglo-Indians are all for cars). Given the fact that not one Anglo-Indian I met in the colony owned a car, this saying reflects a valuing of movement rather than of cars as specific prestige objects. Anglo-Indians have tried to make the vice of mobility that makes them suspect in relation to categories of *jati* and *desh* into a virtue. In these versions of Anglo-Indian selves, their essential nature is associated positively with the power of technology and the mobility of industrial labor.

It is clear from these examples that the general longing among Anglo-Indians for a stable *jati* and *desh*-like foundation for their sense of self, family, and community is hard to resolve. Their inability to find a source or substance of continuity often leaves them feeling invisible, insubstantial, and insignificant. Similarly, historical narratives frequently remain fragmentary and memories are felt to be unanchored and irrelevant. Even the physical spaces of the railway colony begin to lose their solidity. Anglo-Indian genealogies and family histories are therefore dematerialized by the prevailing notions of railway morality. Some Anglo-Indians abandon the quest for *jati* or pedigree altogether in images of individual mobility and freedom. Overall, their lack of *jati* and *desh* leads them to feeling politically illegitimate and irrelevant. When I asked Anglo-Indians about their political commitments, they expressed a hopeless apathy about the local and national situation. At the most they said that they voted Congress, "because when in Rome, you must do what the Romans do." Anglo-Indians link this lack of proficiency with politics to an essential illegitimacy of their community and to their colonial origins. This emerges in their accounts of how Anglo-Indians were offered the Andamans by Nehru as a homeland at Independence. People repeatedly told me this story, which condensed their sense that Anglo-Indians were irrevocably associated by Indians with the brutalities of colonial rule. This made the Andamans, the site of a Raj-era brutal jail regime where nationalists were imprisoned, the natural place for them. The full significance of these stories was made clear to me in a conversation with Colt. One day, when we were sitting with his wife and brother-in-law, he joked that the Anglo-Indians who had stayed back in India were the patriotic Anglo-Indians. His wife and brother-in-law giggled at the idea that such an adjective could apply to their "community." They then talked about how Nehru had offered Frank Anthony (a past president of the Anglo-Indian Association) an Anglo-Indian homeland in the Andaman Islands. Colt said that they would have messed this up because "in truth they were all bastards anyway." The mixed and illegitimate origins of Anglo-Indians embedded in the history of the colonial encounter made it impossible for them to imagine founding any political, national, or community space, even a homeland for themselves in contemporary India. But, as we will see, there is one context in which the chronic instability that besets their projects of attempting to acquire a *jati*-like quality and embedding in place for their selves, family, and community is overcome. This is in the domain of the uncanny.

## DOMESTIC GHOSTS AND DIVINE CITIZENSHIP

I was surprised by the number of Anglo-Indian families in Kharagpur that told ghost stories and had their own personal ghosts in their homes. These domestic ghosts were usually quite benign. They were often associated with a vision of community and of connections between generations founded on the idea of a Catholic community of worship. Overall, experiences of the uncanny were connected to a return of self-being that is impossible to effect in other contexts and to an assertion of connections to the place of the railway colony.

Typical of these ghost tales and their themes were those told in one sitting to me by Gracie, Freddie, and Joseph Dover. One day I began a conversation with them by asking about the Masonic Lodge and its associations. They agreed that spirits were raised there, but they were not particularly interested in pursuing this line of thought. Instead, Gracie began to tell a stream of ghost stories, her tales punctuated by additions from Freddie and Joseph. First, she said that her sister had lived in Anara, and she asserted that most cottages there are haunted. Her nephew, when he was only five, used to get up at night and hide under the bed because he was so worried. She explained that this haunting was because the place was built on a Christian cemetery. Gracie then said that her own neighbor's son fell sick and went to see a Muslim to get a token to cure himself. His elder sister saw the token, got angry, and put it up on the altar. At night things started turning over and the gramophone started playing, when it had not played for years. The boy died a week later. From then on, at night the gramophone used to start up and play a hymn that was the boy's favorite.

Joseph then said to his mother that she should tell me about what had happened to them in the house they had lived in before the current one. He added that the events there had made even him believe in ghosts. Gracie said that in their house in the colony they had an extra member of the family. In the morning she used to be shaken awake so she could get the tea ready for everyone. At night, if you were asleep on a particular bed, then you would feel someone brushing past you. Even Joseph lay there once and woke up startled by the sensation. Gracie and her daughter-in-law saw a little boy of eleven or twelve years old in short black pants and a singlet walking past the house and inside as well. They used to set an extra plate for the ghost at the table during all the meals. At this point Freddie giggled, adding, "I'm not afraid of ghosts; I am one." Everyone laughed, and Joseph said, "that's true enough." Gracie just kept on with her stories. She said that there was a little six- or seven-year-old boy who had holy communion in the church. A photographer took his picture. The boy died at eleven. The photographer later went back to the church to take a picture of something, and the boy was in the resulting photo. He brought it to the mother, who said that her son had been dead for three years. Gracie then said that her mother once told her a true story about that church. The priest in the church didn't say the mass properly and died. One day the choristers heard the church bells ringing and people laughing and singing in the church. They ran in, and there was a ghost of the priest in the church saying mass, and all the people who were dead and gone were at that mass too.

In these stories and experiences of the uncanny, the Dover family, and Gracie in particular, draw a series of connections between ghosts, domestic and religious spaces in Kharagpur, dead family members, and the church. Her stories began with the assertion that the domestic spaces of the railway colony at Adra are constructed on a Christian graveyard. This suggested that there is a potential continuity of Anglo-Indian domestic history underlying these spaces. The houses are founded literally on their ancestors. The importance of graveyards as one of the signs of a rooting in place of Anglo-Indian family history cannot be underestimated. Gracie's emphasis on them was echoed in many accounts, including that of Clarence, who has to return to the graveyard every day. Similarly, people worried about whether they would get spaces in them. Families would carefully preserve and make a point of telling me about papers that guaranteed a right to be buried in Catholic cemeteries. Sometimes people who had with foresight collected a large number of these would hand these on as a treasured inheritance after their death to favorite members of the family. Close family members (reckoned bilaterally) wanted to be buried together in these spaces, and people would tell me proudly about any relatives who were interred in them. Graveyards are more than simply places of memorial where people go to recall lost family members and shared community losses. For Anglo-Indians, the graveyard is proof of genealogical ancestry, a location of generic identification with a place, and a place where authentic family feelings and connections are celebrated and recreated. They described graveyards as locations filled with family members who demand acts of caring from them and that root them in specific places. Ghosts of dead relatives called them to the graveyard. These ghosts articulate people's visceral, emotional relationship both to the deceased person and to the place where they live.

The significance of the graveyard as a place where family history, ancestral continuity, and a connection to place can be asserted is made fully visible during the celebrations of All Souls' Day, on November 2.[6] On this day families go to the church in order to offer prayers for the souls of the dead. They then go to the graveyard and wash the graves of their relatives. They scatter flowers, light candles, and burn incense on them. After the vigil at the grave, they return home and eat simple food with their extended families, including people from both their maternal and paternal lines. This occasion provides a renewal of connections to ancestors and to a place that is contrasted to the lack of family feeling that creates Anglo-Indian diasporas. For example, when I joined Gary and Carol at lunch after the All Souls' ceremony in Kolkata, I found them discussing divided families. Carol and Gary described how one man was coming from England to Kolkata for a tour to try to trace his son and daughter. The mother had died when the children were young, and the father, wanting to get rid of them, sent them to Dr. Graham's Homes in Darjeeling, which was meant for orphans. The son resented the father and led his life independently. The family knew he was now dead. They were debating whether they should tell the returning father this piece of news. The consensus emerged that they had better keep quiet because the father didn't care about his son anyway. He had no, as they put it, "family feeling" in the past, so what was the point of telling him of the death of his son and where he was buried? The moral failings and wanderings of this father were the inverse of the connections to family and place that they had just celebrated in the graveyard. Ghosts and graveyards are therefore assimilated to domestic spaces quite simply because they are one of the only contexts in which a family connection to the place of the railway colony and to the past can be made by Anglo-Indians. The ghost that visited Gracie's nephew in Adra affirmed the links of Anglo-Indians to the railway colony in the form of an externalized and physically experienced manifestation.

The next two stories Gracie told me add another piece to the puzzle of the significance of the uncanny to Anglo-Indians. She described two family hauntings.

In the first, the grief of the loss of a child was externalized in a way that asserted a continuing connection to the dead family member and warned of transgressing the boundaries of an Anglo-Indian Christian community. The cause of the child's death was attributed to his stepping outside of the boundaries of his community of faith, accepting a magic token from a Muslim. But the child's return through the medium of a hymn signaled that in death the ties of family and community are remade. These ties are externalized into an irrefutable force that returns in a domestic space in Kharagpur. The boy's ghost thus helps to affirm the permanence of ties between community, place, and family history. The Dovers' friendly ghost reveals how welcome such domestic presences are and that all ghosts are strongly associated with lost family members. The Dovers incorporated their little boy ghost into the family routines and even laid a plate for him at the table. This ghost is a welcome external sign of temporal and spatial continuity, mediating in his youthfulness an image of the dead past and of the future represented by children. This is why he was welcomed into the family. He was both an ancestral Anglo-Indian presence and an image of the future made manifest in their home. The link of such ghosts to ancestors and family continuity is made explicit by Freddie's comment, "I'm not afraid of ghosts; I am one." This phrase had a double meaning, which is why the family laughed at it. On the one hand, it registered the sense that other Indians have of Anglo-Indians as uncanny remnants. On the other, it expressed the fact that Freddie is the oldest member of the family, almost ancestral, and the next to be a (friendly) ghost. This is why Joseph murmured his appreciation of his father's phrase.

This affection toward ghosts was repeated in many families in Kharagpur. Everyone agreed that Anglo-Indians were great ones for calling the spirits back, but only those of their relatives. As we have seen in chapter 8, the Vanjo family was haunted by the presence of Milly, who returned to assert the veracity of kinship ties and relations of affection despite the suspicions of other Anglo-Indians and the British immigration authorities. Hope recounted how her husband returned to the family. Her granddaughter, whenever she visited Hope at home, heard her grandfather calling to her. Her eldest daughter saw him in dreams bringing sweets and food to their house. When her husband was on his deathbed, he heard his own family calling to him. The day before he died he said his mother called to him, saying, "Son, son, it's your brother's birthday tomorrow. Come home to celebrate it with us." Her husband died the next day, thus fulfilling his kinship obligations. The accounts by Hope of her husband's ghost confirm the association of ghosts with ancestors and connections across the generations. These are welcome presences because they externalize in a physical sensation and felt presence continuities in space and time. They offer a moment of authenticity of self-being in which connections to place and the past are felt acting from outside on the body.

This calling of spirits is perceived as quite distinct from that practiced in the Masonic Lodge. This was made clear in the account of Donna Ahmed of what happened when her uncle, who was a mason, died. First, she agreed that in the Masonic Lodge, "they call up spirits by table rapping and that if you want to talk to anybody that is dead up here you can talk." Then she added that when she was seven years old her uncle died in Kolkata. His body was motored in. Donna then explained with great sadness that the body was kept at the Masonic Lodge in a "full bronze coffin, airtight," rather than being brought home to the family house. The family couldn't go and see it there, and the Masons never opened the coffin so that they could see the Uncle's face. Quite simply, the Masons appropriated her dead uncle, removing him from his family for their own purposes. Their actions blanched all the intimate possibilities from the past and relationships with the dead. By implication, the calling of spirits by railway officers and their relation with the past is marked as profoundly distinct from the personalized relationships of Anglo-Indians.

The forms of Catholicism practiced by Anglo-Indians provide the specific interpretative frame for these accounts of intimate, welcome hauntings that reaffirm the existence of continuities between the past and present and of a community. Gracie's final two stories linked the ghostly presences of ancestors explicitly to the practices of the Catholic Church. In the first story, the church and its ceremony of confirmation provides the site of the return of a lost son. In the second story, when the dead priest returns to say the mass properly, he calls up the whole community of Anglo-Indians who are dead and gone. This event provides a ghostly manifestation of the reality of the past community of Anglo-Indians. They are made present within the walls of the church and in relation to its practices. These stories reflect the more general sense that Anglo-Indians have that the practices of Catholicism provide a means of mediating a relationship to your dead family members, provide the substance of kinship, and give the transcendent authority of divine citizenship to their community.[7] Anglo-Indians, as we have seen, are not recognized as fully Indian by fellow railway families because of their ambiguous *jati*, disconnection from a *desh*, and association with the colonial past. For this reason, it is difficult for Anglo-Indians to articulate their identities to the forms of regional nationalism that surround them. In the context of their exclusion from these forms of belonging, Anglo-Indians particularly emphasize the aspects of Catholicism that reify personal connections and pasts into a divine citizenship.[8] They do this, however, in a manner that serves to give transcendent legitimation to historical connections to a specific place, to ancestors, and to the idea of an Anglo-Indian community. Family origins and continuity with them are founded on the basis of Catholic practices.

We have already seen this dynamic at work in relation to graveyards and the celebration of All Souls' Day. It is also present in the practices surrounding the picture of the sacred heart, which is the image kept on the family altar in most Anglo-Indian houses. The family altar is usually in an intimate space of the house, either the area where the family sits most often or in the bedroom of the core couple of the family (the husband and wife who are still of working age rather than retired, elderly parents). At first light and dusk the wife of the core couple lights incense and puts flowers on the altar and says prayers for the whole family, including deceased relatives. Often, photos of close dead relatives from the maternal and paternal line are placed next to the sacred heart or are the only other images put up on the walls of the house. On the birthday of recently deceased close relatives the priest is called to the house to bless the sacred heart picture. He dresses up in a gold and white robe and sprinkles holy water on the sacred heat picture. Close relatives of the deceased, such as partners, daughters, sons, sisters, and brothers, attend the ceremony and a meal afterward. These events are an occasion to recall the lost family member. These practices around the sacred heart give a transcendent permanence to the presence of dead family members and create a sacred continuity of personal and community history. Catholic practices lend to the Anglo-Indian community a solidity and transcendence that it cannot achieve in other contexts.

As we have seen throughout the second part of the book, Anglo-Indians appropriate Catholic practices and idioms to create a transcendent reality for their fluid substances of relatedness, sentiments of love, and personal origins. These practices do not surpass or oppose nationalist ideas of *jati* and *desh*, but instead cross-fertilize notions of secular citizenship founded in connections to place and to a lineage with ideas of divine communities. The significance of Catholic idioms for these substances of relatedness became most visible to me when Phylis told me of a prayer that she and other Anglo-Indians said when they felt troubled. She said that this prayer should be offered to the Jesus of Mercy at three o'clock in the afternoon on any Friday. It went as follows:

> You expired Jesus, but the source of life gushed forth as an ocean of mercy. Unfathomable, divine mercy envelop the whole world and empty yourself out upon us.
>
> Oh Blood and Water which gushed forth from the heart of Jesus as a fount of mercy for us. I trust in you.

This prayer turns the iconography of the sacred heart into a potent figure of the origins of life, blood, and healing holy water.

The close association of sacred heart pictures with images of ancestral core couples makes clear the links between the healing blood and water of Jesus and the substances of families. In fact, the holy water mentioned in the prayer is often used to heal people when breaches in families have become too acute. It acts as a substitute nurturing medium for the presence of relatives and as a means to reconnect to these lost family members, reviving sustaining ties of affection. Holy water in most general terms is used to cure people of physical-moral ailments, but this curing is strongly associated with the forms of love and nurturance within families. For example, Leslie offered the following account of his miraculous healing on a trip to Our Lady of Health at Velankanni:

From when my mother died in 1952 religion meant nothing to me. After she died I started to drink too much. Then the whole family roamed about and got dissipated. I just started drinking and chasing women in all the stations. But I got very ill in 1984 and was in hospital for one year with stomach complaints. All through the illness I made a vow to go to Velankanni near Madras if I got well. My mother first showed me the place when I went on pilgrimage there with her in 1951. After I was a little better I went there, and I started to feel much worse on the train journey. In the rickshaw I would get bad pains as it moved up and down. On the train as it started moving—clickety-clack—I was in agony and couldn't eat, just asking my friend with me, Davy, for a nip of rum. When we reached Velankanni I was in pain, and we went straight to the cathedral. In the cathedral as the priest said mass I began to feel very thirsty, so I asked Davy to give me some holy water to drink. I drank it and the pain lessened and I felt very hungry. We finished the mass and went to a hotel to eat. Davy couldn't believe how much I ate. Since then whenever I feel a pain I take a little drop of holy water and feel better again. Now religion has come back to me like when my mother was alive.

Other uses of holy water even more explicitly healed breaches caused by the death of or separation from blood relatives. Sandra, Gary's wife, for example, gave the following account of its effects:

I've had ten years of depression, Laura. It only lifted about two years ago. After my mother died and my sister Harriet left for Australia I couldn't stay at home. And every evening when I was doing the housework and everything I would feel a presence come behind me. My mind would go blank and I wouldn't feel nice. Feeling so bad I went to Christ the King to have the priests pray over me—the power of prayer. I used to sit with my Bible open and my rosary with the tears streaming down my face saying my Hail Marys. But one day the priest gave me holy water and I'm alright now, just sometimes it comes over me.

In Anglo-Indian accounts, holy water is the medium that heals breaches in intimate family relations introduced by death and dispersal. The sacred heart prayer of Phylis in particular makes clear that the substances of kinship—life and blood—are interchangeable with the holy water and blood of Christ. But in Anglo-Indian reckonings this life force of Christ is not a substitute for nor does it appropriate the female generation of life and ties of sentiment. Instead, it compliments the generative nurturing power of mothers and revives their influence.[9]

The ghosts described above that haunt Anglo-Indian families such as the Dovers articulate this transcendent community bound by the life of holy blood and holy water to particular places in the railway colony, anchoring it into a topography. Specific experiences of the uncanny provide a context for meditating on temporal and spatial continuities in personal identity, family, and community experience that cannot be asserted elsewhere. The very same ancestors and history that cannot be acknowledged in other social contexts are felt acting on the body as irresistible external forces. The uncanny is a particularly potent context for producing an authenticity of history and community because it is made up of experiences in which the past and spaces are felt to act on you from outside. This sensation of external agency easily transforms into the idea that you as an individual are part of a larger transcendent community, are caught up in long-term forces of history, and are tied to a place that acts on you. Anglo-Indians therefore find solace in it as it provides a source for an authenticity of self-being and belonging that otherwise evades them.

## COLONIAL REMNANTS, THE UNCANNY, AND NATION-STATE HISTORIES

After these discussions of *jati*, divine citizenship, and the uncanny, it would be easy to assume that no secular solidarity of citizenship survives in the railway colony. This would be far from the truth. There are people in the colony that pride themselves on being the representatives of such a political vision. One such example is Abdel Ahmed. As we have seen in previous chapters, he was proud of his "intercaste" marriage to an Anglo-Indian woman. He and his wife founded their identity on a certificate that proved their secular credentials and also held them up as an example to all Indians. He, like his wife, Donna, emphasized his own self-formation into this cosmopolitan self through the cultivation of his physical prowess in sport. His sense of his status as a mediator among communities extended into the practical side of his work as well. He told me that he fixes things with the railway officers for any worker who is in trouble or needs help. Interestingly, Abdel ultimately associated this role as a mediator and his cosmopolitanism with becoming Anglo-Indian. He asserted that through his cultivation of his physical self in sport he had become indistinguishable from them, and that he shared their lack of interest in community distinction. This concept of Anglo-Indians is obviously idealistic, but it shows how a secular narrative of the self can give a positive valuation to the status of being Anglo-Indian. It is, of course, precisely because of Abdel's cosmopolitan self that he took me on the extraordinary guided tour of the railway colony that had revealed so much. On the one hand, he wanted to demonstrate that he had free access (as it said in the certificate on his bedroom wall) to any kind of religious or community space in Kharagpur. On the other, having crossed boundaries with his "intercaste" marriage that provoked controversy, he was acutely aware of the anxieties in other railway families about *jati* and *desh*.

Anglo-Indians often attempted to assert an image of themselves that matched Abdel's sense of them as cosmopolitan citizens. They decried all of the distinctions that Indians traded in based on caste and regional identity. Yet for most of them this did not remove the anxiety of a search for an equivalent of *desh* and *jati*. An exception was Trevor Franklin, a fifty-year-old locomotive inspector, whom I met in Adra when I went for the wedding of Bastian and Michelle. He was an old friend of Gerald, and the Jones family held him in affectionate regard. He lived in one of the rigidly functional new blocks that have been built in the last thirty years on the outskirts of Adra for railway employees. Outside the yellow-stained and cracked concrete flats were mud and dung houses for goats. Inside Trevor's flat the atmosphere paid homage to Jesus, Mary, and the joys of whiskey and the blues. The top of Trevor's *almirah* was a makeshift shrine with figurines of Jesus and Mary honored by incense sticks. Stacked against them were packs of cigarettes and cards. On the wall was a poster of a motorbike, under which was the saying, "Who does not have God is not Strong." Trevor was usually to be found, according to Gary, as I found him the day I met him, surrounded by Indian friends drinking whiskey and listening to Otis Redding. In our conversation Trevor asserted a similar secular identity to that of Abdel, but his version was founded on an explicitly political vision of working class struggle. Whenever I asked Trevor questions about his life, he repeatedly returned to his involvement in founding the All India Locomotive Running Association in 1973 and the events of the 1974 strike called by George Fernandez. This large-scale protest against government policies contributed to the declaration of a state of emergency by Indira Gandhi. Trevor did not want to talk about anything else. Trevor framed his life around an emphasis on his workplace relationships, union activity, and this strike.

He began work on the railways as a *khalasi*, rose to the position of driver, and finally to loco inspector. He said he had a lot of respect from his subordinate workers because he treated them all with money, giving the odd rupee here and there and extra food rations. In return they called him "*saheb*" and respected him, telling him he was "the man," not like the other Anglo-Indian drivers. He got even more respect after the 1974 strike. The union branch that he had helped found made thorough preparations for the strike. The union had code words that were sent through the telegraph network. They said innocuous things like "business is good," and they were sent to the "clog maker" in the colony, not to any employee, because employees were spied on by the Vigilance Department. Once the strike started the arrest order went out from the Railway Police, and Trevor was on the list of those to be arrested. But one of the policemen warned him in advance about his arrest. So, he ran out of the colony and lived in the jungle and village for many weeks. He sneaked into his aunt's house for food and into the Railway Institute at night. He enjoyed hiding right at the heart of the colony. In the villages he and the other union members would encourage the locals who worked on the railways to keep going with the strike and told them about political matters. Trevor did incorporate into this political vision a hierarchical sense of leadership in a manner often characteristic of union officers. He said that he got respect in the villages because of his white skin. But in spite of this invoking of an innate superiority, Trevor proudly told me that it was as a result of his role in the strike that he had so many Indian friends and was respected by his fellow workers. He added that he was proud to be Indian.

Trevor built a connection to India and Adra via his family history as well. He produced a family tree leading back to a Sir Francis Bailey in England via a female relative, and a photograph of his grandfather and grandmother that he had spliced together with a bit of Xerox trickery. But for Trevor the important element of his family history was that it could root him in Adra. He emphasized that Adra was really his family hometown. His grandfather, who had been born in Norfolk, worked for a while in Adra. The first grave in the Adra cemetery was that of one of his grandfather's daughters, Kathleen. It was largely as a result of Trevor's involvement in the strike of 1974 that he had transformed his status and the very shape of his life. The political vision of working class struggle had combined with the building of workplace friendships to enable Trevor to overcome distinctions of *jati* and *desh*. His connections were made even more fluid by the fact that he had never married, so he had never cemented a community link in the all-important domestic sphere. He had never had to found a family with his personal imaginings of genealogy. It might have been more difficult for him to maintain his distance from anxieties about the transmission of *jati* if he had.

Therefore, a kind of secular solidarity in which employees become fellow citizens and workers is possible in the railway colony. Yet this is a possibility largely only open to men. Unions and the workplaces of the railway are male preserves. This egalitarianism is also, as we have seen, countered by other attempts to build hierarchical distinctions based on grounds of *jati* and *desh*. It is these efforts to hierarchically rank citizens on the basis of internal, inherited essences and of links to places that leave Anglo-Indians searching for the solace of the uncanny. This simultaneous appearance in the railway colony of a secular, egalitarian vision of citizenship and hierarchies of essential belonging presents a microcosm of wider processes at work in the Indian nation-state and in all secular nation-states. As I argued in chapter 6, notions of the equality of citizens always have the shadow of genealogical and community origins cast over them, making some citizens more legitimate than others. This book has traced the emergence, from encounters with a colonial bureaucracy, of specific articulations linking the family, community, and nation founded on notions of biomoral substances and genealogical histories. It is these taxonomies that continue to be given life within the unequal rankings of citizens in India today.

Kharagpur also presents a microcosm of another process, of the ways in which the colonial past persists in the present. Despite the stories of the *jadu* house, the colonial past is not an irresistible force that directs action in the present. Nor is it necessarily a vivid source of defining memories that people consciously use as part of their projects of self-fashioning in the present.[10] We saw that Anglo-Indians' accounts of the colonial past were evasive and fragmented due to their ambivalence about using the Raj as a source of their identity. This was related both to their family experiences of this past and to the forms of self-fashioning practiced by other Indians that emphasize ahistorical qualities of *jati* and *desh*. Bengali railway families intentionally sought to suppress their relationship to events of and memories of colonialism in order to preserve an idea of social distinction based on a permanent essence of *jati*. Colonial legacies are in fact present at two other levels in Kharagpur. As we have seen in the previous chapter, they are present as styles of command, procedures of disciplinary action, and ideas of railway morality in the workplace. They are also present in bodily dispositions beyond narrative availability and in sentiments associated with *jati*. The forms of social distinction in the present colony owe much to the structures of feeling associated with and practices of *jati* that emerged in exchange with the railway bureaucracy under the Raj. As people build social hierarchies of belonging and distinction in the colony they draw on these historically constituted forms, reproducing them. Most importantly, the microcosm of Kharagpur has shown that colonial legacies are not inescapable outcomes of colonial history but instead are reproduced in social relationships in the present by specific misrecognitions of the influence of the past on the present. As we have seen, railway families alienate their own ability to alter the legacies of colonialism by making this past into an uncanny presence that acts on them through inanimate objects and other people. The logical consequence of this approach to understanding the postcolonial condition is that we cannot assume that the colonial past is inevitably relevant to understanding all contexts. We have to let go of an assertion that it automatically acts on the present and instead trace exactly how and why elements of it are reproduced within the folds of institutions and domestic spaces. This is what the second part of this book has attempted to do in relation to the interaction between railway families and the railway bureaucracy.

Experiences of the uncanny in Kharagpur also reveal something important about the connections between ghostly appearances and secular nation-state histories. The uncanny in Kharagpur can be linked to a particular nationalist view of the past that perceives it as either a potential origin point for personal belonging or a permanent determining influence on the present, or both. In this view, places manifest and are the anchor for these signs of origins and determining influences. In this chronotope, the relationship of people to the past takes on two characteristics. On the one hand, the present becomes a site of ruins and disappearances that have to be picked over in order to find origin points. This is how Anglo-Indians in the colony experience the past in the present. On the other hand, the past becomes a potent presence that repeats inevitably through the actions of people in the present. This is how Indian railway families in general experience the colonial past. This chronotope of origins and determining influences and of the potency of places as sites for the expression of these is characteristic of many secular nationalist histories. The modern discipline of history is marked by the emergence of the idea of secular, homogeneous time, the malleability of human social forms, and the potential agency of people in making their own history. But in tandem with and simultaneous to this sense of the past is that sense associated with forms of romantic nationalism and ideas of origins that assert natural links between people, territories, and histories. In India, forms of romantic nationalism popularized in songs, poetry, and literature built on notions of *jati*, *bhakti*, and the territorial integrity of *Bharat Mata* (Mother India).[11] These forms of nationalism often rested on an image of emotional connection to a specific place of origin, a *desh*, and to regional languages.[12] In Kharagpur, this popular nationalism interacts with a local process of self-fashioning related to historically produced notions of railway morality and Catholicism. In this case, and perhaps in others, experiences of the uncanny link the chronotopes of romantic nationalism to local forms of ethical self-production. In them, the past and places are materialized as external influences that irresistibly act on individuals. Every ruin (or place) must have its ghost, and that ghost proves the irrefutable connection between the past and the present as a physical experience. The uncanny also can, as in the case of Anglo-Indians, suffuse these links to the past and a place with a religious register connecting secular and sacred notions of history and community.[13] Secular, romantic histories of origins can be authenticated and rendered transcendent in the realm of the uncanny. The very ambiguous quality of the uncanny as not quite the domain of official religion, but as otherworldly, enables such a fusing of secular and sacred concepts. The example of Kharagpur suggests that an exploration of the uncanny in other contexts might reveal important links between the experiences described and the particular content of the shifting chronotopes of romantic nationalism as they are refracted through personal ethical quests of self-fashioning, local meanings of morality, and genealogical reckonings.[14] Nationalist chronotopes do not determine the content or outcome of these quests for ethics, selfhood, and connectedness, but they are part of their frame.

# Conclusion

## ON PEDIGREE, *JATI*, AND GENEALOGY

Much has been written of railways as emblems of social progress, as signs of superiority, and as the locus for the creation of modern forms of subjectivity, yet what marks out the history of the railways in India are repeated attempts to create and challenge the legitimacy of the state. This in itself may not be surprising given the political, economic, and military might produced by the network of railways, but what is important is that this legitimacy was understood by British colonial officials, nationalist politicians, and railway workers as metonymically connected to that other, more intimate sense of legitimacy, a belonging to certain kinds of families with particular moral characteristics and physical inheritances. This kind of legitimacy at one and the same time invokes the innate authority of certain people with particular racial and national provenances *and* class position. As British concepts of pedigree based on agricultural metaphors were put into operation in the practices and institutions of the railway bureaucracy they attempted to naturalize the position of the middle classes, the special qualities of the British nation, and the authority of the race of Europeans to command. Ethnoclimatological medical theories linked the kinship logic of pedigree to the territory of the nation by suggesting that the people of a particular country shared a peculiar bond with the land, which if broken threatened their physical integrity. This could only be compensated for by the rigorous practice of religio-moral ethics.

Ultimately, the fertility and security of populations and the economy in India could only be guaranteed by people with particular genealogies and Christian moral habits. The Indian railways' hierarchies of command, daily practices, and institutions therefore tried to secure the legitimacy of the middle classes at home and abroad and made race and nation present as part of bodies and homes.

The history of the railway bureaucracy in India shows that pedigree is an important term through which to understand the operation of social distinction in Britain as at once about class, racial, and national origins.[1] As we have seen in the historical section of this book, it was in the practices of such institutions in imperial settings that these transcendent social identifications were combined with medical theories and became an inherent part of moral sentiments and bodily substances.[2] The Indian railways were also peculiarly important for this process because their association with technological and entrepreneurial activity gave them a particular significance to the rising manufacturing and capitalist class in Britain. The campaign to persuade the East India Company to introduce railways to India and to provide some protection for the risks involved in such enterprise was widely publicized. When the guarantee was secured by a delegation to the Board of Control containing ten liberal laissez-faire MPs from the Midlands, including John Bright and Richard Cobden, prominent bankers such as Sir Isaac L. Goldsmith, Baron Rothschild and presidents of the Manchester chamber of commerce, and the Blackburn commercial association it was seen as a victory for this new segment of British society.[3] The appetite for histories of the progress of the Indian railways among the Victorian and Edwardian public reflects the continuing importance of those railways as a sign of the reality of British middle-class pedigree. And, of course, the thousands of middle-class British personnel who staffed them were also deeply affected by these practices of legitimation, as we have seen throughout this book in the responses of officers to challenges to their right to control the institution. Their solutions always involved a refusal to abandon their hierarchies of command and turned repeatedly to attempts to administer the various moral and physical qualities of their employees by interventions in their ethical and domestic life. Even when explicit racial categories were apparently removed from the distribution of privilege in the railways in the 1920s in an effort to make institutions more egalitarian, they recurred in adjudications over the rights of Anglo-Indian, domiciled European, and Indian Christian families. Explicit biological racism and eugenics may have long ago been discredited in Britain, but these concepts of the legitimacy and pedigree of the middle classes that enable them to neutrally enact the rule of law, civil society, security, and productive enterprise have not entirely disappeared. The imperial history of pedigree as a form of political legitimacy as practiced by specific institutions should be written into our general understanding of "English" kinship, class politics, and British statecraft.

Equally important are the effects of the railway bureaucracy and its workplaces on Anglo-Indian and Indian employees. They too became caught up in the taxonomies of the bureaucracy and saw issues of political legitimacy and individual justice in terms of moral and physical categories. In the history of railway morality we can see at work an expansive notion of *jati* and of bureaucratic honor that was applied to a new range of social units and relationships. Although the potential to imagine larger social units of power has always been present in ideas of *jati*, in the protests of railway workers against the bureaucracy these idioms were transferred into the designation of class styles of life and onto the scale of the nation.[4] In the process they fused with British ideas of race, pedigree, and "natural" communities of interest. This process is a microcosm of the wider social trends of the late-nineteenth century and the twentieth century that have given terms such as *jati* a broad range of references in the present.[5] In this book I have followed this process specifically in relation to urban middle-class and working class Bengali railway families. In the context of the contemporary workplaces and domestic spaces of the railway in both Anglo-Indian and Bengali homes, as in formal dictionary definitions of the term, *jati* can be broadly understood as referring to a type, sort, or class. The type it indicates can be anything from nation, race, religion, tribe, lineage, and region to breed, pedigree, community, species, and caste.[6] It is a term that suggests that in the flow of social life there exist hidden, shared, and often inherited essences that are revealed by personal demeanor. It is significant that the term easily shifts from an inclusive to exclusionary border marker and that it collapses domestic, public, and physiological or "natural" indicators of commonality. As the term moves in language use from domestic to national and then naturalized contexts it carries with it associations from each. It also links together these discrete ways of forming essential and moral identifications. *Jati* is tied to political belonging through a link to a natural, often specific *desh* that continues however mobile Bengali railway families are through work transfers. The resonances of *jati* are visceral, drawing on the idioms of caste, purity, pollution, and so forth to mark in family inheritances and domestic practices *simultaneously* social status, religious purity, and a natural political belonging. In these concepts of *jati* and *desh* we have backwardly projected lines of genealogy that at once make forms of unequal social relations and the political community of the nation a desired property of bodies, souls, and family life.

It is quite striking that *jati* operated in similar ways in the homes of Anglo-Indian and Bengali railway workers. When I said the word "class" to Anglo-Indians, they always misheard it as "caste" and frequently substituted the word *jati* for caste. For them, as in Bengali railway family homes, caste/*jati* was used to indicate essential regional, religious, national, racial, and traceable lineage identities with time-depth. In spite of their fluid counteridioms of love, strategies of social mobility, and emphasis on ties formed in households, they longed for the secure fixity of a caste/*jati* point of origin. It was the absence of this that led to their attempts to conjure evidence for their kinship substances out of clothing, displays of cosmopolitanism at dances, church documents, ties to "abroad," letters from migrant relatives, idioms of divine Catholic community, embodied signs, and ancestral ghosts. This evidence was always also compromised by the fact that the status of origins was for Anglo-Indians directly linked to economic position. Idioms of class were inseparable from idioms of *jati*, kinship, and origins, making these origins intensely vulnerable to the family fortunes of the present. In Bengali railway families there was a more secure sense of anchored origins in a regional, racial, and caste identity, but this too was perceived as potentially under threat. The public spaces of the railways threatened the status of origins by turning workers into skilled practitioners of the disciplinary practices of the Raj, through the moralizing judgments of superiors on one's fitness for demotion and promotion, and by insisting on ranking purely on the basis of economic role. For both Anglo-Indian and Bengali railway families, the threat of a loss of origins and status was understood through the transactional idiom of permeable persons who can be profoundly affected by the qualities of the places and people with whom they interact.[7] These notions of permeability sometimes enabled social mobility, as in the Jones family, but they also led to elaborate fears about the public spaces of the railway colony and bureaucracy. Although these idioms initially appear familiar from a range of ethnographies of caste, what is visible in the experiences of these railway families is the historical emergence of specific substances of kinship, idioms of status, and notions of national affiliations within a particular institutional space. These are also articulated to other forms of social distinction, such as national and racial identifications. This book has sought to restore one set of bureaucratic practices of legitimation and social reproduction to the historical record and to explore their significance for the emergence of the multiple meanings of shared substance in both "English" and "Indian" kinship, as well as for British and Indian nationalism.

Although the history I have told is specific to the Indian railways, I think it should lead us to interpret a broad range of family histories and genealogies differently. The gradual process of the governmentalization, racialization, and nationalization of the family that I have demonstrated in the institutions of the Indian railways is one that has been widespread in both India and Britain. The experiences of Anglo-Indians push us to confront the category of race as intrinsic to the historical formation of notions of *jati* and pedigree in a manner that is not often enough emphasized in our understanding of both Indian and British kinship. It also forces us to focus on the ways in which family origins and racial affiliations are implicated in languages of class in both countries. In addition, it suggests that in an even wider range of contexts the family histories and stories of kinship that people offer us are in dialogue with existing forms of political community and bureaucratic taxonomies. The accounts that anthropologists collect of family history and genealogical origins cannot be reduced to nationalism or to the notions of race writ small. However, they are often in debate with practices of political community and of genealogy as they have been administered by institutions. They also should be understood as sometimes reaching for a desired form of utopian community that transcends the limits of these public practices. In India and Britain in particular, family histories often contain traces of the historical encounter of colonialism and nationalism either as an explicit reference point, a secret, a sentimental effect, or a desire for pure, traceable, legitimate origins. In this context and in many others, we need to carry out a historical inquiry into the genealogy of genealogies to reveal the effects on families of the appropriation of the substances of kinship by political movements and bureaucracies.

The viscerality of these political genealogies is heightened by the manner in which they link body and soul. In particular, they make an immediate connection between religious practices of commemoration of relatives and political identifications. The commemoration of an ancestor or loved relative becomes in small part also a commemoration of a tie to a nation. Religious idioms and personal emotions of loss and longing become articulated to political communities in these practices. It is not only the war dead or the unknown soldier whose loss creates national sentiment; such sentiments can be evoked by the known and unknown family members who have died before us and are linked to us in our genealogy. In genealogies too political communities can become intimately linked to family sentiments and experiences of fear and awe at the productivity and limits of the body. If our genealogies are so complex that they question the simple boundaries of the nation, we often still feel we have to relate their lines and the inheritances within ourselves to these boundaries. Even if this means using these geneaologies to unravel these boundaries, we find it hard to imagine other ethical projects without first confronting these visceral inheritances. Many of us live in what Povinelli calls "genealogical societies," where we struggle to relate our utopian vision of ourselves as free agents able to love and transact with others on our own terms with a sense that we are constrained by family inheritances from the past.[8] Anglo-Indian railway families demonstrate a peculiarly acute version of this institutionally and politically created dilemma.

To illustrate the broader relevance of these political genealogies of family history, pedigree, and legitimate origins in India and Britain, I would like to offer two short vignettes, one from Kolkata and one from London. Both of these demonstrate the intimate legacies of the encounter between colonialism and nationalism in the languages of class, desires for purity, and notions of propriety in each place. Within families there is a kind of sentimental time lag that does not match the periodizations of historians. Personal duties and emotional attachments to grandparents, parents, and spouses can give continuing life to the stories told by previous generations and the sentiments and idioms of distinction forged among them. Relationships within families often connect people to a living past that profoundly affects their self-fashioning in the present. Stoler and Strassler have made the important point that the aftereffects of colonial experiences may not exist in the form of articulated memories of particular events, but may appear in bodily dispositions beyond narrative availability and in sentiments of nostalgia, longing, and propriety.[9] This is clear in both the stories below. In these accounts, emotional attachments to parents lead to senses of propriety and shame among the storytellers. The stories also reveal the processes of abandonment of illegitimate, unwanted family members that produce genealogies and that have made it hard to trace the historical connections between the sentimental lives of Indian and British families.

The first story was told to me as a cautionary tale by my Bengali teacher and landlady in Kolkata, Mrs. Gupta, a middle-class housewife in her forties. Mrs. Gupta wanted to explain to me the meaning of *jater dosh*—a mistake in the line, a crossbreeding with Anglo-Indians or foreigners that pollutes the lineage. She told me that she had something like that in her family. Her father's uncle went to Glasgow to study to be a doctor. He returned with a British wife with whom he had three children. Nobody in the family liked him; he was too Anglicized. Mrs. Gupta said that he "mentally tortured" his wife, and she ended up dying in Woodlands Nursing Home. The uncle married again, a Bengali woman this time. The family would have nothing to do with the children he had with his British wife. Mrs. Gupta added that she had first met one of his children at his funeral in Nimtollah burning *ghat*. Everyone ignored Shila, his third daughter, as they watched her father's body burning in the flames. No one had told her he had died. She had read an announcement in the newspaper. Mrs. Gupta added that Shila looked so coarse, with a heavy build and white, pockmarked skin, with none of the sweetness of a Bengali face or the freshness of her European mother. Mrs. Gupta felt sorry for her and started to talk to her. Shila told her the whole story of that part of the family, which she'd never heard before. Her eldest brother had been "tyrannized" by his father and he ran away from home. They never heard from him again, but they think he went to Europe to serve in World War Two and died as an enlisted man. Her younger brother married a Bengali woman but divorced her. Shila, just like an Anglo-Indian, added Mrs. Gupta, didn't like studies much and left home at eighteen to be a nurse (a profession associated with Christian and lower-caste groups). She had married a Bengali man and had a son, but she left him and her son for another man. The father sent the son to a boarding school in the hills, but he was like Shila, somehow restless and unable to study. He returned to Kolkata during the 1970s Naxalite movement, and his grandfather couldn't keep him at home. He became involved with the Naxalites and went to live with Shila again. One day, Shila returned to her house to find the door locked. She took a ladder up to open the window and get in, and she found him with a noose around his neck, hanging dead. Mrs. Gupta added as an interpretive frame for this story: "I felt so sorry that her father had started all this mess by marrying a British woman. This is what happens with *jater dosh*." She added conspiratorially that I should be very careful before I thought of having children with my then husband, who was from the Ivory Coast.

In her story, Mrs. Gupta fused a tale of polluted *jati*, domestic disorders, racial difference, and political disorder. This condensation produced for her an irrefutable logic of the necessity of maintaining the racial purity of the modern Bengali subject of extended kinship and the line of male ancestors. This is a postcolonial family story in that it reflects the racialization and nationalization of the concept of *jati*. It also illustrates the intimate processes of separation and abandonment that make such impossible purity possible. It is only by cutting off the lines of connection with Shila and her brothers that Mrs. Gupta's family maintained their romance of an unpolluted lineage.

A companion story to this is that told to me in London by a sixty-year-old woman, Viola, about her own mother, an Anglo-Indian woman, Francis, who went to Britain in the 1930s on a medical scholarship. I met Viola, who is a medical professional, in part because she had read a novel I had written about my experiences of research with Anglo-Indians. Reading this book had made Viola act on her suspicions that her mother was Anglo-Indian, and she attempted to contact her Anglo-Indian relatives, including a lost cousin, John. Francis had never told her daughter that she was Anglo-Indian. Viola had pieced together her origins over the course of her life, largely after the death of her mother in the early 1980s. She had finally confirmed them by meeting her cousin John (her mother's nephew). He has become the family genealogist and has collected an elaborate and detailed family tree going back to a Scottish ancestor who owned a castle in the seventeenth century. What is interesting about Viola's story are the silences and omissions that her mother thought were necessary in order to establish a particular class, racial, and national identity for her daughter and her in Britain. Equally significant is Viola's own disquiet about telling me her mother's story. When I asked Viola about her mother, she immediately launched into a description of her mother's elisions of her origins:

It was clear to me that my mother came from Calcutta, where she was born, in the mid-thirties to do medicine. Her story was that she had passed first in all of Bengal, passed with highest honors in all Bengal, therefore she got a scholarship to Europe, at which point she seems to have severed all connections with her family. Her parents both died, although until I saw my cousin's family tree I had no idea when they had died. Her brother [who was a railway engineer] and sister [who was married to a railway driver] came to England in 1948 after partition, at which point I did meet them, but she was extremely cautious about that. It was difficult partly because her brother was a railway engineer, not a doctor as she was. So she by that time had moved onto another professional level and of course she had completely lost any Indian accent. Whereas my cousin, now seventy, who came younger than she was when she came, still has absolutely clear Indian intonation. She had absolutely abandoned everything.

According to Viola, her mother severed all relationships with her family and carefully managed contacts with them in order to assert a particular kind of racial and class identity in Britain. Francis refused to let John stay with them when he went to settle in Britain. According to Viola: "What my mother would never say was that they were Anglo-Indian. If anyone asked her, she would say, 'Of course not, no!' And so it was a complete taboo, that subject was totally taboo. So the idea that when John came he would stay with us was impossible. He said to me last year, 'Oh no, I was much too brown for your mother to have me to stay.'"

Francis's anxiety about her past transferred itself to Viola. She told me, "It is still difficult to speak of my mother's family background. . . . It was so shameful from her point of view to talk about it. It's as if she is sitting on my shoulder saying, 'Don't do that, don't have this conversation with Laura.'" This necessity for secrecy suffused Viola's childhood for another reason. Her mother had conceived her outside of marriage in a relationship with a man, Richard, whom Viola described as coming from a very grand family related to a well-known nineteenth-century literary figure. This family also had the right kind of connections to empire, members of it serving in the civil service in India and Africa. Her father, according to Viola, later married "a very English woman" instead of her mother. At a girl's private school in the 1950s Viola learned to conceal her double illegitimacy as an Anglo-Indian and as a child of a single mother. She described wanting to assert her own connections to India in the presence of high-class girls whose family members had been important out there but being unable to because her mother did not have quite the right provenance: "Well I might have said, 'Oh my mother was born in Calcutta,' but then there would be a stunned silence, because they would also have family connections and their parents had been sent home to be educated. So I could work out already . . . 'Why was she at school in India . . . ?' So I'd understood fairly early something was not quite kosher."

Viola also related having to bite her tongue and conceal her connections to the well-known literary figure, which also would have given her a social legitimacy. She described her initial naive attempts to claim this origin in the following terms: "At school in the first year there was a rather grand little girl called Susan, who said she was the great-great-great-granddaughter of [literary figure], which she was. And I said, 'Well I'm the great-great-grandniece,' but then that was very difficult as to how I got the . . . to trace that history, how was I to demonstrate that we were in fact [sharing] common ancestors?"

The whole time Viola was at this school she felt like an "outsider," "incomer," or "go-between." She related how this double secrecy and illegitimacy that made her dubious in terms of her class status in the school led to a particular kind of shame: "I had all sorts of guilt. . . . I found the whole thing . . . the word that comes to mind is 'disfigurement,' interestingly. The first word that emerges is 'dis-figurement.' I don't know whether that is the illegitimacy or the Anglo-Indian." The early 1960s, when she left school for a secretarial course at Oxford, was a partial liberation from these judgments of social distinction. In the context of the political and social movements of the time, her origins seemed less of a problem. Also, by that time her father and half brothers had claimed her, and they all went on holidays together. Yet since then Viola's life has involved a long, slow, tentative process of piecing together everything that her mother erased. Her mother kept an album of unlabeled photographs. When Viola asked who the people were, she said that she had forgotten or didn't know. When Viola recently sent the album to her cousin John in order to find out if they were family members, she discovered that they were her mother's sisters and parents. It was in particular when she saw the picture of her grandfather, whom Francis had described as a strict Presbyterian Scot, that she realized the extent of her mother's concealment. To Viola he looked like a very dashingly dressed Indian man. Viola says that she still feels a sense of shame about her origins, particularly when she meets Indians. She can't explain this, but she feels she has a secret that shouldn't be told. Her husband also suggests, much to Viola's annoyance, that she feels ambivalent about being included in John's genealogy and about maintaining contact with her newly found Anglo-Indian relatives.

Viola's account suggests that the ideas of legitimacy and pedigree that un-derpin concepts of relatedness and languages of class in Britain can be seen as postcolonial too. When Francis moved to Britain she, as many Anglo-Indians did in India, concealed her origins and cut herself off from her relations in order to refound her racial, national, and class identity. We can see her disowning as an extreme version of the present-oriented kinship that remains characteristic of Anglo-Indian family practices. That such an abandoning of her family was neces-sary in order to enable her acquisition of a professional status in Britain speaks of the continuities between social distinctions in the metropole and colony. It points to the importance of pedigree, legitimacy, the right kind of connections to empire, and a purity of racial origins to asserting middle-class identity in the Britain of the 1930s as well as in India. Viola's sense of shame speaks of the continuing significance of these status differentials. In particular, her sense of herself as essentially "disfigured" reveals the importance of a purity of racial origins and legitimate pedigree to the marking out of a middle-class body.

Viola tells stories of her experiences at school in order to meditate on the continuing problematic internal frontiers of her citizenship and of her class position. She returns to her concealment of her illegitimacy and suspected Anglo-Indian status in this context as a way of puzzling over the nature of her origins and of her place in the world now. She is attempting to tease out whether she should continue to desire an appropriate pedigree or abandon this wish altogether and formulate a different vision of class, racial, and national community. Since the 1960s she has been able to claim her father's pedigree in the literary family as the social stigma of illegitimacy receded and he incorporated her into his family. But in recent years her curiosity about her mother's origins suggests that she is searching for a more radical reformulation of her senses of class, nationality, and race. Her attempts to do this are tentative, restrained by her mother's prohibitive voice and her experiences of only half-belonging at school. As Carsten has shown in her recent work on adoptees retracing their links to their families of birth, Viola's efforts to rediscover her family origins reflect broader desires for a continuity of self and for a frame for telling stories about the past.[10] They also represent an attempt to reach for a utopian, alternative notion of what it means to be middle class and British, which would move beyond the postcolonial notions of pedigree and legitimacy that haunt notions of English kinship and citizenship. By reclaiming the complex origins that her mother abandoned Viola also offers the possibility of revealing the shared history of the nationalization and racialization of Indian and British families in the context of the Raj.

## ON NATIONALISM, BUREAUCRACY, AND INTIMACY

Since the 1990s the study of bureaucracy, kinship, and intimacy has been productively combined to trace the links between nationalism, morality, and familial metaphors.[11] Other work has importantly added the insight that colonial and other states have sought to administer sentiment and form certain kinds of families.[12] Histories of imperialism and nationalism in India have shown that the family has been a public site of intervention central to a wide range of political projects. Kinship studies have also begun to insist on historical studies that trace the emergence

of ideas of relatedness in medical, biological, and scientific institutions.[13] I want to
end by suggesting how anthropological histories such as the one I have carried out
in this book can enrich the arguments about the relations between public institutions and domestic spaces that have been made in these arenas.

It is clear from the history that I have charted that moralizing bureaucracies
do not produce moral orders, but instead create ethical dilemmas for bureaucrats and clients alike. They never fully legitimize bureaucratic action, nor make
its transcendent indifference believable. Instead, their appropriation of idioms
of kinship, community, and religion create a volatile domain of public emotions in which both iconic and indexical signs of identity are simultaneously
at work. When these idioms are appropriated by institutions, far from producing a seamless taxonomy of order and disorder, what occurs is the enfolding of
other principles of association and ethical sensibilities into the context of bureaucratic practices. At work in the history of the railway bureaucracy was not
only the racial, protestant, and medical theorizing of British officials centered
on notions of pedigree, but the notions of *jati* and bureaucratic honor among
Indian employees and those of Catholic divine citizenship and fluid, temporally
shallow genealogical reckoning of Anglo-Indian railway castes. Most importantly,
bureaucracies such as the one described here do not seamlessly produce a taxo-
nomic order and domain of alienating, transcendent rationality. Instead, they
are a place for the production of emotion and the emergence of incoherent and
fragmented identifications, temporal disjunctures, and uncanny presences. Even
the most emblematic artifacts of bureaucracies, the file and document, are not
simply de-individualizing, timeless, or reifying. As part of social strategies, nos-
talgias, and longings, they can become, as they did for Anglo-Indians, the most
potent and intimate material symbol of self-fashioning, memory, and sentiment.
Technocratic bureaucracies such as the Indian railways are not a realization of an
individualizing rational modernity or of a moral order but in their practices set
loose an unpredictable series of fraught negotiations of the social inequalities and
ethics they produce.[14]

The history of the railway bureaucracy also illustrates the complexities of the
institutional emergence of substances of relatedness. Despite the colonial context
for my analysis, at no point were kinship or race naturalized as a purely biological
or medical phenomenon or simply understood as a quality of blood. Instead, for
colonial bureaucrats and Anglo-Indian and Bengali railway families, there was a
complex layering of religious, physiological, emotional, and political ideas in the
formation of families. There were also potentially a range of substances and forms
of material culture through which connections could be manifested and proved.
Long before the involvement of medical and scientific institutions in the parsing
and reconstruction of kinship definitions, colonial and national institutions such

as the railway bureaucracy were central to changing understandings of "English" and Indian kinship *as well as* to the administration of familial status and origins. On the frontiers of empire the distinctions between British and Indian family formation were defined using an eclectic range of signifying substances in a manner that directly affected the political rights and social status of families. Here also the links of British and Indian concepts of kinship to historically produced notions of race and nation are revealed. Idioms of kinship such as *jati* and pedigree should more often be considered in relation to such practical institutional interventions in the lives of families. Anthropological histories in particular have the great potential to make visible these intimate, unnoticed effects of colonialism and nationalism as part of the ontology of and desire for race, pedigree, *jati*, and class. This is because they can move among archives, institutions, and lived experience, allowing us to trace the cross-fertilization of private and public moralities and to question the nature of the boundaries between them.

Most important of all, the history of the railway bureaucracy and the dilemmas of Anglo-Indian railway families demonstrate the importance of genealogy to nation-states and political communities. The material presented here would suggest that the self-creating subject of national political communities is frequently guaranteed by particular genealogical inheritances and domestic practices. It is also through these genealogies that rights, privileges, and access to resources are unequally distributed. Genealogical lines, importantly, relate particular historical visions and social relations to family inheritances.[15] This is certainly true of the way that railway morality, *jati*, and pedigree have operated in the past and present railway colony. Significantly too the embedding of political community in genealogy and domesticity anchors it in an anxious domain of emotion, universal human fears, and nonsecular idioms of love and care. It will also often tie this community to religious sentiments and emotional longings.[16] We need to follow in a wider range of contexts the consequences for people and institutions as the nation enters peoples' experiences of fear and wonder at the generative potential and existential limits of the body. We also should trace the transformation of political community in the practices of genealogy into other nonsecular and emotional forms, such as the commemoration of ancestors, appearances of ghosts, and strategies of forging connections through love. The experiences of Anglo-Indians ultimately speak of the predicaments and inequalities produced when political communities are made part of family lines and sentiments.

# Notes

INTRODUCTION

1. For an early account asserting this view before the railways were built, see the arguments of the railway entrepreneur Stephenson in *Report Upon the Practicability and Advantages of the Introduction of Railways Into British India*, which were part of the campaign that successfully led to the setting up of the East Indian Railway.

2. See, for example, Davidson, *The Railways of India: With an Account of Their Rise, Progress, and Construction*, Bell, *Railway Policy in India*, Huddleston, *History of the East Indian Railway*, and the later, more muted, nostalgic version of this kind of history in Westwood, *Railways of India*, and Berridge, *Couplings to the Khyber*. For discussions of the railways as an emblem of progress in India that legitimated British rule, see Arnold, *The New Cambridge History of India*, vol. 3, no. 5, *Science, Technology, and Medicine in Colonial India*, and Kerr, "Representation and Representations of the Railways of Colonial and Post-Colonial South Asia." On technology more generally as proof of Western progress, see Adas, *Machines as the Measure of Men*.

3. Naoroji, *Poverty and Un-British Rule in India*; Dutt, *The Economic History of India*; Ranade, "Indian Political Economy." See Kalpagam, "Colonialism, Rational Calculations, and Idea of the 'Economy,'" and Chandra, *The Rise and Growth of Economic Nationalism in India*.

4. Marx, "The Future Results of British Rule in India."

5. This idea is drawn from Chakrabarty, "Postcoloniality and the Artifice of History."

6. Mukherjee's work was further consolidated into suggestions for nationalist administrative policies in the 1930s and 1940s in, for example, Shiva, *The Industrial Worker in India*, Gupta, *Labour and Housing in India*, and Lokanathan, *Industrial Welfare in India*.

7. See the important essays in the collection in Parry, Breman, and Kapadia, *The Worlds of Indian Industrial Labour*. Also relevant here is the work of Chandavarkar, which argues for the intermittent making of class identity in response to particular historical events, in *The Origins of Industrial Capitalism in India* and *Imperial Power*

*and Popular Politics.* See also the volume edited by Robb, *Dalit Movements and the Meanings of Labour in India.* On the creative ground of tradition and the formation of identities counter to those of capitalism and nationalism, see Daniels's accounts of the historical sensibility and antimodern resistance of Estate Tamils in *Charred Lullabies.* Chakrabarty, *Rethinking Working Class History*, explores at times the enfolding of "non-capitalist" social relations in capitalist workplaces under colonial rule. For more recent historical work that pays close attention to issues of gender, see Gooptu, *The Politics of the Urban Poor in Early Twentieth-Century India*, Sen, *Women and Labour in Late Colonial India*, and Fernandes, *Producing Workers.*

8. For examples of economic analyses of the railways that emphasize the arrival of capitalism in an alien social landscape, see Hurd, "Railways: The Beginnings of the Modern Economy," and Morris, "The Growth of Large-Scale Industry to 1947." For detailed analysis of the economic impact of railways on one region, see Derbyshire, "Economic Change and the Railways in North India, 1860–1914." On markets, see Hurd, "Railways and the Expansion of Markets in India, 1861–1921." On investment, see Thorner, *Investment in Empire.* For general administrative and managerial accounts that contain an embedded nationalist critique of economic imperialism, see Sanyal, *The Development of Indian Railways*, Srinivasan, *The Law and Theory of Railway Freight Weights*, and Natesan, *State Management and Control of Railways in India.* For later work on the same lines, see Lehman, "Great Britain and the Supply of Railway Locomotives in India," and Rao, "Political Economy of Railways in British India, 1850–1900." For debates about railway economy in a Marxist frame, see Sen, "Marx on Indian Railways." On the issues of technology transfer, see Lehman, "Railway Workshops, Technology Transfer, and Skilled Labour Recruitment in Colonial India," and Headrick, *The Tentacles of Progress.* On managerial issues and capitalism, see Kerr, *Building the Railways of the Raj, 1850–1900.*

9. On the impossibilities and dilemmas of the notion of the "transfer" or translation of modernity to colonial contexts, see Prakash, *Another Reason.* For popular hopes and doubts about the applicability of modernity to Indonesia, see Mrazek, *Engineers of a Happy Land.* For a more general theoretical discussion of the translation of modernity, see Chakrabarty, *Provincializing Europe.* My work differs from Chakrabarty's in the emphasis on the emergence of "difference" and translated forms of modernity as a project *within* the colonial bureaucracy produced by exchanges between bureaucrats and workers. The paradoxical forms produced by these have much in common with the "mediators" described by Latour in *We Have Never Been Modern.* Too often in accounts of Indian history the rationality and capitalist logic of colonial bureaucracies and interventions has been assumed. This is inherent to a large amount of the otherwise important early work of the subaltern studies school of thought. It leads to the suggestion that subaltern responses to these bureaucracies and work environments use a temporality and logic that is radically other to them. This is not always true; these responses may look "other," but they can be a direct engagement with the peculiar moral universe of these institutions. For examples of this, see the petitions in chapter 5.

10. Goswami, *Producing India*; Jagga, "The Emergence of the Railway Labor Movement in India" and "Colonial Railwaymen and British Rule." See also Kerr, *Railways in Modern India*.

11. The new names for cities (Kolkata, Chennai, and Mumbai) are used in the ethnographic sections in part 2 and the introduction and conclusion of this text. The old names for cities (Calcutta, Madras, and Bombay, respectively) are used in part 1.

12. This aspect of my project is inspired by Stoler's *Race and the Education of Desire* and *Carnal Knowledge and Imperial Power*.

13. See Hertzfeld, *Cultural Intimacy* and *The Social Production of Indifference*. I do not translate the term *jati* into its usual referent of caste here, or in the rest of the book, unless I am referring to the academic debates about the relationship between caste and religious ideas of purity and pollution. I am addressing a domain that is not central to these debates, that is, the expansion of languages of distinction associated with *jati* and *desh* into new contexts of race, nation, community, class, democratic politics, and bureaucracy. These new contexts, however, are expressed by the term *jati* as it is now commonly used in India, especially in Bengal and in urban working class and middle-class Bengali families as explored in this book. For example, see the definition in Biswas, *Samsad Bengali-English Dictionary*.

14. See Schivelbusch, *The Railway Journey*; Marx, *The Machine in the Garden*; Freeman, *Railways and the Victorian Imagination*; Carter, *Railways and Culture*; Den Otter, *The Philosophy of Railways*; Kirby, *Parallel Tracks*.

15. See Kahn's arguments about the emergence of racism as a product of modern national political institutions in "The Making and Unmaking of a Malay Race."

16. In exploring this moral universe and the ethical projects of families and people, I follow the approach suggested by Laidlaw, "For an Anthropology of Ethics and Freedom." I have followed his method by tracing, on the one hand, the moralizing practices of the institutions of the railways and political movements and, on the other, the specific ethical projects of families and individuals. One cannot be collapsed into the other.

17. It is impossible to define the term "Anglo-Indians" or "Eurasians" out of historical context. The boundaries and visibility of this "community" shifted according to the provision of state institutions to regulate their identity. One cannot trace their presence or even their community name as a continuous object through history because their definition changed with each local administrative decision on employment qualifications or suitability for admittance to European systems of education. The same individual would often be defined differently according to which part of the state bureaucracy he or she applied to for recognition. This contradictory classification continued even after the ruling of the government of India in the Montagu-Chelmsford electoral reforms of 1919, which defined an Anglo-Indian as any individual who had a European citizen in the male line. This definition was incorporated into the Constitution of India and is the current official definition of the community (although Anglo-Indians see themselves differently from this, as I outline

in this book). "Domiciled Europeans" were a group often affiliated politically with Anglo-Indians, and they were administratively defined as people who had settled in India but could demonstrate links with Europe in terms of property and family in both male and female lines of descent.

18. "Petition to the Minorities Commission of the Domiciled European and Anglo-Indian Community," in *Report of the Indian Statutory Commission (Simon Commission)*, vol. 16; Hassan, *Report on the Representation of Muslims and Other Minority Communities in the Subordinate Railway Service.*

19. For example, see Stark, *Call of the Blood* and *Hostages to India*, Anthony, *Britain's Betrayal in India*, Dover, *Half-Caste*, and Maher, *These Are the Anglo-Indians.*

20. Thurston, "Eurasians of Madras City and Malabar"; Mahalanobis, "Anthropological Observations on the Anglo-Indians of Calcutta."

21. See Sen, "Anglo-Indians of Calcutta."

22. Abel, *The Anglo-Indian Community*; Gaikwad, *The Anglo-Indians*; Dutt, *In Search of a Homeland*; Varma, *Anglo-Indians.*

23. Here I mean specifically the substance discussed in recent kinship studies. I follow the important arguments of Carsten, "Substantivism, Antisubstantivism, and Anti-antisubstantivism," Weston, "Kinship, Controversy, and the Sharing of Substance," Feeley-Harnik, "The Ethnography of Creation," Bouquet, "Making Kinship, with an Old Reproductive Technology," and Tapper, "Blood/Kinship, Governmentality, and Cultures of Order in Colonial Africa," who all trace the multiple and historical meanings of substance in different contexts.

24. Ghosh, "Making and Unmaking Loyal Subjects" and "Household Crimes and Domestic Order." For a less critical history, see Hawes, *Poor Relations.* For a fascinating, important, and nuanced discussion of the family life of a "mixed-race" family, the Bleychyndens, in the early period of colonial rule, see Robb, "Children, Emotion, Identity, and Empire."

25. See Chatterjee, *Colouring Subalternity, Gender, Slavery, and Law in Colonial India*, and *Unfamiliar Relations.* See also Singha, "Making the Domestic More Domestic," Mody, "Love and the Law," and Sturman, "Property and Attachments."

26. Caplan, *Children of Colonialism.* See also Blunt, *Domicile and Diaspora.* See also my earlier discussion of Anglo-Indians and the politics of domesticity and empire in Gbah-Bear, "Miscegenations of Modernity." My argument differs from these important books because it relates the situation of Anglo-Indians to the formation of both Indian and British nationalist communities and to the practices of bureaucracies. It also differs in terms of the interpretation of kinship, family relationships, and politics among Anglo-Indians. Caplan and Blunt both suggest that their family life aspired to and followed "British" rather than "Indian" domestic forms. The limits of this argument are shown in the second half of my book.

27. See Mondal, "The Emblematics of Gender and Sexuality in Indian Nationalist Discourse"; Devika, "The Aesthetic Woman"; Raychaudhuri, "Love in a Colonial Climate"; Hancock, "Home Science and the Nationalization of Domesticity in Colonial India"; Burton, *Gender, Sexuality, and Colonial Modernities* and "House/Daugh-

ter/Nation"; Ramaswamy, *The Pleasures of the Tongue*. This claim of separation and then active intervention in the domestic sphere is also shown in British history by Davidoff and Hall, *Family Fortunes*, Davin, "Motherhood and Imperialism," and Rose, *Limited Livelihoods*. On colonial settings, see in particular Tranberg Hansen, *Distant Companions*, and Clancy-Smith and Gouda, *Domesticating the Empire*.

28. Munasinghe, "Narrating a Nation Through Mixed Bloods"; Kahn, "The Making and Unmaking of a Malay Race"; Baca, "Politics of Recognition and Myths of Race."

29. See Young, *Colonial Desire*, and the important critique of the use of the idea of hybridity by Scott in his article "Hybridity, Vacuity, and Blockage," which both emphasize that specific images of disorder especially in relation to hybridity reflect particular cosmologies of humanity and its relation to nature. Also see the important arguments about the naturalization of particular nationalist views of history in genealogical metaphors in Bryant, "The Purity of Spirit and the Power of Blood."

30. Kharagpur is part of the network of the South-Eastern Railway. My historical research was carried out in the records of the Eastern Railway as well as in the higher-level government records in the India Office Library, National Library, and National Archives in Kolkata and the National Archives in Delhi. The South-Eastern Railway had no colonial records preserved. I finally got permission to see inside an old godown at the railway's headquarters in Garden Reach, only to discover from the *dufteri* (office watchman) in charge that all pre-1950 records had been destroyed the previous year. However, the South-Eastern Railway was jointly administered from the Eastern Railway Headquarters during the crucial period from 1930 to 1950 addressed in chapters 4, 5, and 6. I also pieced together aspects of Kharagpur's history from the more general records available in public archives. The specific history of the East Indian Railway is, of course, vitally relevant to the whole story I tell because it was the first and largest railway administration, and it set the pattern for all other railway companies throughout its history.

31. Thomas argues contra Strathern that the letters written by colonists from the edge of empire should be seen as elements of partible persons. See Thomas and Eves, *Bad Colonialists*. It is Hertzfeld who argues that the documents, forms, signatures, emblems, and stamps on bureaucratic documents all help to create the permanence of nation-state authority. He suggests that such documents are deindividualizing and reifying in *The Social Production of Indifference*. Here I wish to supplement this idea with an emphasis on these effects as just one aspect of these documents. Their use is suffused with strategy, personalization, and attempts to project social personas into the circuits of the bureaucracy. In particular, this works with a logic familiar from ideas of *jati* in other contexts in which persons are permeable and can transmit elements of their substance in material forms to others.

32. For an important discussion of personalizing idioms through which people attempt to redirect bureaucratic power, see Osella and Osella, "The Return of King Mahabali." For work that addresses documents as part of social strategies, see Tarlo, "Paper Truths."

33. Hertzfeld provides an important discussion of the qualities of bureaucratic time and the strategic uses of it in *The Social Production of Indifference*.

34. On the spatial formations of the state as a series of institutions and ideas, see Radcliffe, "Imagining the State as Space," and Nugent, "Before History and Prior to Politics." On the claims to scalar and spatial ideology of the state, see Ferguson and Gupta, "Spatializing States." This work is, of course, part of the wide-ranging debate on space within the discipline of geography inspired by the work of Lefebvre, *The Production of Space*.

35. See Benei's introduction to *Manufacturing Citizenship*.

36. For similar attempts to deconstruct the reifications of "the state," restore the emotional life of institutions, and personalize their practices, see Navaro-Yashin, *Faces of the State*, Verkaaik, "The Captive State," and Taussig, *The Magic of the State*.

37. For examples of this in other contexts, see Palsson, "The Life of Family Trees and the Book of Icelanders," and Tapper, *In the Blood*. These accounts concentrate on the traffic between scientific, biological, and cultural ideas of kinship. In my account I particularly emphasize the role of institutions of the nation-state in reconfiguring our understandings of family history and relatedness. This represents an attempt to restore the political and colonial history of both Indian and English kinship.

38. The range of idioms that we use for the substances of kinship are very broad. For example, see Feeley-Harnik's discussion of the richness of Morgan's imagery of the courses of blood that underlie social groups, "The Ethnography of Creation." This imagery drew on folk physiology, livestock breeding, the life cycle of the beaver, the watery landscape of Michigan, desires to touch and reconnect with dead family members, and nonconformist religion.

## 1. THE INDIAN RAILWAYS AND THE MANAGEMENT OF THE MATERIAL AND MORAL PROGRESS OF NATIONS, 1849–1860

1. Thorner, *Investment in Empire*.
2. Kerr, *Building the Railways of the Raj, 1850–1900*.
3. Goswami, *Producing India*.
4. Kalpagam, "Colonialism, Rational Calculations, and Ideas of the 'Economy.'"
5. Chandra, *The Rise and Growth of Economic Nationalism in India*.
6. Jagga, *The Emergence of the Railway Labour Movement in India* and "Colonial Railwaymen and British Rule." Also see Goswami, *Producing India*, and Prakash, *Another Reason*.
7. These forms of action provide a specific historical example of Chatterjee's point that the actual history of capital has involved its realization in governmental technologies that give authority to technical expertise. See *The Politics of the Governed*.
8. Dalhousie, "Railway Reports from India."
9. See Ghosh, *Dalhousie in India, 1848–1856* and "The Utilitarianism of Dalhousie and the Material Improvement of India."
10. See Hari Rao, *The Indian Railways Act (IX of 1890)*, pp. 117–22.

11. Arnold, "White Colonisation and Labour in Nineteenth Century India."

12. Clarke, *Colonisation, Defence, and Railways in Our Indian Empire.*

13. See Harrison's discussion of theories of ethnoclimatology and their development into contradictory ideas of deep racial difference and social improvement by 1850 in *Climates and Constitutions.* Harrison importantly addresses the impact of these theories on medical understandings of disease and the management of the army. This book extends on Harrison's by examining how adaptations of these ideas were practiced within a bureaucracy and their effect on popular understandings of genealogies, bodies, and families.

14. Arnold, "White Colonisation and Labour in Nineteenth Century India."

15. Evidence of Major General G. B. Tremeheere in "Committee on Colonisation and Settlement," IV:2.

16. Evidence of William Theobald, "Committee on Colonisation and Settlement," IV:58.

17. Evidence of John Ochterlony, "Committee on Colonisation and Settlement," IV:12.

18. Evidence of Major General Tremeheere, "Committee on Colonisation and Settlement," IV:40.

19. See the discussion in Harrison, *Climates and Constitutions.*

20. Ritvo, *The Animal Estate*; Cassidy, *The Sport of Kings*; Wolfram, *Inlaws and Outlaws.*

21. David Arnold addresses this class politics in his pioneering "White Colonisation and Labour in Nineteenth Century India."

22. "Committee on Colonisation and Settlement," V:263.

23. This is a different finding from the arguments of Manning, "Owning and Belonging," although I do very much agree with his *historical* analysis of the category of belonging in English kinship.

24. Evidence of James Ronald Martin, "Committee on Colonisation and Settlement," VII:II, 23. On the history of hill stations, see Kennedy, *The Magic Mountains.*


## 2. AN INDIAN TRAVELING PUBLIC, 1850–1900

1. "The Railways of Great Britain," p. 401.

2. De Certeau writes of the railway carriage as a utopian space of laissez-faire individualism and modernity. He in fact just gives a twist to an already common argument of the 1840s—the insight that he adds is that this subjectivity dissolves and disappears once the journey is over. See *The Practice of Everyday Life.*

3. Schivelbusch, *The Railway Journey.*

4. Davidson, *The Railways of India*, p. 39.

5. Goswami writes of the railway carriage and railway station in general as forms of colonial mobile incarceration in which distinctions of race were maintained in *Producing India.* This chapter shows that the new public sphere of the railways took different historical forms and had complex effects. The hierarchies of class and *jati* in

Indian society, for example, were also enfolded into this sphere. This chapter is intended as a contribution to the debates on the colonial and Bengali nationalist public sphere in the work of Chakrabarty, *Habitations of Modernity*, and provides a different understanding of the related class politics.

6. Schivelbusch, *The Railway Journey*.

7. See the images reproduced in Desmond and Satow, *Railways of the Raj*. This is the book in which I first saw photographs of Kharagpur, in 1992, and partly on the basis of this I began my research.

8. Captain C. Young, officiating general engineer, Lower Provinces, to secretary to the government of Bengal, April 23, 1859, *Bengal Proceedings: Public Works Department*, no. 72.

9. Ibid.

10. Captain Impey, officiating civil architect, ibid.

11. Captain Stanton, executive engineer, Grand Trunk Road, ibid.

12. Captain C. Young, ibid. Emphasis added.

13. Colonel R. Baird Smith, officiating secretary to the government of India, Public Works Department, conveying views of the governor-general in council, October 7, 1859, *Bengal Proceedings: Public Works Department*, no. 85.

14. Colonel R. Strachey, junior secretary to the government of India, Public Works Department, to chief commissioner of Oudh, March 30, 1864, *India Proceedings: Public Works Department*, no. 33.

15. Captain R. De Bourbel, assistant secretary to the government of the North West Provinces, March 15, 1864, *India Proceedings: Public Works Department*, no. 171.

16. Major J. Hovenden, assistant secretary to the government of Bengal, Public Works Department, Railways, reporting views of the lieutenant governor of Bengal to secretary to the government of India, Public Works Department, "Defences of Railway Stations in Bengal," *India Proceedings: Public Works Department: Railways*, July 1865, nos. 23–24.

17. Ibid.

18. Lieutenant Colonel C. H. Dickens, secretary to the government of India, Public Works Department, on behalf of the governor-general, to the joint secretary to the government of Bengal, Public Works Department, Railways, July 5, 1865, *India Proceedings: Public Works Department: Railways*, no. 543 R.

19. Minute by Sir W. Muir, lieutenant governor of the North West Provinces, March 21, 1868, *Bengal Proceedings: Public Works Department: Railway Branch*, no. 85.

20. Ibid.

21. Ibid.

22. Hari Rao, *The Indian Railways Act (IX of 1890)*, p. xiii.

23. E. Palmer, agent, East Indian Railway, to the consulting engineer, government of Bengal, Railway Department, June 1, 1869, *Bengal Proceedings: Railway Branch*, September 1869, nos. 8–13.

24. See also Arnold, "European Orphans and Vagrants in India in the Nineteenth Century."

25. Memorandum by the Honorable James Minchin, March 15, 1868, "Report on and Text of Act XXI of 1868 to Provide Against European Vagrancy," *Legislative and Judicial Proceedings/5/11*.

26. S. Hogg, commissioner of police, Calcutta, to the officiating secretary to the government of Bengal, Judicial Department, June 1, 1871, *Bengal Proceedings: Judicial*, September 1871, no. 68.

27. Ibid.

28. Ibid.

29. H. Harrison to the commissioner of Bhaugulpore, September 13, 1871, ibid., no. 81.

30. H. C. Williams, chairman of the Corporation of Calcutta, to secretary to the government of Bengal, Municipal Department, October 23, 1896, reporting H. H. Risley's comments to the corporation meeting, *Bengal Proceedings: Municipal, Medical*, February 1897, nos. 115–16.

31. Ibid.

32. J. P. Hewett, secretary to the government of India, Home Department, to secretary to Bengal, Municipal Department, reporting on the Epidemic Diseases Act and instructions of the governor-general, *Bengal Proceedings: Municipal, Medical*, February 1897, nos. 139–40.

33. H. H. Risley, secretary to the government of Bengal, Municipal Department, to secretary to the government of India, Home Department, February 25, 1897, ibid., no. 270.

34. J. P. Hewett, secretary to the government of India, Home Department, to secretary to the government of Bengal, Municipal Department, reporting on the government of India's decision on the implementation of land quarantine against plague-infected areas, *Bengal Proceedings: Municipal, Medical*, March 1897, no. 160.

35. Ibid.

36. "Notes on the Arrangements in Connection with the Plague Observation Camp at Khana, on the East Indian Railway," published for general information under orders of H. H. Risley, March 22, 1897, ibid., no. 228.

37. *East Indian Railway Dress Regulations*.

38. See the comments of Ram Gopal Ghosh, partner in the trading firm Kelsall and Ghosh, in Stephenson, *Report Upon the Practicability and Advantages of the Introduction of Railways into British India*, p. 36.

39. R. P. Jenkins, officiating commissioner of Patna, to the officiating joint secretary to the government of Bengal, reporting on his consultations with native gentlemen residing in his districts, June 21, 1869, *Bengal Proceedings: Public Works Department: Railway Branch*, September 1869, no. 99.

40. V. Taylor, officiating magistrate of Hooghly, to the commissioner of Burdwan, reporting on suggestions of eight Hindu gentlemen residing near the line of the East Indian Railway or passing through this district, May 27, 1869, ibid., no. 211.

41. Baboo Dwarkanath Mitter to the magistrate of Burdwan, June 4, 1869, ibid., no. 102.

42. V. Taylor to the commissioner of Burdwan, May 27, 1869, ibid., no. 211.

43. Baboo Hit Lall Misser, zemindar of Mancoor, to the magistrate of Burdwan, May 21, 1869, ibid., no. 101.

44. Baboo Dwarkanath Mitter to the magistrate of Burdwan, June 4, 1869, ibid.

45. Baboo Hit Lall Misser, zemindar of Mancoor, to the magistrate of Burdwan, May 21, 1869, ibid.

46. Ibid.

47. Baboo Dwarkanath Mitter to the magistrate of Burdwan, June 4, 1869, ibid.

48. Bayly, *Caste, Society, and Politics in India from the Eighteenth Century to the Modern Age.*

49. V. Taylor, officiating magistrate of Hooghly, to the commissioner of Burdwan, May 27, 1869, *Bengal Proceedings: Public Works Department: Railway Branch*, September 1869, no. 211.

50. Ibid.

51. Ibid.

52. Babu Sreenath Ghose, personal assistant to the commissioner, presidency division, July 29, 1869, ibid., no. 107.

53. Baboo Hit Lall Misser, zemindar of Mancoor, to the magistrate of Burdwan, May 21, 1869, ibid., no. 101.

54. Minute by Sir William Muir, lieutenant governor, North West Provinces, July 17, 1869, ibid.

55. Ibid.

56. Ibid.

57. Ibid. The introduction of the Contagious Diseases Act in 1868 had led to the adoption of measures to watch the arrival of women at stations. In 1871, for example, the officiating commissioner of the Patna division issued orders to the magistrate at Dinapur instructing him that police officers should visit each train as it arrived at Dinapur station to ascertain whether any "European prostitutes or suspicious women alighted for Dinapore Bazaar or the cantonments." The numbers were reported to the magistrate and the residences of the women were watched for suspicious activity. File 34B/10–11, August 11, 1876, *Bengal Proceedings: Medical*, December 1876, no. 355.

58. C. Stephenson, agent, East Indian Railway, to the consulting engineer to the government of Bengal, Railway Department, August 27, 1869, reporting on minutes of official board meeting on reservation of female carriages, *Bengal Proceedings: Public Works Department: Railway Branch*, September 1869, no. 114.

59. Commissioner of Agra to Bengal Public Works Department, Railways, June 21, 1869, ibid., no. 100.

60. Schivelbusch, *The Railway Journey*, p. 103. Whereas we may choose to disagree with his version of U.S. society in an era of slavery and the conquest of the West, his point about the contemporary comments on the difference in design of U.S. railway carriages from European models still stands.

61. *Report on the Railway Conference*, 1871, p. 10.

62. Ibid., p. 17.

63. *Report on the Railway Conference*, 1888, p. 7.

64. "Railway Outrages."

65. "The Indian Association and the Assensole Outrage Case."

66. No. 8554, from the officiating general traffic manager, East Indian Railway, to agent, November 18, 1895, file P1-R/4–1, *Bengal Proceedings: Judicial: Police*, May 1896, nos. 32–33.

67. From the deputy inspector of police, North West Provinces and Oudh Railway branch, to agent, East Indian Railway, no. 2766, October 19, 1895, ibid.

68. No. 8554, from the officiating general traffic manager, East Indian Railway, to agent, November 18, 1895, file P1-R/4–1, ibid., nos. 32–33.

69. From assistant inspector-general government railway police, Howrah, to agent, East Indian Railway, no. 4362, November 6, 1895, ibid.

70. From deputy inspector of police, North West Provinces and Oudh Railway branch, to agent, East Indian Railway, no. 2766, October 19, 1895, ibid.

71. Ibid.

72. "The Indian Association and the Assensole Outrage Case."

73. For examples of these, see the following issues of *The Bengalee*: September 26, November 21, November 28, and December 5 of 1891; January 5, May 18, June 1, June 22, July 27, August 24, September 21, and November 30 of 1895; January 11, March 14, April 4, April 18, May 2, May 9, and August 22 of 1896; April 24, June 28, and August 21 of 1897; and January 22, 1898.

74. "Facts Relating to an Attempted Outrage on a Lady in a Railway Carriage," p. 2.

75. "The Indian Association and the Assensole Outrage Case."

76. Ibid.

77. In the general traffic manager of the East Indian Railway's report to the agent on cases of assault on females traveling by rail prompted by the Asansol Rajabala Dasi case, he stated that of eighteen cases over the past year, thirteen had been committed by native staff. In the Asansol outrage case an Indian nonrailway employee, Cartes Ali, was also arrested by the police. "Report on Asansol Outrage Case," *Bengal Proceedings: Judicial: Police*, May 1896, nos. 22–23.

78. Ibid., no. 21.

79. Ibid., nos. 22–23.

80. Report from the assistant inspector-general government railway police, Howrah, to the chief secretary to the government of Bengal, "Report on Asansol Outrage Case," nos. 22–23.

81. Guha, "Chandra's Death." This section of my argument is a critique of Guha's arguments about a subaltern realm of tradition beyond the enfolding of the colonial state.

82. "Report on Asansol Outrage Case," nos. 32–33.

83. Ibid.

84. R. Gardiner, agent, East Indian Railway, to the consulting engineer to the government for railways, December 20, 1895, ibid.

85. J. A. Bourdillon, officiating commissioner of the Burdwan division, to the chief secretary to the government of Bengal, August 12, 1895, ibid., no. 25.


3. GOVERNING THE RAILWAY FAMILY, 1860–1900

1. For a recent example, see Kerr, *Building the Railways of the Raj, 1850–1900*, although this only covers the construction of the railways so does not fully address the day-to-day running of the bureaucracy.

2. Bickersteth, in "Appendix to the Report to the Secretary of State for India on Railways in India," p. 71.

3. *East Indian Railway Rules and Regulations and Act for Regulating Railways in British India.*

4. E. H. Lushing on behalf of the lieutenant governor to the officiating consulting engineer to the government of India, Railway Department, July 14, 1859, *Bengal Proceedings: Public Works: Railway Branch*, July 1859, no. 104.

5. Schivelbusch, "The Accident," in *The Railway Journey*.

6. See governor-general's minute, "Recruitment of Engine Drivers and of Mechanics from Men Trained Exclusively in India," May 3, 1861, *Bengal Proceedings: Public Works Department: Railway Branch*, June 1861, nos. 1–7, and "Training of Engine Drivers," July 13, 1860, *Bengal Proceedings: Public Works Department: Railway Branch*, August 1860, no. 1897.

7. "Recruitment of Engine Drivers and of Mechanics from Men Trained Exclusively in India," May 3, 1861, *India Proceedings: Railway Department: Railway A*, nos. 1–7, and "Question of the Appointment of Natives in the Superior Grades of the Traffic Department," *India Proceedings: Public Works Department: Railway Establishment*, December 1879, no. 5.

8. L. Stokes, locomotive superintendent, to agent, East Indian Railway, December 1, 1860, *Bengal Proceedings: Public Works Department: Railway Branch*, May 1861, no. 920.

9. "Report on the Question of the Appointment of Natives in the Superior Grades of the Traffic Department," *India Proceedings: Public Works Department: Railway Establishment*, December 1879, no. 5, p. 155.

10. Traffic manager to agent, January 29, *Agent's Letters to the Home Board of the East Indian Railway*, January 1875, no. 11.

11. August 8, *Agent's Letters to the Home Board of the East Indian Railway*, August 1876, no. 206, and February 2, *Agent's Letters to the Home Board of the East Indian Railway*, February 1877, no. 16.

12. April 16, *Agent's Letters to the Home Board of the East Indian Railway*, April 1875, no. 75.

13. June 20, *Agent's Letters to the Home Board of the East Indian Railway*, June 1876, no. 153.

14. *Official Meetings of the Board of the East Indian Railway*, September 13, 1878, no. 49, and May 16, 1878, no. 27.

15. "Regulations for Pay and Promotions," in *Report on the Railway Conference,* 1900, p. 45.

16. For example reports from traffic managers and locomotive and carriage superintendents, see *Bengal Proceedings: Public Works Department: Railway Branch,* August 1860, no. 1897; *India Proceedings: Railway Department: Railway A,* May 1861, nos. 1–7; *Bengal Proceedings: Public Works Department: Railway Branch,* December 1866, nos. 157–58; "Question of the Appointment of Natives in the Superior Grades of the Traffic Department," *India Proceedings: Public Works Department: Railway Establishment,* December 1879, no. 5.

17. Agent to board of East Indian Railway, November 7, *Agent's Letters to the Home Board,* November 1854, no. 1977.

18. *East Indian Railway Rules and Regulations and the Act for Regulating Railways in British India.*

19. Circular from Edward Palmer, agent, East Indian Railway, July 20, 1859, *Bengal Proceedings: Public Works Department: Railway Branch,* September 1859, no. 21.

20. See entries in *Agent's Letters to the Home Board of the East Indian Railway,* 1858–1860.

21. Agent to board of East Indian Railway, April 3, *Agent's Letters to the Home Board of the East Indian Railway,* 1862, no. 69.

22. *Handbook of Rules and Regulations for All Departments of the East Indian Railway.*

23. Letter from chief operating superintendent to agent, East Indian Railway, September 18, 1925, AE230.

24. Ibid.

25. Letter from agent, East Indian Railway, to Lieutenant Colonel Baker, consulting engineer to the government of India, October 6, *India Proceedings: Public Works Department,* November 1854, no. 64.

26. "Text of Act No XIX of 1850," *India Proceedings: Legislative Consultations/11/4,* 1850.

27. Advocate general's comments on the Draft Act to secretary to the government of India, December 12, 1846, *India Proceedings: Legislative Consultations,* 4 April–10 May 1850, no. 13.

28. Letter from George Turnbull to agent, East Indian Railway, July 13, 1859, in enclosures to letter from agent to the officiating consulting engineer to the government of Bengal, July 23, 1859, *Bengal Proceedings: Public Works Department,* September 1859, no. 64.

29. Ibid.

30. D. W. Campbell, superintendent, Locomotive and Steam Boat Department, East Indian Railway, to S. Power, chief engineer, East Indian Railway, December 20, 1866, *Bengal Proceedings: Public Works Department: Railway Branch,* February 1867, no. 44.

31. Ibid.

32. *The Engineers Journal,* October 2, 1858, p. 15.

33. Memorandum by Captain Hodgson, officiating consulting engineer to the government of Bengal, Railway Department, "Rent to be Paid by the Company's Servants When Living in Houses the Property of the Company," *Bengal Proceedings: Public Works Department: Railway Branch*, December 1859, no. 32.

34. "Sanitary Condition of Railway Stations in Bengal and Punjab: Report of Committee Appointed by His Honour the Lieutenant Governor of Bengal," *India Proceedings: Public Works Department: Railways*, July 1865, nos. 49–56.

35. Clark, "The Atmosphere of Buildings and Their Ventilation."

36. "Sanitary Condition of Railway Stations in Bengal and Punjab: Report of Committee Appointed by His Honour the Lieutenant Governor of Bengal."

37. March 28, *Agent's Letters to the Home Board of the East Indian Railway*, 1874, no. 52.

38. *Official Meetings of the Board of the East Indian Railway*, September 14, 1875, no. 190.

39. One of many examples is that created in Jamalpur in 1888; see agent to board of East Indian Railway, May 19, 1888, *Agent's Letters to the Home Board*, 1888, no. 53.

40. Lieutenant governor of Bengal in "Government of India's Sanction to the Provision of Clergymen at Suitable Stations on the East Indian Railway," August 10, 1860, *India Proceedings: Public Works Department*, nos. 7–8.

41. James Irving to H. P. Lemesurier, officiating chief engineer, North West Provinces, enclosure in "Consideration of the Question of Providing Swimming Baths and Other Means of Recreation for Railway Employees," *India Proceedings: Public Works Department: Railways*, November 1860, nos. 41–44.

42. Undersecretary to the government of Punjab, Public Works Department, Railway Branch, to secretary to the government of India, Public Works Department, "Means of Recreation for Servants of Railway Companies in India," *India Proceedings: Public Works Department Proceedings: Railways*, August 1865, nos. 18–22 A.

43. "Inspection Report of East Indian Railway," July 24, 1865, *Agent's Letters to the Home Board*, 1865, no. 70.

44. T. Gatehouse to J. Strachan, enclosure to letter from agent, East Indian Railway, to the officiating consulting engineer to the government of Bengal, Railway Department, September 24, 1867, *Bengal Proceedings: Public Works Department: Railway Branch*, October 1867, no. 116.

45. B. Gower, district superintendent, East Indian Railway, Howrah, to consulting engineer, East Indian Railway, London, enclosure in "Inducements to Engine Drivers and Fitters of the East Indian Railway to Remain in the Service After the Expiry of Their First Term of Service," *India Proceedings: Public Works Department: Railways*, April 1868, no. 139.

46. Danvers, in "Report to the Secretary of State for India on Railways in India," *Parliamentary Papers* 56, 1876, p. 13.

47. Memorandum by H. R. Maddocks, officiating commissioner of the Bhaugulpore division, to secretary to the government of Bengal, Judicial Department, June 30, *Bengal Proceedings: Judicial*, September 1871, no. 72.

48. Evidence of Thomas McGuire, superintendent, District Charitable Society Alms House, September 30, 1890, "Report of the Pauperism Commission," file 4L/1, *Bengal Proceedings: Miscellaneous*, September 1892, nos. 1–2.

49. Evidence of Mr. Wyllie McCready, inspector, Calcutta police, Lilotollah section, to Subcommittee on Statistics, September 28, 1891, "Report of the Pauperism Commission," nos. 1–2.

50. Evidence of Thomas McGuire, superintendent, District Charitable Society Alms House, September 30, 1890, ibid.

51. Evidence of A. B., evidence of Thomas McGuire, superintendent, District Charitable Society Alms House, September 30, 1890, ibid.

52. G. N. Barlow, commissioner of Bhagulpore division, to secretary to the government of Bengal, General Department, March 13, *Bengal Proceedings: Education*, June 1875, file 70–38, p. 187.

53. G. Lorimer, secretary, Imperial Anglo-Indian Association, Calcutta, to secretary to the government of India, Public Works Department, January 31, 1902, *India Proceedings: Public Works Department: Railways Establishment B*, February 1903, pp. 240–42.

54. The following material is based on interviews with Anglo-Indians and Indian Christians who lived in Kharagpur, Adra, and Jamalpur in the period from 1930 to the present.

55. Westridge, *Railway Life in India*.

56. I am grateful to Indrani Chatterjee for pointing me to these references. Colonel James Emerson, cantonment magistrate, Dinapur, to magistrate of Patna, August 26, 1876, file 34B (1)-10–11, *Bengal Proceedings: Medical*, December 1876, no. 77.

57. Dr. Jameson, extract in letter from C. T. Metcalfe, officiating commissioner, Dinapur, to secretary to the government of Bengal, Judicial Department, March 10, 1876, file 34B-37/38, *Bengal Proceedings: Medical*, August 1876, no. 92 J.

58. Station staff surgeon, Dinapur, to magistrate of Patna, August 19, 1876, ibid.

59. A. Mackenzie, officiating secretary to the government of Bengal, Judicial Department, to agent, East Indian Railway, "Dacoities by Railway Coolies in Hooghly," *Bengal Proceedings: Judicial*, July 1872, no. 88.

60. "Quarters for Menial Staff at Stations," *Official Meetings of the Board of the East Indian Railway*, 1876, no. 21.

61. *Report on the Railway Conference*, 1871.

62. "House Accommodation for Native Staff," in "Official Meeting of the East Indian Railway," August 20, 1878, *Minutes of Official Board Meetings of the East Indian Railway*, 1878, no. 46, resolution 1150.

63. "Screen Walls and Enclosures to Native Quarters at Stations," April 12, 1888, *Minutes of Official Board Meetings of the East Indian Railway*, 1888, no. 14, resolution 400.

64. January 10, *Agent's Letters to the Home Board of the East Indian Railway*, 1901, no. 6.

65. Huddleston, *History of the East Indian Railway*, p. 15.

66. Archbishop Bayly, "Suggestions for Supplying the Educational Requirements of East Indians and Europeans of the Working Class in India," file 70–68/69, *Bengal Proceedings: Education*, June 1875.

67. Richard Temple, "Minute by the Lieutenant-Governor of Bengal 25 February 1875 on the Educational Means for the Poorest Classes of Europeans and East Indians," file 70–68/69, *Bengal Proceedings: Education Department*, March 1875.

68. E. E. Lowis, commissioner of Chittagong division, to secretary to the government of Bengal, no. 12G, April 6, file 70–55, *Bengal Proceedings: Education*, June 1875, p. 203.

69. Resolution by the government of Bengal, General Department (Education), May 29, file 26–58, *Bengal Proceedings: Education*, July 1876.

70. "Schools for Europeans and Eurasians," file 13–17–19, no. 16T, June 30, *Bengal Proceedings: Education*, July 1879.

71. Sir Ashley Eden's opinion referred to in A. W. Croft to secretary to the government of Bengal, September 4, file 26–42, "Schools for Europeans and Eurasians," *Bengal Proceedings: Education*, November 1880.

72. Ibid.

73. Minute by Lord Lytton, March 25, 1879, quoted in appendix to *Committee on the Financial Condition of Hill Schools for Europeans in Northern India*, pp. 336–39.

74. R. Roberts, acting agent, East Indian Railway Company, no. 201G, March 23, file 26–82/98, *Bengal Proceedings: Education*, September 1876.

75. J.C. Oman, "On Training and Industrial Schools for Children of Railway Employees," in *Report on the Railway Conference*, 1871, p. 30.

76. *East Indian Railway Report on Oak Grove School* and *Report on the East India Railway Aided Schools*.

77. Inspector of European schools in Bengal to director of public instruction in Bengal, October 10, *Official Meetings of the East Indian Railway Board*, October 1884, no. 375.

78. Sir Ashley Eden, governor-general in council, extract from proceedings of the government of India, Home Department: Education, no. A, Simla, October 1881, *Committee on the Financial Condition of Hill Schools for Europeans in Northern India*.

79. *Committee on the Financial Condition of Hill Schools for Europeans in Northern India*.

80. Agent, "The Unsatisfactory Financial Position of Oak Grove Hill School, September 3, *Agent's Letters to the Home Board of the East Indian Railway*, September 1903, no. 134.

## 4. INDUSTRIAL UNREST AND THE CULTIVATION OF RAILWAY COMMUNITIES, 1897–1931

*Epigraph*: AE1386/6.
*Epigraph*: I am grateful to Johnny Parry for this reference.

1. Confidential, n. 133, Commissioner's Office, Allahabad, February 13, 1922, *India Proceedings: Railway Establishment B*, May 1922, nos. 215/1–91, cited in Jagga, "Colonial Railwaymen and British Rule." This article is a pioneering account of the nationalist nature of strike action on the Indian railways to which I am greatly indebted in some of my interpretations here.

2. *Report of the Royal Commission on Labour*, p. 285.

3. Alter, *Gandhi's Body*.

4. Ibid.

5. Chandavarkar, *Imperial Power and Popular Politics*.

6. See Jagga, "Colonial Railwaymen and British Rule."

7. President, Railway Defence Committee, to secretary to the government of India, Military Department, "Appointment of a Railway Defence Committee and its Findings," March 17–43B, *India Proceedings: Public Works Department: Railway Construction*, 1902.

8. "Measures for Extending the Employment of Anglo-Indians on the Railways," *India Proceedings: Public Works Department: Railways Establishment B*, February 1903, nos. 240–42.

9. F. R. Upcott, secretary to the government of India, Public Works Department, Railways, to agents of the railways in India, March 14, 1900, ibid.

10. Manager, East Bengal Railway, to secretary to the government of India, Public Works Department, December 29, 1900, ibid.

11. F. B. Herbert to Captain W. J. McElhinney, undersecretary to the government of India, Public Works Department, ibid.

12. Agent, Southern Mahratta Railway, to J. Willcocks, officiating consulting engineer for railways, Bombay, April 13, 1900, ibid.

13. J. Willcocks to G. H. LeMaistre, August 9, 1901, ibid.

14. A. Muirhead to agent, May 31, 1900, ibid.

15. "There is one class not alluded to in these papers and rapidly growing in numbers whose members live or can live as cheaply as natives generally and who have comparatively little objection to leave their districts. I refer to the native Christians. . . . These men are entirely outside the caste combinations of the caste natives." A report on the number of native Christians on the various railways was then called for. Arundel comments on file 13/8/1902, ibid.

16. Minutes of meeting held on January 2, 1903, *India Proceedings: Public Works Department: Establishment A*, July 1903, nos. 17–25.

17. February 24, *Agents Letters to the Home Board of the East Indian Railway*, February 1921, paragraph 9.

18. Varma, *Anglo-Indians*.

19. "Petition to the Minorities Commission of the Domiciled European and Anglo-Indian Community," in *Report of the Indian Statutory Commission (Simon Commission)*, vol. 16; Hassan, *Report on the Representation of Muslims and Other Minority Communities in the Subordinate Railway Service*.

20. R. W. Carlyle, chief secretary to the government of Bengal, Political Department, to secretary to the government of India, Home Department, no. 2141PD, September 19, *India Proceedings: Home Department: Public A*, December 1906, no. 74.

21. R.W. Carlyle, chief secretary to the government of Bengal, to secretary to the government of India, Home Department, September 17, 1906, *India Proceedings: Home Department: Public*, April 1907, nos. 1–5.

22. "Proceedings of Board of Conciliation Appointed by the Government of India to Deal with the Representation from the Drivers of the Howrah Jah-Jah District," *Agent's Letters to the Home Board of the East Indian Railway*, April 1907, no. 88.

23. Letter from agent, Bengal-Nagpur Railway, to secretary to the Railway Board, July 16, 1910, in *Railway Board: Railway Construction A*, September 1911, nos. 34–42.

24. Ibid.

25. Jagga, "Colonial Railwaymen and British Rule."

26. De, "Believer in Brotherhood, Love and Emancipation, Renunciation and Service."

27. Mitra, "From Pages of Past," pp. 319–20.

28. Basu, "A Human Chain Along the Railroad from Calcutta to Burma," p. 226.

29. "Strikes of Indian Staff of Locomotive Department," January 1922, *Agent's Letters to the Home Board*, 1922, no. 10.

30. Jagga, "Colonial Railwaymen and British Rule."

31. Giri, *My Life and Times*.

32. "Policy to be Adopted in Connection with the Housing of Workshop Staff," November 20, 1923, AE1239.

33. *Report of the Royal Commission on Labour*, p. 285.

34. Ibid., p. 284.

35. "Petition to the Minorities Commission by the Anglo-Indian and Domiciled European Community," in *Report of the Indian Statutory Commission (Simon Commission)*, vol. 16, p. S3.

36. Ibid., p. S2.

37. Ibid., p. U4.

38. Ibid., p. U5.

39. Ibid., p. S2.

40. Ibid., p. S3.

41. Speech by K. C. Neogy, MLA, in Legislative Assembly, February 24, 1928, quoted in ibid., p. S4.

## 5. AN ECONOMY OF SUFFERING

1. AE763/4, p. 40.

2. My interpretations of petitions here are informed by Davis, *Fiction in the Archives*, Forge and Foucault, *Le desordre des familles*, Van Voss, ed., *Petitions in Social History*, and Zaret, *Origins of Democratic Culture*.

3. "Staff Councils and Welfare Committees," *India Proceedings: Railway Department: Labour A*, October 1929, case 3-L/1–15, p. 35.

4. Ibid., p. 37.

5. *Memorandum by the Railway Board to the Royal Commission on Labor*, p. 35.

6. Anderson, "Work Construed."

7. *Handbook of Rules and Regulations for All Departments of the East Indian Railway*, pp. 175, 179.

8. *Memorandum by the Railway Board to the Royal Commission on Labor*, p. 151.

9. "Rules Regulating the Discharge and Dismissal of State Non-Gazetted Railway Servants," *East Indian Railway Rules for Employees*, p. 31.

10. Bell, "The Idea of a Patriot Queen?" p. 4.

11. Ibid.

12. J. W. Mitchell, *The Wheels of Ind*, pp. 63, 67.

13. *Memorandum by the Railway Board to the Royal Commission on Labour*, p. 189.

14. May 12, 1934, AE763/5, p. 124.

15. January 4, 1935, AE518/1, p. 53.

16. September 16, 1930, AE578, p. 15.

17. July 1, 1930, AE763/3, p. 67.

18. August 29, 1935, AE578, p. 105.

19. July 1, 1930, AE763/3, p. 67.

20. April 6, 1928, AE1205, p. 43.

21. June 3, 1931, AE763/5, p. 24.

22. November 23, 1933, AE1386/6, p. 102.

23. September 2, 1931, AE1386/4, p. 89.

24. June 11, 1934, AE763/6, p. 164.

25. March 1, 1932, AE386/5, p. 100.

26. See Wadley, "Power in Hindu Ideology and Practice," and Price, *Kingship and Political Practice in Colonial India*.

27. Chatterjee, "History as Self-Representation."

28. May 12, 1934, AE763/5, p. 124.

29. November 28, 1933, AE1386/6, p. 91.

30. Undated, AE763/3, p. 98.

31. September 8, 1930, AE763/3, p. 103.

32. Ibid.

33. May 12, 1934, AE763/5, p. 124.

34. June 24, 1931, AE763/5, p. 78.

35. Chatterjee, "History as Self-Representation."

36. *Memorandum by the Railway Board to the Royal Commission on Labor*, p. 57.

37. Ibid., p. 61.

38. Ibid., p. 101.

39. Ibid., p. 90.

40. Ibid., p. 91.

41. February 26, 1934, AE763/5, p. 85.

42. Undated, AE763/5, p. 213.

43. Undated, AE763/5, p. 34.

44. Ibid.

45. July 18, 1933, AE763/5, p. 67.

46. Undated, AE763/5, p. 34.

47. Ibid.

48. Ibid.

49. Ibid.

50. Ibid.

51. Ibid.

52. Undated, AE763/3, p. 41, and undated, AE763/4, p. 25.

53. May 12, 1934, AE763/5, p. 124.

54. Undated, AE763/4, p. 25.

55. April 26, 1934, AE763/6, p. 115.

56. *Indian State Railways Magazine* 1, no. 1 (October 1927): 12.

57. From (in order of quotation) December 1927, AE761/1, p. 87, March 11, 1933, AE1386/6, p. 68, and undated, AE763/4, p. 23.

58. November 8, 1935, AE1386/6, p. 30.

59. October 12, 1931, AE386/5, p. 14.

60. March 31, 1932, AE386/5, p. 35.

61. Undated (probably September 1930), AE763/3, p. 90.

62. June 27, 1930, AE763/3, p. 67.

63. May 5, 1930, AE763/3, p. 89.

64. June 1932, AE763/4, p. 98.

65. Undated, AE763/9, p. 63.

66. Undated, AE763/3, p. 101.

67. July 15, 1931, AE1478/3, p. 200.

68. May 15, 1933, AE578, p. 267.

69. September 8, 1931, AE578, p. 192.

70. June 11, 1934, AE763/6, p. 164.

71. Ibid.

72. Ibid.

73. Lahiri, "Truth is Stranger than Fiction," p. 409.

74. October 1929, *Sadai Mazhum*, in AE763/11, p. 40.

75. In this respect we can see among working class railway workers a similar process of the formation of the Indian modern self embedded in the morality of *jati* and kinship ties that Chakrabarty describes for the Bengali middle classes in *Provincialising Europe: Postcolonial Thought and Historical Difference*. But unlike in Chakrabarty's example, railway workers were also fusing these notions with ideas of respectability, pedigree, and community current in the railway bureaucracy, which also embedded the British modern self in family moralities.

76. Ibid.

77. October 8, 1930, AE763/3, p. 78.

78. Undated, AE763/4, p. 40.

## 6. PUBLIC GENEALOGIES

*Epigraph*: AE80/1, p. 81.

*Epigraph*: AE80/1, p. 83.

1. The lack of a category of "Indian" and its substitution by a caste designation in this list of nationalities is, of course, a classic colonial reading of Indian society—lacking in unity and simultaneously divided and unified by a logic of caste.

2. August 9, 1916, AE80, p. 118.

3. AE80, p. 109.

4. AE80, p. 118.

5. From the little evidence I have of forms filled in by Indian workers, the kind of designation they wrote in the space assigned for "nationality" was rarely what colonial authorities or anthropologists would describe as a "caste" category. Usually, they wrote down regional place of origin, religion, or language. This illustrates further the new logics of *jati* emerging in interaction with the bureaucracy.

6. November 8, 1929, AE80, p. 12.

7. Ibid., p. 14.

8. September 23, 1947, AE80/3, p. 267.

9. Ibid., p. 268.

10. This would conform to Chatterjee's visions of the nature of nationalism as founded on a universal unbound seriality but crosscut by a contradictory logic of class, i.e., property vs. community, but as we will see in this chapter this is not the only segmentation of the community of the nation. See *The Politics of the Governed*.

11. February 8, 1940, AE80/1, p. 17.

12. In *After Nature: English Kinship in the Late Twentieth Century*, Strathern argues that an uncertainty about the naturalness of kinship is a relatively recent event in British society that has intensified in the context of recent technological and scientific definitions of the person and interventions into the process of reproduction. However, this example suggests (as does Stoler's work) that this uncertainty about what aspects of persons made them of a certain family, community, and nation was generated earlier in colonial situations. The historical experience of these institutional attempts to parse origins related to racism and nationalism needs to be rewritten into the anthropological story of English kinship. I am grateful to Pete Gow for pointing me toward these issues.

13. July 27, 1929, AE80, p. 20.

14. Undated, AE80, p. 24.

15. May 9, 1940, AE80/3, p. 35B.

16. June 6, 1940, AE80/3, p. 53.

17. See Viswanathan, *Outside the Fold: Conversion, Modernity, and Belief*. Viswanathan suggests that conversion entails an oppositional logic to that of the secular

state. Here, I want to suggest something more akin to the argument of Van Der Veer in *Imperial Encounters*. This is that the secular and religious self are deeply entangled and mutually productive rather than radically oppositional. Notions of community and selfhood formed in secular nationalism both partake of and become translated into notions of self and community from religious contexts. This cross-fertilization is what I am trying to capture in the idea of divine citizenship in the ethnographic section of the book. This cross-fertilization, as Van Der Veer has shown, is particularly visible in the interaction of the moral and religiously inflected project of the Raj with Indian notions of religious community. Although, as Kantorowicz has shown in *The King's Two Bodies*, over several centuries in Europe there has also been a gradual transposition of Christian polity onto an earthly, this-worldly one and vice versa, with the consequence that patriotism has been endowed with highly sacred qualities (I am grateful to Veronique Benei for this last reference).

18. See Ballhatchet, *Caste, Class, and Catholicism in India, 1789–1914*, and Bayly, *Saints, Goddesses, and Kings: Muslim and Christians in South Indian Society, 1760–1900*.

19. Mr. Robertson, deputy agent, East Indian Railway, September 7, 1934, AE2(34), p. 123.

20. September 24, 1940, Mrs. G. Hayler to general manager, East Indian Railway, AE80/3, p. 17.

21. November 19, 1939, AE80/1, p. 122.

22. March 14, 1945, AE80/2, p. 159.

23. July 28, 1941, AE80/2, p. 141.

24. January 11, 1946, AE80/2, p. 223.

25. This historical summary is from the *Imperial Anglo-Indian Association Report*, 1900–1912.

26. The following historical summary of the Anglo Indian Association is from issues of *The Anglo-Indian Review* from 1932 to 1947.

27. Wallace, "Asil Anglo-Indians," pp. 10–11.

28. See Sukumar Rai's poem *Tash Goru*, published in *Sandesh* and *Abol-Tabol*, 1923.

29. "What is an Anglo-Indian?"

30. Mahalanobis, "Anthropological Observations on the Anglo-Indians of Calcutta."

31. April 26, 1934, AE763/6, p. 115.

32. Gandhi, *The Collected Works of Mahatma Gandhi*, pp. 184–85.

33. Balibar, "The Nation Form."

34. See my novel Roychowdhury, *The Jadu House*.

## 7. UNCERTAIN ORIGINS AND THE STRATEGIES OF LOVE

1. Bouquet, "Making Kinship, with an Old Reproductive Technology."

2. See Benei, *Nationalizing Children*, and Ramaswamy, *The Pleasures of the Tongue*.

## 8. TRACES OF THE ARCHIVE

1. Sealy, *The Trotter-Nama*, p. 55.

2. Ibid., pp. 277, 394.

3. Ibid., p. 572.

4. Ibid., pp. 307–8.

5. Derrida, *Archive Fever*. Derrida suggests that all archives are haunted by ghosts or specters of the living substrates of culture, persons, and memories that they seem to refer to, but which can never be made present in their writing. Archives provoke and are provoked by a desire to make the past of sensuous memories present again in the form of writing. This desire can, of course, never be fulfilled. Derrida uses many examples of family and personal losses in his account, from Hamlet's vision of the ghost of his father to Freud's diary. He also deploys metaphors that emphasize the relationship between the domestic and the public archive. Yet by making a general theoretical point about the uncertainties of all archives, he misses the important opportunity of addressing historical questions about the variable effects of specific archives and their relationship to particular kinds of families. I want to suggest that this discussion of archives in general hides the historical processes by which certain people's memories, families, and bodies have been placed in unequal relationships with specific archives.

6. Carsten, *The Heat of the Hearth*; Lambert, "Sentiment and Substance in North Indian Forms of Relatedness."

7. See Caplan, *Children of Colonialism*, chap. 6, for a similar finding in Chennai.

8. For examples of this in Chennai, see ibid.

9. For examples of this in Chennai, see ibid.

10. Parry criticizes arguments about caste that polarize dividuals/individuals and suggest that notions of *jati* represent a solely being-based idea of a fluid transactional self. He points out that ideas of caste contain both a strong idea of inherited essences and a notion of a transactional self, as does the "Western" idea of the self. He suggests that caste ideology works on a dynamic in which this self, although inherited, has to be maintained by the nature of social interactions. See Parry, "The End of the Body." My perspective on ideas of *jati* among Anglo-Indian and Indian railway workers follows this approach.

11. In some respects their situation is similar to that described for adoptees in Britain by Carsten, *After Kinship* and "Knowing Where You've Come From."

12. I am assuming he sits in the National Library from the violet-colored stamp and the reference to fans, familiar to me from trips I took there during my research.

13. Derrida, *Archive Fever*, p. 20.

## 9. RAILWAY MORALITY

1. Moshin, *Chittaranjan: A Study in Urban Sociology*.

2. Proceedings of conference quoted in Chakravarty, ed., *Tales of Railwaymen's Chivalry*, p. 282.

3. *Report of the Indian Railway Inquiry Committee*, pp. 161–62.

4. See Chakravarty, "A Struggle to Live with Courage, Dignity, and Pride."

5. "Eastern Railwaymen's Union General Secretary's Annual Report, 1959," p. 110.

6. *Report of the Railway Corruption Enquiry Committee, 1953–55*, p. 6.

7. Ibid., p. 127.

8. Ibid., p. 120.

9. Ibid., p. 11.

10. Ibid., p. 122.

11. Chakravarty, "A Struggle to Live with Courage, Dignity, and Pride," p. 176.

12. This enactment of hierarchy is, of course, visible in other Indian bureaucracies such as the civil service, police, etc. This suggests that we need to investigate more widely the continuation and extension of colonial regulations, bureaucratic moralities, and workplace practices in order to understand the contemporary forms of the Indian state.

13. For a very different example, in which class identities override other forms of distinction, see Parry's account of Bhilai in "Nehru's Dream and the Village 'Waiting Room.'" The difference is due to the different caste and class background of my informants and their long involvement in railway work. If I had carried out research with scheduled caste employees who had no previous family connection with the railways, it is very likely that I would have found a similar emphasis to that among Parry's informants on class status. Here, I concentrate on Bengali families of middle-ranking caste with long connections to the railways because I want to trace what has happened to the ideas of *jati* that I saw expressed in previous generations on the railways.

14. On the miniature see Stewart, *On Longing*.

## 10. RUINS AND GHOSTS

1. Self-fashioning is, of course, Steven Greenblatt's term, which he coined to describe the self-conscious attempt to become a particular kind of man characteristic of Renaissance poets, artists, and playwrights in *Renaissance Self-Fashioning*. It is appropriate here because of the self-consciousness with which people in Kharagpur formulate their projects of becoming certain kinds of people. Of course, the self here is different from that described by Greenblatt. As I make clear, it is a self conceived through the historically produced categories of *jati*, *desh*, pedigree, and the secular citizen-subject. The emphasis on ethical projects of self-formation is also indebted to James Laidlaw's "For an Anthropology of Ethics and Freedom."

2. A sensation of the nearness and relevance of the past can indicate a flight from dealing with the inequalities of present political and social relationships. See Todorov, *Les abus de la memoire*.

3. On the relationship between transactional and essentialized notions of caste identity, see Parry, "The End of the Body."

4. On the alienation of memory into places and objects of memory in contemporary France, see Nora, *Conflicts and Divisions*. On the opposite sensibility, in which the past inheres only in creative acts of human agency and renovation of monuments carried out by spirit mediums and priests in the present, see Lambek, *The Weight of the Past*.

5. Carsten, *After Kinship*.

6. This, as Rowena Robinson points out, echoes the practice of Hindus during the month of Bhadrapadh (August/September) in which they remember their dead lineal ancestors. It is commonly practiced among Goanese Christians with a much more directly Hindu and patrilineal inflection. In Kharagpur, it links families to a place as well as a family line and commemorates not just distant ancestors of the patriline but the recent dead and bilaterally reckoned kin. Also, Robinson does not report ghosts as a regular feature of her informants' lives; much more commonly found among her informants was the idea of possession by spirits of the dead. For them, the past and places are an external influence rather than an internal one (see note 4). See Robinson, *Conversion, Continuity, and Change*.

7. In spite of claims about Christianity's otherworldly orientation and disembedding of kinship relations, Fenella Cannell has shown that in practice it is often associated with family relationships. For Mormons it is inextricable from a this-worldy orientation toward the family and a sense of a divinized personal genealogy. See Cannell, "The Christianity of Anthropology." Cannell argues that on the basis of Mormonism we should rethink both the nature of the link between Christianity and kinship and the secular nature of genealogy and kinship in Europe and the United States. See her important and pioneering work, "'Loving the Dead,'" My thinking on these issues and the nature of Catholicism among Anglo-Indians is inspired by her approach and many conversations with her. Anglo-Indians carry out a double move in relation to Catholicism. They use its sense of transcendent community to give substance to the idea of a generic Anglo-Indian community that cannot be fully founded in any secular ideas of Indian community, and they also use practices of Catholicism to memorialize specific kinship relationships. I would not have begun to think of their approaches in these terms without conversations with Fenella Cannell.

8. I want to make a similar move to that of Van Dijk in his analysis of conversion to Pentecostalism in Malawi. He contextualizes the attraction of certain forms of Christianity for a particular group of people in relation to the temporalities of nationalism as institutionalized in state practices in Malawi. See his "Pentecostalism, Cultural Memory, and the State."

9. This is a counterexample to Carol Delaney's argument that the Abrahamic tale of sacrifice fundamentally appropriates the generative power of women to the patriline; see her "Cutting the Ties That Bind."

10. This section owes much to Stoler and Strassler, "Castings for the Colonial."

11. See, for example, for the case of middle-class Bengalis, Chakrabarty, *Provincializing Europe*.

12. See, for Maharashtra, the work of Benei, *Nationalizing Children*, and for Tamil Nadu, Ramaswamy, *Pleasures of the Tongue*.

13. This idea comes from Cannell. She makes the important point that secular history and genealogical imaginings may share structures of feeling and content with Christian chronotopes.

14. We might ask questions about the late-nineteenth-century German idea of the home and nation (*heimat*) through Freud's case studies of the uncanny. Why is it that family and the space of the home are suffused with such a determining power to act on people in Freud's patients' accounts and in his analysis? Does this reflect a similar reification in German nationalist chronotopes of origins?

## CONCLUSION

1. For discussions of pedigree and English kinship in general, see the following important works: Ritvo, *The Animal Estate*; Cassidy, *The Sport of Kings*; Wolfram, *Inlaws and Outlaws*; and Edwards and Strathern, "Including Our Own." The history of the railways contributes a different emphasis to the wider discussion of English kinship by exploring the transformation of ideas of pedigree, blood, and belonging into forms of nationalism and race in imperial contexts. These then affected concepts and practices of nationalism and racism in Britain as well. The work carried out on Victorian ideas of pedigree and use of agricultural metaphors and on contemporary understandings of pedigree among racing families and concepts of belonging in British towns can then be refracted through a different historical prism and institutional history. The political history of kinship idioms can be incorporated.

2. See the very significant argument of Robb about the importance of the British Empire in India and race to the creation of the ideas of British nationalism at home in "Children, Emotion, Identity, and Empire."

3. Thorner, *Investment in Empire*.

4. On the precolonial imagination of power in idioms of caste, see the work of Dirks, *The Hollow Crown* and *Castes of Mind*. His work explains part of the elective affinity among new political ideas of the public sphere, bureaucratic honor, and *jati* in colonial India in popular sentiment and nationalism. Contrary to colonial images of caste, these were already an important part of the idioms of power in precolonial India. However, current forms of *jati*, of course, are profoundly distinct from precolonial idioms in the important ways that Dirks's books and this work trace.

5. See Beteille, "Caste in Contemporary India."

6. See Biswas, *Samsad Bengali-English Dictionary*. It is certainly true that Bankim Chandra Chattopadhyay used this broad notion of *jati* to satirize the literalist understanding of caste by a British judge in *Kamalakanta*, as Chatterjee suggests in *The Nation and Its Fragments*. Yet the Bengali use of this term has also been repeatedly used to close down the boundaries of belonging and to mark class distinction. For a comic literary example of this, see Ray, "Tash Goru," in *Abol-Tabol*. The figure of the Eurasian clerk in this poem is satirized for its petty class position and grander aspirations

and for its physical weakness. Here, the lineage, species, race, and class meanings of *jati* all combine to make the clerk not quite "right" and not quite "one of us."

7. For other examples and contexts for this idea of permeable persons, see Daniels, *Fluid Signs*, and Busby, *The Performance of Gender*. For an important discussion of the variable meanings of substance in anthropological theories and English language use, see Carsten, "Substantivism, Antisubstantivism, and Anti-antisubstantivism."

8. See the discussion in Povinelli, "What's Love Got to Do with It?" The history of the railway bureaucracy provides a concrete example of her argument that we live in genealogical societies in which inequalities are produced through the opposition of a self-creating sovereign subject and its "other," the subject limited by genealogical inheritances. She suggests that "genealogy consists of concrete practices and regulatory ideas that, no matter their internal incoherences, have three major topographies: the materiality of genealogy, the symbolics of genealogy, and the economy of genealogy" through which the limits on the self-creating politically free citizen are imagined and "life goods and values" are distributed "across social space" (p. 177). The material from the railway bureaucracy shows most strongly that particular legitimate genealogies provide the foundation for the ideal citizen who can act as a fully autonomous and fair agent in the public sphere, unlike those "others" handicapped by limiting inheritances and moral sensibilities.

9. Stoler and Strassler, "Castings for the Colonial."

10. For example, Hertzfeld, *Cultural Intimacy*, and Delaney and Yanagisako, *Naturalizing Power*.

11. Stoler, *Race and the Education of Desire* and *Carnal Knowledge and Imperial Power*.

12. For example, Franklin and McKinnon, *Relative Values*.

13. See the recent discussion of the uncertainties created by bureaucratic documents in Kelly, "Documented Lives."

14. See the argument of Bryant in "The Purity of Spirit and the Power of Blood."

15. This important insight comes from my conversations with Fenella Cannell, although she might not agree with my interpretations here in relation to the politics of kinship. See "'Loving the Dead.'"

# Bibliography

NEWSPAPERS AND MAGAZINES

Clark, W. "The Atmosphere of Buildings and Their Ventilation." *The Engineers Journal and Railway Public Works and Mining Gazette of India and the Colonies* 6 (May 1, 1863).

"Colonisation in India." *Calcutta Review* 30 (1858): 175–79.

*The Engineers Journal and Railway Public Works and Mining Gazette of India and the Colonies*. October 2, 1858.

"Facts Relating to an Attempted Outrage on a Lady in a Railway Carriage." *The Bengalee*. August 21, 1897.

Gidney, H. "Eleventh Annual General Meeting of the Anglo-Indian Association, Calcutta." *The Anglo-Indian Review*. February 1938. Pp. 16–18.

"The Indian Association and the Assensole Outrage Case." *The Bengalee*. September 21, 1895.

*Indian State Railways Magazine* 1, no. 1 (October 1927).

Marx, K. "The Future Results of British Rule in India." *New York Daily Tribune*. August 8, 1853.

"Railway Outrages." *The Bengalee*. October 31, 1891.

"The Railways of Great Britain." *The Edinburgh Review* 108 (July 1858–October 1858): 399–419.

Stephenson, R. M. "The World's Highway." *Calcutta Review* 26 (1856).

"What Is an Anglo-Indian?" *The Modern Review* 24 (1923): 203–4.

## SOURCE MATERIALS

*Anglo-Indian Association, Kolkata*

*Anglo-Indian Review.* Calcutta, 1932–1947.


*Agent's Record Room, Eastern Railway Headquarters, Kolkata*

Bundles of files from 1890 to 1947, including:
AE2(34)
AE80/1
AE80/2
AE80/3
AE230.
AE386/5.
AE518/1
AE578.
AE761/1.
AE763/3.
AE763/4.
AE763/5.
AE763/6.
AE763/9.
AE763/11
AE1205.
AE1239.
AE1386/4.
AE1386/6.
AE1478/3.
*Minutes of Official Board Meetings of the East Indian Railway.* Volumes from 1878 to
    1940.


*India Office Library, London*

*Bengal Proceedings: Education.* June 1875.
——. July 1876.
——. July 1879.
——. September 1876.
——. November 1880.
*Bengal Proceedings: Education Department.* March 1875.
*Bengal Proceedings: Judicial.* September 1871.
——. July 1872.
——: *Police.* May 1896.
*Bengal Proceedings: Medical.* August 1876.

———. December 1876.

———. July 1877.

*Bengal Proceedings: Miscellaneous.* September 1892.

*Bengal Proceedings: Municipal, Medical.* February 1897.

———. March 1897.

*Bengal Proceedings: Public Works Department.* April 1859.

———. May 1859.

———. September 1859.

———. October 1859.

———: *Railway Branch.* July 1859.

———: *Railway Branch.* September 1859.

———: *Railway Branch.* December 1859.

———: *Railway Branch.* August 1860.

———: *Railway Branch.* May 1861.

———: *Railway Branch.* June 1861.

———: *Railway Branch.* December 1866.

———: *Railway Branch.* February 1867.

———: *Railway Branch.* October 1867.

———: *Railway Branch.* March 1868.

———: *Railway Branch.* April 1868.

———: *Railway Branch.* September 1869.

*Committee on the Financial Condition of Hill Schools for Europeans in Northern India.*
    Simla: Government of India Press, 1904.

*East Indian Railway Rules and Regulations and Act for Regulating Railways in British
    India.* Calcutta: Sanders and Coomes, 1854. European manuscripts, F133/140.

*India Proceedings: Legislative Consultations.* April 4–May 10, 1850.

*India Proceedings: Public Works Department.* March 1864.

———: *Railways.* July 1865.

———: *Railway Establishment.* December 1879.

*Memorandum by the Railway Board to the Royal Commission on Labour.* 1930.

*Report of the Indian Railway Inquiry Committee.* New Delhi: Railway Board, 1948.

*Report of the Pauperism Commission.* File 4L/1, nos. 1–2.

*Report of the Railway Corruption Enquiry Committee, 1953–55.* New Delhi: Govern-
    ment of India Press, 1955.

*Report of the Royal Commission on Labour.* London: Her Majesty's Stationery Office,
    1931.

"Report on and Text of Act XXI of 1868 to Provide Against European Vagrancy."
    *Legislative and Judicial Proceedings/5/11,* 1868.

"Text of Act No XIX of 1850." *India Proceedings: Legislative Consultations/11/4,* 1850.


*Mechanical Engineering Library, Eastern Railway, Kolkata*

*Agent's Letters to the Home Board of the East Indian Railway.* Volumes from 1854 to 1921.

*East Indian Railway Dress Regulations.* March 3, 1927.

*East Indian Railway Rules for Employees.* 1930.

*Handbook of Rules and Regulations for All Departments of the East Indian Railway.* Calcutta: East Indian Railway Press, 1916.

*Official Meetings of the Board of the East Indian Railway.* Volumes from 1875 to 1888.


### National Archives, New Delhi

*India Proceedings: Home Department: Public.* April 1907.

———: *Public A.* December 1906.

*India Proceedings: Public Works Department.* November 1854.

———. August 1860.

———: *Establishment A.* July 1903.

———: *Railway Construction.* 1902.

———: *Railways.* November 1860.

———: *Railways.* July 1865.

———: *Railways.* August 1865.

———: *Railways.* April 1868.

———: *Railways Establishment B.* February 1903.

*India Proceedings: Railway Board: Railway Construction A.* September 1911.

*India Proceedings: Railway Department: Labour A.* October 1929.

———: *Railway A.* May 1861.


### National Library, Kolkata

*East Indian Railway Report on Oak Grove School.* 1915.

Hassan, K. M. *Report on the Representation of Muslims and Other Minority Communities in the Subordinate Railway Service.* Simla: Government of India Press, 1932.

*Imperial Anglo-Indian Association Report.* 1900–1912.

*Report on the East India Railway Aided Schools.* 1906.

*Report on the Railway Conference.* Simla: Government of India Press, 1871.

———. Simla: Government of India Press, 1888.

———. Simla: Government of India Press, 1900.


### University of Michigan Library

"Appendix to the Report to the Secretary of State for India on Railways in India." *Parliamentary Papers (House of Commons)* 43, no. 353 (1864).

Dalhousie, Lord. "Railway Reports from India." *Parliamentary Papers* 86 (1852–1853): 114–15 (594–95).

"Report of the Committee on Colonisation and Settlement." *Parliamentary Papers (House of Commons)* 7, no. 2 (1857–1858).

———. *Parliamentary Papers (House of Commons)* 4 (1859).

———. *Parliamentary Papers (House of Commons)* 5 (1859).

*Report of the Indian Statutory Commission (Simon Commission)*, vol. 16 (1930).
"Report to the Secretary of State for India on Railways in India." *Parliamentary Papers* 56 (1876).


## BOOKS AND ARTICLES

Abel, E. *The Anglo-Indian Community*. New Delhi: Chanakya, 1988.

Adas, M. *Machines as the Measure of Men: Science, Technology, and Ideologies of Western Dominance*. Ithaca: Cornell University Press, 1989.

Alter, J. *Gandhi's Body: Sex, Diet, and the Politics of Nationalism*. Philadelphia: University of Pennsylvania Press, 2000.

Anderson, M. R. "Work Construed: Ideological Origins of Labour Law in British India to 1918." In P. Robb, ed., *Dalit Movements and the Meanings of Labour in India*, pp. 87–120.

Anthony, F. *Britain's Betrayal in India*. New Delhi: Allied Publishers, 1969.

Antze, P. and M. Lambek. *Tense Past: Cultural Essays in Trauma and Memory*. New York: Routledge, 1996.

Arnold, D. "European Orphans and Vagrants in India in the Nineteenth Century." *The Journal of Imperial and Commonwealth History* 7, no. 2 (1979): 104–27.

——. "White Colonisation and Labour in Nineteenth Century India." *The Journal of Imperial and Commonwealth History* 9, no. 2 (1983): 133–58.

——. *The New Cambridge History of India*. Vol. 3, no. 5, *Science, Technology, and Medicine in Colonial India*. Cambridge: Cambridge University Press, 2000.

Baca, G. "Politics of Recognition and Myths of Race." *Social Analysis* 49, no. 2 (Summer 2005): 147–54.

Balibar, E. "The Nation Form: History and Ideology." In E. Balibar and I. Wallerstein, eds., *Race, Nation, Class: Ambiguous Identities*, pp. 000. London: Verso, 1991.

Ballhatchet, K. *Caste, Class, and Catholicism in India, 1789–1914*. London: Curzon, 1998.

Basu, P. K. "A Human Chain Along the Railroad from Calcutta to Burma." In R. Chakravarty, ed., *Tales of Railwaymen's Chivalry*, pp. 226–50.

Bayly, S. *Saints, Goddesses, and Kings: Muslims and Christians in South Indian Society, 1760–1900*. Cambridge: Cambridge University Press, 1989.

——. *Caste, Society, and Politics in India from the Eighteenth Century to the Modern Age*. New York: Cambridge University Press, 1999.

Bell, D. "The Idea of a Patriot Queen? The Monarchy, the Constitution, and the Iconographic Order of Britain, 1860–1900." *The Journal of Imperial and Commonweath History* 34, no. 1, (2006): 3–21.

Bell, H. *Railway Policy in India*. London: Rivington, Percival, 1894.

Benei, V. *Manufacturing Citizenship: Education and Nationalism in Europe, South Asia, and China*. London: Routledge, 2005.

——. "Nationalizing Children: An Ethnography of Schooling, Gender, and Violence in Contemporary India." Manuscript.

Berridge, P. S. A. *Couplings to the Khyber: The Story of the North-Western Railway*. New York: Augustus M. Kelley, 1969.

Beteille, A. "Caste in Contemporary India." In C. J. Fuller, ed., *Caste Today*, pp. 150–77. Delhi: Oxford University Press, 1996.

Biswas, S. *Samsad Bengali-English Dictionary*. 2d ed. Calcutta: Shishu Sahitya Samsad, 1992.

Blom Hansen, T. and F. Stepputat. *States of Imagination: Ethnographic Exploration of the Post-Colonial State*. Durham, N.C.: Duke University Press, 2001.

Blunt, A. *Domicile and Diaspora: Anglo-Indian Women and the Spatial Politics of Home*. Oxford: Blackwell, 2005.

Bouquet, M. "Making Kinship, with an Old Reproductive Technology." In S. Franklin and S. McKinnon, eds., *Relative Values*, pp. 54–85.

Bryant, R. "The Purity of Spirit and the Power of Blood: A Comparative Perspective on Nation, Gender, and Kinship in Cyprus." *Journal of the Royal Anthropological Institute*, n.s., 8 (2002): 509–30.

Burton, A. "House/Daughter/Nation." *Journal of Asian Studies* 56 (1997): 921–46.

——. *Gender, Sexuality, and Colonial Modernities*. London: Routledge, 1999.

Busby, C. *The Performance of Gender: An Anthropology of Everyday Life in a South Indian Fishing Village*. London: Althone Press, 2000.

Cannell, F. "The Christianity of Anthropology." *Journal of the Royal Anthropological Institute* 11, no. 2 (June 2005): 335–56.

——. "'Loving the Dead': Mormon Kinship and the Work of Mourning." Manuscript.

Caplan, L. *Children of Colonialism: Anglo-Indians in a Postcolonial World*. Oxford: Berg, 2001.

Carsten, J. *The Heat of the Hearth: The Process of Kinship in a Malay Fishing Community*. Cambridge: Cambridge University Press, 1997.

——. "Knowing Where You've Come From: Ruptures and Continuities of Time and Kinship in Narratives of Adoption Reunions." *Journal of the Royal Anthropological Institute* 6, no. 4 (December 2000): 687–703.

——. "Substantivism, Antisubstantivism, and Anti-antisubstantivism." In S. Franklin and S. McKinnon, eds., *Relative Values*, pp. 29–53.

——. *After Kinship*. Cambridge: Cambridge University Press, 2004.

Carter, I. *Railways and Culture: The Epitome of Modernity*. Manchester: Manchester University Press, 2001.

Cassidy, R. *The Sport of Kings: Kinship, Class, and Thoroughbred Breeding in Newmarket*. Cambridge: Cambridge University Press, 2002.

Chakrabarty, D. *Rethinking Working Class History: Bengal, 1890–1940*. Princeton, N.J.: Princeton University Press, 1989.

——. "Postcoloniality and the Artifice of History: Who Speaks for 'Indian' Pasts?" *Representations* 37 (1992): 1–26.

——. *Provincializing Europe: Postcolonial Thought and Historical Difference*. Princeton, N.J.: Princeton University Press, 2000.

———. *Habitations of Modernity: Essays in the Wake of Subaltern Studies*. Chicago: University of Chicago Press, 2002.

Chakravarty, R. "A Struggle to Live with Courage, Dignity, and Pride." In R. Chakravarty, ed., *Tales of Railwaymen's Chivalry*.

———, ed. *Tales of Railwaymen's Chivalry*. Calcutta: S. B. Lahiri, 1993.

Chandavarkar, R. *The Origins of Industrial Capitalism in India: Business Strategies and the Working Classes in Bombay, 1900–1940*. Cambridge: Cambridge University Press, 1994.

———. *Imperial Power and Popular Politics: Class, Resistance, and the State in India, c. 1850–1950*. Cambridge: Cambridge University Press, 1998.

Chandra, B. *The Rise and Growth of Economic Nationalism in India*. Delhi: People's Publishing House, 1966.

Chatterjee, I. "Colouring Subalternity: Slaves, Concubines, and Social Orphans in Early Colonial India." *Subaltern Studies* 10. New Delhi: Oxford University Press, 1999.

———. *Gender, Slavery, and Law in Colonial India*. New Delhi: Oxford University Press, 1999.

———. *Unfamiliar Relations: Family and History in South Asia*. New Brunswick, N.J.: Rutgers University Press, 2004.

Chatterjee, K. "History as Self-Representation: The Recasting of a Political Tradition in Late Eighteenth-Century Eastern India." *Modern Asian Studies* 32, no. 4 (1998): 913–48.

Chatterjee, P. *The Nation and Its Fragments: Colonial and Post-Colonial Histories*. Princeton, N.J.: Princeton University Press, 1993.

———. *The Politics of the Governed: Reflections on Popular Politics in Most of the World*. New York: Columbia University Press, 2004.

Clancy-Smith, J. and F. Gouda. *Domesticating the Empire: Race, Gender, and Family Life in French and Dutch Colonialism*. Charlottesville, Va.: University of Virginia Press, 1998.

Clarke, H. *Colonisation, Defence, and Railways in Our Indian Empire*. London: John Weale, 1857.

Daniels, E. V. *Fluid Signs: Being a Person the Tamil Way*. Berkeley: University of California Press, 1984.

———. *Charred Lullabies: Chapters in an Anthropology of Violence*. Princeton, N.J.: Princeton University Press, 1996.

Davidoff, L. and C. Hall. *Family Fortunes: Men and Women of the English Middle Class, 1780–1850*. London: Hutchinson, 1987.

Davidson, H. *The Railways of India: With an Account of Their Rise, Progress, and Construction: Written with the Aid of the Records of the India Office*. London: E and F. N. Spoon, 1868.

Davin, A. "Motherhood and Imperialism." *History Workshop* 5 (1978): 9–57.

Davis, N. Z. *Fiction in the Archives: Pardon Tales and Their Tellers in Sixteenth Century France*. Stanford: University of California Press, 1987.

De, B. "Believer in Brotherhood, Love and Emancipation, Renunciation and Service." In R. Chakravarty, ed., *Tales of Railwaymen's Chivalry*, pp. 401–8.

De Certeau, M. *The Practice of Everyday Life.* Berkeley: University of California Press, 1984.

Delaney, C. "Cutting the Ties That Bind: The Sacrifice of Abraham and Patriarchal Kinship." In S. Franklin and S. McKinnon, eds., *Relative Values*, pp. 445–67.

—— and S. Yanagisako. *Naturalizing Power: Essays in Feminist Cultural Analysis.* New York: Routledge, 1995.

Den Otter, A. A. *The Philosophy of Railways: The Transcontinental Railway Idea in British North America.* Toronto: University of Toronto Press, 1997.

Derbyshire, I. "Economic Change and the Railways in North India, 1860–1914." *Modern Asian Studies* 21, no. 3 (1987): 521–45.

Derrida, J. *Archive Fever.* Chicago: University of Chicago Press, 1996.

Desmond, R. and M. Satow. *Railways of the Raj.* New York: New York University Press, 1980.

Devika, J. "The Aesthetic Woman: Re-forming Female Bodies and Minds in Early Twentieth-Century Keralam." *Modern Asian Studies* 39, no. 2 (2005): 461–87.

Dirks, N. *The Hollow Crown: The Ethnohistory of an Indian Kingdom.* Cambridge: Cambridge University Press, 1987.

——. *Castes of Mind: Colonialism and the Making of Modern India.* Princeton, N.J.: Princeton University Press, 2001.

Dover, C. *Half-Caste.* London: Secker and Warberg, 1937.

Dutt, K. L. *In Search of a Homeland: Anglo-Indians and McCluskiegunge.* Calcutta: Minerva Associates, 1990.

Dutt, R. C. *The Economic History of India.* Delhi: Publications Division, Ministry of Information and Broadcasting, Government of India, 1960.

"Eastern Railwaymen's Union General Secretary's Annual Report, 1959." In R. Chakravarty, ed., *Tales of Railwaymen's Chivalry.*

Edwards, J. and M. Strathern. "Including Our Own." In J. Carsten, ed., *Cultures of Relatedness: New Approaches to the Study of Kinship*, pp. 149–66. Cambridge: Cambridge University Press, 2000.

Feeley-Harnik, G. "The Ethnography of Creation: Lewis Henry Morgan and the American Beaver." In S. Franklin and S. McKinnon, eds., *Relative Values*, pp. 54–84.

Ferguson, J. and A. Gupta. 'Spatializing States: Towards an Ethnography of Neoliberal Governmentality.' *American Ethnologist* 29, no. 4 (November 2002): 981–1002.

Fernandes, L. *Producing Workers: The Politics of Gender, Class, and Culture in the Calcutta Jute Mills.* Philadelphia: University of Pennsylvania Press, 1997.

Feuchtwang, S. "Remnants of Revolution in China." In C. Hann, ed., *Postsocialism: Ideals, Ideologies, and Practices in Eurasia*, pp. 196–213. London: Routledge, 2002.

Forge, A. and M. Foucault. *Le desordre des familles: Lettres de cache des archives de la Bastille au XVIIIe siecle.* Paris: Editions Gallimard Julliard, 1982.

Franklin, S. and S. McKinnon. *Relative Values: Reconfiguring Kinship Studies*. Durham, N.C.: Duke University Press, 2001.

Freeman, M. *Railways and the Victorian Imagination*. New Haven, Conn.: Yale University Press, 1999.

Fuller, C. J. and V. Benei, eds. *The Everyday State and Society in Modern India*. New Delhi: Social Science Press, 2000.

Gaikwad, V. *The Anglo-Indians*. New Delhi: The Asia Publishing House, 1967.

Gandhi, M. "Hind Swaraj." *The Collected Works of Mahatma Gandhi*. Vol. 21. 1909. Reprint, Delhi: Publishing Division, Ministry of Information and Broadcasting, Government of India, 1970.

Gbah-Bear, L. "Miscegenations of Modernity: Constructing European Respectability and Race in the Indian Railway Colony, 1857–1931." *Women's History Review* 3, no. 4 (1994): 531–46.

Ghosh, C. *Dalhousie in India, 1848–1856: A Study of His Social Policy as Governor-General*. New Delhi: Munshiram Manoharal Publishers, 1975.

——. "The Utilitarianism of Dalhousie and the Material Improvement of India." *Modern Asian Studies* 12, no. 1 (1978): 97–110.

Ghosh, D. "Making and Unmaking Loyal Subjects: Pensioning Widows and Educating Orphans in Early Colonial India." *The Journal of Imperial and Commonwealth History* 31, no. 1 (January 2003): 1–28.

——. "Household Crimes and Domestic Order: Keeping the Peace in Colonial Calcutta, c. 1770–1840." *Modern Asian Studies* 38, no. 3 (2004): 599–623.

Giri, V. V. *My Life and Times*. New Delhi: Macmillan, 1976.

Gist, N. and R. Wright. *Marginality and Identity: Anglo-Indians as a Racially-Mixed Minority in India*. Leiden: E. J. Brill, 1973.

Gooptu, N. *The Politics of the Urban Poor in Early Twentieth-Century India*. Cambridge: University of Cambridge Press, 2001.

Goswami, M. *Producing India: From Colonial Economy to National Space*. Chicago: University of Chicago Press, 2004.

Greenblatt, S. *Renaissance Self-Fashioning: From More to Shakespeare*. Chicago: University of Chicago Press, 1980.

Guha, R. "Chandra's Death." In R. Guha, ed., *Writings on South Asian History and Society*, Subaltern Studies 5, pp. 135–65. Delhi: Oxford University Press, 1987.

Gupta, R. *Labour and Housing in India*. Calcutta: Longmans, Green, 1930.

Hancock, M. "Home Science and the Nationalization of Domesticity in Colonial India." *Modern Asian Studies* 35, no. 4 (2001): 871–903.

Hari Rao, P. *The Indian Railways Act (IX of 1890)*. Mylapore: The Madras Law Journal Office, 1930.

Harrison, M. *Climates and Constitutions: Health, Race, Environment, and British Imperialism in India, 1600–1850*. New Delhi: Oxford University Press, 2002.

Hawes, C. *Poor Relations: The Making of a Eurasian Community in British India, 1773–1833*. Richmond: Curzon, 1996.

Headrick, D. *The Tentacles of Progress: Technology Transfer in the Age of Imperialism*. New York: Oxford University Press, 1998.

Hertzfeld, M. *The Social Production of Indifference: The Symbolic Roots of Western Bureaucracy*. New York: Berg, 1992.

——. *Cultural Intimacy: Social Poetics in the Nation State*. New York: Routledge, 1997.

Holmstrom, M. *South Indian Factory Workers: Their Life and Their World*. Cambridge: Cambridge University Press, 1976.

——. *Industry and Inequality: Towards a Social Anthropology of Indian Labour*. Cambridge: Cambridge University Press, 1984.

Huddleston, G. *History of the East Indian Railway*. Calcutta: Thacker, Spink, 1906.

Hurd, I. "Railways and the Expansion of Markets in India, 1861–1921." *Explorations in Economic History* 12, no. 3 (1975): 263–88.

——. "Railways: The Beginnings of the Modern Economy." In D. Kumar and M. Desai, eds., *The Cambridge Economic History of India*, vol. 2, *c. 1757–1970*, pp. 737–61. Cambridge: Cambridge University Press, 1983.

Jagga, L. "The Emergence of the Railway Labour Movement in India, c. 1899–1925, a Preliminary Study." Master's thesis, Jawaharlal Nehru University, 1980.

——. "Colonial Railwaymen and British Rule: A Probe Into Railway Labour Agitation in India, 1919–1922." In B. Chandra, ed., *The Indian Left: Critical Appraisals*, pp. 103–45. New Delhi: Vikas, 1983.

Kahn, J. "The Making and Unmaking of a Malay Race." *Social Analysis* 49, no. 2 (Summer 2005): 164–72.

Kalpagam, U. "Colonialism, Rational Calculations, and Ideas of the 'Economy.'" *Economic and Political Weekly* 32, nos. 1–2 (1997): 000.

Kantorowicz, E. *The King's Two Bodies: A Study in Mediaeval Political Theology*. Princeton, N.J.: Princeton University Press, 1997.

Kelly, T. "Documented Lives: Fear and the Uncertainties of Law During the Second Palestinian Intifada." *Journal of the Royal Anthropological Institute*, n.s., 12 (2006): 89–107.

Kennedy, D. *The Magic Mountains: Hill Stations and the British Raj*. Berkeley: University of California Press, 1996.

Kerr, I. *Building the Railways of the Raj, 1850–1900*. New Delhi: Oxford University Press, 1995.

——. *Railways in Modern India: Themes in Indian History*. Delhi: Oxford University Press, 2001.

——. "Representation and Representations of the Railways of Colonial and Post-Colonial South Asia." *Modern Asian Studies* 37, no. 2 (2003): 287–326.

Kipling, R. "Among the Railway Folk." *The City of Dreadful Night*. Calcutta: Calcutta Wheeler Railway Library, 1891.

Kirby, L. *Parallel Tracks: The Railroad and Silent Cinema*. Durham, N.C.: Duke University Press, 1997.

Kolatkar, A. "Jejuri." In A. Mehrota, ed., *The Oxford India Anthology of Twelve Modern Indian Poets*, pp. 62–75. New Delhi: Oxford University Press, 1992.

Kostal, R. W. *Law and English Railway Capitalism, 1825–1875.* Oxford: Oxford University Press, 1997.

Lahiri, S. B. "Truth is Stranger than Fiction: Kanchrapara Branch of the Union Has a Glorious Chapter to Add To." In R. Chakravarty, ed., *Tales of Railwaymen's Chivalry*, pp. 409–35.

Laidlaw, J. "For an Anthropology of Ethics and Freedom." *Journal of the Royal Anthropological Institute*, n.s., 8 (2002): 311–32.

Lambek, M. *The Weight of the Past: Living with History in Mahajanga, Madagascar.* Basingstoke, Eng.: Palgrave Macmillan, 2002.

Lambert, H. "Sentiment and Substance in North Indian Forms of Relatedness." In J. Carsten, ed., *Cultures of Relatedness: New Approaches to the Study of Kinship*, pp. 000. Cambridge: Cambridge University Press, 2000.

Latour, Bruno. *We Have Never Been Modern.* Hemel Hempstead, Eng.: Harvester Wheatsheaf Press, 1993.

Lefebvre, H. *The Production of Space.* Cambridge, Mass.: Blackwell, 1991.

Lehman, F. "Great Britain and the Supply of Railway Locomotives in India: A Case Study of 'Economic Imperialism.'" *The Indian Economic and Social Review* 2, no. 4 (1965): 297–306.

——. "Railway Workshops, Technology Transfer, and Skilled Labour Recruitment in Colonial India." *Journal of Historical Research* 20, no. 1 (1977): 49–61.

Lokanathan, P. S. *Industrial Welfare in India.* Madras: Methodist Publishing House, 1929.

Mahalanobis, P. C. "Anthropological Observations on the Anglo-Indians of Calcutta." *Records of the Indian Museum* 23 (1922).

Maher, R. *These Are the Anglo-Indians.* Calcutta: Swallow Press, 1962.

Manning, P. "Owning and Belonging: A Semiotic Investigation of the Affective Categories of a Bourgeois Society." *Comparative Studies in Society and History* 46, no. 2 (2004): 300–25.

Marx, L. *The Machine in the Garden: Technology and the Pastoral Ideal in America.* New York: Oxford University Press, 1964.

Mitchell, J. W. *The Wheels of Ind.* London: Thorton and Butterworth, 1934.

Mitra, S. R. "From Pages of Past." In R. Chakravarty, ed., *Tales of Railwaymen's Chivalry*, pp. 319–71.

Mody, P. "Love and the Law: Love-Marriage in Delhi." *Modern Asian Studies* 36, no. 1 (2002): 223–56.

Mondal, A. "The Emblematics of Gender and Sexuality in Indian Nationalist Discourse." *Modern Asian Studies* 36, no. 4 (2002): 913–36.

Morris, M. D. "The Growth of Large-Scale Industry to 1947." In D. Kumar and M. Desai, eds., *The Cambridge Economic History of India*, vol. 2, c. *1757–1970*, pp. 553–676. Cambridge: Cambridge University Press, 1983.

Moshin, M. *Chittaranjan: A Study in Urban Sociology*. Bombay: Popular Prakashan, 1964.

Mrazek, R. *Engineers of a Happy Land: Technology and Nationalism in a Colony*. Princeton, N.J.: Princeton University Press, 2002.

Mukerjee, R. *The Indian Working Class*. Bombay: Hind Kitabs, 1951.

Munasinghe, V. "Narrating a Nation Through Mixed Bloods." *Social Analysis* 49, no. 2 (Summer 2005): 155–63.

Naoroji, D. *Poverty and Un-British Rule in India*. London: Swan, Sonnenschein, 1901.

Natesan, A. *State Management and Control of Railways in India: A Study of Railway Finance Rates and Policy*. Calcutta: University of Calcutta, 1964.

Navaro-Yashin, Y. *Faces of the State: Secularism and Public Life in Turkey*. Princeton, N.J.: Princeton University Press, 2002.

Nietzsche, F. *On the Genealogy of Morals*. New York: Vintage Books Edition, 1989.

Nora, P. *Conflicts and Divisions*. Vol. 1, *Realm of Memory: Rethinking the French Past*. New York: Columbia University Press, 1996.

Nugent, D. "Before History and Prior to Politics: Time, Space, and Territory in the Modern Peruvian Nation-State." In T. Blom Hansen and F. Stepputat, eds., *States of Imagination*, pp. 257–83.

Osella, F. and C. Osella. "The Return of King Mahabali: The Politics of Morality in South India." In C. J. Fuller and V. Benei, eds., *The Everyday State and Society in Modern India*, pp. 139–62.

Palsson, G. "The Life of Family Trees and the Book of Icelanders." *Medical Anthropology* 21 (2002): 317–67.

Parry, J. P. "The End of the Body." In M. Feher, ed., *Fragments for a History of the Human Body*, vol. 2, pp. 490–517. New York: Urzone, 1989.

——. "Lords of Labour: Working and Shirking in Bhilai." In J. P. Parry, J. Breman, and K. Kapadia, eds., *The Worlds of Indian Industrial Labour*, pp. 107–40.

——. "Two Cheers for Reservation: The Satnamis and the Steel Plant." In R. Guha and J. P. Parry, eds., *Institutions and Inequalities: Essays in Honour of Andre Betelle*, pp. 129–69. New Delhi: Oxford University Press, 1999.

——. "The 'Crisis of Corruption' and 'The Idea of India': A Worm's Eye View." In I. Pardo, ed., *Morals and Legitimacy: Between Agency and System*, pp. 27–56. Oxford: Berghahn Books, 2000.

——. "Ankalu's Errant Wife: Sex, Marriage, and Industry in Contemporary Chhattisgarh." *Modern Asian Studies* 35, no. 4 (2001): 783–820.

——. "Nehru's Dream and the Village 'Waiting Room': Long Distance Migrants to a Central Indian Steel Town." *Contributions to Indian Sociology* 37, nos. 1–2 (2003): 217–49.

——, J. Breman, and K. Kapadia. *The Worlds of Indian Industrial Labour*. New Delhi: Sage, 1999.

Povinelli, E. "What's Love Got to Do with It? The Race of Freedom and the Drag of Descent." *Social Analysis* 49, no. 2 (Summer 2005): 173–81.

Prakash, G. *Another Reason: Science and the Imagination of Modern India*. Princeton, N.J.: Princeton University Press, 1999.

Price, P. *Kingship and Political Practice in Colonial India*. Cambridge: Cambridge University Press, 1996.

Radcliffe, S. A. "Imagining the State as Space: Territoriality and the Formation of the State in Ecuador." In T. Blom Hansen and F. Stepputat, eds., *States of Imagination*, pp. 123–45.

Ramaswamy, S. *The Pleasures of the Tongue: Language Devotion in Tamil Nadu, 1891–1970*. Berkeley: University of California Press, 1997.

Ranade, M. G. "Indian Political Economy." In M. G. Ranade, *Essays on Indian Economics*, pp. 1–42. Madras: G. A. Nateson, 1906.

Rao, G. "The Political Economy of Railways in British India, 1850–1900." *Artha Vijanana* 20, no. 4 (December 1978).

Ray, S. *Abol-Tabol: The Nonsense World of Sukumar Ray*. Trans. Sampurna Chattarji. New Delhi: Puffin Books, 2004.

Raychaudhuri, T. "Love in a Colonial Climate: Marriage, Sex, and Romance in Nineteenth-Century Bengal." *Modern Asian Studies* 34, no. 2 (2000): 349–78.

Ritvo, H. *The Animal Estate: The English and Other Creatures in the Victorian Age*. Cambridge, Mass.: Harvard University Press, 1987.

Robb, P. *Dalit Movements and the Meanings of Labour in India*. Delhi: Oxford University Press, 1993.

——. "Children, Emotion, Identity, and Empire: Views from the Bleychyndens' Calcutta Diaries (1790–1822)." *Modern Asian Studies* 40, no. 1 (2006): 175–201.

Robinson, R. *Conversion, Continuity, and Change: Lived Christianity in Southern Goa*. New Delhi: Sage, 1998.

Rose, S. *Limited Livelihoods: Gender and Class in Nineteenth Century England*. Berkeley: University of California Press, 1992.

Roychowdhury, L. *The Jadu House: Intimate Histories of Anglo-India*. London: Anchor, 2001.

Sanyal, N. *The Development of Indian Railways*. Calcutta: University of Calcutta, 1930.

Schivelbusch, W. *The Railway Journey: The Industrialisation of Time and Space in the Nineteenth Century*. Berkeley: University of California Press, 1986.

Scott, M. "Hybridity, Vacuity, and Blockage: Visions of Chaos from Anthropological Theory, Island Melanesia, and Central Africa." *Comparative Studies in Society and History* 47 no. 1 (2005): 190–216.

Sealy, A. I. *The Trotter-Nama*. Delhi: Penguin, 1990.

Sen, J. "Anglo-Indians of Calcutta." *Human Science* 32, no. 1 (1983): 33–56. Reprint by the Anthropological Survey of India, Calcutta.

Sen, S. "Marx on Indian Railways." In M. Sen and M. B. Rao, eds., *Das Kapital Centenary Volume: A Symposium*. New Delhi: People's Publishing House, 1968.

——. *Women and Labour in Late Colonial India: The Bengal Jute Industry*. Cambridge: Cambridge University Press, 1999.

Shiva, B. R. *The Industrial Worker in India*. London: Allen and Unwin, 1939.

Singha, R. "Making the Domestic More Domestic: Criminal Law and the 'Head of the Household,' 1772–1843." *Indian Economic and Social History Review* 33 (July–September 1996): 309–44.

Srinivasan, K. C. *The Law and Theory of Railway Freight Rates*. Madras: B. G. Paul, 1928.

Stark, H. *Call of the Blood*. Rangoon: British Burma Press, 1932.

——. *Hostages to India*. Calcutta: The Calcutta Fine Art Cottage, 1962.

Stephenson, R. M. *Report Upon the Practicability and Advantages of the Introduction of Railways Into British India*. London: Kelly, 1845.

Stewart, S. *On Longing: Narratives on the Miniature, the Gigantic, the Souvenir, the Collection*. Durham, N.C.: Duke University Press, 1993.

Stoler, A. "Sexual Affronts and Racial Frontiers: European Identities and the Cultural Politics of Exclusion in Colonial Southeast Asia." *Comparative Studies in Society and History* 34, no. 3 (1992): 514–51.

——. *Race and the Education of Desire: Foucault's 'History of Sexuality' and the Colonial Order of Things*. Durham, N.C.: Duke University Press, 1995.

——. *Carnal Knowledge and Imperial Power: Race and the Intimate in Colonial Rule*. Berkeley and Los Angeles: University of California Press, 2002.

—— and K. Strassler. "Castings for the Colonial: Memory Work in 'New Order' Java." *Comparative Studies in Society and History* 42, no. 1 (2000): 4–48.

Strathern, M. *After Nature: English Kinship in the Late Twentieth Century*. Cambridge: Cambridge University Press, 1992.

Sturman, R. "Property and Attachments: Defining Autonomy and the Claims of Family in Nineteenth-Century Western India." *Comparative Studies in Society and History* 47, no. 3 (2005): 611–37.

Tapper, M. *In the Blood: Sickle Cell Anaemia and the Politics of Race*. Philadelphia: University of Pennsylvania Press, 1999.

——. "Blood/Kinship, Governmentality, and Cultures of Order in Colonial Africa." In S. Franklin and S. McKinnon, eds., *Relative Values*, pp. 329–54.

Tarlo, E. "Paper Truths: The Emergency and Slum Clearance Through Forgotten Files." In C. J. Fuller and V. Benei, eds., *The Everyday State and Society in India*, pp. 70–90.

Taussig, M. *The Magic of the State*. New York: Routledge, 1997.

Thomas, N. and R. Eves. *Bad Colonialists: The South Sea Letters of Vernon Lee Walker and Louis Becke*. Durham, N.C.: Duke University Press, 1999.

Thorner, D. *Investment in Empire*. Philadelphia: University of Pennsylvania Press, 1950.

Thurston, E. "Eurasians of Madras City and Malabar." *Records of the Indian Museum* 23 (1922).

Todorov, T. *Les abus de la memoire*. Paris: Arlea, 1998.

Tranberg Hansen, K. *Distant Companions: Servants and Employers in Zambia, 1900–1985*. Ithaca, N.Y.: Cornell University Press, 1989.

Van Der Veer, P. *Imperial Encounters: Religion and Modernity in India and Britain.* Princeton, N.J.: Princeton University Press, 2001.

Van Dijk, R. "Pentecostalism, Cultural Memory, and the State: Contested Representations of Time in Postcolonial Malawi." In R. Werbner, ed., *Memory and the Postcolony: African Anthropology and Critique of Power,* pp. 155–74. London: Zed Books, 1998.

Van Voss, L. ed. *Petitions in Social History.* International Review of Social History, supplement 9. Cambridge: Cambridge University Press, 2001.

Varma, L. B. *Anglo-Indians.* New Delhi: Bhasha Prakashan, 1979.

Verkaaik, O. "The Captive State: Corruption, Intelligence Agencies, and Ethnicity in Pakistan." In T. Blom Hansen and F. Stepputat, eds., *States of Imagination,* pp. 345–64.

Viswanathan, G. *Outside the Fold: Conversion, Modernity, and Belief.* Princeton, N.J.: Princeton University Press, 1998.

Wadley, S. "Power in Hindu Ideology and Practice." In K. David, ed., *The New Wind: Changing Identities in South Asia,* pp. 133–58. The Hague: Mouton, 1977.

Wallace, K. E. "Asil Anglo-Indians." *The Anglo-Indian Review* (August 1938): 10–11.

Weston, C. N. *Anglo-Indian Revolutionaries of the Methodist Episcopal Church.* Bangalore: Scripture Literature Press, 1938.

Weston, K. "Kinship, Controversy, and the Sharing of Substance: The Race/Class Politics of Blood Transfusion." In S. Franklin and S. McKinnon, eds., *Relative Values,* pp. 147–74.

Westridge, R. *Railway Life in India.* Calcutta: Telegraph Association Press, 1935.

Westwood, J. N. *Railways of India.* Newton Abbot, Eng.: David and Charles, 1974.

Wolfram, Sybil. *Inlaws and Outlaws: Kinship and Marriage in England.* Beckenham, Eng.: Croom Helm, 1987.

Wood, J. C. *British Economists and the Empire.* London: Croom Helm; New York, St. Martin's Press, 1983.

Young, R. *Colonial Desire: Hybridity in Theory, Culture, and Race.* London: Routledge, 1995.

Zaret, D. *Origins of Democratic Culture: Printing, Petitions, and the Public Sphere in Early-Modern England.* Princeton, N.J.: Princeton University Press, 2000.

# Index